HEADING OUT

HEADING OUT

A History of American Camping

TERENCE YOUNG

Cornell University Press
Ithaca and London

First published 2017 by Cornell University Press

Printed in the United States of America

Library of Congress Cataloging-in-Publication Data

Names: Young, Terence (Terence G.), author.
Title: Heading out : a history of American camping / Terence Young.
Description: Ithaca : Cornell University Press, 2017. | Includes
    bibliographical references and index.
Identifiers: LCCN 2016047309 (print) | LCCN 2016050292 (ebook) |
    ISBN 9780801454028 (cloth : alk. paper) | ISBN 9781501712821
    (epub/mobi) | ISBN 9781501712838 (pdf)
Subjects: LCSH: Camping—United States—History.
Classification: LCC GV191.4 .Y68 2017 (print) | LCC GV191.4
    (ebook) | DDC 796.540973—dc23
LC record available at https://lccn.loc.gov/2016047309

Cornell University Press strives to use environmentally responsible suppliers and materials to the fullest extent possible in the publishing of its books. Such materials include vegetable-based, low-VOC inks and acid-free papers that are recycled, totally chlorine-free, or partly composed of nonwood fibers. For further information, visit our website at www.cornellpress.cornell.edu.

For Pat and Jack—who introduced me to camping when I was an infant. Thank you for a lifetime of roughing it.

CONTENTS

ACKNOWLEDGMENTS

To write a book an author needs much support and incurs many obligations. Near the outset of this endeavor, the Smithsonian Institution's National Museum of American History provided a one-year fellowship. I am indebted to this marvelous organization for its backing; to Cheney Moss, Jennifer Loux, and Richard Wicka, who acted as my interns at the time; to Roger White, who generously shared his thoughts with me; and to Jeffrey Stine especially for his support and leadership from the beginning. Before anyone, including me, Jeffrey saw that camping might have more to do with heading out of a city than into nature. His insight transformed my research. I am also grateful to the Huntington Library, Art Collections, and Botanical Gardens for providing two fellowships, and especially to Robert C. Ritchie for his continuing support and encouragement. Moreover, I benefited from grants provided by the Adirondack Museum's Warder and Julia Cadbury Travel-to-Collections program, by the Benson Ford Research Center's Clark Travel-to-Collections program, and by Cal Poly Pomona's Research, Scholarship, and Creative Activities program, the Center for Professional Development, and the John T. Lyle Center for Regenerative Studies.

As critical as funding to any historical project is the knowledge and assistance of the librarians, archivists, curators, and institutional historians who collect, organize, and preserve the documents, maps, and other materials necessary to reveal our past. Over the course of two decades I have benefited from the hard work of many, including Joseph Schwartz, Ann Cummings, David A. Langbart, Paul Wormser, and John Hedger of the U.S. National Archives; Barry Mackintosh, Dwight Pitcaithley, Reed Engle, Ward Eldridge, William Tweed, Thomas A. Durant, David Nathanson, Nancy Flanagan, and Wade Myers of the U.S. National Park Service; Linda Lux of the U.S. Forest Service; Jerrold Pepper, Hallie Bond, Jim Meehan, Angela Snye, and Caroline M. Welsh of the Adirondack Museum; Jeff Flannery and Patrick Kerwin of the Library of Congress, Manuscripts Division; Karren Elsbernd and Michelle Wellck of the California Academy of Sciences; Ann T. Walden and Laura Nicholson of the Coleman Company; Elijah Carder and Jini Keasling of the Airstream Company; Cathy Hunter of the National Geographic Society; Judith E. Endelman and Linda Skolarus of the Benson Ford Research Center; Cheryl Oakes of the Forest History Society; John Gerber of the Appalachian Mountain Club; Claudia Jensen of the Denver Public Library; and most especially, Peter Blodgett of the Huntington Library. On more occasions than I can possibly recall, Peter provided suggestions, insights, assistance, and friendship.

Many friends and supportive colleagues have also provided feedback, shared materials, and offered technical assistance. Among them are Warder F. Cadbury, Mark Cioc, Craig Colten, Lary Dilsaver, Janet Fireman, Ron Foresta, Martin Hogue, Linda McClelland, Joe Peplinski, Miles Richardson, Judy Scales-Trent and her mother Viola Scales Trent, Dale Schwamborn, Peggy Shaffer, Mark Stoll, Bill Wyckoff, and Yolonda Youngs. Phil Terrie was especially helpful with his critical feedback and guidance as the manuscript neared completion. Jonathan Cobb deserves special recognition for his early and invaluable suggestion that I organize each chapter around an individual or two in order to humanize the overall story. I believe the result to be a far more engaging tale of American life. Versions of chapters 4 and 5 appeared previously in the journals *George Wright Forum* and *Environmental History* respectively. The editors and reviewers of those earlier efforts greatly improved this book.

Michael McGandy has been an outstanding editor, at once both supportive and insightfully critical. Similar services have been provided by other members of the Cornell University Press staff, especially Karen Hwa, Susan Barnett, and Bethany Wasik. Together this team has been organized, responsive, and consistently professional. It's been a true pleasure to work with them. A related professional, Bill Nelson, produced the maps without hesitation and in a timely fashion.

Finally, I thank my parents, who taught me to camp, my sisters and brother, and my friends, especially Tony Cruz, Izzy Schwartz, Greg Story, and Gary Woods, whose steady queries about "the book" kept me pressing forward. You will never know how much your interest and curiosity led directly to a successful outcome. In the same vein, Kitty Connolly has my utmost affection for her steadfast support and patience, her frequent and thoughtful comments, and her mutual pleasure in camping. This book is a reality because of you.

To everyone above and to the many more who were helpful at a moment when I needed bracing, I am deeply grateful.

HEADING OUT

ROUGHING IT SMOOTHLY

We had been looking forward to this camping trip for more than a month and were now comfortably settled into our favorite campsite. Kitty and I discovered this eastern Sierra Nevada idyll in our usual fashion. We pored through the older camping guides on our bookshelves and explored the Internet for suggestions. Finally settling on a general area near Bridgeport, California, we drove for seven hours and then spent several more exploring the forest's rather remote camping areas before choosing one. The site appealed to us because it was spacious, isolated, and adjacent to a lovely gallery of trees and a mountain stream that was home to beavers. Nearby sprawled a meadow that stretched away toward the towering mountains. Nothing in our everyday world compared to this attractive scene. We felt as though we were, like some earlier Americans, "roughing it" in a picturesque, quiet, fragrant, and untamed wilderness. At the same time, though, we also enjoyed this campsite because it was accessible by car.

We take pleasure in car camping and have enjoyed many satisfying camping trips in state parks, national parks, and national forests. Unlike the majority of car campers, however, we prefer primitive areas over developed ones, and this Sierra Nevada site became our favorite because it is an attractive blend of "roughing it" and comfort. Our ideal camping area is on public land without designated campsites, fire pits, tables, potable water on tap, toilets (flush or earthen), or trash services. Instead, we enjoy having to manage these challenges ourselves. Yes, we have to dig our own toilet, but since we are car camping, we can also surround ourselves with a variety of conveniences. We have an easily assembled two-person tent, sleeping pads, and sleeping bags; all are quite light and can be packed into small spaces. These particular items are part of our household's camping kit because they can do double duty: when we are feeling more adventurous and head out on the occasional backpacking trip, they also come along. Nearby stands our aluminum folding table plus two five-gallon water containers and a steel ice chest for storing perishable items. We have the usual assortment of (somewhat) mismatched cooking and eating utensils, including pots and pans, cups, plates, bowls, and can opener. On the table we have a two-burner, white-gasoline pressure stove that allows us to begin cooking a meal in less than a minute. With just a small amount of hand pumping, this century-old technology comes to life every time. The longer we own it, the more impressed I am by its reliability. Close at hand sits the most memorable piece of our gear—a 1948 Coleman white-gasoline pressure lantern that I inherited from my parents, who were avid campers. Coming up on its seventieth birthday, this antique continues to light the darkness whenever we wish to read, play cards, or engage in some other game in the evening. Although it is too cumbersome and heavy for backpacking, I am attached to it and continue to be impressed by its light-producing capacity. As a part of our campsite building ritual, we assembled a few rocks into a makeshift fire ring and have placed our firewood, purchased in nearby Bridgeport, nearby.

Our love of camping is not unusual. Millions of Americans enjoy camping trips as much as we do, and they have been doing so for more than a century. But camping is not a universally attractive leisure activity. *Heading Out* explores attitudes toward camping by focusing on the three long-term trends that quietly shaped the American camping experience. First, campers lived in a world that was undergoing modernization. The cities and towns where they resided grew larger, more complex, polluted, and less green. Like us, they temporarily retreated from their workaday lives to an attractive natural setting that counteracted a world that too often left them tired, tense, and alienated. Second, camping has restored and refreshed campers since the nineteenth century because it is a form of pilgrimage. Like any pilgrim, campers travel away from their daily lives into an alternative, transformative place—in our case, the eastern Sierra Nevada—where they are rewarded with rest and relaxation. Finally, Kitty and I car camp with equipment that would have been technological marvels to a nineteenth-century camper. Ironically, while camping has been an antimodern reaction to a modernizing world, it has also been subject to modernization itself. The clothing, utensils, and other gear that early campers employed were bulky, heavy, and in general little different from those items used in daily life. But over the decades gear diversified, became lighter, specialized, and more easily transportable as manufacturers redesigned equipment to smooth out some of camping's roughness and in the process enhance their sales. These three trends—modernization, pilgrimage, and technological change—quietly shaped camping from its beginning.

Modern and Antimodern

Camping, of course, is not new, but it did not become a widespread form of recreation until after the Civil War. That conflict spurred industrialization, urbanization, and a variety of social changes that swept through the country during and after the war, accompanied by a decades-long, mass migration toward America's cities. Urbanization offered more employment options, improved leisure amenities, and a host of other attractive opportunities. However, city dwellers were also assaulted by smoke, noise, crowding, shifting gender, class, ethnic, and other social relations, increased social diversity and stratification, production schedules, pervasive regulation, and more. Unsurprisingly, many found America's modernizing cities to be confusing and alienating even as they were attracted to them. Yearning for a sense of belonging and connection in the cacophony of modern urban life, some embraced camping, which from its outset was clearly antimodern.

In common parlance, "modern" often means contemporary or recently developed, but in the social sciences this word and especially the related but more culturally oriented "modernity" suggest "a process by which society constantly renews itself." Generally, these terms refer to the historical period, starting around the year 1500 in Europe, when capitalism, industrialization, rationalization, and their associated institutions slowly transformed existing, relatively traditional societies into "modern" ones. In the nineteenth century there came a growing awareness among modernizing peoples that they lived in a time of rapid and revolutionary change, yet they remembered more premodern times. It was at this moment of rising awareness that recreational camping appeared in America. On the one hand, camping is an expression of modernity and is shaped by modern institutions, but on the other hand it is premodern in its sentiment and the nature it reveres. What drives modernity? Economic forces are critical, but they are neither the exclusive cause nor the focus of *Heading Out*. Instead, this book explores the meaning of camping, especially as expressed through noneconomic social relations, science, and technology, and values, attitudes, and beliefs. Indeed, when attitudes, values, and beliefs, rather than economic forces, are in the foreground, modernity ceases to be a process that happened to a society. Instead, it becomes clear that modern people rationalized, embraced, and self-consciously produced it through their belief in progress.

People expected that modernization's changes, however disturbing, would generally be for the better. The resulting fusion of cultural, social, economic, and technological aspects made modernity a vibrant force for change, with its focus on the future rather than the past.[1] Consequently, modernity has been pervasive and taken many forms.

The American response to modernity was complex. As manufacturers, for instance, embraced arduous work schedules to enhance production and as work was rationalized and working hours became fixed, labor demanded limits and regular hours off. Decades of agitation and labor actions were organized around a slogan that expressed a strongly antimodern attitude: "Eight hours for work, eight hours for rest, and eight hours for what we will." Modern production techniques also transformed the manufacturing process into a series of discrete and highly ordered steps. This segmentation of production left many workers, in both labor and management, with a reduced sense of connectedness to the products they created. In response, many Americans, in search of personal fulfillment, embraced such trends as the antimodern Arts and Crafts movement with its focus on simplicity, aestheticism, and education. Nor were the impacts of modernity and anti-modern reactions limited to the workplace; they could be found throughout society. For example, modernity emphasized rationality and secularization, which tended to undermine the authority and mystical aspects of liberal Protestantism, leaving many Americans feeling a loss of individual meaning and purpose. One antimodern response came in the appearance of "muscular Christianity," which emphasized vigorous exercise and physical action, especially through competitive sports, as a means to achieve intense, meaningful experiences.[2]

While antimodernism was widespread during the nineteenth and twentieth centuries and was expressed in many forms, antimodernist views in general tended to mirror and merge with the contemporary romantic movement. This movement was not so much a single philosophy or ideology as a period in Western cultural history. It stretched through the eighteenth and nineteenth centuries, influencing the arts, sciences, politics, religion, and many aspects of daily life. It had diverse expressions, which ranged along a broad continuum, but generally could be recognized by a rejection of rationalism, a regard for history, and a focus on perception and beauty, particularly the beauty of nature. Moreover, a belief that the folk spirit or character of a group of people grew organically and over a long period of time rather than as the product of any planning runs through this era. Romanticism is often a part of these centuries' concerns with nationalism, patriotism, nature, and design. Romanticism, however, was not an exclusively antimodern movement. It also contributed to the growth of democracies, to a belief in progress, and to the more open societies that are common features of modern life. Nonetheless, antimodernists frequently drew on the conventions of romanticism in their struggles with modernity's advance.[3]

Romantic antimodernism was strongly felt in America during the latter half of the nineteenth century, and the city and urban life often seemed the battleground of modernity. Of course, cities had been present in America from early colonial days, but even then they were often disdained. In 1787's *Notes on the State of Virginia*, Thomas Jefferson argued that the ideal society would endure where the economy was agricultural and the settlements small and dispersed. Farmers, he insisted, were the backbone of America. "Those who labor in the earth are the chosen people of God, if ever he had a chosen people, whose breasts he has made his peculiar deposite [*sic*] for substantial and genuine virtue," he wrote. Manufacturing and cities, in contrast, were sources of vice. Drawing a particularly repulsive word picture, Jefferson suggested that "the mobs of great cities add just so much to the support of pure government, as sores do to the strength of the human body." After the Civil War, the rapid growth and increasing complexity of modern cities compounded Americans' discomfort with them, but the expression of that discomfort took a new turn. Jefferson had condemned cities as politically destructive and urged residents to move back to the land in order to farm. In the land, not the city, lay the roots of the republican nation, stated Jefferson. But late nineteenth-century romantic antimodernists only rarely mentioned farming, and they were not adamantly opposed to cities. Instead, they tended to be ambivalent about urban life because it resulted in both benefits and costs. Even as they denounced many aspects of urban life, they praised efforts to get back to nature through art, natural history, gardening, travel, and more because these compensated for and counteracted the trials of city life.[4]

The nature-loving antimodernism of the nineteenth and early twentieth centuries was shaped by innumerable actors, including writers, painters, philosophers, pastors, politicians, architects, landscape architects, and others, but one of the most influential was John Ruskin. Born in England in 1819, Ruskin was renowned in England and America as an art critic and moral crusader. His *Modern Painters* of 1843, which praised contemporary landscape artists for their ability to properly express both the moral and material "truths" of water, clouds, air, vegetation, and the other aspects of nature, prompted many English tourists to visit France, Italy, and Switzerland to see and explore the region's mountains. Wealthy Americans also flocked to the Alps, and as they did so boosters at home took to favorably comparing their local mountains to Switzerland's. Moreover, after mountain art encouraged mountain tourism, the latter quickly branched out to evolve into the international sport of mountaineering. Ruskin published a second volume of *Modern Painters* in 1846, but this work was more theoretical than the first. He argued that truth, beauty, and the divine are inseparably linked. "Now, in whatever is an object of life, in whatever may be infinitely and for itself desired, we may be sure there is something of divine; for God will not make anything an object of life to His creatures which does not point to, or partake of, Himself." If something is beautiful, argued Ruskin, it must express the divine, which is inherently good. Therefore, travels into beautiful nature and viewing landscape paintings true to nature were beneficial. With these two volumes, Ruskin established his reputation as a polemicist, aesthetician, scientific observer, and ethicist within the romantic mold, but his next book would make him influential as a social thinker as well.[5]

In *The Stones of Venice*, a multivolume treatise published between 1851 and 1853, Ruskin continued along a romantic path when he looked to the past to denounce modernity's degradation of contemporary labor. In a notably antimodern turn, he contrasted the individual creativity allowed the medieval craftsmen, such as those who had worked on Gothic cathedrals, with the demand for mindless precision and order in the factory system of his day. According to Ruskin, "men were not intended to work with the accuracy of tools," and having been forced to do so, modern laborers had been reduced to "a heap of sawdust."[6] Moreover, he warned, this morally contemptible situation was also a social threat because it would likely lead to revolution. The creative impulse, in Ruskin's view, arose naturally, and modern laborers, like their medieval counterparts, needed opportunities to be expressive and to find joy in their work. Where such joy existed, they would be satisfied with their material and social conditions; where it was absent, violent change could occur. Ruskin suggested various reforms, but they generally took the form of voluntarist efforts that had little immediate impact. Nonetheless, his overt rejection of modern mechanization and standardization and his romantic praise for what he saw as a medieval reverence for nature and natural forms in art, plus his earlier praise for nature, encouraged a host of antimodernists.

William Morris and the Arts and Crafts movement in England and America is probably the best known of the romantic antimodern movements that drew on Ruskin's work, but Ruskin's voluminous writings on nature, art, and society also stirred a wide range of similarly romantic and antimodern practices in America, including political movements, historic preservation organizations, and the broad field of urban planning. Andrew Jackson Downing, an influential and early proponent of urban parks, suburbanization, and landscape gardening in America, considered Ruskin a "favorite author." Downing, in his turn, encouraged a young contemporary,

Frederick Law Olmsted, who became one of the two designers of New York City's Central Park and numerous other urban parks, suburbs, and grounds. Olmsted read widely and drew on many sources to inform his romantic antimodern plans, but he regarded Ruskin as a "mentor" and one of "the real prophets." Ruskin's influence in America can also be detected in such American landscape painters as Frederick Edwin Church and William James Stillman and the transcendentalist authors Ralph Waldo Emerson and Henry David Thoreau. The latter pair wrote poetry and prose that praised the ability of sublime nature to elevate the mind and spirit, and, unsurprisingly, they were both frequent hikers, and Thoreau seems to have camped out fairly often.[7]

Less well known but equally representative of the period's shifting attitudes was a book by Susan Fenimore Cooper. The eldest daughter of James Fenimore Cooper, she had authored a novel, *Elinor Wyllys; or, The Young Folk of Longbridge*, in 1846 but became best known for her *Rural Hours*, published in 1850. She was fascinated by nature and natural history, which she read avidly, and *Rural Hours* was a contemplation of domestic life and the shifting natural landscape around her home in Cooperstown, New York. Organized around the four seasons, the book embeds the elements of her domestic life into nature's cycles. In many ways she offered a fairly conservative commentary on women's lives, but she also drew on nature as a source for moral education. In particular, she suggested that women look to nature as a resource for mitigating the worst aspects of America's expanding urban life and as a model for building family harmony. In the words of historian Vera Norwood, *Rural Hours* put Cooper "on the public stage." Her book was read and favorably reviewed by many of her best-known contemporaries, including William Cullen Bryant, Washington Irving, Andrew Jackson Downing, and Henry David Thoreau. Like them, she contributed to the slow awakening of middle-class Americans to romantic antimodernism and to the attractiveness and value of their wilder lands.[8]

By the 1840s, romantic antimodernism could be found in myriad forms in America, although one expression stands out: the rising regard of urban Americans for the wild areas of the Northeast, and in particular the Adirondacks. American tourists had begun to travel to natural areas such as the White Mountains, the Hudson Highlands, and, after the opening of the Erie Canal in 1825, Niagara Falls, but the less accessible Adirondacks did not receive their first tourists until the late 1830s. One of these earliest travelers, Charles Fenno Hoffman, an author and editor well known on the New York literary scene, published the first Adirondack book, *Wild Scenes in the Forest and Prairie*, in 1839. A series of "sketches" about his "ramble" through the region, it subsequently inspired additional writers to visit the

Adirondacks and recount their own experiences in print. Among this next generation were the Reverend Joel T. Headley and T. Addison Richards. Headley's 1849 book, *The Adirondack; or, Life in the Woods*, described his mountain climbing and boating during the 1840s. Like many Americans who were consciously or unconsciously aware of Ruskin's impact on Alpine tourism, Headley frequently compared the Adirondacks to the mountain glories of Switzerland. No comparable scenery, he offered, was "to be found [elsewhere] in our picturesque country. . . . None . . . will match it this side of the Alps." Apparently suffering from exhaustion, Headley had taken to the Adirondack wilds because, in a romantic antimodernist turn, he feared that urban life was more malignant than benign. "I believe," declared Headley, "that every man degenerates without frequent communion with nature." Then, sounding a great deal like Ruskin, he explained why. Nature "is one of the open books of God, and even more replete with instructions than anything ever penned by man. A single tree standing alone, and waving all day long its green crown in the summer wind, is to me fuller of meaning and instruction than the crowded mart or gorgeously built town." For Headley, a visit to God's handiwork, the natural world, was the key to personal regeneration. Richards's account also described the excitement of outdoor sports, the meaning of wilderness, the beauty of wild scenes, and day-to-day life in the woods with guides. Intriguingly, however, he recorded meeting another party in the backwoods that included three women. According to Richards, together they hunted deer and other game and then spent three days ascending and descending Mount Marcy during the summer of 1858. The men and women treated each other more equally and with fewer socially dictated restrictions than would have been typical at home. Moreover, it is clear that Richards and the other men enjoyed the women's company.[9]

At around the same time that Headley and Richards published their books, Thoreau narrated his Massachusetts and New Hampshire odyssey in 1849's *A Week on the Concord and Merrimack Rivers*. Largely an extended musing about history, poetry, and religion, it was also an account of his boat trip, and it had a distinctly romantic antimodern sensibility as Thoreau lamented the effects that modern factories had on the rivers. A few years later, in August 1858, the popularly named "Philosophers' Camp" took place in the Adirondacks at Follensby Pond (fig. I.1).

Organized by William James Stillman, this summer camping trip included Ralph Waldo Emerson, the Harvard professor Louis Agassiz, the judge Ebenezer Rockwood Hoar, the poet James Russell Lowell, and five additional members from Boston's prestigious Saturday Club. Described by a *New York Times* journalist as a "congregation of philosophers, *savans* [*sic*], authors, artists, and ordinary human beings," this trip by some of America's

Figure I.1. The "Philosophers' Camp" of August 1858, based on a sketch made by Charles E. Whitehead after he unexpectedly encountered Ralph Waldo Emerson, Louis Agassiz, and their compatriots camping in the Adirondacks. From F. S. Stallknecht and C. E. Whitehead, "An August Sporting Tour," *Frank Leslie's New Family Magazine*, November 13–20, 1858, 336. Courtesy of the Adirondack Museum, Blue Mountain Lake, NY.

best known (and urban residing) individuals into the frontier-like wilds of the Adirondacks made national news both during and after the event.[10]

American camping was born in this modernizing milieu in 1869. Many thoughtful, educated, and influential people sensed that the pace of change was quickening, and they were uncomfortable with the emerging world. In reaction, they embraced a variety of antimodern correctives, including a camping trip into the Adirondack woods. Although romantic painting and park making slowly faded as antimodern responses, camping endured because it continued to bring regeneration to legions of campers who unquestioningly assumed that travel to and a temporary stay in nature would restore them. That is, campers felt sure that a pilgrimage into nature would activate camping's antimodern power.

Pilgrimage

Camping, the practice of living in a temporary shelter, has been present intermittently throughout human history, but only in recent times did it become an antimodern feature and socially approved custom of American culture. Military campaigns may require encampments, and unsettled, non-urban people may camp by necessity, but only a people who had become city dwellers would adopt this temporary retreat into the outdoors as an acceptable form of leisure.[11] A key insight of *Heading Out* is that recreational camping takes Americans away from their ordinary urban (or suburban) lives. In other words, campers "head out" of the city, out of their daily routine. From recreational camping's outset, campers have enjoyed three principal modes of camping—on foot, on horseback, or with a wheeled vehicle. But no matter which mode was employed, camping remained an antimodernist activity designed to visit "nature," and often, either consciously or unconsciously, one that recapitulated the frontier experience, which many campers perceived as a crucial chapter in the formation of the American nation. As the following chapters demonstrate, nature turned out to be ocean beaches, forests, lakeshores, mountains, grasslands, deserts, and many more types of places. No single sort of natural environment dominated among campers. Moreover, a campsite could be distant from a camper's home or just beyond the edge of town. This diversity of destinations is a distinctive feature of camping, because it prompts us to look beyond any differences between seashore and mountains to see that all these destinations shared an essential element—they were *not* a part of ordinary life; they were *not* city. The camper who chose to visit the Great Smoky Mountains was likely just as satisfied as the one who chose to camp along the Southern California coast. The physical differences between these places remain significant, but they must not distract us from understanding what campers did and why.

Like the motivations of all migrants, campers' movements were shaped by both "pull" and "push" factors. They were pushed away from a place associated with something undesirable and pulled toward another where they imagined they could find what they wanted. That is, campers moved into nature because it provided them relief; but if we were to focus only on the places they were pulled to, their differences would make it difficult for us to recognize what bound these locations together. However, when we also recognize that all campers were pushed away from their everyday modern lives, which were complex and multifaceted, then we can better understand why a variety of "natures" were satisfactory destinations. It is critical to understand campers' motivations for heading out, because when a camping trip satisfied, the camper was transformed by his or her immersion into nature/not-city and then returned home having been changed in a positive way. In other words, camping is a form of pilgrimage.

This statement may seem jarring, since the term "pilgrimage" will more likely bring up images of Christians on the *camino* to Santiago de Compostela or Muslims on the *hajj* to Mecca than anything to do with camping.

However, pilgrimage need not be a religious act. In essence, a pilgrim is someone who leaves home, journeys to a sacred place as an act of devotion, and returns home changed. As anthropologist Barbara Myerhoff pithily put it, a pilgrim is someone who goes "in-out-in with a difference." Such persons step out of their normal social milieu, depart on a pilgrimage, and then return to the everyday world having undergone some sort of change. Many pilgrims, of course, are religiously motivated, but in America they have tended not to be, because America's initial, seventeenth-century colonists were Protestants who had overtly rejected the religious pilgrimage practices of Roman Catholicism. Setting a pattern in the culture, they spurned the geographic movements and trappings of traditional Roman Catholic pilgrimage, which in their eyes supported the idea of salvation through good works and vows fulfilled rather than by faith and God's grace. Instead, as illustrated by John Bunyan's *The Pilgrim's Progress* of 1678, America's founding Puritans embraced the concept of pilgrimage as an allegory for the individual's lifetime struggle to achieve spiritual redemption in the afterlife. The impulse toward renewal through geographic pilgrimage, however, is not easily repulsed, and it emerged in America in secular guises. Beginning in the mid-nineteenth century, Americans performed pilgrimages to such historic destinations as Mount Vernon, the home of George and Martha Washington, and to natural sites like Niagara Falls. Such pilgrimages remain popular today. In recent decades, many Americans also took to traveling to more commercialized destinations like Graceland, the home of Elvis Presley, or to Walt Disney World, and, most poignantly, many Americans felt the urge to visit the scene of tragic deaths. Countless "grief pilgrims" have traveled to the bombed-out Alfred P. Murrah Federal Building in Oklahoma City, to the mass-shooting site at Sandy Hook Elementary School in Newtown, Connecticut, and to the site of the former World Trade Center twin towers. Moreover, American pilgrimage developed as a reversal of traditional medieval and Roman Catholic pilgrimage in many instances. Unlike these earlier pilgrims, who often traveled from rural homes to urbanized sacred sites where churches, shrines, and subsidiary structures had developed, Americans just as often headed out of the cities where they pursued their material fortunes to the rural areas and wildlands that contained few if any structures and which they perceived as their spiritual "homes."[12]

Pilgrimage is ancient and transcultural, but three fundamental beliefs generally account for why any pilgrim departs onto the path. First, he or she is convinced that powerful forces exist and that these forces can influence people's lives. Second, the pilgrim believes it is potentially possible to have meaningful relationships with these forces. They are not beyond reach. And, finally, the pilgrim trusts that there are unique and special places where the unmatched power of these forces feels close enough to touch. Examples of these places include Jerusalem, where such power is spiritual; Washington, D.C., where it is historical; or Yosemite, where it resides in nature.[13]

Places of pilgrimage, of course, vary by society, by era, and even from individual to individual. Nevertheless, pilgrimage is basically a journey to a sacred setting where both the journey and the destination are significant for the pilgrim. Her or his intention is to undergo the kind of experience that will bring about a change in one's life or spirit. Moreover, the experience of pilgrimage involves a number of recurrent elements, including the pilgrim's motivations; the route traveled and the physical, mental, or other challenges faced; the destination (and why it is sacred); the outcome once the pilgrimage is complete; and the relationship between pilgrimage and the pilgrim's sense of personal and group identity. When we apply these common elements to American campers, we find that they generally sought to visit "nature," which varied in its locations and forms. That nature could lie at the end of the journey, or it could suffuse the journey itself.[14] They took many routes, some more demanding than others, but always they had to journey from their homes (that is, they could not camp successfully in their own backyards). Campers' motivations varied, as we will see as we examine the distinctions between the various camping modes. Most modes of camping were inexpensive, but camping was often mentally taxing, physically punishing, or both. As a consequence, camping has long been colloquially known as "roughing it." The end result sought by campers also varied, but a common refrain was release from modern life's tensions and the opportunity to relax. Likewise, campers sought to reinforce a variety of identities, but a frequently shared pursuit was the reinforcement of the camper's sense of belonging, especially of being an American. Many returning campers felt closer to the nation for the experience.

While camping fits into the overall pattern of pilgrimage, pilgrimage itself is rarely a pure practice. Instead, pilgrimage and tourism often are wound together, and the differences between them can be hard to discern. Tourism is generally regarded as secular and as the seeing of new things or the experiencing of new places for the sake of recreation. It is not thought to have a strong spiritual component or to be pursued in order to produce some fundamental change in the traveler. Nonetheless, pilgrims travel, which can expose them to enough new sights and experiences to satisfy any inclinations they may have toward tourism. Moreover, many of the world's pilgrimage shrines have become enmeshed in nearby tourism facilities. Conversely, tourism often involves the sort of temporary displacement from home and exposure to a potentially transforming experience that is a routine part of pilgrimage. A tourist might become a pilgrim while traveling.

Tourists are not usually prevented from visiting most pilgrimage sites, which results in an often confusing blend of the two. Anyone who has ever visited a major pilgrimage site open to the public, for instance Saint Peter's Basilica in Rome, understands how difficult it is to distinguish the pilgrims from the tourists.

To address the blurred overlap between tourism and pilgrimage, religious and other institutions have sometimes formalized and regularized the spiritual conditions that a proper pilgrim is supposed to achieve or the physical actions one should complete. The pilgrim, for example, would only be able to obtain a certificate of visitation from the established "authority" after performing a series of steps in the prescribed order. Such strictures, however, are of limited effect, because what sets someone apart as a true pilgrim is contested in both meaning and practice. Pilgrims to Santiago de Compostela, for example, generally have little regard for individual motivations and consider only those who have walked (and perhaps bicycled) or ridden a horse long distance along one of the traditional paths as true pilgrims. Pilgrims' collective embrace of these nonmotorized and challenging forms of travel generates authenticity because it links them to the community of religious pilgrims whose paths stretch across Europe and back deep in time; traveling under one's own power recalls and confirms the traditional method these pilgrims have used for more than a thousand years. As anthropologist Victor Turner put it, "One gains more merit or grace by ignoring modern means of transportation." Travelers who instead choose to ride in automobiles, buses, and airplanes to the city and its shrine are cut off from the past, judged ersatz, and dismissed by the nonmotorized pilgrims as "tourists," no matter how much the former may feel they are authentic pilgrims.[15]

Campers similarly contest what is authentically camping and what is tourism. Like the pilgrims to Santiago, campers rarely question individual motivations but instead hitch their judgments to differences in mode and equipment. Today's backpackers routinely reject car and recreational-vehicle camping as too easy and inauthentic. For their part, motorized campers may respect the physical challenge of backpacking, but they fail to see it as transformative because in their view it demands too much exertion. "Are you kidding me?" snorted one recreational-vehicle camper after *New York Times* writer Timothy Egan asked if he would consider camping in a tent. "I've got a whole house with me. My wife likes to shower every day. Why would I ever go camping in a tent?"[16]

In the same way that few campers would consciously describe camping as an antidote for modernity, few of them would frame a weeklong trip to the Lake Michigan shoreline as pilgrimage. Nonetheless, such a trip fits comfortably within the cultural form of pilgrimage. When camping is unpacked from its popular descriptions, how-to manuals, and summertime advertisements, what remains is a leisure-time activity that moved people from their familiar homes and into a special place in order for them to return home transformed. A devout Catholic would hope for nothing less from her travels to Lourdes. As a consequence of its qualities as pilgrimage, camping is a "rough" activity, but campers disagree about the appropriate degree of challenge in the same way that they disagree about what qualifies as a "natural" destination.

Technology and Modernization

Campers' concerns about authenticity and their attitudes toward various camping modes and equipment point to another issue explored in *Heading Out*—the interaction between camping and modernization. Earlier I noted that modernity has been a vibrant force for change, but are antimodern practices and antimodernists themselves beyond the reach of modernity? Were any of the romantic antimodern movements mentioned above altered by this vibrant force? The simple answer is yes. The Arts and Crafts movement, which took inspiration from John Ruskin, was a critique of the modern way of life that split routine work and passive leisure. It inspired some antimodernists to step away from their urban lives in order to restore wholeness "by living a hard but satisfying life on the land." Generations of Americans have repeatedly reenacted this antimodern impulse, most recently in the communes and craft communities of the late twentieth century. Others, however, ambivalent in their antimodernism, were unwilling to relocate to small towns and rural areas. For many of them, the Arts and Crafts movement led to a rise in personal crafting as a way to engage in what historian Stephen M. Gelber termed "productive leisure." Early twentieth-century crafters, he argued, "did not seek financial justification for their hobby but understood it as a healthful and productive relief from regular work." But even as this strain of Arts and Crafts retained echoes of its antimodern origins, it also underwent modernization, spawning a love of collecting, personal gadgets, "tinkering," the suburban workshop in garage or basement, Home Depot superstores, and numerous handicraft and hobby shops in America's malls.[17]

Camping followed a similar trajectory. No matter which mode of camping was chosen, all campers headed out of town for a restoring but temporary stay in nature. Backpackers, for instance, sought to counteract the worst aspects of modern life by embracing the most physically challenging and historically rich mode of camping. Like earlier backpackers and the pedestrian pioneers before them, they continued the tradition of walking while carrying one's equipment and supplies—although these have become smaller, lighter, and more effective as backpacking modernized. Other kinds of campers, by contrast, were unwilling to rough it as much as backpackers. Camping continued to be an antimodern practice for them, but modern life held more appeal. As with backpackers, their equipment and supplies modernized, but unlike the backpackers, they embraced a new and highly transformative transport—the automobile—which allowed for a massive flowering in the size, range, and types of camping equipment used.

To explain how traditional and antimodern practices came to be modernized, the sociologist George Ritzer developed the notion of "McDonaldization." According to him, it is "the process by which the principles of the fast-food restaurant are coming to dominate more and more sectors of American society as well as the rest of the world." The process, Ritzer argues, is an outcome of modernity's rationality and consists of four dimensions that have made it alluring to many institutions. "It offers consumers, workers, and managers efficiency, calculability, predictability, and control." *Efficiency* refers to the identification and employment of the optimum method for completing a task, traveling from location to location, and the like. Systems often function efficiently by moving through a series of pre-designated steps. *Calculability* plays up a service or product's quantitative aspects. In the modern world, he insists, "quantity has become equivalent to quality." It is easy to imagine an American quipping that "more is better." At the same time, calculability can denote how quickly an activity might take to complete or how far one might need to travel. In terms of production, calculability tends to shift the emphasis from the qualitative aspects of a product to the number produced. Typically, workers will be expected to work a lot and quickly (and perhaps for low pay). *Predictability* means that "products and services will be the same over time and in all locales." Consumers can take comfort in the fact that when they make a purchase, no surprises will occur. Producers can rely on their systems working in a regular fashion, which allows them to forecast rates of output. Finally, *control* is exerted over the consumers, workers, and suppliers that participate in a system. Methods are employed that will lead people to do what management wishes and when. Technologies and organizational structures are also often engaged to enhance control and achieve management's desired outcomes. According to Ritzer, modernization has become "inexorable" and widespread throughout American society because McDonaldization is capable of impacting even such "seemingly impervious institutions" as religion.[18]

Like other elements of American society, camping was not beyond the reach of this modern process, which has slowly altered the practice and material culture of camping. In particular, modernization shaped camping in terms of comfort and convenience. As mentioned, camping was pilgrimage away from routine modern life and into a timeless nature where someone who "roughed it" could be transformed before returning to his or her permanent home. Nevertheless, offered manufacturers and retailers who provided camping equipment, and administrators who managed camping areas, a camper need not be completely bereft of modern devices and techniques in order to achieve transformation. If a camper chose to use a particular appliance, convenience, time- or effort-saving procedure or the like, then she could have a more efficient, calculable, predictable, or controlled experience that would eliminate the "unnecessary" roughness. Some of these innovations were aimed at increasing a camper's safety or health in the wild. Horace Kephart, for example, dedicated a chapter in 1917's *Camping and Woodcraft* to "Accidents and Emergencies: Their Backwoods Treatment." Along with the latest techniques for treating unconsciousness, convulsions, and poisoning, he dictated the components of a modern first-aid kit.[19] Most new technologies, however, were directed toward a camper's comfort. Sleeping on the ground was wonderful, for example, but an inflatable-mattress manufacturer would suggest that when a camper used its product, sleeping on the ground would be reliably restful.

Almost as soon as camping appeared as a popular recreation, some equipment manufacturers and retailers started to develop new camping products, while others adapted existing ones to camping. Nearly all began to advertise how their "gear" reduced bulk, prolonged food freshness, kept campers drier, warmer, cooler, bite-free, and more. The authors of new camping manuals similarly informed their readers how to avoid discomforts by purchasing particular products, by the use of special techniques, and by selecting the best locations. And, in the same vein, early twentieth-century campground managers modernized their areas by installing infrastructure, for example piped water, and by instituting such regulations as designated campsites. In each instance, these efforts included the inducement of reducing camping's challenges. By the 1920s, modernization had so impacted camping that one of the era's best-known authors, Elon Jessup, avoided any ambiguity by titling his how-to-camp manual *Roughing It Smoothly; How to Avoid Vacation Pitfalls.*[20]

Despite its antimodern roots, camping increasingly modernized. Some Americans, of course, continued to enjoy a challenging and often uncomfortable camping trip where they had to exert themselves and experience nature in a relatively unmediated state—backpacking, horse packing, and canoe camping come to mind. The majority, however, instead embraced equipment that reduced camping's potential discomforts. As the variety of comfort and convenience-enhancing gear expanded, camping and camp-grounds became increasingly like the domestic spaces from which campers had headed out. Concurrent with this development, camping increasingly attracted more people who enjoyed its social aspects as much as or more than its natural ones. Early campers frequently had written about their aesthetic responses to nature but said little about any other campers they met. For them, a beautiful natural landscape was enough to lift the spirit. Such reactions continued into the twentieth century, but by the 1950s many of the more socially oriented campers were also quick to praise their encounters with other campers, too. Like camping's material culture, its social aspects shifted as well.

Modernity impacted every mode of camping, but it is difficult to judge whether it undermined a camper's ability to achieve the personal transformation that he or she sought. Did an 1880 camper in the Adirondacks who used simple equipment and met few other campers feel more like he had successfully entered sacred nature than did a motor-home camper at a crowded campground on California's Pacific Coast Highway in 1980? Did one of them feel more refreshed, fulfilled, or in some way transformed than did the other? It is not for this author to decide whether one camper's experience was more authentic and transformative than another's when the outcome sought by all campers was an interior change. The best judge of the experience and its outcome has to be the camper. Did she set out because she was tired of "city life"? Did she travel to a place she considered "natural," properly set up the campsite, and after an acceptable amount of time feel transformed and better able to return to everyday life? If the answer was an honest yes, then we are compelled to accept it. It was, after all, the camper who wished to be revitalized. Consequently, campers are heavily quoted in *Heading Out*, because they can best speak for themselves about what they desired, what they experienced, and what it meant for them.

At the same time that camping modernized, a tension developed between the different modes of campers. Traditionally, camping was a pilgrimage that involved challenge, a rejection of the mundane, and an embrace of many premodern methods for interacting with nature. When antimodern camping first appeared, the differences between the modes were minimal, and little tension existed. However, as camping modernized, some modes became much less challenging, much safer, and relatively comfortable, as these campers were happy to accept more of everyday life's aspects when experiencing nature. Consequently, a contradiction developed as antimodern camping modernized, and it was largely expressed as disrespect or anxiety between the practitioners of camping's several modes. Backpackers, packhorse campers, car campers, and recreational-vehicle campers often felt antipathy toward the other camping modes and would overtly dismiss them as somehow pointless or worse. Many fundamentally disagreed about the authenticity, value, and appropriateness of the modes they did not enjoy. This book suggests, for example, that one explanation for why backpackers were often uncomfortable with car campers lay in the backpackers' view that an automobile and much that it could carry on a camping trip did not belong in nature. It was too much a part of conventional urban life and thus a violation of how backpackers felt that one should camp. Furthermore, campers went to great lengths to promote their preferred mode and sometimes engaged in conflicts with those who practiced another mode. According to the authors of one park management textbook, the park manager's job had become so fraught with challenges by 1983 that the authors felt compelled to warn students that "by far the greatest clash of personalities and the most vigorous forwarding of mutually exclusive objectives" did not develop between non-recreationists and recreationists, but among the latter group alone, including campers.[21] In other words, even though a motorhome camper and a backpacker might enjoy similarly transformative journeys, they also could view the other's camping mode as a threat and expend much energy to see that their mode in particular was secure and, where possible, enhanced in America's parks, forests, and other protected areas.

Overview

Heading Out is not a full, comprehensive history of American camping. That story is too large and complex to tell in a single volume.[22] Instead, this book explores the origin, expansion, and meaning of camping through a series of linked chapters. Each chapter is a vignette with its focus on a particular camping mode during a period when that mode's development, impact, and elements were in flux. Each chapter also revolves around individuals who shaped camping, clearly revealed its status and character at the moment, or in some other way were in the middle of representative events as they unfolded. This somewhat biographical method is used because the culture that is explored here is a shared set of beliefs, ideas, attitudes, and judgments. At the same time, these elements are part of individual lives and ways of life. Consequently, this sort of research requires that we find a camper, a camping advocate, an equipment manufacturer, and the like who incorporated camping's ideas into her or his life and expressed them in a letter, report, diary, advertisement, how-to manual, or policy statement. From this perspective, camping is a performance that must be acted out, and the campers, who are the actors on this stage, can best tell us what it means.

Heading Out attempts to historically bookend the principal cultural characteristics of American camping. On the one hand, the story begins just after the end of the Civil War because camping emerged as a recreation at that moment. For the first time, Americans began to talk about "going camping" as a leisure activity. On the other hand, the later chapters come to a close by the 1970s because today's camping patterns were more or less set during the post–World War II years. The social turbulence of the 1960s and 1970s swept through camping as it did throughout American society (and deserves a book of its own), aspects of camping's material culture changed after 1980, and events like the oil embargo of the 1970s and the recent Great Recession altered the balance between the camping modes, but camping in the early twenty-first century is not much different from what it was fifty years before. The total number of campers is greater today than in 1965, but the principal modes of camping, the equipment used, and the destinations visited remain about the same.

Heading Out begins with the launch of recreational camping during the summers of 1869 and 1870. During this "rush," thousands of campers first headed out from America's northeastern cities to the wilder areas of central New York's Adirondack Mountains. At the forefront of this multitude was an unexpected leader, William H. H. Murray, a well-known Congregationalist minister. Following the appearance of recreational camping, we turn in chapter 2 to the era of camping before the automobile came onto the scene. Camping persisted as a largely upper-middle-class and white activity during this time, but its popularity grew rapidly as magazine accounts, how-to manuals, and guidebooks taught more urban people how and where to camp. We meet several camping advocates, including Horace Kephart, a tortured soul who became America's best-known camping author during the twentieth century's first decades. Pre-automobile camping was not, however, just discussed; it was also experienced. We follow two camping parties—historian Frederick Jackson Turner out with his family on a month-long canoe trip to Ontario's Lake Nipigon and the writer Mary Bradshaw Richards, who with her husband traveled from Massachusetts to the young but distant Yellowstone National Park.

With chapter 3 we turn our attention to the appearance of the single most significant technological innovation in the history of camping—the inexpensive automobile. By the 1920s, millions of Americans, from Henry Ford to "Paw and Maw," were "hitting the motor camping trail." In addition, automobiles became a platform and facilitator for an enormous range of changes in camping gear. As an instance of these changes, the chapter examines the Coleman Company's move into the camping market. In addition, this chapter introduces the reader to some of the era's best-known camping promoters, including Elon Jessup and Frank Brimmer, as well as to the personal accounts of two continent-crossing campers, Mary Crehore Bedell and Frederic Van de Water.

In chapter 4 we read how the millions of campers who swarmed public facilities around the country led to their rapid deterioration. By the 1920s, campgrounds were being abandoned as uninhabitable, while some natural features were irreparably damaged by campers. Into this breach stepped E. P. Meinecke, who developed the auto campground plan that was quickly adopted by public agencies around the country and dominates car campgrounds to this day. The inexpensive automobile also extended camping to the mass of middle- and working-class Americans, but chapter 5 reveals that not everyone who could camp was welcome. When several new national parks opened in southern states during the 1930s, the campgrounds were racially segregated. For one African American, William J. Trent Jr., this was unacceptable, and he waged a long and often lonely campaign to officially desegregate all national park campgrounds.

Chapter 6 investigates the development and use of camping trailers. In particular, the history of Airstream trailers and the company's colorful founder, Wally Byam, are featured. Byam initially came to Southern California in the 1920s to make his fortune in Hollywood, but he found success only after he began to sell trailer plans and trailers themselves during the early 1930s. After Byam passed away in 1962, the Wally Byam Foundation worked with the Airstream Company and the U.S. State Department to create several programs that used trailer camping as a means to familiarize foreign diplomats and others with the "real America." Chapter 7 turns to the subject of backpacking to explore the emergence and meaning of a central infrastructural element of this mode—the long-distance trail. In particular, the chapter examines the motivations of Clinton C. Clarke and Warren L. Rogers, whose efforts ultimately led to the creation of the Pacific Crest Trail. Finally, *Heading Out* concludes with a review of the key notions developed in the earlier chapters and draws upon this enhanced understanding to offer an explanation for why camping's popularity has begun to waver.

The chapters in *Heading Out* open a doorway onto the historical development and meaning of camping in America. The modes of camping and their shifting technologies provide the central pivot for each chapter, but the changes that occurred steadily involved the ongoing but normally unconsidered elements of modernity, pilgrimage, and technological modernization. The first two, in particular, were central to the emergence of camping as a leisure activity in the summer of 1869.

CHAPTER ONE

ADVENTURES IN
THE WILDERNESS

William H. H. Murray and the
Beginning of Recreational Camping

In the late spring of 1870, with summer rapidly approaching, the editors of the *New York Daily Tribune* decided to send a reporter into the Adirondack region north and west of the city. Their correspondent had traveled to the area the summer before and with his second arrival was pleased to report that it remained an "Enchanted Ground." High-altitude lakes and higher mountains made it cool and refreshing during the hot summer months. The paths were quiet, green, and mossy, drawing out hikers onto seven- or eight-mile walks between breakfast and lunch. And everywhere the views were exquisite, varied, and captivating to the eye. If someone chose to camp in this delightful region, the reporter promised, he would "take back with him at the Summer's close the happiest, brightest, freshest memories of his life."[1]

A newspaper report that praises the qualities of a natural place is unremarkable today, but it would have been unknown only a few years prior to 1870. Even the correspondent admitted that the area of mountains and lakes had recently seemed far-off and marginal, with news accounts of it sounding "like legends from a distant and mythical country." But now, he reported, "this wild region is much more definitely known" and growing rapidly in popularity. This change to the region's status had come about primarily because an unlikely author, William H. H. Murray, the pastor of Boston's "Brimstone Corner," better known as the Park Street Church, had published a groundbreaking book, *Adventures in the Wilderness*, in April 1869. "Last summer," continued the reporter, "Mr. Murray's book, with its fresh, vigorous descriptions . . . alive with his own intense vitality . . . and with a sportsman's love of adventure—drew a throng of pleasure-seekers into the

Figure 1.1. William H. H. Murray, circa 1872. Courtesy of the Adirondack Museum, Blue Mountain Lake, NY.

lake region. It was amusing to see the omnipresence of this book. It seemed to be everywhere. Hawked through the cars; placarded in the steamers; for sale in the most unlooked-for places; by every carpet-bag and bundle lay a tourist's edition of Murray."[2] With the publication of this book, American camping had begun.

William Henry Harrison Murray

William Henry Harrison Murray came from a modest New England family whose ancestors had been among the first to settle his hometown of Guilford, Connecticut. The fourth child in a family of three girls and two boys, Murray was born on April 26, 1840, in Guilford, to Sally and Dickinson Murray. His mother, who had been a public school teacher before her marriage, possessed a sharp mind and a tendency toward seriousness, and like the other members of her family, she was religious. In her case, religious fervor sometimes prompted ecstatic visions. Murray's father, a hardworking ship carpenter, was energetic, buoyant, talkative, and engaging but rather improvident. The son would inherit many of his parents' qualities.[3]

Murray's boyhood was an enthusiastic mixture of study, farmwork, and outdoor recreation, leavened by the occasional prank. On one occasion, he tossed a small charge of gunpowder into his school's potbellied stove, while on another he ignited a newspaper held by his sister Sarah's beau, apparently thinking the young man's attentions were proceeding at too leisurely a pace. Young "Bill" came to love the outdoors, learning to shoot, hunt, and fish in the forest and meadows that lay near his family's home. During these same years, he developed a voracious reading habit, a taste for Latin and literature, and a desire to enter college. It may have been at about this time that Murray had his initial exposure to romanticism. One of Murray's biographers, Harry V. Radford, related that Fitz-Greene Halleck, a renowned American poet and member of the Knickerbocker Group, "was a fellow townsman of Murray's, and though much his senior in years, they were intimate friends, mutual admirers, and frequent visitors at each other's homes. It is said that Halleck taught Murray much of literature and poetry." It seems likely that Halleck would have introduced Murray to such American romantic authors as Emerson and Thoreau, but he might also have acquainted Murray with the English romantic John Ruskin. Halleck may also have been the source for Murray's desire to learn, because according to the younger man, his educational ambition was not his parents' doing. "I had no help, no encouragement. My father opposed me in my efforts, and my mother said nothing." Nonetheless, they must have felt their son had potential, because Dickinson did not stop Sally from sending Bill to the Guilford Institute, a private Yale preparatory school, soon after it opened. The family, however, had few resources, so young Murray worked on neighbors' farms to pay his tuition. Nor was he discouraged by the four miles he had to walk each way to the institute or by his need to carry his shoes in order to economize. Instead he leapt into his education, becoming a school leader, a member of the debating society, and the organizer of squirrel-hunting excursions into nearby woods.[4]

The fall of 1858 found Murray entering Yale College with not quite five dollars in his pocket and all his belongings—a few books and clothes—squeezed into two small carpetbags. Tuition continued to be a challenge for Murray and his family, so he contributed by selling bread, butter, and other goods baked and prepared by his mother and sisters. In addition, he continued to labor on Guilford farms, especially during summer breaks. As earlier in life, Murray was a devoted student in college, but he quickly turned his prankish nature against a distasteful Yale tradition—hazing the freshman. Murray had entered Yale with the largest freshman class in its history. Recognizing an opportunity, and with the college president's approval, Murray organized his fellow freshmen to frighten away the sophomores, who were seriously outnumbered. The next year Murray continued with his iconoclastic ways by persuading his classmates not to haze the entering freshman. It would not be the last time that Murray demonstrated his lack of patience with traditions he thought outmoded.

Upon graduating from Yale in 1862, Murray, strong, energetic, and good looking (fig. 1.1), married Isadora Hull, an East River, Connecticut, woman who shared his love of the outdoors. Bright and thoughtful, Isadora assisted Murray with his studies after he entered the Congregationalist East Windsor Hill Theological Seminary (now the Hartford Seminary) in East Windsor, Connecticut, and she supplemented the family's income by teaching school when Murray apprenticed as a pastor's assistant in New York City. Once he had finished his theological studies, Murray served in a succession of increasingly prosperous and prestigious churches in Connecticut and Massachusetts between 1864 and 1878, most famously at the Park Street Church in Boston. During these years, Murray developed a reputation as a church leader, a public defender of temperance, and an eloquent, engaging speaker. His eulogy of President Lincoln so moved his friends that they had it published. At the same time, however, Murray became notorious for his outdoor sporting activities, which were met with resistance at each of his new churches. The members of his Washington, Connecticut, church were reportedly shocked when Murray once arrived late to an evening service still carrying his game bag and dressed in hunting clothes. He apparently had forgotten about the service and, rushing back to church, had no time to change. Although he explained his tardiness and apologized, his parishioners were not amused. Opposed to a leisure ethic and of two minds about wild nature, Puritanical New Englanders had long rejected field sports as an unseemly recreation for any proper person and felt them especially unsuited for a minister.[5] But unlike his peers, Murray would not be contained.

Adventures in the Wilderness

It is unclear how Murray came to visit New York State's Adirondack Mountains, but he took his first summer vacation there in 1864 and then returned annually for the next fourteen years. He canoed and hiked widely, exploring some of the region's wildest and remotest corners, but his favorite campsite was small Osprey Island on Raquette Lake across from Woods Point, near the mouth of the Marion River. Occasionally he brought parties with him, which could number as large as thirty, and among them would be not only his friends but his wife and his friends' wives. "He had a strange notion (or is it so strange?) that women were as strong or stronger than men," wrote Murray's daughter about forty years after his death. Custom dictated that middle-class women should stay at their homes, but an iconoclastic Murray felt that they could benefit from wilderness as much as men. Moreover, he "reasoned that the Indian women were able to stand hardships, so why not white women."[6]

Smitten by the Adirondacks' beauty and the outdoor recreations he had enjoyed there with Isadora and their friends, Murray chose to make them the subjects of a series of what he termed "vivacious" essays composed during the mid-1860s. He neither intended them for publication nor even to share with friends, but as a writing exercise to make himself "more perfect in English composition, and . . . to keep my mind buoyant and out of conventional ruts of expression." At the time, Murray was the new pastor of the Congregational church in Meriden, Connecticut, which had a "large and intelligent" congregation. Feeling somewhat insecure about his ability to meet their expectations, Murray began to practice his writing each day. Over time he produced "a collection of original [essays] that were unique, and being rewritten time and again, were . . . as perfect as I could make them." However, since Murray had no plan to publish them, they would never have seen daylight if not for an accident. Luther G. Riggs, the owner-editor of the *Meriden Literary Recorder* and a friend of Murray's, burst into the minister's office one morning "in a state of mind not easily appreciated save by some country editor in like circumstances." Riggs had to go to press in four hours, and three empty columns remained to be filled. "You must give me something, Parson," he begged in desperation. "A section of an old sermon, a portion of a Sunday school address, a bit of temperance talk, a report of a Sunday school convention which was never held—something you have never used—any worthless stuff to fill up the space." Laughing at his comrade's consternation, Murray replied, "I have the very thing you want." Tossing Riggs a copy of "Crossing the Carry," one of his practice essays on the Adirondacks, Murray assured the editor that "I have never used it and never shall. You are welcome to it." Riggs hastily printed it on August 14, 1867, and then five more of Murray's Adirondack essays before the end of October. These sometimes humorous, sometimes serious adventure stories received only a subdued and local response. To Murray's mind, his Adirondack essays now had reached the largest audience they would, but he was wrong.[7]

In early 1869, shortly after Murray had become pastor of Boston's prestigious Park Street Church, a visiting college friend, Josephus Cook, paid him a visit. Cook would become a well-known public orator within a few years, but at the time he was struggling to begin his career. Viewed suspiciously by Boston's orthodox Congregationalists, Cook was unable to obtain an invitation to speak in church. Murray, however, thought Cook "the ablest man . . . since Jonathan Edwards," so he gave his friend the Park

Street Church's pulpit the following Sunday.[8] The congregation's response to Cook's sermon was strongly positive, and he was swiftly accepted by the city's other Congregationalists. A few weeks later and in a state of exuberance, Cook again visited his friend to tell him that his becoming pastor of the Park Street Church was a tremendous accomplishment, but that he would never be able "to look upon Boston as captured" until he had spoken in Music Hall, lectured before the Total Abstinence Society, and published a book with the "aristocratic" house of Fields, Osgood and Company, whose list included Longfellow, Emerson, and Hawthorne. Not wishing to publish anything and with no plans to speak in either setting, Murray good-naturedly dismissed Cook's proposition. To Murray's complete surprise, that same afternoon brought first a delegation inviting him to speak some evening at the Music Hall and then another asking him to give the annual address before the Total Abstinence Society! Stunned by the turn of events, Murray was standing at the open door as the second committee departed when he happened to spot clippings from his Adirondack articles in the *Meriden Literary Recorder*. In that instant, he knew what he would next do.

By his own admission, Murray was "utterly ignorant of the conventional way of procedure in such a matter," but, standing in the doorway with the clippings, he said to himself, "Why not take them across the street [to Fields, Osgood and Company] and see if they will do anything with them." A few minutes later Murray was being ushered into the office of James T. Fields, the firm's director, where he briefly stated who he was and why he had called. Despite the impropriety of Murray's sudden appearance, Fields remained courteous but discouraging. "I regret to say, Mr. Murray, that our list of publications was closed last week, and it would be against the custom of the house to enlarge it."[9] However, having heard of Murray's "love of outdoor life" and not wishing to embarrass the minister, Fields asked if he and his wife might be allowed to read the manuscript. Murray agreed, and two days later he received a request to return to the publisher's office. According to Murray, he never forgot "a single phase of that interview," and it is best told in his own words.

> He received me standing with several chapters of my manuscript lying loosely on the desk before him. "Mr. Murray," he said, "both Mrs. Fields and myself have read these papers attentively. They are very unique. We do not recall anything that is just like them. Here," he added, picking up several leaves, "is a descriptive bit entitled 'A Ride With a Mad Horse in a Freight Car.' May I ask, did you write that piece?" "I certainly did," I replied. "And here is a piece," he added, taking up another set of leaves called "Fantom Falls." "May

I ask, did you write that?" My reply was again in the affirmative. In like manner he questioned on the chapter called "Crossing the Carry," and I gave him the same answer. Now, friends, in all my pulpit career I had never in all the ups and downs of it allowed myself the privilege of getting mad, and up to this point in the conversation I held myself perfectly in hand. But now I said, "Mr. Fields, you are aware that your interrogations are most unusual for one gentleman to address to another in our position, and I feel at liberty to ask what you mean by it?" "Simply this, Mr. Murray," he said, "your method of interpreting nature and your humor are unlike anything that we have ever seen. This little book, I am confident, is destined to a great career. We have decided to reopen our list this spring and illustrate it in the best manner that time will permit."

Murray and Fields signed a contract on February 10 that promised the author royalties of ten cents per copy after the first thousand sold and then fifteen cents per copy for any sales over five thousand.[10]

Near the beginning of April 1869, Fields, Osgood and Company released *Adventures in the Wilderness; or, Camp-Life in the Adirondacks*, but the critics were more mixed in their opinions than Fields. The *Overland Monthly* dismissed the book as "breathless," a "gratuitous advertiser," and as "a succession of views of insignificant details." As far as the reviewer was concerned, Murray apparently had gone into the wilderness for only one thing—to eat, especially trout. The description of the catching of these fish was, in the critic's view, "without exception the most extravagant piece of writing we have ever met. . . . It is gorgeous French, badly translated." The *Nation* was more generous, finding *Adventures* to have both attractive and repellent elements. "It would be hard for the honest lover of woods and waters and forest sports to find a book concerning them which should not please him more than Mr. Murray's. And it would be harder for the person with tolerable taste in literature to find a book the tone of which would very much more displease him." Murray's voice was unsettling, a "falsetto," and "screechy," which did not inspire confidence. Still, they found his practical advice "to be sensible and worth taking." Elsewhere, the *New York Times* described *Adventures* as "fresh, lively and exhilarating," while another early newspaper critic found the book charming: "The Adirondacs [sic] have been the summer resort of the author for several years, and he writes of their beauties and advantages with hearty enthusiasm. According to his description it is a most delightful region, and he gives ample particulars for rendering it accessible to all who would enjoy the health-giving air and exhilarating spirits of its wide solitudes.

Mr. Murray is a sportsman in the highest sense of the term, and he imparts to the sportsman's life a refined and elevating spirit which is exceedingly pleasing. . . . The book will be read with pleasure by all who feel an interest in woodland life."[11] And so it was.

The Murray Rush

Despite the mixed reviews, *Adventures in the Wilderness* was a cultural event, hugely popular with the public and a tremendous commercial success. Murray was both famous and wealthy by June. We likely may never know exactly how many copies were sold, but the numbers probably rose into the tens of thousands. The book was in its tenth printing by July 7 (although we do not know the size of the printings), and later in life, Murray reported that *Adventures* had sold at a rate of five hundred per week.[12] Without a doubt, the book was a best seller.

Within months of the book's release, the sleepy Adirondack region, which had sat at the edge of both northeastern U.S. maps and northeasterners' imaginations, was transformed by an unprecedented horde of approximately two to three thousand recreational hunters, anglers, and campers from New York, Boston, Hartford, and other cities. This stampede, which continued unabated through the summers of 1869 and 1870, came to be called the "Murray Rush," a title it retains, and its instigator gained a nickname—"Adirondack" Murray. By July 1869, demand for *Adventures* was so great that publishers produced a "Tourist's Edition," with twelve pages of timetables and a map in the back pocket. To stimulate their business, railroads began to offer a free copy of Murray's book with each round-trip ticket to the Adirondacks.[13] Soon, as this chapter's opening vignette related, it seemed that everyone traveling to the Adirondacks owned "a copy of Murray."

Among the crowd were reporters, including one, "Wachusett," whose pseudonym referred to a central Massachusetts mountain that was a popular hiking spot. Under a title of "With the Multitude in the Wilderness," Wachusett described the arriving legions for his Boston readers.

> Mr. Murray's pen has brought a host of visitors into the Wilderness, such as it has never seen before—consumptives craving pure air, dyspeptics wandering after appetites, sportsmen hitherto content with small game and few fish, veteran tourists in search of novelty, weary workers hungering for perfect rest, ladies who have thought climbing the White Mountains the utmost possible achievement of feminine

strength, journalists and lecturers of both sexes looking for fresh material for the dainty palate of the public, come in parties of twos and dozens, and make up in the aggregate a multitude which crowds the hotels and clamors for guides, and threatens to turn the Wilderness into a Saratoga of fashionable costliness.[14]

Most of these adventurers followed Murray's prescribed route from wherever they started to Plattsburgh on the New York shore of Lake Champlain (usually reached by boat) and then by train to Ausable River and Port Kent, where they transferred to whatever surface transport they could find (fig. 1.2). Here the travelers encountered their first obstacle—the regular twice-weekly stage was wholly inadequate to the suddenly expanded task. Coaches might carry "sportsmen and outers" with their rods and rifles, but "trunks, portmanteaus, tents, bales of blankets, and other baggage" could not get aboard. Seizing the opportunity, enterprising teamsters filled the gap, often earning an impressive fifteen dollars for the thirty-five miles to the settlement of Saranac Lake on the edge of Murray's Adirondack wilderness.[15]

Once in the forest, travelers found few if any accommodations available, even though seemingly every small "hotel," cabin, log lean-to, and tent had been put into service. Overcrowding and skyrocketing rates resulted, producing a bumper crop of woeful tales both true and enhanced. According to one,

A New Yorker arrived late one night at an overcrowded hostelry. He found people lying in the parlors and on the piazzas [porches]. He was told there was only one place in the house where he could sleep—on an old pool-table. As it was either that or nothing, he accepted, merely remarking, "This is hard!" He awoke early the next morning, sore in mind and body, and bent on returning to civilization at the first opportunity. He sought the landlord, and met him emerging from a barn.

"How much do I owe you?" asked the guest.

"Lemme see," reflected the landlord. "What room was you in?"

"Room!" ejaculated the other in disgust. And then, with expletives, he explained where he had spent the night and how he had retired supperless.

"Five dollars," was the laconic verdict.

"Five dollars!" came the dull echo of indignant surprise.

"Sure thing," said mine genial host. "Dollar an hour is the regular charge for the pool-table after midnight."[16]

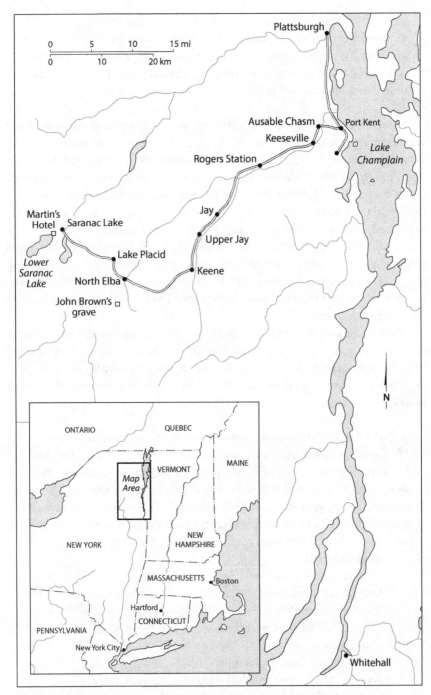

Figure 1.2. Murray's recommended route from Plattsburgh, New York, to Lower Saranac Lake on the edge of the Adirondack wilderness.

Figure 1.3. Lakeside campers enjoy an early version of an "Adirondack shelter." From H. P. Smith and E. R. Wallace, *The Modern Babes in the Wood or Summerings in the Wilderness* (Hartford, CT: Columbian Book Co., 1872), i.

Watercraft and guides, twin necessities for venturing into the Adirondack wilderness, were equally in great demand but were equally insufficient. Boys who could be spared from farmwork became guides overnight, often receiving wages far higher than experienced men who were already engaged. During the Murray Rush of 1869 and 1870, as well as the several following seasons, campers thronged to the Adirondacks, gathering at every log shelter or picturesque campsite near a lake or riverbank (fig. 1.3).

From our perspective at the beginning of the twenty-first century we can see that *Adventures in the Wilderness* was the watershed book in the history of American camping. For decades before its publication, books, magazines, and newspapers had enticed readers into the wilds of New York, New Hampshire, and elsewhere in New England, but these inducements did not have the impact of *Adventures in the Wilderness* because of factors both internal and external to the latter's publication. Externally, the population of New England and the mid-Atlantic states expanded by more than 40 percent between 1850 and 1870, while the number of U.S. cities with populations greater than twenty-five hundred increased from 236 to 663 nationally. Many, if not most, of these expanding and newly urbanized settlements were in the Northeast. It was from among these city dwellers that campers were most likely to appear. The post–Civil War economy also boomed, with estimates of growth averaging around

6 percent per year. This rapid increase in wealth was accompanied by a surge in the number of middle- to upper-middle-class professionals, many of whom could afford a vacation. Together they made it possible for more people to buy Murray's book and then to act on his advice. Moreover, the waging of the Civil War, which had concluded only four years before *Adventures* was published, had taught thousands, perhaps tens of thousands, of urban men how to camp. The era's limited and expensive transportation meant that few urban dwellers ever had contact with natural settings, so they were, somewhat paradoxically, farther from the wild than are today's urban Americans, who can travel to wildlands easily and cheaply. The war, however, had changed that relationship. As one camping guidebook noted only a couple of years after Murray published his book, it was easy to learn how to camp because, no matter what questions might arise, "nearly every one can get valuable hints on the subject of out-of-door life from men of army experience." Finally, it was only in 1868 that two railroads and a telegraph line reached the region's margin, greatly improving Adirondack access.[17]

Internal to Murray's book, it is noteworthy that the author who opened the Adirondacks to the middle classes by emphasizing a need for outdoor recreation and vacations was a liberal Protestant clergyman. Referring to ministers as stressed and overworked, and by implication other professions as well, he declared that "a visit to the North Woods could not fail of giving them precisely such a change as is most desirable, and *needed* by them [emphasis added]. In the wilderness they would find that perfect relaxation which all jaded minds require." With this argument, Murray became an early advocate for a social as well as a physical space for leisure in a society founded on a work ethic. According to historian Philip Terrie, antebellum authors had been "literate, Eastern men, who actually camped in and achieved intimacy with a wild landscape." However, the wilderness that they experienced "was far less appealing than the wild landscapes so glowingly depicted in Romantic literature and art." As a consequence, argued Terrie, these authors developed "a profound ambivalence about the existence and future value of wilderness." This ambivalence was absent from *Adventures*. An enthusiastic Murray delivered his positive message as a set of lively and appealing stories in a simple, direct, and engaging style that communicated the pleasures of wilderness camping. He wrote with a vigor and pacing and an ebullience that well conveyed his grasp of the wilderness.[18]

In addition, we must credit Murray's appeal to the substance of his book. The Adirondack travel literature published prior to *Adventures in the Wilderness* had attracted few campers to the region because writers had offered readers little *useful* information. One of the most informative and more popular books, Joel T. Headley's *The Adirondack; or, Life in the Woods*, had limited its practical advice to three pages at book's end, and most of this was information on how to get to the region. In terms of camping gear, Headley's advice was less than terse—"A good rifle, a knife, three or four shirts, and a blanket or overcoat, making a package of only a few pounds weight, must be all that you take with you." More memoirs than guides, books before *Adventures in the Wilderness* had successfully evoked wilderness feelings but had offered few practical insights on how to act once there. In sharp contrast, the fifty-six-page opening chapter in Murray's book provided a nascent camper with hands-on information and advice. Murray told his readers how to get to the Adirondacks, how to avoid pesky insects, where to buy equipment, the names of local guides and which qualities to value in one, and what accommodations were available, as well as what to bring and what not. As the scholar Warder H. Cadbury remarked, "A reader could not help but come away from reading Murray with the belief that he too could rough it in the wilderness." Moreover, Murray published *Adventures* just as guidebooks were beginning to shape and enhance wilderness recreation. Literacy was rising among Americans, and while city dwellers could no longer learn traditional skills from families and neighbors, they could and did seek assistance from written guidebooks.[19]

Finally, *Adventures* produced its dramatic popular response because Murray, while similar to his literary predecessors, more forcefully introduced camping within the American pilgrimage pattern. The wilderness books written before Murray can generally be described as fitting within the romantic tradition when they presented nature as sacred and emphasized its beauty, emotional power, and connections to divinity. They dwelled on landscape and scenery rather than people, reducing the latter to insignificance, and provided few if any geographic connections between a reader and the described settings. Like the lush romantic paintings of Asher B. Durand and John Kensett, who also were working in the Adirondacks in the decades before Murray, books by Thoreau, C. F. Hoffman, or J. T. Headley tended to describe idealized settings of an attractive and benevolent nature. Even when they focused on specific landscape features, their narratives often lacked a strong sense of place, leaving them beyond the grasp of most readers.[20]

Murray fell within the romantic tradition when he described an Adirondack morning sky as "overspread as with a thick silvery veil, with the least trace of amber and gold amid the threads," or the mountains as "among the first to rise out of the Profound," but he also stepped outside it. Murray helped to calm readers' anxieties about entering the wild through lighthearted language and tension-relieving humor. In one chapter, "Jack-Shooting in a Foggy Night," Murray related what occurred after his deer-hunting partner, Martin, came to be holding a deer by its very short tail. "Now and then the buck would take a short stretch into the fog and darkness, only to reappear [in their lights] with the same inevitable attachment of [Martin's] arms and legs streaming behind. The scene was too ludicrous to be endured in silence." So Murray shouted to Martin as he again went by, "That's *your* deer. I quit all claim to him." Nature, Murray indicated to his readers, was not just dramatic; it could also be comedic. In addition, Murray did not simply praise Adirondack nature. He gave it a more definite location than his predecessors, which helped to transform this dimly perceived and marginal region into an accessible and circumscribed place. *Adventures in the Wilderness* stimulated a throng of campers because Murray, more than his predecessors, held out the Adirondacks as the sacred place that would act as a balm to the iniquities of city life. In straightforward, guidebook language, he told readers where and how they could step out of the workaday world for a brief immersion into that other world of nature and then return to their everyday lives refreshed.[21]

While writers before Murray generally had made some reference to the value of getting into nature, he took these references further. According to J. T. Headley, who was clearly wearied by modern life, "The mask that society compels one to wear is cast aside . . . and the soul rejoices in its liberty and again becomes a child in action." For him specifically, his first visit to the Adirondacks was prompted by a physician who had prescribed it as the cure for "an attack on the brain." Thereafter, Headley went to the Adirondacks "with pleasure." A decade later, the well-known humorist, painter, illustrator, author, and veteran sportsman Thomas B. Thorpe began his description of an 1859 Adirondack journey with an exclamation: "Bless the invention of a short trip into the country!" Such excursions, he declared, provided "relief from mental activity" as well as "healthful exercise."[22]

Murray, in comparison, enhanced and extended his predecessors' concerns when he explicitly blamed modernity's primary symbol, the city, for his readers' yearnings or aches and then prescribed a wilderness cure. In the wake of the Civil War, Murray sensed how the movement of rural residents into cities would feel personally and how the newly urbanized might long for that more vigorous and "rougher" life. He introduced his book to the "large number of people who, born in the country, and familiar in boyhood with the gun and rod, still retain, in undiminished freshness and vigor, their early love for manly exercises and field sports." *Adventures*, he declared, was written for those "who, put up in narrow offices and narrower studies, weary of the city's din, long for a breath of mountain air and the free life by field and flood." These misplaced ideals, he assured his readers, were not forever lost but could be found on a camping trip into the Adirondacks. Moreover, Murray did not settle for a sentence or two about the generic value of nature at the outset of *Adventures*, but included numerous, specific references scattered throughout. Repeatedly, he detailed how one's health and happiness increased during an Adirondack outing. If one was healthy, he related, the beauty and grandeur of the Adirondack scenery would please "the gazer's eyes," with its "lakes gleaming amid the depths of the wilderness like gems of purest ray amid the folds of emerald-colored velvet." If one was weak or ill, "the spruce, hemlock, balsam, and pine, which largely compose this wilderness, yield upon the air, and especially at night, all their curative qualities."[23] For Murray, the Adirondacks' wilds were a sacred place that stood apart from and in opposition to campers' everyday world in the developing cities.

Another element in *Adventures* that is common to pilgrimage was a sense of *communitas*, an equalizing of the social divisions that occur in ordinary life. In the city, Murray's readers lived and worked in hierarchical institutions where their social status situated them above or below others. On a camping trip, much of this distinction disappeared. Outdoor recreation writers before Murray usually had treated camping as a means to support hunting, fishing, or some other activity. Murray revised this relationship by suggesting that Adirondack camping was a pleasant and beneficial recreation itself and by noting that it was available to the middle classes, not just the wealthy.[24]

Murray offered a reduction in gender distinctions too by insisting that camping was "delightful to ladies. There is nothing in the trip which the most delicate and fragile need fear. And it is safe to say, that, of all who go into the woods, none enjoy the experiences more than ladies, and certain it is that none are more benefited by it." Other writers had characterized women as "fragile" and physically unable to endure time in the wilderness, but Murray regarded this view as nonsense. "Acquainted as I am with many ladies, some of them accustomed to every luxury, and of delicate health, who have 'camped out' in this wilderness, I have yet to meet with a single one who ever 'caught cold,' or experienced any other inconvenience to the bodily health in the woods." To cement women's interest, he detailed the components of a "Ladies Outfit" that "a lady at my elbow" had provided him. After five years' experience, she had found that the "most appropriate and serviceable [outfit] for a lady to wear in the wilderness" included gloves with "armlets," a felt hat, a "flannel change throughout," waterproof foot-wear, and a "short walking-dress, with Turkish drawers fastened with a band tightly at the ankle."[25] No woman, in Murray's opinion, was to avoid camping because she feared for her health or safety.

Murray also went well beyond his predecessors when he provided the miracle often associated with a sacred place. A young, consumptive man, he related, "the son of wealthy parents in New York . . . lay dying in that great city." A friend came by the young man's home to tell him that "many had found help from a trip to [the Adirondack] region." At first, the young man's family would not allow him to travel, but ultimately they relented. When this consumptive arrived in the Adirondacks during the first week of June, he could no longer walk and had to be carried into the forest lying in a canoe. After two weeks of camping, however, he was walking. In three, he lost his cough. And, during the second week of November, after a summer camping in the woods, he walked out sixty-five pounds heavier and "bronzed as an Indian." Such an extraordinary episode amplified readers' perception of the Adirondacks as a place apart and prepared them for similarly remarkable events on their own camping trips. At the same time, Murray sought to dampen unreasonable expectations when he cautioned readers to remember that the young New Yorker's experience was "an extreme case." Nonetheless, others, he assured them, had enjoyed similar, if less dramatic results, including his wife. "There is one sitting near me, as I write, the color of whose cheek, and the clear brightness of whose eye, cause my heart to go out in ceaseless gratitude to the woods, amid which she found that health and strength of which they are the proof and sign."[26]

Finally, while Murray provided directions on how to get to favored Adirondack areas, he also included stories about the route and events that had occurred there. One stop stands out—John Brown's grave—which was located on the road to Saranac Lake. Brown was a renowned abolitionist who, in October 1859, had led twenty-one men, including five African Americans and three of his sons in an attack on the federal armory and arsenal at Harpers Ferry, Virginia, in order to start an antislavery insurrection. Although the raid failed to achieve its goal and was disastrous for Brown and his followers, it hastened the onset of the Civil War. When a camper reached Lake Placid, Murray recommended a visit to the nearby North Elba farm, where "the martyr of the nineteenth century sleeps." Here, he suggested, travelers, especially Americans, should stop for a day "to enter the house he built, to see the fields he and his heroic boys cleared, the fences they erected and others standing incomplete as they left them when they started for Harper's Ferry." Such details and interpretations are another common element in pilgrimage. Pilgrims seek historically saturated pathways on which to recapitulate others' endeavors and to partake in rituals because they support and reinforce identity. Murray not only recommended camping in the sacred wilds; he infused the route with a post–Civil War, national significance and prescribed a ritual visit to a place specifically sacred to Americans—the site of a martyr's tomb. With this knowledge, the Adirondack campers' journeys took on deeper meaning as they fused their identities into the imagined community of past, present, and future American campers.[27]

The Response to *Adventures*

The skyrocketing sales of Murray's book and the subsequent "rush" partly reveal the degree to which *Adventures in the Wilderness* seized the popular imagination, but we can also gauge its impact by noting the abundance and range of comments, critiques, and spoofs it inspired. Newspaper editors soon heard about the Murray Rush and quickly sent their correspondents into the Adirondacks. Some may even have suspected that something like the rush would occur, because the *Boston Daily Advertiser*'s Wachusett filed his series of eight reports during the last two weeks of July 1869. Yes, he noted, crowds of people were daily arriving in the Adirondacks from a variety of cities, but these "companions of travel" easily dropped the conventional social order of home. Instead, we can see that they embraced the *communitas* common to campers on their way to sacred space. According to Wachusett, arriving travelers "burst the withes of ceremony as they sniff the atmosphere of the woods, make the first advances toward that acquaintance and good fellowship which is the rule in the Wilderness. The talk begins to run on the four great subjects of the Adirondacks,—game, Murray, guides and mosquitoes; the world of newspapers, stock markets, hurry and headaches fades away with the disappearance of the telegraph wires; and one realizes that he is entering a new atmosphere." Nevertheless, Wachusett found the long route into the region to be tiring and the final carriage ride so brutal that "the weary traveler cannot even enjoy the poor luxury of being bruised in a new spot."[28]

After arriving at Martin's hotel on the northeast shore of Lower Saranac Lake, Wachusett generally enjoyed himself and supported Murray's contentions about the beautiful scenery, the exciting fishing and hunting, and the pleasures of camping. However, he also repeatedly questioned the author's descriptions in light of the sudden appearance of a "multitude" that had altered the individual and small-group situations presented in *Adventures*. Accommodations might have been easy to find during the summer of 1868, before Murray's book was published, but now, Wachusett pointed out, they were difficult to obtain at hotels like Martin's. Worse still, guides, who were necessary if one wished to camp in the wilderness, were nearly impossible to hire.

> As you mingle with the guests of the inn, you discover that one thought is dominant with all. People collect into knots to talk over their chances of guides; they form combinations to secure the desired end; they watch each other jealously to see that no individual gets an unfair advantage; they stand guard on the pier to catch the first glimpse of an incoming boat; they make furtive expeditions up the Lake on the dim chance of catching a disengaged guide coming down. . . . One would think that Mr. Martin's pleasant hostelry was a prisonhouse, by the eagerness of its inmates to secure the means of getting away.[29]

In spite of his critique about hotel accommodations and the hiring of guides, Wachusett found Murray "in the right" on the matter of mosquitoes and blackflies. They could be managed, and the majority of people would get along without serious inconvenience, but he warned everyone against them just the same. "Either the insects have not read Mr. Murray's book; or they have mislaid their almanac; or, what is more probable, the lateness and the wetness of the season has prolonged their term of life." Some visitors, he reported, had come prepared for extended stays, only to be driven out by insects within a few days of arriving. Still, the blackflies were in decline, and if one could visit in September, then "the guides assure me, there are no poisonous insects in the woods."[30]

Elsewhere, a letter received by the *New York Daily Tribune* strongly supported Murray. The author, "H.H.," began by explaining that he had "visited the North Woods eight times within the last 13 years" and so knew the conditions in the Adirondack region. In his opinion, "Mr. Murray has not overrated the fishing and hunting" but in fact had understated the opportunities for adventure and field sports. Mr. Murray's successes, stated H.H., did not begin to describe the possibilities for pleasure and quite simply had not "come quite up to my own." The problem, he decided, was ignorant visitors. Typically, he wrote, the summer season would have brought the area a handful of small parties of two to six people before the publication of *Adventures in the Wilderness.* "Now, because 3,000 persons could not find accommodations, boats, and guides, in the center of a pathless wilderness . . . Mr. Murray is set down as a deceiver. . . . I hold that Mr. Murray is not responsible for these disappointments. The tourists should have informed themselves what facilities there were for getting into the woods, and what accommodations could be obtained . . . before they left home, and should have taken into the woods with them all the little necessaries and what provisions they expected to want, except trout and venison." With a few precautions, preparations, and prudence, "very few, if any, will return dissatisfied."[31]

H.H.'s defense of Murray exposes a tension common to pilgrimages—determining who is authentic. H.H. dismissed those Adirondack visitors who complained about the inadequacy of accommodations and camping equipment or the shortage of fish as uninformed and unprepared for the wilds. Using the worst description he knew, H.H. did not refer to them as imprudent campers or sportsmen, but spurned them as "tourists." When disappointed Adirondack visitors questioned Murray's veracity and doubted his expertise, many of his defenders responded that these critics were not really campers. Such a response is not unusual. Pilgrimage authorities, including someone like H.H., can attempt to control the definition of who is "real" or not by proclaiming that "true" pilgrims will visit a special site, possess a particular spirit or symbol, or follow a prescribed route or ritual; yet any definition will remain contested and frequently change over time. Someone may try to define the authentic camping experience for himself and others, but the reality is that campers, like other pilgrims, find authenticity in place and in practice. Consequently, those who feel camping to be most authentic when practiced at a particular location or type of place and in a particular fashion are most likely to feel that variations are inauthentic and a form of desecration. H.H. undoubtedly was wise to suggest greater preparation and foresight before entering the wilderness, but neither he nor anyone else could control who qualified as a camper. There can be no single camping practice, place, or meaning, only contested degrees of authenticity.[32]

Other newspaper accounts and letters, however, were not as supportive or as evenhanded as H.H. and Wachusett. "Murray is a humbug." "Murray is a liar." "Murray ought to be assassinated." "I am one of Murray's fools." Reports came in that the woods had been overhunted and overfished, and that the guides, when they could be found, were incompetent and extortionate. As one wag wisecracked, nothing could be more obvious to someone who had read *Adventures* and had recently visited the Adirondack wilderness than that "there are two sides to every question."[33]

In particular, critics brought up the issue of who was an authentic camper by focusing their ire on the presence of amateurs and women in the Adirondacks. Thomas B. Thorpe was particularly aggrieved about the impact of *Adventures*, provocatively titling his piece in *Appletons' Journal* "Abuses of the Backwoods." For Thorpe, "the genuine sportsman and the true lover of Nature" shared Murray's opinion that the Adirondack wilderness was sacred space, but he dismissed Murray's descriptions of it as "fashionable

Figure 1.4. Kate Field in 1865. From Lilian Whiting, *Kate Field: A Record* (Boston: Little, Brown, 1899), 147.

twaddle." Worse, Thorpe was deeply offended that the book had attracted urban "pretenders and superficials" who possessed neither a proper understanding of the wild nor the appropriate abilities to enter it. "The highly cultivated mind which rejoices in the wilds of Nature, is too sensitive to remain unmoved when they see 'those temples of God's creation' profaned by people who have neither skill as sportsmen, nor sentiment or piety enough in the composition, to understand Nature's solitudes, and sympathize with the 'home of the Great Spirit.' "[34] Before entering the Adirondacks, Thorpe insisted, city amateurs needed to become skilled and educated to nature's meaning so as not to violate it.

Kate Field, by contrast, suggested that people like Thorpe were upset simply because "their favorite hunting and fishing grounds have been made known to the public."

A renowned and highly regarded journalist, travel writer, actor, and lecturer (fig. 1.4), Field had read *Adventures in the Wilderness* when it was first released and decided to camp in the Adirondacks with three female companions and no men for the month of July 1869. Through sheer coincidence, she traveled along the way with Murray, who was himself headed to the region for a two-month vacation. After this experience, Field publicly embraced the equality and openness that camping promoted rather than the hierarchy and exclusivity Thorpe demanded. "The greatest good of the great-est number is," she declared in August 1869, "the true democratic platform, and if several hundred men think that the life-giving principles of the North Woods was [*sic*] instituted for the benefit of a few guns and rods, they are sadly mistaken."[35]

Field's declaration for open wilderness was salt in Thorpe's wound because, unsurprisingly, he was as incensed by the presence of women in the Adirondacks as he was by novices. Early in July 1869, Wachusett had reported that women were camping and that other campers (presumably men) were upset, asserting that the wilderness was "no place for women." "But I cannot join this crusade," declared the reporter. "I think there is no lady who could not heartily enjoy" camping. Moreover, "they may even dispense, if they choose, with the inconvenient appendage of male escort,—going, of course, in parties of two or more of their own sex. The experiment, I think, has never been tried before; but its feasibility has been tested this year, and with entire satisfaction to the parties interested." Among those testing this feasibility was, of course, Field herself, who took to the public lecture stage in the fall of 1869 to praise the Adirondacks and to argue that women should camp. On one occasion, she told a large audience at New York's Steinway Hall that her Adirondack camping trip without any men had gone very well. Oozing sarcasm, she admitted that "it was agreeable to women to be accompanied on such excursions by the tyrant man; but when there was no such tyrants at hand to rescue her, it is surprising what powers of rescue she finds within herself." She and her companions, who called themselves the Black Fly Club, had no trouble "rescuing" themselves, leaving Field to report simply that the Adirondack scenery was grand, the local men were "unmitigated 'roughs,'" and that mosquitoes were "like the poor, 'always with you.'" Nevertheless, she had successfully fished and hunted, and besides, "the flapjacks, eaten with maple syrup, made up . . . for all inconveniences." A few months later, Field published another piece where she argued that women should camp because "they are in greatest need of just such a life." Most, she admitted, would not enjoy themselves "because of their horror of the bare ground, a little dirt and freedom from restraint." But for that handful "who are willing to be tanned, freckled, and even made to resemble antique statuary, for the sake of renewed youth . . . try the wilderness."[36]

Field's lecture and print campaign rankled Thorpe, who snorted that "now the wilds . . . have been invaded by Miss Kate Field." According to Thorpe, who in contrast to Murray and Wachusett saw the wild as a place to escape the growing feminization of American culture, "Miss Kate's" public lectures misrepresented wilderness when she "softened" the Adirondacks with "her womanly imagination." The authentic backwoodsman tested his manliness through hunting and fishing; he did not pursue "soft breezes, pretty cascades, charming evening effects, lovely Nature, and all that sort of thing." Anyone who engaged in these activities was not camping, he sneered, but "sight-seeing," and likely a woman. "The wild woods," he proclaimed, were not "a place for fashionable ladies of the American style; they have, unfortunately, in their education, nothing that makes such places appreciated, and no capability for physical exercise that causes the attempt to be pleasantly possible. . . . Let the ladies keep out of the woods (even such male ladies as admire Mr. Murray's book)." Field ignored Thorpe's diatribe and continued to lecture, prompting an increased, if still small, number of women to camp in the Adirondacks during the summer of 1870.[37]

The most biting and painful attack by the critics, however, was that Murray was "responsible for more than one death" and "a murderer of helpless invalids." Murray's story about the young New York consumptive who recovered from his tuberculosis while camping had regrettably inspired similar and worse sufferers to hasten to the Adirondacks. Despite Murray's caveat that such miracles could not be expected by everyone, many deeply desperate sufferers came anyway. Sadly, "numbers have died far from home, and one, at least, without a friend to soothe his dying hour." The arrival of tuberculosis sufferers is unsurprising when one recognizes that the disease was killing approximately one in seven Americans around the middle of the nineteenth century and that its diagnosis was considered a death sentence. Anyone who even hinted at a cure or some relief got a hearing and some support.[38]

The viciousness of these attacks quickly prompted several writers to defend Murray from the accusation that he was responsible for such unreasonable expectations. Kate Field warned her *New York Daily Tribune* readers in July 1869 that "no invalid will go into the wilderness unless advised to do so by the family physician, and no physician will advise the step without due consideration." Furthermore, she wrote, it was unfair to Murray to blame him for the deaths of consumptives who, "with both legs in the grave, visit the Adirondacks, . . . Yet this is being done." Nor were there many of these deaths in the first place. Instead, she contended, "newspaper writers multiply two or three dead men by a fertile imagination, and produce 'numbers of dead and dying.'" During her recent camping in the wilderness, Field had seen no dying consumptives but had met an Ohio woman who had arrived at Martin's hotel with "every symptom of quick consumption" and after three weeks had "passed from death to life" as her symptoms receded.[39]

Despite his defenders, when Murray returned home from his own Adirondack vacation in the fall of 1869, he felt compelled to respond to the critics. His eighty-five-hundred-word "Reply to his Calumniators," published first in the *New York Daily Tribune* of October 23, 1869, and a week later in the *Boston Journal*, largely took the same tack as Kate Field and Wachusett—vindicating the area rather than the author. He had not lied, Murray contended, about the characteristics, size, or accessibility of the Adirondacks. They were nearby, easy to enter, and large enough to hold thousands of campers. He once again defended women and amateur campers, calling the region "of value to the country at large," not just to the "two or three hundred gentlemen who would selfishly monopolize the Adirondack Wilderness." Moreover, Murray emphasized that the region was not "filled with lamentation" for a multitude of dead and dying consumptives—only three had passed away during the summer of 1869. Instead, both the suffering and their physicians had written Murray in gratitude for his having directed them to the wilderness and to express their indignation at the rumors of rampant deaths. "It is not in my power," noted Murray fairly, "to say who will be benefited" by a journey to the Adirondacks, but he was correct when he predicted "that the Wilderness will be more and more frequented by invalids, as accommodations are provided for their reception and comfort, and that the region will become the resort of thousands each year seeking restoration to health." Positive comments about the healing power of the air by Murray, Field, and others were repeated by other writers and observers during following years. Consequently, tuberculosis sufferers continued to travel to the Adirondacks for their health, eventually prompting Dr. Edward Trudeau, himself a consumptive, to establish the nation's first tuberculosis sanatorium in Saranac Lake in 1884.[40]

At the same time, Murray stepped away from Field, Wachusett, and his other defenders to again emphasize the value of the region for urban dwellers seeking a restorative camping trip.

This wilderness, lying as it does within two days' ride of our great cities, is not for us to selfishly appropriate. It is, and is to be regarded in the future, a place to which not only the artist, and the lover of nature in her grandest aspects, but the business man and the professional man, weary and jaded by months and years of overwork, can go and find in its recesses rest and recuperation for body and mind. There are thousands of men in our cities—clergymen, lawyers, physicians, merchants and bankers—men whose lives are too valuable to the country to be shortened by a day, to whom a month's annual sojourn in this wilderness would bring a renewal of all their powers and a vast increase of all their energies. The overworked student and professor in our colleges, the clerks in our stores, and every young man whose habits or occupation put a heavy strain upon his body

THE RUSH FOR THE WILDERNESS.

Figure 1.5. "The Rush for the Wilderness" ridiculed the crowds of new Adirondack adventurers who boarded steamships at Whitehall, New York, during the summer of 1870. From Charles Hallock, "The Raquette Club," *Harper's New Monthly Magazine,* August 1870, 325.

and mind, should visit this region; not to sit down in idleness at the hotels along the margin of the wilderness, but to take a guide and penetrate into its recesses, and by steady, daily work at the oar, and by learning that most beautiful of aquatic arts, the art of paddling, build up his body in muscular power, and add to the strength and vigor of his brain.[41]

Despite the flurry of detractors and supporters during the fall of 1869, reporters, advocates, critics, and humorists continued to comment on Murray and the Adirondack camping phenomenon. During the second year of the Murray Rush, in August 1870, *Harper's Magazine* published a Charles Hallock story, "The Raquette Club," that lampooned Murray's book and the rush that followed (fig. 1.5).

Echoing the complaints of Thorpe, the story drew a bead on the outdoor inexperience of Murray's followers with a series of outrageous sketches and misadventures. From the formation of the club, through the boat, train, and

BEFORE GOING TO THE ADIRONDACKS.   AFTER GOING TO THE ADIRONDACKS.

Figure 1.6. Mocking William H. H. Murray's tale of recovery, "The Raquette Club" included these caricatures of someone "Before" and "After" a visit to the Adirondack wilderness. From Charles Hallock, "The Raquette Club," *Harper's New Monthly Magazine*, August 1870, 334–35.

wagon rides of wholly overprepared or underprepared visitors, the questionable guides, and the fishing and hunting blunders, to the impact of camping on one's health, nearly every element of *Adventures in the Wilderness* and its sometimes bewildered followers was satirized, mocked, and ridiculed.

On the article's first page, for instance, the "celebrated club of incipient anglers" holds its first meeting. The club president, also known as "the venerable fish-persuader," begins by putting all potential club members on notice. "Before we proceed to business I must state that no candidate can be admitted who has ever fished. . . . Are all present novices? We are," cheered the assembled crowd. "Then I greet you in the name of the immortal Izaak, whose mantle I wear. You now enter fairly upon what may be aptly termed your *no-fishiate*." For anyone who disliked puns, irony, ridicule, and sarcasm, the story only deteriorated from this point on.[42] Nevertheless, the article probably drew still more campers to the region (fig. 1.6).

By contrast, Winslow C. Watson's *A Descriptive and Historical Guide to the Valley of Lake Champlain and the Adirondacks* of 1871 clearly moved into Murray's corner by foregrounding the healthfulness of the Adirondack climate and the number of sufferers who had arrived "in advanced stages of pulmonary affection" and then found themselves "restored to comparative health" by the air. Watson also dismissed many of those who had expressed disappointment during the rush as "embryo sportsmen" who, "ignorant of the art, fished and hunted without science." Instead of "upbraiding" Murray, he suggested, "they might have referred their disappointment to personal and peculiar causes." Three years later, however, Seneca Ray Stoddard, an Adirondack photographer, cartographer, and rival guidebook author, questioned Murray's veracity in 1874's *The Adirondacks Illustrated* when he related that the guides "have come to the conclusion generally that if his preaching is not a better guide to heaven than his book to the Adirondacks, his congregation might manage to worry through with a cheaper man."[43] Nonetheless, Murray's book had made its mark, permanently opening the region as a camping destination.

In the years following the release of *Adventures in the Wilderness*, the number of Adirondack campers increased even as the romantic and literary portions of camping books dwindled, the practical elements expanded, and the justification for camping continued, albeit usually in brief. For example, in 1872, H. Perry Smith and E. R. Wallace published *The Modern Babes in the Wood or Summerings in the Wilderness; To Which Is Added a Reliable and Descriptive Guide to the Adirondacks*. Like Murray's book, it was a combination of literature (Smith's *The Modern Babes in the Wood*) and "how to" (Wallace's *Reliable and Descriptive Guide*). Three years later, Wallace separated from Smith to publish his own book, *Descriptive Guide to the Adirondacks*, without the latter's adventure stories.[44] In only a few years, publishers had come to realize that campers would more readily purchase reliable, current, and useful information about camping's sites, equipment, and routes than the nature literature that described and encouraged camping. Many campers already knew that they would enjoy themselves in the wild; they wanted to know where and how.

After *Adventures*

The Reverend William H. H. Murray had given an occasional public lecture about the Adirondacks before the release of *Adventures in the Wilderness*, but soon after its publication, he leapt to the task. During the next three years, "Adirondack" Murray spoke to approximately half a million people throughout New England, earning himself the considerable fortune of nearly $50,000. These speaking events undoubtedly stimulated many nascent campers, and Murray himself felt his lectures most influential. "The little book on the Adirondacks through ignorance of the facts of the case has been credited with exerting a greater influence than it ever did," he recorded in his personal papers. Instead, he insisted, "it was the Lecture and its delivery in five hundred principal cities and villages that did the work." This lecture, more than any of the others he regularly delivered, "captured the lyceum platform." Although he spoke primarily about the attractions of the Adirondack region, his audience wanted more. "At the close of its delivery," Murray would normally have stepped off the stage, but instead he "was compelled often to remain on the platform an hour, giving practical information and advice." For the remainder of his life, Murray continued to lecture and write, but nothing he accomplished ever again approached the cultural impact of *Adventures*. Indeed, by his own admission, "it was perhaps the most influential utterance I ever made."[45]

Ironically, Murray's Adirondack camping, ministry, marriage, and money did not last much longer. As he rode the wave of popular adulation, his labors expanded to include the composing of new, secular books and the creation of a stock farm that included his birthplace in Guilford, Connecticut, and which was dedicated to the breeding of horses. For several years his situation was tenable, but in late 1874, long-simmering tensions between Murray and the more conservative members of the Park Street Church reached the boiling point. Unable to reach an agreement, Murray resigned as pastor, but within a year he was back in the pulpit, this time of an independent Congregational church he organized, the New England Church. This Boston church prospered and, being more liberal than his previous one, offered no resistance to his also publishing a religious magazine, *The Golden Rule*, and the popular "John Norton" stories. Meanwhile, his real estate and horse-breeding ventures continued to expand. In May 1878, Murray took a year's leave from the New England Church and made a last and relatively short trip to the Adirondacks. When that vacation was done, Murray turned his attention to yet another new enterprise—the manufacturing of horse carriages. Unfortunately, Murray had spread himself and his resources too thin. In late summer 1879, his financial bubble burst, and his marriage broke up. It was all too much for him. In an effort to make a clean break, Murray retired from the ministry, left all his property "wholly to my creditors," and departed Boston.[46]

For several years Murray traveled widely, but the scope and nature of his activities during this period are unclear. At one point, he owned a ranch and a lumber business in Texas, but they ultimately failed. He subsequently traveled widely, eventually visiting most of the United States, as well as England and the European continent. In time he ended up in the city of Montreal, where his situation began to improve. In September 1886 he remarried, and the couple soon moved to the United States, where Murray again became a successful author and lecturer, albeit with new topics. Oddly enough, in 1890 he was able to once again purchase his family's farm in Guilford. Here he spent the remainder of his life, quietly writing, republishing earlier works, and raising his four daughters. Murray died in his boyhood home in March 1904, only a month short of his sixty-fifth birthday.

Although camping is often associated with quiet and calm, it started with a "rush." *Adventures in the Wilderness* was a well-written and practical book, but more than that, the public was ready for the message. When Murray told the increasingly prosperous middle classes that the cities they occupied were profane and that the noise, smoke, regulation, and crowding would incapacitate minds, hearts, and bodies, these urbanized antimodernists agreed more than anyone, even Murray, had suspected was possible. Thousands who had never previously visited the region embraced his prescribed cure of a short journey and a long vacation in the Adirondacks' sacred wilderness. But a profane-city/sacred-nature contrast alone would not have been enough to start the movement. Romantically inclined writers before Murray had also sketched out the contrast, yet no surge had resulted. Murray initiated the rush when he first insisted that the best way anyone, including women, could enjoy nature's restoration was on a camping excursion, and then he told them how and where to camp, as well as how to get there. Murray even saturated the routes into the wild with historic and national significance by encouraging campers to visit the grave of John Brown, an American martyr. With this combination of nature as spiritual and physical cure, camping as an open and equal activity, and holy routes of travel from profane to sacred space, "Adirondack" Murray's book presented camping as pilgrimage, and it transformed a previously small and narrow coterie of wilderness travel-book readers into a mass exodus. Not everyone agreed with Murray's characterization of the proper pilgrim—some did not want women camping, others demanded greater skills, and still others expected campers to possess more understanding and awareness of nature's physical and spiritual qualities—but such disagreements about the authentic camper continue to the present. For as we shall see in the next chapter, camping grew rapidly and diffused widely as Americans discovered what an adventure it could be.

CHAPTER TWO

THE ART OF CAMPING

Roughing It during the Decades before Automobiles

While William H. H. Murray's *Adventures in the Wilderness* began American camping with a rush into the Adirondacks, this region did not remain their exclusive destination for long. For the next forty years, campers headed out by foot, horse, wagon, and canoe into wild areas both near and far, and often with hired guides, as interest grew and as travel and outdoor writers promoted the benefits of this new activity. Before Murray, outdoor writers had treated camping only as a necessary adjunct to hunting and fishing, not the primary mode for a vacation, while travel writers simply did not mention it as they waxed exuberant over railroads and destination hotels. The Murray Rush transformed this situation, prompting both regional outdoor guidebook and travel authors to include increasingly extensive sections on camping.

In Murray's Footsteps

Among the earliest books to piggyback on Murray's *Adventures* was H. Perry Smith and E. R. Wallace's *The Modern Babes in the Wood, or Summerings in the Wilderness*, published in 1872. This awkward combination of Adirondack travelogue and guide was largely descriptive, but it did dedicate 9 of its 444 pages to a camping "appendix." This brief section aimed to prepare novice campers by recommending clothing outfits for men and women, specialized equipment, insect "preparations," and a list of basic provisions. It appears to have been reasonably successful, but three years later, Wallace began publishing a guidebook without Smith's travelogue, and his enhanced, 265-page manual to the Adirondacks and surrounding areas expanded the camping appendix to 23 pages. This augmented section included amplified advice on the same topics covered previously—clothing, hunting and fishing equipment, insect control, and food—but it also now incorporated new information on a variety of ancillary equipment like boats, lamps, and stoves.[1]

A similar transformation occurred with another successful guidebook, John B. Bachelder's *Popular Resorts, and How to Reach Them*. Bachelder had launched his reputation as a travel writer with a particularly successful series of books about understanding and visiting the Civil War battlefield at Gettysburg, Pennsylvania. With his books selling well, Bachelder branched out in 1873 to publish *Bachelder's Illustrated Tourist's Guide of the United States*, a two-volume compendium about northeastern U.S. resorts, but one that also included a special focus on the Gettysburg site. This publication seems to have sold more unevenly than his previous efforts, so in 1874 he pared it down into a single volume, *Popular Resorts*, which he announced would be updated annually. This guidebook continued the earlier volumes' focus on northeastern railroad and hotel travel, but it opened with a three-page "Camping Out" section that began with a short but powerful declaration concerning the value of camping. "Beyond all question, the most delightful and healthful way to spend one's summer vacation is in 'camping out.'" Conventional life, Bachelder observed, was filled with "stiff formalities" that constrained both mind and body. Camping, in contrast, liberated. "The body is left free for any sort of dress except fashionable styles; and the mind is in constant and cheery repose." Recalling Murray's testimony, but with less caution, he similarly promised that "health comes to the invalid" who camped, and that eventually all campers felt "an electric energy, daily renewed, unknown in great cities." In sum, he promised, a camper would return home heavier, stronger, and with a sense of having had a "glorious vacation."[2]

With this pitch complete, Bachelder offered some brief and simple advice about the size of camping parties ("scarcely . . . less than three, nor more than five") as well as equipment ("two grand essentials . . . plenty of dishcloths and a hatchet"). Going to greater lengths, he provided general recommendations for camping in the mountains of Pennsylvania or Virginia because they were "quiet and subdued," the Canadian provinces of Prince Edward Island ("unsurpassed in natural charms"), Nova Scotia ("abounds in novelties"), and New Brunswick ("some of the loveliest as well as the grandest and most romantic attractions to be found on any portion of our continent"), as well as Maine, Vermont, the White Mountains, and the

Adirondacks. Nonetheless, he demurred on specific site recommendations, noting that it was "impossible, and useless to attempt, to describe particular spots, which would tempt a 'camping-out' party. . . . They are numbered by thousands." Here we must be careful to understand that his reference to "thousands" did not mean *developed* campsites. At this time and for many decades to follow, campers would establish themselves at *any* attractive location, not just ones with tables, benches, piped water, and other amenities. These features would not become common at camping grounds for another fifty or more years. Consequently, a campsite could be on nearly any riverside, lakeshore, or oceanfront, in virtually any forest. Bachelder concluded that campers could, so far, be found only here and there "in the warm months. . . . But it cannot be commended too earnestly, nor pressed too persistently upon public notice."[3]

Good to his word, Bachelder produced an 1875 edition of *Popular Resorts* that included even more recommendations. As before, he began with camping, but placed it under the more revealing heading of "Summer Recreation." The practice of taking a two-week to two-month summer vacation "as a respite from labor" was "fast gaining popularity," he reported. Each year increased the number of urban Americans who temporarily left their everyday lives to "seek rest and recuperation for mind and body among the hills and deep green woods of the country, or at the sea-shore." The few "whom fortune has favored" could travel as long as they liked and to any natural wonder they chose. "Such have only to select the points of interest, and the most pleasing routes by which they may be visited." Another group of travelers, which was "a far larger number," was not so blessed and so had to carefully choose the route and destination where they could "secure the desired change and rest, at cheaper rates even than they could remain at home." These two groups of travelers, Bachelder announced, would find much of interest in his book's chapters on hotels, railroads, and sightseeing, but this opening chapter was "devoted to another class, who, from economy or adventure, choose more freedom in their movements. I refer to the . . . camping-out party."[4]

Like William H. H. Murray and succeeding camping advocates, Bachelder linked the camping vacation to values perceived as absent in readers' ordinary lives. Residence in a city was expensive, he implied, while camping was "economical." Urban life was routine and unremarkable, but camp life provided "adventure." And, most telling, an urban existence (as well as the resort vacations described elsewhere in his book) was constrained, regulated, and inhibited, even as camping offered "freedom."[5] Camping, Bachelder insinuated, occurred in sacred, not mundane space, and campers were not simple travelers, but travelers who could return home rested and recuperated in spirit and body from having been immersed in powerful nature.

Bachelder also addressed the issue of technique. If a party intended to spend its entire vacation at one campsite, he began, then "it matter[ed] little how the place is reached." But if the party sought "the advantages of tour and camp," alternatives were available. These alternative camping techniques, with some variations and additions, continue today. First, one could practice "pedestrianism," or what we would call backpacking (see chapter 7). If a camper were physically up to the challenge and had a strong sense of adventure, pedestrianism was recommended. Of course, admitted Bachelder, not everyone would want to pedestrian camp. While it was physically challenging and so appealed to young men, a few years later in life "the same parties will prefer a horse to facilitate their movements; and, later yet, a carriage will be required to complete their happiness." Mounted campers could travel where pedestrian campers went and pass more quickly through the uninteresting sections of a trail; but more importantly, packing with a horse allowed for an easing of camping's challenges because "additional clothing and equipments can be taken." And if a little smoothing was good, Bachelder suggested, more would be better. "Another very popular plan," he declared, was to hire a horse and wagon, which possessed additional advantages while including "the pleasures of those [camping techniques] already described." We cannot know if Bachelder sincerely believed this latter claim, but it was an exaggeration. A wagon, even a small, light one, could not travel across wet or rocky ground, or through dense vegetation or uneven terrain that backpackers and packhorse campers could traverse. Given the primitive roads of the 1870s, especially those in rural and wild areas, wagon campers were commonly restricted to areas with at least a minimum of infrastructure and so missed the wilder nature that backpackers and horse packers relished. Conversely, the true advantage of the horse and wagon, which Bachelder admitted, was that an even "larger supply [of clothing, food, and equipment] can then be taken." Furthermore, with a good pair of horses and a wagon, a camping party could bring along "an experienced cook for driver and 'man of all work' [to] complete the outfit."[6]

For the next four decades, a growing army of campers would head out of cities from across the United States, but most of the earliest ones came from the Northeast, where populations were largest and densest. Consequently, the destinations recommended in the first guidebooks tended to be in the same region. Wallace, for instance, focused on upstate New York and nearby Vermont, while Bachelder's 1874 version of *Popular Resorts* covered an area from the beaches of southern Maine, through New York and Pennsylvania, to the mountains of Virginia. Soon, however, authors' sights stretched farther, as camping caught on with the public. Charles Hallock, a well-known sportsman and author, produced *Camp Life in Florida: A Handbook for Sportsmen and Settlers*. A compilation of articles that had appeared in Hallock's *Forest and Stream* magazine, the book stressed Florida's hunting and fishing opportunities but also supported camping itself. One chapter, Fred Beverly's "Three Months in Florida for a Hundred Dollars," began by declaring that people could camp in Florida for less money than if they stayed home. Like Bachelder, Beverly understood that many readers would hesitate to camp because they feared that their household budgets could not absorb the cost of a vacation residence while continuing to cover the expense of their regular domicile. But a Florida camping trip, he insisted, would not be burdensome, because it was so cheap that a household's total expenses would be lower than if one stayed home. Even the cost of a tent, he insisted, could be skipped if one was "handy with an axe and knife, and an old campaigner" (that is, a veteran), because then one could build a shelter from palmetto stems and leaves.[7] Having made his point about the expense of a Florida vacation, Beverly proceeded to explain how to camp inexpensively and the minimum of equipment and supplies that were needed.

Bachelder's *Popular Resorts* also expanded the geography of its recommendations when the 1875 edition appeared. As he had in 1874, Bachelder emphasized the Northeast, but this time incorporated sections on Kentucky, Illinois, Wisconsin, Minnesota, and the western states, including California. Moreover, after he presented the three common camping techniques, he admitted that "still another species of camping-out" existed—"the real camp of the explorer, the hunter, or adventurer." Instead of recapitulating the encounters of pioneers who had once come through Pennsylvania and similarly settled areas, one could camp on the current frontier and have the most authentic experience possible. From Canada to Mexico, urged Bachelder, stretched "a border of wild partially explored country, which affords a rich field of adventure." He distinguished this region from New York, Pennsylvania, and the other resort destinations by a simple fact—along this wild border camping was "a real necessity." You could not choose between hotels, or even between a hotel and a camp, because no hotels existed; camping was the only way to experience this wilderness. Bachelder urged caution and "thorough study" before embarking on such an excursion, but he simultaneously encouraged all readers to go. "There are so many interesting localities on our frontier to visit that one can hardly go amiss."[8]

Additional publications explaining how to camp and where to camp, as well as personal accounts of camping trips, soon appeared in magazines and on bookshelves. A short report in the "Home and Society" section of

Scribner's Monthly magazine for August 1874 described a recent camping trip by "eight or ten families." No regional or local destination was identified, only that they had camped on a lakeshore about six miles from a city. The children had turned out "to romp and gather flowers, and climb trees, and delve in the dirt to their hearts' content." The adults had enjoyed the lake's rowing and fishing, taking "excursions" in every direction, rejoicing in the clean air and picturesque scenery. "At the end of the six weeks, the party voted unanimously to return to the same place in the succeeding summer."[9]

The year 1877 brought the first book-length, nonregional publication dedicated solely to the practice of camping, John M. Gould's *Hints for Camping and Walking*, but unlike most guidebooks of the time, it included no romantically oriented tales from the author's life and little justification for camping. Instead, Gould drew upon his civilian and military experience to objectively provide practical advice on preparation, clothing, cookware and cooking, tents, and the arrangement of campsites. Like Bachelder, Gould organized camping along lines of technique and gender. Either one walked and carried his own equipment and supplies, or one employed a horse, or a horse and wagon to do the job. In terms of technique or mode, the vast majority of the book focused on backpacking, but he recommended it only for youthful men, who should carry but a handful of supplies on relatively short journeys. Only a small portion of the book addressed camping with a horse or a horse and wagon, and most of this was dedicated to the latter. A horse and wagon could carry more supplies and equipment, he readily pointed out, but its best advantage came for "a party of different ages, rather than for one exclusively of young men. It is especially suitable for ladies who wish to walk and camp, or for an entire family, or for a school with its teachers" (fig. 2.1).

Mixed groups were likely to include people with differing stamina, and a wagon provided them with the opportunity to walk or ride at will. At the same time, Gould specifically encouraged women to camp, providing details for their outfit, but limiting their appropriate activities. Women, he declared, could walk and camp, but "they must have a wagon, and do none of the heavy work." Invoking a common descriptive phrase that would come to epitomize camping, Gould told women that "they ought not to 'rough it' so much as young men expect to." Edwin L. Godkin, editor of the *Nation*, found Gould's book to be an excellent guide to this new activity. "Major Gould" covered all the important concerns for campers, announced Godkin; "nothing that the novice ought to be told is omitted." The author understood what he wrote about, and although the book was aimed at young men, "there is no age nor sex that cannot profit by its practical directions."[10]

Figure 2.1. An 1880 party camping with horses and wagons at Bridalveil Fall in Yosemite Valley, California. Courtesy of National Park Service Historic Photograph Collection, Harpers Ferry (WV) Center for Media Services; photographer Gustav Fagersteen.

The Continuing Pilgrimage

In contrast to John M. Gould's nearly exclusive focus on utility, most new guidebooks, how-to articles, and personal accounts that appeared presented camping in expressions that suggest pilgrimage and justified it in terms reminiscent of William H. H. Murray's *Adventures in the Wilderness.* "With the coming of summer," noted *Outing* magazine's Dillon Wallace in July 1909, "the vexing question arises as to how and where the vacation period can be spent to best advantage." One could visit a resort or remain home in town, but these would not provide a connection to the true source of rest and recovery. "Let me suggest going camping for a change." Two weeks of camping, Wallace promised, would wash away the suffocating veneer of modernity and liberate "that bit of primitive instinct which slumbers 'way down deep in the heart of everyone, no matter how conventionalized he or she may be." This instinct, which recognized what one's rational mind might miss, "calls us away from the crowded city to green fields or mountain retreats when brain and heart are tired." Camping, unlike those other vacations, took one out of the city's profane world and into sacred space where normal restrictions were absent even as spiritual and physical satisfaction thrived. "Nowhere," advised Wallace, "can one get so close to nature and God's out-of-doors as in camp, and nowhere else can the city toiler so surely find that rest and complete change from the routine of his daily life that he mentally craves and he physically needs."[11]

Camping advocates during these decades also sometimes described nature in the suggestive, sentimental language of romanticism, just as Murray had done before them. According to Thomas Appleton, when one camped in the Adirondacks, one did not simply visit nature but was "enveloped by her." Mixing nature and gender metaphors, Appleton told his primarily male readers that "you lie on her breast, and her arms are around you. She mixes your blood with the balsam of her caresses. All that she loves—her happy solitude, the floor of glassy lakes, her woodland song and odors,—She gives to you." More frequently, writers identified the spiritual and physical transformations, such as health, rest, and strength, that would come to the camper. Helen Clark's account of her party's 1891 Adirondack camping trip ended on just this note. "The head guide," she reported, "waved . . . in token of farewell [as we left the woods], and we betook ourselves to our new electric-lighted, telephone-connected habitat, where we put on again the yoke and garments of civilization, and in the strength of our ten-days' camping wore them merrily many a day."[12]

Nevertheless, the most common element in these publications was an indictment of modernity's urban life. Cities, authors contended, were overpopulated, rushed, smelly, noisy, ugly, and worse. George Washington Sears, who published under the name Nessmuk, and who was particularly leery of urban life, even prefaced his 1884 book, *Woodcraft*, with a deeply cautionary poem for his readers.

> For brick and mortar breed filth and crime,
> With a pulse of evil that throbs and beats;

And men are withered before their prime
By the curse paved in with the lanes and streets.
And lungs are poisoned and shoulders bowed,
In the smothering reek of mill and mine;
And death stalks in on the struggling crowd—
But he shuns the shadow of oak and pine.

Another author, who wrote from his campsite, suggested that just reading about camping in nature was better than urban life alone. He half-humorously admitted that his essay could not transport an urban reader into the wild, but if the reader had "not been out of the city, if you've been pinned to your desk, even a second-hand glimpse of the wildwood will be worth having."[13]

These decades' writers also presented camping as a pilgrimage when they linked it to home, national identity, and values like freedom. In the July 1895 issue of *Outing*, Hubert Dyer described how he and three other "collegians" had decided to pack camp "with three little donkeys" through California's Sierra Nevada. The young men had been "lately released from the grind of the year's hard work," and now they sought to maximize their freedom "by roughing it to our heart's content." Emily Palmer made a similar connection in *Outing*'s September 1895 issue, asserting that "the sense of freedom begotten by breathing fresh air for a few weeks . . . is alone worth the effort necessary to make such an outing possible." Palmer also linked camping to family life. "Happy the home where father, mother and children can gather together their needful belongings, betake themselves to the shores of some lake or stream, and raising their temporary home of white tents, find their best pleasure in being together and leaving behind them the care of conventional life." Moreover, in each of these instances, the author situated the value gained while camping against its opposite setting—everyday life. For Dyer it had been the "year's grind," while Palmer contrasted camping with "the care of conventional life." Also, like Murray, authors of the 1870s and following decades sometimes argued that camping confirmed and fortified American identity. In his 1878 book, *Windfalls*, Thomas Appleton declared that a camping trip to the Adirondacks would clarify the identity of anyone who had "half-European nerves." If one spent time at the Atlantic seashore, it would always be whispering, " 'Come back to Mother England; you are her child,' . . . but in the Adirondacks, we are wholly American. No trick of the old civilization is here. No imported habit, no daily custom, borrowed from a sunless land, here exists. It is American to the core."[14]

Finally, some writers presented camping as a form of pilgrimage when they revealingly reversed the normal relationship between home and away. In the *Outlook* magazine for June 3, 1905, Elisabeth Woodbridge concluded her story about camping with her husband with the following observation: "As

I have said, all the really important things about camping out can never be told. People who try the life will either grow impatient in it, and soon drift back to their proper home in a civilized world . . . or they will find themselves really at home, really alive, they will go back to a so-called home only when they must, and always their hearts will be restless for the free life of the woods and rivers." The anthropologist Gwen Kennedy Neville tells us that Woodbridge's reversal of home's location fits a pattern. Americans, Neville argues, regard home as impermanent because they are supposed to leave home's warmth and comfort to fulfill their individual destinies. This practice has produced many successful world citizens, but it has also left a host of Americans feeling displaced and disconnected. From this perspective, campers were not so much going away from home as heading back to it to escape the depersonalization and placelessness experienced in an often anonymous urban society. Moreover, writes Neville, for the American pilgrim "the journey is a sacred one to a sacred place," but the holiness did not come so much from the martyrs or saints that would have sanctified a Roman Catholic site, as it came from "a community of believers over time."[15] As a consequence, as increasing numbers of Americans camped at a national park, state forest, or any other location, their geographic choices sanctified these natural "home" sites, which subsequently attracted still more campers in a self-nourishing cycle.

The Ritual of Camping

In addition to presenting camping in the language of pilgrimage, books and magazines served a triple role in this leisure form's development. First, they provided the practical information and advice needed by novice and intermediate campers, the majority of whom were middle class to upper middle class, lived in cities, and consequently tended to lack useful outdoor skills. As Dan Beard, one of the future founders of the Boy Scouts of America, put it in the "The Art of Camping," in 1903, "Most of us are so accustomed to having other people build our fires, make our beds and cook our meals that we are more or less helpless in the woods, where we are away from the butcher, baker, candlestick-maker, doctor and trolley-cars." Even the many campers who had migrated to their urban dwellings from rural areas were often in need. Their earlier experiences frequently would have been on farms, which did not prepare them for life in the wild. Moreover, they might have forgotten any skills they once possessed.[16]

Second, the explosion in camping literature fostered the growth of camping by stimulating campers' imaginations. Long before would-be campers headed out of their city, they likely had read at least one of these publications and envisioned themselves camping on nearby lakeshores, in the distant

Adirondacks or even at far Yellowstone National Park. Prior to arriving physically at a destination, many campers had already mentally begun their journey to transform some distant and abstract natural space into a place that was personally meaningful.[17]

Third, the practices described in these publications at first merely suggested how to experience sacred nature, but through repetition they imparted and then became reflections of camping's customs. For example, in "A Glimpse of the Adirondacks," an anonymous personal account of camping along New York's Ausable River during the summer of 1876, the writer commented on the striking scenery ("a rocky hollow of wildest beauty"), the comforts of a campfire ("a splendid fire . . . kept up all night"), and a hike up Mount Marcy ("the ascent . . . was decidedly a 'pull' "). He found these elements noteworthy enough to mention, but he never stated that any of them were necessary components during someone else's camping vacation. If writers during the next few years had ignored their own experiences of scenery, campfires, or hikes, these three elements might have disappeared from camping, but as all were noted repeatedly in later descriptive accounts, new campers associated them with the practice of living in wild places. As more of these early campers practiced and interpreted camping along the same lines, they fostered a community of people who shared a body of rituals. Furthermore, the observation of camping's rituals became more essential with repetition, suggesting that by staying within the confines of custom, campers could more easily find the ideals they sought as they left their conventional urban worlds to enter sacred nature.[18]

The manuals, guidebooks, advertisements, and other prescriptive publications that taught campers how they should camp fostered its ritualization. Instead of casually mentioning how to camp within a larger, often personal narrative, the prescriptive literature zeroed in on camping's practice. Manuals told campers what clothing, tents, and other equipment and supplies to bring on a journey, the techniques for using them properly, what behaviors were proper in the wild, and what sort of places qualified as campsites. Some publications, especially magazine articles, would focus on a single concern, such as building a campfire, winter camping, or cooking equipment; but others, like John Gould's *Hints for Camping and Walking*, provided a general manual that covered a variety of topics.[19]

Horace Kephart and the Frontier

The most influential of these how-to-camp manuals combined their prescriptions with explanations of why a proper camper practiced camping in a particular fashion. In each case, the emerging rituals, to be performed in

Figure 2.2. Horace Kephart relaxing at his campsite, circa 1905. Courtesy of Hunter Library, Western Carolina University.

the sacred space of wild nature, came to embody the way things "ought to be." Generally short, these narratives often situated specific acts in a larger historical, social, environmental, or other context. One of the best known of the prescriptive authors during the early twentieth century was Horace Kephart (1862–1931), who beginning in 1894 wrote hundreds of popular magazine articles on camping and the outdoors (fig. 2.2).

Kephart's articles covered a range of topics, including animals, shooting, camp bedding, how to tell directions, and many others, but it was 1906's *The Book of Camping and Woodcraft* that made him famous among campers. It went through several revisions and dozens of printings during Kephart's lifetime, dozens more printings after his death in 1931, and remains in print today. Kephart's reputation grew so large that he became known as the "Dean of American Campers" and was unanimously elected to the National Council of the Boy Scouts of America in 1929.[20]

Kephart's publications commanded respect for a variety of reasons, but the first was his insightful, detailed, and practical advice, which clearly demonstrated his experience. In *The Book of Camping and Woodcraft*, he addressed issues in the order that they naturally arose for a novice camper—preparing an appropriate camping "outfit" before departure, packing it for travel, campsite selection and design, and, finally, hunting, cooking, pests, forest travel, and a variety of other activities likely to occur on a camping trip. Each of these topics, and many more, were given pages and pages of attention in the book.

Tents and the equipment that supported and furnished them, for instance, received an entire chapter. A tent, Kephart intoned, must satisfy in multiple ways. It "should be easy to set up. It should shed heavy rains, and should stand securely in a gale. It should keep out insects and cold draughts, but let in the rays of the camp-fire and plenty of pure air. It should be cool and airy on summer days, but warm and dry at night. All of which is easily said." (This last sentence illustrates another of Kephart's endearing characteristics—a joking self-awareness that camping was not always simple and sometimes difficult.) Kephart identified seven categories of tents (wall, lean-to, A, miner's, Sibley, teepee, and canoeist's), the positive and negative attributes of each, the variety of textiles used to make them, and how any tent could be waterproofed. A wall tent, he declared, was generally preferred "for a fixed camp, or any camp that can be reached by wagon. . . . It is easy to set up, and has plenty of headroom. . . . It can be made cozy in any kind of weather." This same tent, however, had its limitations. "With its necessary poles," Kephart warned, it "is too heavy and bulky for anything but a wagon trip. Men who travel in untracked forests, deserts, or mountains, usually require a more portable shelter." For horse packers, canoe campers, and backpackers, he especially recommended the A tent (fig. 2.3). "For extreme portability, lightness, and ease of pitching, the A tent is recommended. Nothing is better, in the long run, for a trip in summer, where portages must be made and camp shifted at frequent intervals." In addition to his advice about tent types, Kephart occasionally went so far as to recommend a specific manufacturer's brand or a specific equipment design, but only when it was notably effective. "The Hudson Bay form of A or wedge tent," he noted, "economizes cloth and weight. . . . A waterproof silk tent of this pattern, 6x9x7 feet, weighs only 6 pounds."[21]

Kephart also stood apart from such previous authors as John Bachelder by his careful attention to the ideal campsite's characteristics. Bachelder had noted in passing that "thousands" of possible campsites existed but had offered little guidance on how to select one. Kephart filled this gap, again demonstrating his deeply practical knowledge. "The essentials of a good campsite," he declared on the first page of a chapter in *The Book of Camping and Woodcraft* titled "The Camp," are

1. Pure water.
2. Wood that burns well. . . .

Figure 2.3. An *A* or "wedge" tent. From Horace Kephart, *Camping: A Handbook for Vacation Campers and Travelers in the Wilderness* (New York: Macmillan, 1917), 92.

3. An open spot, level enough for the tent and campfire, but elevated above its surroundings so as to have good natural drainage. . . . Observe the previous flood marks.
4. Grass or browse for the horses (if there are any) and bedding for the men.
5. Straight poles for the tent, or trees convenient for attaching the ridge rope.
6. Security against the spread of fire.
7. Exposure to direct sunlight during part of the day, especially during the early morning hours.
8. In summer, exposure to whatever breezes may blow; in cold weather, protection against the prevailing wind.

When one followed these guidelines and invested the proper "time and hard work," he promised, the resulting campsite would be "snug and trim."[22]

Although Kephart's publications focused on practical matters and reflected his sense of humor, he also attracted a large following by peppering his writing, especially *The Book of Camping and Woodcraft* and its subsequent variations, with elements that presented camping as pilgrimage. In 1906, Kephart began *The Book* by highlighting a value he found in wild nature but one that, by implication, was missing from urban life. "It is not here my purpose to dwell on the charms of free life in a wild country; rather, taking all that for granted, I would point out some short cuts, and offer a lift, here and there, over rough parts of the trail."[23] Campers, Kephart implied, were distant from the urban arena, so they did not have to respond to that life's requirements. Unlike the average urban worker who had little control over his life, campers were free to select (or neglect) their chores, to fish (or not) when they chose, to eat whatever they wanted, and to camp with whom they preferred. Few restrictions contained the camper, making it easier to restore a flagging spirit, and to exercise the all-American right to pursue happiness.

A little further into *The Book of Camping and Woodcraft*, Kephart made camping's spiritual and restorative nature even more explicit as he discussed the selection of camping companions. "The joys and sorrows of camp life, and the proportion of each to the other, depend very much upon how one chooses his companions. It may be noticed that old-timers are apt to be a bit distant when a novice betrays any eagerness to share in their pilgrimages." A camping trip was likely to restore and refresh most anyone, admitted Kephart, but the transformation was never guaranteed. As he cautioned, "not every good fellow in town makes a pleasant comrade in the woods." Novice campers should, like the old-timers, show "commendable caution" before agreeing to head out with someone new.[24]

In a 1909 article, "A Month in the Woods for $30," Kephart highlighted some other values—cleanliness, purity, and social equality—that he found when camping. Earlier in his life, Kephart recalled, when he had first camped, he had decided to camp alone for as little cost as possible. Starting with no equipment (he may have been referring to his initial camping trip), he had purchased a few items (a gun and a tent, for example), made some others (a cotton bed "tick" that could be filled with grass to act as a mattress), and gathered the remainder from his house (clothing and bedding). This outfit had cost merely twenty-five dollars, so the remaining five dollars he spent on transportation to and from the campsite. Fully prepared and about to depart, he nonetheless found himself second-guessing the decision to camp. "I had doubted in my heart," he admitted, "if I could stand a fortnight of this solitary life in the woods." What would he do to fill the days? Would he find nearby campers difficult? To his delight, "there was never an hour of boredom, never a worry or care. I stayed a month." He explained his abundant camping pleasure in part by reference to the satisfaction he discovered while fishing, studying the woods, and other activities, but also he gave credit to the place's sacred qualities. Camping, he declared, was "a clean life. Pure air to breathe, pure water to drink, clean food to eat, and all the surroundings wholesome." Furthermore, the social order among campers was more equitable than at home. Unlike the urban life he had left, Kephart found, "the woods had no paupers to depress my spirits, no autocrats to stir my wrath."[25] Like the pilgrims who travel to religious destinations, Kephart found himself to be equal to the other campers.

Nor was the contrast between camping and ordinary life limited to the social order or to an individual's spirit; it had a material aspect that extended as far as the taste buds. "To season camp dishes as a French chef," Kephart warned in 1910's *Camp Cookery*, would be "a blunder of the first magnitude." The urban chef had to work with materials made inferior by "cold storage" and by "chemical preservatives." Consequently, the various foods were "insipid" and had to be "corrected by spices, herbs, and sauces to make them eatable." At the campsite, by contrast, "our fish is freshly caught, our game was hung out of doors, and the water and air used in cooking (most important factors) are sweet and pure." Camp food was neither bland, nor did its flavors need to be masked. "The only seasoning required," reported Kephart, was "pepper and salt, to be used sparingly."[26]

Finally, in 1917's *Camping and Woodcraft*, Kephart foregrounded the fundamental transformation that camping had on its adherents. In a chapter titled "Vacation Time," he noted the deteriorating consequences of urban life. The "hurry and worry" of modern life, Kephart cautioned readers, "would age [a man] before his prime." One could travel to a resort, but why not, he asked, "exorcise the devil of business and everything that suggests it?" If an exhausted urban dweller intended to achieve "his dream of peace and freedom from every worldly care, let him keep away from summer resorts and even from farms; let him camp out." Only when camping could someone escape the anomie of daily life to rediscover the heritage of personal skills and self-reliance that modern man had lost. "In cities," Kephart observed, "our tasks are so highly specialized, and so many things are done for us by other specialists, that we tend to become a one-handed and one-idead race." Camping, he suggested, counteracted this abnormal overspecialization. "The self-dependent life of the wilderness nomad brings bodily habits and mental processes back to normal, by exercise of muscles and lobes that otherwise might atrophy from want of use."[27] If an urban American, Kephart promised, would leave his city and camp in wild nature, then he will return home improved by his pilgrimage.

In addition to introducing camping as a form of pilgrimage, Kephart repeatedly linked it to an emerging American concern—the frontier and its pioneers—as well as to the nationalist fervor wrapped up with these issues.[28] Americans had begun to save their history around the middle of the nineteenth century as they began to see it as uniquely American. The history of the frontier became especially attractive during the last third of the century as the nation grew more self-consciously aware of the positive and negative effects of its embrace of industrialization and urbanization. Modern life offered many charms, but it came at a high price for America's uncomfortable urban population. By the turn of the century, frontier history, the challenges of frontier life and the exploits of frontier women and men, had grown into outsize myths as rapidly urbanizing Americans responded to their new lives in an industrializing society.

Frederick Jackson Turner, a historian at the University of Wisconsin, was the first intellectual to capture America's imagination about the frontier's influence on the national character. In an 1893 speech to the American Historical Association, he argued that the ideal American society, one consisting of democratic, courageous, independent, and self-reliant individuals, had been created by the frontier experience and that it needed to be regenerated continuously through contact with the frontier's wild nature. According to Turner's "frontier thesis," it was a vital, transformative place and experience, but also one that was transient. The frontier had, inevitably, receded and disappeared before an advancing society, leaving many Americans anxious about the future of the nation. From the perspective of the twenty-first century, we can see that this interpretation produced what historian Lee Clark Mitchell termed "an irresolvable contradiction at the heart of America's self-conception." As the twentieth century dawned, American intellectuals concluded that the nation was threatened by the loss of the frontier that had created it.[29]

At about this same time, many local and state historical societies were producing accounts of pioneer days. The American fascination with frontier history was neither limited to a handful of professors and artists, nor was it restricted to reports about famous people, places, and events. Instead, interest was widespread through American society, and broadly focused. Many local organizations recorded local developments that had involved only local actors, but unlike their more intellectual counterparts, they were less anxious about America's future. One element connecting these various local history societies was their commitment to preservation, which took such forms as genre painting, photography, personal accounts, fiction, and the physical preservation of texts, documents, and objects as small as a thimble and as large as a building. Together, the intellectual and popular concerns about the recent past forged an enduring enthusiasm for the nation's frontier heritage.[30]

Horace Kephart's outdoor writings participated fully in this fascination with a vanishing America, while suggesting that camping was a method for generating and regenerating the American identity in a modernizing America. Few of his publications failed to tie modern camping to Native Americans or to white frontier life. In 1901's "Bits of Woodcraft," Kephart detailed the many possible uses for American trees, suggesting how each might assist a camper. He noted that the fiber of the inner bark of the red mulberry tree, for example, is "so fine that the Indians made twine of it fit for weaving."[31] Five years later, his *Book of Camping and Woodcraft* contained a wide variety of frontier references. In the foreword, as he explained his book's purpose, he offered a definition of camping's woodcraft by way of comparison to the practices of a famous American frontiersman.

> Woodcraft may be defined as the art of getting along well in the wilderness by utilizing nature's storehouse. When we say that Daniel Boone, for example, was a good woodsman, we mean that he could confidently enter an unmapped wilderness, with no outfit but what was carried by his horse, his canoe, or on his own back, and with the intention of a protracted stay; that he could find his way through the dense forest without man-made marks to guide him; that he knew the habits and properties of trees and plants, and the ways of fish and game; that he was a good trailer and a good shot; that he could dress game and cure peltry, cook wholesome meals over an open fire, build adequate shelter against wind and rain, and keep himself warm through the bitter nights of winter—in short, that he knew how to utilize the gifts of nature, and could bide comfortably in the wilderness without help from outside.[32]

Further on, Kephart again referred to a wilder America as he described how to travel in the dark. Lanterns were fine, but sometimes torches might be needed. Should that be the case, he reminded the reader, "Southern Indians, when exploring caves, used joints of cane filled with deer's tallow and supplied with wicks." Later still, when writing about "emergency foods," Kephart praised the light weight and nutrition of a traditional Native American food, rockahominy. "The best of our border hunters and warriors, such as Boone and Kenton and Crockett, relied upon this Indian dietary when starting on their long hunts, or when undertaking forced marches more formidable than any that regular troops could have withstood. So did Lewis and Clark on their ever-memorable expedition across the unknown West."[33]

With each reference to Native Americans or white pioneers, whether in *The Book of Camping and Woodcraft* or another publication, Kephart drove home his message—the authentic camper was as prepared, self-assured, and self-reliant as any wildland native. Like his pioneer forebears, the true camper knew

> how to outfit, how to select and make a camp, how to wield an axe and make proper fires, how to cook, wash, mend, how to travel without losing his course, or what to do when he has lost it; how to trail, hunt, shoot, fish, dress game, manage boat or canoe, and how to extemporize such makeshifts as may be needed in wilderness faring. And he should know these things as he does the way to his mouth. Then is he truly a woodsman, sure to do promptly the right thing at the right time, whatever befalls. Such a man has an honest pride in his own resourcefulness, a sense of reserve force, a doughty self-reliance that is good to feel.[34]

In other words, a true camper was a true American.

One could easily, however, have an inauthentic experience. On page 1 of *The Book of Camping and Woodcraft*, Kephart noted that in some large cities one could simply pay a professional outfitter to prepare everything for a camping trip. "When your party reaches the jumping-off place it will be met by professional guides and packers, who will take you to the best hunting grounds and fishing waters." They would do all the work, even showing their employer "where the game and fish are 'using' and how to get them." But like William H. H. Murray before him, Kephart dismissed this comfortable and unchallenging approach as "touring, not campaigning." It required "little practical knowledge of the wilderness" and would not develop in the camper the self-reliance and independence of the pioneers. Kephart, like John Bachelder, linked camping's authenticity to past practices that had required greater sacrifice, endurance, and austerity than were necessary in 1906. Moreover, when a camper persisted in taking this comfortable and easy approach to the out-of-doors, "the day of disaster may come . . . and the city man may find himself some day alone. . . . Then it may go hard with him indeed."[35]

At the same time, Kephart never suggested that the truest camper was the one who simply suffered the most. "Let me not be misunderstood," he appealed, "as counseling anybody to 'rough it' by sleeping on the bare ground and eating nothing but hardtack and bacon." Camping was a matter of skill, experience, and preparation; a seasoned camper knew that comfort was not the central issue. "Only a tenderfoot will parade a scorn of comfort and a taste for useless hardships. As Nessmuk says: 'We do not go to the woods to rough it; we go to smoothe it—we get it rough enough in town.'" The experienced and authentic camper could be recognized by the simplicity of his outfit and his comfort with the situation.[36]

Camping as Deliverance

Horace Kephart's success as a camping author did not derive solely from the utility of his advice, his allusions to pilgrimage, and his frontier references. It also arose from the personal passion that he brought to these issues. John Bachelder had become a camping author to expand his guidebook offerings, and John Gould had transformed his military experiences into a useful guide for campers, but Kephart embraced camping as a form of personal salvation. Like many in his generation, Kephart had experienced the frontier early in life, but later on it was camping that restored his damaged spirit and body.

Horace Sowers Kephart was born September 8, 1862, in central Pennsylvania to Mary Elizabeth Sowers Kephart and the Reverend Isaiah Kephart. His ancestors had emigrated from Switzerland to the Allegheny Mountain wilderness in 1747, and the family had remained in the area since. Kephart's parents valued the family's traditions and history, and from birth Horace had imbibed his family's passion for wilderness and the frontier life. In particular, Horace's father enjoyed reminiscing to his son about the exploits of his father, grandfathers, and great-grandfathers and the world in which they had lived. Late in life, Isaiah went so far as to publish a series of articles on the family's history, which he titled "Pioneer Life in the Alleghenies."[37]

Despite the family's long Allegheny residence, Isaiah and Mary decided to move west with their young son in 1867 to Jefferson, Iowa, where they established a farm. Horace's new home, as he recalled it in 1922, was "a frontier village set in a prairie wilderness. . . . There was little to be seen from our front door but a sea of grass waving to the horizon. Behind the house was one of the few groves of trees in all that region. . . . For a couple of years, I was actually in the heart of a region where game birds of every description swarmed in myriads, as they never will again, and I soon became a good shot with real guns."[38] Shooting and hunting would remain a lifelong pleasure for Kephart.

Mary taught her only child to read, and when he was seven (and able, in his own words, to comprehend "almost anything"), she gave him his first book, *Robinson Crusoe*. The romantic, isolated, and self-sufficient main character strongly appealed to Horace, who had no siblings or playmates, and the book would set him along the path of the solitary adventurer, a role he was still playing when he published *The Book of Camping and Woodcraft* in 1906. In 1875, at the age of thirteen, Horace entered Western College near Cedar Rapids, Iowa, but once the school year ended in the spring of 1876, the family returned to Pennsylvania. That fall, Kephart enrolled at Lebanon Valley College, a Methodist-affiliated liberal school near Harrisburg, and he remained there to graduate in the spring of 1879, although "not without misgivings on the part of the faculty as to my orthodoxy and sundry other qualifications." Despite his professors' doubts, Kephart continued to pursue his education by enrolling that fall at Boston University, where he studied under the renowned evolutionary zoologist Alpheus Hyatt and enjoyed "the blessed privilege of studying whatever I pleased in the Boston Public Library."[39] This latter experience was so exhilarating, Kephart chose librarianship for his career.

Kephart's interlude in Boston was short, however. In 1880 he landed the post of assistant librarian at Cornell University in Ithaca, New York, where he also enrolled as a graduate student in history and political science. As the decade unfolded, he continued to work as an assistant librarian, first for a private book collector in Italy and then at Yale University, which he found particularly appealing. "New Haven," he wrote his confidant and former employer, Willard Fiske, "isn't a bad sort of place. . . . There is an *atmosphere* about New Haven that stimulates a man to use his mental powers profitably," which Kephart did. He recalled later in life that his spare time "was given to historical research, chiefly along the line of American frontier history." It had been his family's passion, and now was increasingly his own. At this time, Kephart also began his long publishing career. Most of his early publications related to library issues rather than camping, but his writing steadily improved, and in 1888 he landed his first literary sale, earning three dollars for a brief piece in the *Nation*.[40]

In addition to supporting Kephart's research and writing interests, his position at Yale University secured his financial position so he could now pursue his love, Laura White Mack. He and Mack had become engaged before his departure for Italy in December 1884, but after his return and establishment in New Haven, they were wed on April 12, 1887, and their first child was born in August 1888. Parenting, however, seems to have rested uncomfortably on Kephart's shoulders, for within weeks of baby Cornelia's birth, he bought a rifle, began shooting regularly at a New Haven rifle range, and took to roaming the nearby hills to shoot at anything his travels offered. "This may not become me as a gentleman and a scholar," he admitted to his friend Fiske, "but it fills my lungs, steadies my nerves, and gives me an appetite to be proud of."[41] Such outdoor activities would increase in frequency and duration as Kephart's family grew in number.

Many people would have been satisfied with such a life at this point, but Kephart, like *Robinson Crusoe*, longed for more adventure. To satisfy his restlessness, he began searching for a job with greater responsibilities, and in September 1890 he became head librarian at the St. Louis Mercantile Library.[42] The Mercantile was the oldest library west of the Mississippi, but that alone does not explain why Kephart chose it over the posts he was offered at Princeton and Cornell Universities. We must connect St. Louis, which had long been the gateway to the American frontier, to the man. For Kephart, the Mercantile stood above any other library because it was the primary collection of scholarly books in the Mississippi Valley. Kephart could blend his passion for pioneer life with his professional skills to create an outstanding special collection of western Americana.

In his accustomed manner, Kephart leapt to this task with a sharp mind and intense energy. Clarence Miller, an assistant librarian, described his supervisor as "the most brilliant man I have known, and, almost as a matter of course, the least assuming." Recollecting Kephart later in life, Miller remembered him as "a man of medium height and build, with quick decisive movements that bespoke muscular strength and coordination . . . neither introverted nor austere. . . . Any legitimate question got either a direct answer or concise information as to where the answer could be found. . . . All of his answers revealed a broad basis of understanding as well as a photographic memory." During these early St. Louis years, Kephart built the library's general collections and pursued rare materials. Often, he remembered decades later, "I was rewarded by finding diaries or other records of actual participants in the stirring events of the Old West." Kephart, however, wanted to be more than a collector of western history; he wanted to contribute to it. He had published a number of professional articles by this point, but now, he said, he "was ambitious to take up the story of 'The Winning of the West' where [Theodore] Roosevelt had left it, and continue it to the last frontier."[43]

Unfortunately, while Kephart's professional life was on the ascent, his personal life was in a slow decline. In an 1894 letter to Willard Fiske, the perpetually restless Kephart suggested that his home life had lost any spark. "Our little family is getting along nicely," he deadpanned; "we have a pleasant home and are laying by a little something every pay-day. In short, I am in a blessed rut."[44] Furthermore, Kephart's family continued to grow, swelling to include six children by 1897. In an apparent effort to retain some personal control and assert his masculinity in the face of this increasing domesticity, he joined a local hunting club and took frequent, often solitary, and increasingly long camping excursions into the Ozarks. Moreover, Kephart's general unease and anxiety about his everyday existence prompted two sweeping changes in his life. First, he developed a drinking problem, one he sadly would wrestle with for the rest of his life. And, second, his professional publications ceased in 1897, to be replaced by sporting and camping articles (he called them "snake stories") and by popular histories in *Harper's New Monthly Magazine*, *Forest & Stream*, *Outdoor Life*, and other magazines. One particularly revealing piece of writing was an unpublished notebook titled "The Joys of Barbarism": during 1901, Kephart copied approximately one hundred pages of excerpts from a wide range of authors. Standard writers like Longfellow and Shakespeare appeared, but the majority focused on outdoor adventures, exploration, and sports: George Ruxton, Lewis and Clark, Nessmuk, Theodore Roosevelt, and others. The linking theme was one well known to Kephart's camping contemporaries—the decadence of a materialistic urban life, and the virtue, integrity, and restorative possibilities of the primitive living experienced by frontiersmen and Native Americans.

According to Clarence Miller, "Kephart's aura of loneliness deepened in the years 1902 and 1903." He was drinking heavily, and his Ozark camping trips increased in frequency and duration, which "soon began to alienate the library's directors." In the memory of daughter Margaret, who was approximately twelve at the time, her father "couldn't stop drinking by then, couldn't manage his troublesome nerves, and couldn't sleep or work." Then, late in 1903, Kephart's life collapsed on all fronts. The library discharged him, he was physically exhausted and broke, and shortly before Christmas, he and his wife separated, with Laura taking the children and moving to her parents' home in Ithaca. These events shattered Kephart, and he "suffered a complete nervous collapse and was taken to the hospital," according to Miller.[45] Kephart's father, Isaiah, soon arrived from Dayton, Ohio, and returned home with his son.

In Dayton, Kephart struggled with his future as he slowly recovered. His professional career was over. Besides being fired from his job, he had abandoned bibliographic writing seven years before. Still, literary writing about the out-of-doors, firearms, and the American frontier continued to appeal to him. He could hope to restore himself and his life, as well as earn a living, with this sort of writing, but the issue was *where*. Nine years after Kephart had pondered this question, he offered a brief explanation for his decision to move to western North Carolina.

When I went south into the mountains I was seeking a Back of Beyond. This for more reasons than one. With an inborn taste for the wild and romantic, I yearned for a strange land and a people that had the charm of originality. Again, I had a passion for early American history; and, in Far Appalachia, it seemed that I might realize the past in the present, seeing with my own eyes what life must have been to my pioneer ancestors of a century or two ago. Besides, I wanted to enjoy a free life in the open air, the thrill of exploring new ground, the joys of the chase, and the man's game of matching my woodcraft against the forces of nature, with no help from servants or hired guides.

Knowing no one who had been to the southern Appalachian Mountains, Kephart recalled in 1922 that he had used a topographic map to find "what seemed to be the wildest part of this region; and there I went. It was Swain County, amid the Great Smoky Mountains, near the Tennessee line."[46]

In late July or early August 1904, Kephart departed Dayton for Asheville, North Carolina. Traveling with but a handful of possessions, he planned to establish a temporary camp in the mountains. Consulting a physician, C. D. W. Colby, upon his arrival in Asheville, Kephart was declared "a physical wreck," but the doctor also recognized someone determined to recover. Moving into the woods, Kephart found an appealing site about forty-five miles from Asheville, where he set up camp in a Baker tent and then set about searching the region for a more attractive, permanent home. In October, having found what he wanted, Kephart departed for "a little log cabin on the site of a disused copper mine . . . on Hazel Creek, deep in the virgin woods." Here Kephart found the pioneer people he sought, and as his condition improved, he began to publish camping articles in *Sports Afield*, *Forest and Stream*, and other popular magazines. By 1906 he had compiled enough material with these publications to produce the first edition of *The Book of Camping and Woodcraft*. The most enduring of his publications, the book was published by the Outing Publishing Company, one of the leading American firms in the area of outdoor recreation, and positively reviewed in the *New York Times* at the beginning of summer 1907. According to the *Times* reviewer, Kephart's book was practical, well-illustrated, and taught one "how to get along without the appliances of civilization." And, unlike so many other camping authors, Kephart's writing was "animated by a delicate appreciation of the poesy of the woods and the outdoor life that far removes it from the dull guide book it so easily might have been." In sum, the reviewer suggested, "Mr. Kephart's little book on camping should be the friend of every intending sojourner in the wilderness." Over the next decade, the book sold very well and Kephart regularly revised it, resulting in at least seven American editions.[47]

Despite Kephart's longing to escape the present and to live a frontier life, he found his new home to be a "strange environment." In 1917's *Woodcraft*, he described his initial response: "To one coming from cities, it was . . . almost as though [I] had been carried back, asleep, upon the wings of time, and had awakened in the eighteenth century, to meet Daniel Boone in flesh and blood." Kephart, now "awake" in the past, heartily embraced his dream of living as a frontiersman.

> In such a situation it was natural, nay imperative, that one should pick up and practice certain arts long lost and forgotten by civilized communities but quite essential in our backwoods way of living. I began, to be sure, with the advantage of experience gained on many hunting and camping trips in other lands; but in this new field I had to make shift in a different way, and fashion many appliances from materials found on the spot. The forest itself was not only my hunting-ground but my workshop and my garden. . . . To what degree I was reverting to the primitive came home to me one day when a white dame, finding Will Tahlahlah giving me a lesson in Cherokee, remarked rather sourly to the redskin: "You needn't teach *him* anything; he's more of an Indian than you are."

At the same time, Kephart's literary side flourished, and he found that it acted as a balm.

> Seldom during those three years as a forest exile did I feel lonesome in daytime; but when supper would be over, and black night closed in on my hermitage, and the owls began calling all the blue devils of the woods, one needed some indoor occupation to keep him in good cheer: and that is how I came to write my first little book on camping and woodcraft.[48]

Once Kephart had explored his western North Carolina environment, felt that he understood it, and had transformed this knowledge and his experience into a successful camping guidebook, he decided to pursue his interest in the region's residents. This investigation he pursued with the same vigor and intensity he had brought to *The Book of Camping and Woodcraft* and earlier projects. The result was a series of 1912 articles in *Outing Magazine* and a 1913 book, *Our Southern Highlanders*, which remains in print today. In his introduction to the 1995 printing, George Ellison calls this last book "the classic study of the Southern mountains, and the authors of virtually every book written about the region since the publication of

Kephart's volume owe and usually acknowledge a debt to him." From 1913 to 1931, Kephart lived a modestly successful and relatively settled life in Bryson City, North Carolina. He edited volumes for the Outing Adventure Library, wrote articles for a variety of outdoor magazines, and published *Camping* (a revised and much expanded portion of *The Book of Camping and Woodcraft*) in 1916, then a similarly expanded version of *Woodcraft* in 1917. In 1921, his publisher combined these two enhanced volumes into a single book, *Camping and Woodcraft*, which is still available in print. Finally, Kephart published his last major volume in 1923, *The Camper's Manual: For the Novice and the Expert*, but he continued to publish newspaper and magazine articles for the remainder of his life. He also became an authority on camping equipment and firearms, prompting manufacturers to send him products for field evaluation and to seek his advice on design and performance.[49]

Kephart might have continued in the new life and career he had developed, but his restlessness kept him open to new challenges, which appeared as his reputation swelled. During the mid-1920s he became actively involved in the effort that led to the creation of the Great Smoky Mountains National Park. He did not live to see the movement succeed, but without his efforts, the park might never have developed.[50] And, in the late 1920s and early 1930s, he helped plot the route of the Appalachian Trail through North Carolina's Smoky Mountains and into northern Georgia. On April 2, 1931, Horace Kephart died in an accident in Bryson City when the taxi he had hired lost control on a curve. He was sixty-eight. Although Kephart and his estranged wife Laura never fully reconciled, she, two of their sons, and a grandson attended the burial services on April 5, which were held in a packed Bryson City high school auditorium with hundreds outside standing. He was interred in Bryson City Cemetery, which lay next door to the school.

The Growth of Camping

Supported by the guidebooks and articles of John Bachelder, John Gould, Horace Kephart, and others, the popularity of camping expanded between 1870 and 1915. Most camping trips went unrecorded during the period, but some sense of the increase can be obtained from visitor numbers to national parks and from the number of camping publications. Guidebooks, how-to articles, and personal accounts were few in number at first. From 1877 to 1890, only five camping and related articles appeared in magazines, while eighteen books were published. During the 1890s, the number of magazine articles rose noticeably to twenty-six, but new book releases declined sharply to only two. This reversal between books and magazines may represent a glutted book market, but more likely reflects the rising popularity of magazines and the impact of the 1893 Panic. The latter was the largest economic reversal in the United States prior to the Great Depression that began in 1929. The 1900s, however, brought a tremendous increase in camping publications (and campers presumably), with more than 180 magazine articles produced and eleven new books. Park visitor numbers disclose a similar pattern. Yellowstone National Park received a total of only 3,105 visitors in 1895, and approximately 1,500 of them camped using their own or hired transportation. Five years later, park visitation had nearly tripled to 8,928 total, with just over 4,500 camping. By 1906, total visits had doubled again to 17,182, and almost half of these camped. In the twelve national parks as a whole, 1906's visitation was approximately 31,000, but it increased sixfold to 199,000 in 1910 and to 335,000 in 1915. A conservative estimate would be that almost 50,000 of these visitors camped in 1910 and nearly 85,000 of them in 1915.[51]

While camping's popularity expanded, its diversity remained unremarkable. The large majority of campers were adult, white, and middle- to upper-middle-class men who were independent businessmen or held jobs as managers or professionals. Moreover, as an outgrowth of traditionally masculine hunting and fishing, camping appealed most strongly to men. Perhaps in reaction, magazines and outdoor organizations published a steady stream of articles encouraging women, albeit from the middle and upper middle classes, to camp. M. F. Whitman, for example, informed her 1878 Appalachian Mountain Club audience that her writing was "chiefly for the benefit of women, and I desire to let them know that they may, if they will, do almost the same mountain work as men." Martha Coman's "The Art of Camping: A Woman's View" was even more encouraging to members of her gender and class. With the exception of the guides, only women filled the photographs and populated the accounts of camping's pleasures in her 1902 magazine article. She encouraged women to "camp out" so that they could live like pioneers—"simply and naturally with a mind and heart ready for the benediction of the woods." At the same time, Coman warned her readers away from camp cooking. "Many a camping trip have I known to be utterly spoiled because that part of the duties was assigned to one of the feminine members of the party." If a woman accepted the chore, Coman warned, she could be sure that some appealing hike or similarly strenuous event would draw her away from camp for the day and that when she returned she would be "exhausted and ready to drop." Collapsing, however, would be impossible if she was the cook. "The rest of the party are starved and clamor for food—not a hastily gathered makeshift meal because your back aches and your legs are leaden-weighted; no, they want plenty, more than plenty, and they hover about anxiously inquiring 'if it isn't nearly ready,' and 'how much longer must they wait?' until you could just sit down and weep for shear weariness." The solution, Coman suggested, was simple. "Don't attempt to do the cooking yourself. You'll regret it if you do, for it is one of the duties that is never at an end, and there are so many other things you want to be doing when you get into the woods and find yourself in the thrall of nature." Instead, she recommended, hire someone whose "sole duty" is to cook for everyone. Of course, many adult women had children, so the accounts of Whitman and Coman were unlikely to persuade them to camp. To reach these skeptics, articles like Mrs. N. E. Corthell's tale of her "Family Trek to the Yellowstone" with husband and seven children were published. During two months of 1903, the Corthells "traveled twelve hundred miles, stood the journey well and never, never had such a wonderful, delightful summer." As a consequence, while women remained the minority, their ratio to men tended to even out as the size of a camping group increased.[52]

McDonaldization Begins

Even as camping's popularity grew, its appeal remained limited because, for several reasons, it remained too "rough." First, the equipment was often designed for domestic use, making it awkward, bulky, and difficult to move. The earliest guides, such as John Bachelder's *Popular Resorts* of 1876, provided few details about what one should bring, unless one was backpacking, which prompted a warning—weight was a particularly knotty issue for anyone on foot. "It is of the greatest importance to reduce the stock of clothing and equipment to actual necessities, for 'every ounce becomes a pound' at the end of a long jaunt." The camper should consider carefully each piece of equipment, Bachelder urged, and not include "new and elaborately equipped knapsacks, heavy rifles . . . patent ammunition and fishing tackle." In a very short time, he cautioned, they will become a burden, "and the pleasure of the excursion is spoiled."[53] Despite the cultural connections to the frontier and the high status and authenticity of this, the most primitive camping technique, the total number of backpacking Americans stayed small. Other camping techniques—on horseback, in canoe, or with a horse and wagon—allowed for more latitude, but the weight of such objects as tents, tent poles, plates, cutlery, frying pans, pails, cups, and axes, as well as food-stuffs, rapidly developed into a heavy load. Horace Kephart, for example, estimated that the average person on a two-week camping trip would eat from twenty-eight to fifty pounds of food—plus some fresh trout, venison, or other wild game (fig. 2.4).

As mentioned earlier, campers have tended to judge the authenticity of themselves and other campers based on the degree of difficulty faced. Were they truly "roughing it"? All modes of camping in this era were arduous, but backpacking was harder than the others, so Bachelder had ranked it highest and most likely to result in a "romantic" experience of the wild. At the same time, not every camper or potential camper wished to experience a maximum of roughness. Many sought greater comfort, which explains why backpacking had the fewest practitioners. As a consequence of the major-ity's willingness to allow more of modern domestic life into their camp if it reduced or removed some unwanted aspect of camping's roughness, equipment manufacturers quickly developed new, specialized products. The consumerist desire to "smooth out" camping's adventures was soon met with "improved" versions of tents, sleeping gear, stoves, cookware, lighting devices, and myriad other items. Moreover, the new items were often pro-duced and sold in standardized versions, which reduced production costs and potentially provided manufacturers with greater profits and a larger market share.

This tendency for many campers to embrace greater comfort and for manufacturers to pursue more profits and market share is an early exam-ple of modernity's impact on camping. Despite its romantic antimodern roots, camping began to be shaped by "McDonaldization"—society's desire for greater efficiency, calculability, predictability, and control—soon after *Adventures in the Wilderness* was published. Of course, any camper who wanted to reduce the weight of his or her camping "kit" did not necessarily know what innovations might be available, especially early in camping's development. In order to make campers aware of the new equipment and to calm any concerns about its use, manufacturers and suppliers initially relied heavily on endorsements and promotions in guidebooks and maga-zine articles. E. R. Wallace included both laudatory language and illustra-tions about several products in his *Descriptive Guide to the Adirondacks* in 1875. "We must not omit," he reminded himself and his readers, "to call attention to an ingenious contrivance recently invented." Do you remember, Wallace inquired, how awkward it had been to transport utensils when you last had to portage? This challenge, he assured readers, could be eliminated by using a "Patent Sportsman's Kit," which held a frying pan, plates, cups,

	Light		Heavy	
	Summer	Winter	Summer	Winter
Meats, etc.				
Salt pork		10 lbs.		10 lbs.
Bacon	12 lbs.	12	10 lbs.	10
Ham	5	5	5	5
Corned beef (canned)	4	4	4	4
Concentrated soups	2½	2½	1½	1½
Canned consommé			2	2
Fresh eggs			5 (4 doz.)	5
Butter			6	6
Cheese	1	1	1	1
Lard	3	3	3	3
Dried milk (or evaporated				
cream, 6 cans)	2½	2½	2½	2½
	30	40	40	50
Bread, etc.				
Fresh bread			5	5
Hard biscuit	5	5		
Flour	25	25	25	25
Cornmeal (yellow)	3	10	3	10
Buckwheat flour		3		3
Rolled oats	3	3	3	3
Rice	3	3	3	3
Macaroni	1	1	1	1
Baking powder (Royal)	1	1	1	1
Baking soda	1	1	1	1
	42	52	42	52
Vegetables				
Potatoes (fresh)			30 (½ bu.)	30
" (evaporated)	4	4		
Onions (fresh)	4	6	4	6
Beans	4	6	4	6
Split peas	4	4	4	4
Tomatoes (canned)			5 (2 cans)	5
Sweet corn (canned)			2½ (1 can)	2½
	16	20	49½	53½
Beverages				
Coffee (roasted, whole,				
_or_ 5 lbs. ground)	3	3	3	3
Tea	½	½	½	½
Whitman's cocoa	½	½	½	½
	4	4	4	4

Figure 2.4. Horace Kephart's summary of the rations needed by four men on a two-week camping trip. From Horace Kephart, _The Book of Camping and Woodcraft_ (New York: Outing Publishing Co., 1906), 65–66.

silverware, and other items (fig. 2.5). Moreover, it "weighs but 16 lbs. And costs only $17." As effective as these endorsements were, manufacturers and retailers like Lewis & Conger, Abercrombie & Fitch Company, and Sears, Roebuck & Company also began to run advertisements in popular magazines like _Outing, Forest and Stream_, and _Collier's_ even as they distributed product catalogs and brochures.[54]

	Light		Heavy	
	Summer	Winter	Summer	Winter
Sugar, etc.				
Sugar (granulated)	5	5	5	5
Maple sugar	5	5		
Maple syrup			3 (1 qt.)	6 (½ gal.)
Preserves, jam, marmalade			5	5
	10	10	13	16
Acids				
Vinegar		1 (1 pint)		1
Pickles			2	2
Lemons			4 (2 doz.)	
Citric acid	¼			
	¼	1	6	3
Fruits, etc.				
Evaporated apples, peaches, apricots	2	4	2	2
Prunes (stoned)	1	1	2	2
Raisins (seeded)	1	1	1	1
Canned peaches, plums, cherries, pears, cranberries			10 (4 cans)	10
Shelled nuts	1	1	1	1
	5	7	16	16
Condiments				
Salt (if allowing for curing skins, etc., take 10 lbs.)	2	2	2	2
Pepper (white)	1 oz.	1 oz.	1 oz.	1 oz.
Cayenne or chili	1 oz.	1 oz.	1 oz.	1 oz.
Worcestershire sauce			1 bot.	1 bot.
Olive oil			1 bot.	1 bot.
Mustard			x	x
Sage			x	x
Parsley			x	x
Mixed herbs			x	x
Nutmeg			x	x
Curry powder			x	x
Ginger			x	x
	2⅛	2⅛	5	5
Total	109⅜ lbs.	136⅜ lbs.	176 lbs.	200 lbs.

Add soap, matches.

Figure 2.4. (continued)

These product testimonials, magazine advertisements, and the catalogs and brochures also contributed to the creation of a camping imagination. Along with personal accounts and guidebooks, these images and texts filled a novice's mental blanks with "Sportsman's Kits," "Baker Tents," and "Acme Folding Canvas Boats." They prompted incipient campers to

"PATENT SPORTSMAN'S KIT,"

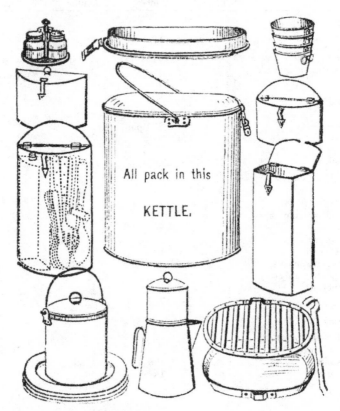

All pack in this

KETTLE.

Figure 2.5. The "Patent Sportsman's Kit" of 1875 promised greater convenience, making it an early example of the impact of modernity on camping. From E. R. Wallace, *Descriptive Guide to the Adirondacks and Handbook of Travel* . . . (New York: American News Co., 1875), 249.

mentally transform "nature" and "campsite" from vague and abstracts spaces into the increasingly clear and detailed places that drew them out of their ordinary urban lives and onto their antimodern pilgrimages.[55]

In spite of the numerous developments that lightened, shrank, and increased the effectiveness of equipment, camping gear remained cumbersome, leaving many campers to rely on horses and wagons, as well as hired staff, to assist them with their adventures. This workforce was a major source of the limited ethnic and racial diversity that might have been found at campsites and, as we shall see, sometimes became embroiled in controversy. Backgrounds varied by region, but Native Americans, African Americans, Asians, and Latinos worked as cooks, guides, and general laborers

Tent, 16 x 18, with 5 ft. wall, and fly with 4 ft. extension $27.50
Tent, 12 x 16, 2½ ft. wall, no fly, second-hand 5.00
Canvas sheet for dining floor, 8 x 16 ft. 2.50
Platform for dining floor, 8 x 12 ft. 12.00
Platform for large tent, with 12-inch side wall 33.00
Well, 15 feet piping, point, labor, and pump 10.00
Gasolene [sic] stove and oven 3.50
2 chests drawers, secondhand, and paint 2.50
Camp chairs, one arm and two small 3.40
Lumber and labor on three bedsteads, table, and benches 5.00
4 excelsior mattresses at $1.75 .... 7.00
Lumber and labor on closet 2.50
Freight and carriage 12.00
Lantern 1.60
4 bedsprings at $2.25 .... 9.00

$136.50

Figure 2.6. Clara Gamble and family's camping outfit and costs. From "Camping on the East Shore, Lake Michigan," *Country Life in America*, July 1909, 310.

on many camping trips. Although frequently unmentioned in personal accounts, such staff and their ethnic diversity were common enough that fiction writers sometimes included them in their stories. Kate Douglass Wiggin, for instance, included Hop Yet, "a Heathen Chinee" cook, and Pancho Gutierrez, "a Mexican man-of-all-work," in her 1889 novel *A Summer in a Cañon: A California Story*. Despite their low status, some of these employees, especially the guides, developed reputations that drew many campers. One of them, Mitchell Sabattis, an Abenaki Indian, became renowned throughout the Adirondacks, was much sought by outdoorsmen, and has often been recorded as one of the region's top guides.[56]

Of course, the cost of camping with packhorses or in a wagon with equipment and support staff was substantial and provided the second reason that camping's appeal was limited to a relatively small, if growing, group. Clara Gamble and her family, for instance, had camped for seven summers on the eastern shore of Lake Michigan when she published a description of the equipment they had purchased and the campsite design they had devised for an optimal, low-cost, family experience. According to her July 1909 article in *Country Life in America*, their camping outfit, "which we had used two seasons and which is good for several more," cost a total of $136.50 (fig. 2.6).

A small figure today, the capital investment was sizable in its day, even when we assume that the equipment might last from five to ten years. Furthermore, the annual freight and cartage charge for moving the equipment and supplies (plus the family's personal travel costs, which were not mentioned) would recur.[57]

In the Woods with a Canoe

In addition to being expensive, wagons and railroad itineraries narrowed the paths that campers could explore. A backpacker or horse packer might travel freely through thick woods or across rough terrain, but wagons needed open, smooth surfaces, and although trains dropped backpacking campers along some lines, most usually stopped only at settlements that might be some distance from wildlands. Campers on foot or horse, however, could not travel across the wild marshes, rivers, and lakes that are common across the northern tier of the United States and in southern Canada. Only a canoe or small boat could liberate campers to roam freely, and it did so relatively inexpensively. Small watercraft had been employed for war and for work in the region since the seventeenth century, while recreational fishermen and hunters had relied on them since the early nineteenth century. Modern-day boat camping may have begun in the Adirondacks—William H. H. Murray was an avid canoe camper—but it quickly diffused from there, even as it developed its own subsection within the camping literature.[58]

The 1882 edition of E. R. Wallace's *Descriptive Guide to the Adirondacks* assumed his readers would engage in waterborne camping trips and included advertisements for a variety of vessels, including folding canvas boats. A decade later, Nessmuk, the renowned outdoor magazine writer of the 1860s and 1870s, dedicated a chapter in his 1884 guidebook, *Woodcraft*, to canoeing, which he saw as "gaining rapidly in popular favor."[59] The next year, 1885, Seneca Ray Stoddard produced his *Canoe and Camp Cookery: A Practical Cook Book for Canoeists, Corinthian Sailors and Outers*, and in 1897 Perry D. Frazer released *Canoe Cruising and Camping*. None of the last three publications focused exclusively on the Adirondack region, but instead they considered issues that would be common wherever someone boat camped.

This increase in literature stimulated interest in boat camping even as the new publications reflected an increasing enthusiasm for it. Among these enthusiasts was no less a figure than Frederick Jackson Turner. Although the historian had expressed a concern for the "closing" of the American frontier, pockets of wild nature nonetheless remained, and he frequently canoe camped through them as an escape from his everyday life. Turner's taste for camping and fishing began during his youth in Portage, Wisconsin, a small town near the frontier when he was born in 1861. His father, Andrew

Jackson Turner, loved the out-of-doors, especially fishing and hunting. The younger Turner, who considered himself and his father to be "comrades," similarly embraced outdoor activities wholeheartedly, especially fishing. As he grew into a college student and then a professor (at the University of Wisconsin at Madison from 1890 to 1910 and at Harvard University from 1910 to 1922), Turner frequently spent his summers fishing and camping. One biographer noted that Turner often began fall semester "trim and tanned" because of these summer outdoor vacations.[60] Many of these vacations, such as the one he enjoyed during the summer of 1908, relied on canoes. On August 10 of that year, Turner, his wife (Caroline) Mae, and their daughter Dorothy departed on a canoe camping trip through southern Ontario Province with Charles Van Hise, a geologist and president of the University of Wisconsin, and his two daughters Mary Janet and Hilda. Paddling and portaging from Basswood Lake on the Minnesota-Ontario border to Lake Nipigon north of Thunder Bay, they covered nearly four hundred miles.

Both Turner and his wife left accounts of their vacation—a later letter by him to fellow historian and friend Max Farrand, and a personal journal by her—which occasionally reveal how their wilderness travels were a voyage into sacred space. According to Turner, the campers "had a bully taste of the real wilderness" on this canoe-camping adventure. They had slept in beds only once, had cut their own trails at times, saw no one new for three weeks, encountered moose and bear, and caught and ate so many fish that "we filed the barbs off our hooks to keep from getting too many to eat." The six campers were assisted by four men Van Hise had "borrowed from the force of the Oliver mining company which let us pay them and use them in a dull season." In Turner's view, these men were not effeminate, urban types whose ethnic heritage had been erased, but "real bullies of the northern woods" whose experiences had made them into rugged, pioneer-like individuals. "Erick the head guide was a canny Swede who has lived in the woods some thirty years and can do anything. . . . Dow was a Canadian Scotch man—a true sport. . . . McCabe was a fine Irish man, strong as the propeller of an ocean liner at the stern paddle, and then there was the cook [Fred Landry], a French Canadian, with the gasconade of his people, but clever with the frying pan." These four men supported the camping party for the entire time by being the principal paddlers in three of the four canoes, by portaging most of the approximately one thousand pounds of supplies and gear, by almost daily erecting and striking their encampments, and by preparing all meals. Although the campers were generally "roughing it," they had time to relax and ate well (fig. 2.7).

One dinner, Mae Turner recounted, was an especially elaborate delight, since they had been camping for more than three weeks at the time. Dinner,

Figure 2.7. Caroline Mae Turner found time to relax on her canoe camping trip on the Nipigon River in the summer of 1908. From Dorothy Turner, image 66, box 58c, album 1, Frederick Jackson Turner Papers, Huntington Library, San Marino, CA.

she noted in her journal for September 2, was "pea soup—very good. Trout and bacon—sweet potatoes . . . hot baking powder biscuit—blueberry pie— blueberries—cheese—coffee." This sumptuous meal was followed the next morning by a similarly impressive repast: "blueberries, prunes, Oatmeal, trout, bacon, toast & coffee—and some left over blueberry pie." However rough other elements may have been, the cook made their meals quite smooth.[61]

As the ten traveled their route, they sometimes admired the landscape, just as other, romantically inclined campers had before them. A few days into their trip, for instance, Van Hise termed the scene at one lake a "Hog-arthean line of beauty from mountain to valley," which prompted Turner to remark, "My I love these trees. Look at those leafy isles." On another occasion, a landscape feature recalled the fading frontier for Turner. "We had a little taste of the old Dawson Route from Fort William to the Rainy river," he happily reported to his historian friend Farrand. The Dawson route had been a wide trail that ran from Thunder Bay to the Red River district of southern Manitoba. Initially surveyed by S. J. Dawson in 1858 and opened about 1870, it was slowly being reclaimed by the forest and largely unused, except for local traffic, when the Turners and Van Hises encountered it in 1908. "The old portages cut out for teams and with corduroy road in places," observed Turner, "made a contrast with the Indian portages we had been following." The former were more open and easier to travel, but "not altogether to our taste." The Dawson route, it seemed to Turner, was out of place and an invasion of sacred wilderness because "it looked like civilization."[62]

Ethnicity and race also challenged Turner, his companions, and their guides as they canoed across southern Ontario. Parts of this wilderness were home to Canada's First Peoples, but evidence of their presence distressed Mae Turner. On one occasion, she recorded in her journal, the company established camp "on a point commanding all the area," but she wished it was elsewhere. "Attractive" pine groves on other points caught her eye, but more importantly, nearby their campsite sat "the frame of an Indian tepe." Where the Dawson route had inspired Mae's husband to recall frontier history, the native structure gave her "the feeling that the place is unclean," even though it had not been occupied for years. "Camping on virgin ground," she concluded, "spoils one."[63]

A few days later, as the campers prepared to head their canoes up the Nipigon River, they faced a dilemma that again involved First Peoples. The superintendent of the river and the local populace "protested against our party going up with light canoes and no Indians," recounted Turner. Van Hise and the hired men dismissed these protestations, telling Turner that they could do it on their own. Turner, however, disagreed with the other men, insisting that his family had to have a "Nipigon canoe" (a twenty-foot, dory-like boat) and an Indian guide who knew the river and where to fish. Turner's stance, he lamented, "greatly disgusted Van Hise who hates Indians," but Turner held firm nonetheless. Then, to his surprise, "Dow [the guide] kicked and would not paddle [in the same canoe] with an Indian." Turner, finally revealing his own feelings, admitted that he "sympathized with [Dow]. He was a true sport; but I had made up my mind." Subsequently, the party obtained its Nipigon canoe, and Dow, who had been at the stern of Turner's canoe, exchanged with "amiable Mike" McCabe, who had been paddling in a canoe with the cook. The campers then departed upriver toward the next camp, where an outfitter had promised they would meet their expert aboriginal guide. Ironically, when the new man appeared the next day, "he proved to be a clever young bluffer, a white lad" with little experience, it later turned out. Perhaps Van Hise's disgust, Dow's "kicking," and Turner's sympathy had reached the ears of the locals, but for whatever reason, Turner admitted, "No Indian could be gotten to work with whites." Consequently, the campers missed some good fishing "by not having an expert Indian who could take us into one or two places where prior knowledge was requisite." Nevertheless, after the canoe campers completed their vacation on September 10, Turner judged his travels a success because, like all true pilgrims, he had returned in a transformed state. "I am 20 pounds lighter & much more muscular," he crowed. Only forty-six at the time, Turner would continue to camp and fish for many years to come.[64]

The fact that the Turner and Van Hise families' canoe-camping vacation had covered nearly four hundred miles was noteworthy, but its duration— one month—was unexceptional. Many, if not most, camping trips taken during this era tended to stretch to thirty or more days, making duration the third factor that restricted camping's appeal to a relatively small group of adherents. Few Americans possessed sufficient leisure time to vacation in any form. For most people, if they had the time to camp, it came as a result of the sort of ill health that would confine them to the house or because they were unemployed and without the money. Only as the nineteenth became the twentieth century did paid vacations begin to be won by working people.[65]

In the Yellowstone

As a consequence of the era's bulky equipment, high costs, and extraordinary time demand, most Americans camped near their homes or at natural sites easily approached on public transport. Nevertheless, a small number of them began to journey to the country's first wildland preserve, Yellowstone National Park, shortly after Congress created it in 1872. From its beginning, the park was sacred space where the everyday was generally excluded. In the words of the authorizing legislation, Yellowstone was not normal, profane space, but "dedicated and set apart . . . for the benefit and enjoyment of the people." Moreover, anyone who thought otherwise was warned away: "All persons who shall locate or settle upon or occupy the [park], or any part thereof, except as hereinafter provided, shall be considered trespassers and removed therefrom." Congress protected the park for campers and other visitors, not for settlers, and it soon attracted the former. Local residents had camped in the Yellowstone during its first summer as a park, and then Harry J. Norton, followed by the colorful Earl of Dunraven (Windham Thomas Wyndham-Quin), pack-camped through the park in the summers of 1873 and 1874 respectively. In 1876, only four years after the park's creation, John Bachelder recommended "the great National Park" and Colorado's "Garden of the Gods" to his readers.[66]

By 1910, the federal government had sanctioned and enshrined seven additional sites—Sequoia, Yosemite, Mount Rainier, Crater Lake, Wind Cave, Mesa Verde, and Glacier—with all of them receiving campers. These new parks, like Yellowstone before them, were dedicated to the *nation*, rather than to any specific group, sect, or view. Each was, in the terminology of historian Mircea Eliade, an *imago mundi*, that is, an outstanding example of the wild nature that had helped create the American nation during its pioneer period and for that reason an environment where campers could recapitulate that formative experience. All were, however, in the West, quite distant from America's eastern population centers. As a consequence, the national parks were beyond the reach of most Americans; only locals could head out to them frequently.[67]

One among the handfuls of easterners who made the long trek to camp in Yellowstone National Park was an adventuresome Mary Bradshaw Richards, who arrived with her husband, Jesse Mayne Richards, in the summer of 1882. The Richardses were not wealthy, but sufficiently upper middle class to afford the steep costs of travel from New England. Mary's father had been a printer and the founder of a newspaper, the *Salem Observer*, while Jesse had run a successful grocery business in the same Massachusetts city when the two were married in 1855. The couple moved to New York City sometime between 1856 and 1876, where apparently Jesse's transplanted business flourished. It was during these two decades that the couple took to traveling—a socially acceptable leisure activity that people of their class saw as an opportunity for self-improvement.[68]

Mary and Jesse were not young when they camped through Yellowstone— she was fifty-seven and he fifty-three—but they were experienced and determined travelers. Their previous adventures had taken them as far as Italy and Switzerland, and it appears that they also had toured the Holy Land. Moreover, this was the Richardses' second attempt to visit the new national park. Five years earlier, in 1877, they had made it as far as Salt Lake City and had set out for Yellowstone when they were turned away by General Philip Sheridan's troops, who were chasing approximately eight hundred Nez Perce through the park as they attempted to flee to Canada.[69]

After traveling by train from New York, the Richardses arrived in Salt Lake City on July 27, 1882, but Mary found the once "peaceful" settlement dismaying, having become "busier" and more "bustling" than it had been in 1877. Nevertheless, she and Jesse toured the town for three days, taking in the graves of Brigham Young and his first wife, the Great Salt Lake, and the tabernacle during Sabbath services. They also, by necessity, purchased blankets and provisions and hired the equipment, transportation, and guides for their camping trip through the park. According to Mary Richards, her and her husband's outfit "consisted of a wall tent, blankets, buffalo skins, axe, hatchet, nails, ropes, hammer and wheel grease; flour, sugar, lard, ham, eggs packed in oats, canned meats, fruits and jellies; a long tailed frying pan, bake kettle, coffee pot, tin plates, cups and spoons, knives and forks; a capital driver, an accomplished cook, two large balky horses and lastly the all-important spring wagon, canvas-covered, large, strong, rather stiff in the joints, but possessing a fitness for its purpose which we soon learned to appreciate. This outfit cost us eighteen dollars per day." The total expense for the Richardses' rental alone—$252—points to their class standing, because it was a tremendous sum when the U.S. Gross National Product per capita was a mere $204.[70]

Mary and Jesse departed Salt Lake City by the Utah and Northern Railroad on the afternoon of July 30. Heading north along the lake, Mary enjoyed the scenery, calling it "wild and beautiful." At Ogden they changed to a sleeping car that carried them until noon the next day when they would meet their guides and begin their camping trip through the Yellowstone Park from August 1 to August 15, 1882. We know about Mary's park experiences because beginning on August 1 she composed a daily "letter" for publication in the *Salem Observer*.[71] These lively reports undoubtedly stimulated many readers' imaginations as well as their feet, and they reveal an educated, thoughtful, and playful correspondent, whose comments were a blend of careful observation and engaging interpretation. Furthermore, they clearly demonstrate that even though Richards and her husband never declared it, they were on a pilgrimage.

At noon on July 31, the Richardses reached Beaver Canyon (now Spencer), Idaho, where, Mary noted, "our camp life commenced." Mary's comment here suggests that Beaver Canyon represented the transition out of their ordinary lives and into the sacred space where she and Jesse could perform their devotions to wilderness and, hopefully, achieve their desired objectives. Who would direct them through this transformative space? The Richardses undoubtedly had read at least one Yellowstone guidebook before departing, but when in the park they chose to be guided by the Basset brothers, whom Mary described as "fine enterprising fellows of the true pioneer stamp." In the care of these guides, Mary suggested to her readers, she and Jesse would enjoy an authentic adventure that would recapture the frontier experience.[72]

Mary Richards's belief that the frontier transformed people is revealed by her description of a local resident the party met on their second day in the park. They had gathered around a sunset campfire when an unexpected horseman came galloping rapidly toward them. Mary initially assumed that the rider must be a Native American, because "who, save an Indian . . . could ride like the coming guest!" When the stranger drew near, Richards was amazed and pleased. "A man, once white, dressed in buckskin, leather fringed, and red flannel, shouted a greeting to our boys, calling them by name." With the veneer of civilization stripped away from him by a life in wilderness, she found the result to be a true and handsome man. "He was of fine form and feature; thin, agile, brown as a chestnut and with uncombed hair and beard. His eyes were clear and sharp, looking through instead of at you while he spoke." Independent and self-sufficient for the past fifteen years, this "fair specimen of an Idaho frontiersman" caught and sold fish and game to traveling parties and the railroad to earn enough money to "hibernate" through winter "in some den of a country saloon." He stayed with them for the night, but Richards was unsurprised that he had departed in the morning before she arose, leaving only the shawl he had borrowed from her to cover up his rifle and pistol, along with a half dozen trout as a "thank you." This theme—the national park as a transforming frontier and campers as pioneers—runs steadily through Richards's letters and was one of her most reliable tropes.[73]

While at Beaver Canyon, Richards also recorded her initial recognition that campers had to reduce their accustomed material possessions and adopt a more austere lifestyle. She and Jesse had brought trunks filled with clothes, towels, and other personal items, but like the pioneers before them, they now faced rugged conditions and had to select the few that they would carry through the wilderness. Weighing the value and purpose of each, Mary and Jesse chose their "thickest and oldest clothing, a change of boots, a few towels, gloves, and our rubber coats," which they then packed into a hamper "scarcely larger than a champagne basket." Stowed with their blankets and rubber sheets, their much reduced kit fit "exactly under a seat of our wagon."[74]

The Richards and their two guides—a driver, Ernest, and Peter their cook—entered the park on August 1 near the current West Yellowstone entrance. Having traveled about twenty miles, they were pleased to reach Camas Meadows and to set up their first full encampment. Again, Mary Richards dwelt on the contrast between her normal surroundings and the more primitive conditions that she and Jesse now faced. Inside their tent, she related, sat "our furniture, viz.: a bed of blankets folded on a rubber sheet, our hamper for a table, a wagon seat for a sofa, a candle set in a bottle for an electric light, a tin wash basin, soap and towels on a pile of grass for a toilet room—only these and nothing more." Although Mary seemed somewhat surprised by these spartan quarters, she voiced no complaint and turned quickly to camping's joys—the beauty of the scenery, the pleasure of their first supper, and the satisfaction arising from "sleep so close to the bosom of mother earth." The next morning began with a crackling fire that the guides had started before dawn, and while their moist blankets dried on a frame of sticks, Mary focused on one of camping's most notable physical pleasures—breakfast. "Never was coffee so delicious," she cheered; "its aroma sweetened even that morning atmosphere! 'Condensed Milk, Eagle Brand,' a sigh shall lie down with every emptied can that goes to mark the trail of campers to Yellowstone National Park!" Like William H. H. Murray before her, as well as Horace Kephart and many others after, Mary Richards had discovered how camping made food become tastier and more aromatic.[75]

Richards's heightened gustatory satisfaction on that initial day of camping was only the first of many moments when she would signal readers that she and Jesse had departed their everyday world and entered a place apart. As they traveled from Fire Hole Basin to Mammoth Hot Springs, Yellowstone Lake, and the Upper Geyser Basin, accounts of the park's outstanding elements recurred in Richards's letters. On August 2, for example, she recounted how that day's campsite had a notable history. It was "close to a battle ground" where U.S. cavalry had defeated the Nez Perce in 1877, but at a high cost to the military. "We are shown graves, marked by stakes, of soldiers who were killed during the fight."[76] They were heroes, she implied, who had hallowed this ground with their lives. On most occasions, however, Richards followed the same path as most writers before and after her, presenting Yellowstone's unique character as a function of its natural features rather than its past.

As she described the geysers, hot springs, mud pots, and other features, Richards regularly employed such terms as "indescribable," "great," "strange," and "sublime," but one term in particular, "wonder," occurred most frequently. Yellowstone National Park had been referred to as "Wonderland" for at least a decade when the Richardses visited in 1882, so Mary's word choice is unsurprising. Such terms recall the romantic language employed by William H. H. Murray and others. But one feature most amazed Richards: on August 4, the camping party was on the road from Fire Hole Basin to Mammoth Hot Springs when a display in the Gibbon

River Canyon seized their attention. The moment is best recounted in Richards's own words.

> We stopped in mute astonishment before one of the most awful spectacles of the Park. At the top of a great half cone of solid stone projecting into the river below, from the walls of the canyon, is the "Devil's Den," "Blower," "Roarer," or it can be called any other pet name. From a horizontal orifice five or six feet wide and equally high, a torrent of boiling water completely filling the space poured in a basin directly below, whose depth all soundings have failed to determine. This cavity is forever full and overflowing. Frightful sounds, explosions of pent up water and steam, hissings, roarings, and earth shaking generally, made conversation or remark inaudible. In fact, one finds very little to say in presence of such a monstrous exhibition. Every blade of grass and leaf trembled as if in terror.

Clearly, Yellowstone was unusual and a place remote from the conventional world of Mary Richards and her readers, but more than that, it was God's handiwork.[77]

On August 10, as the party prepared to depart from its campsite on Yellowstone Lake, Richards linked the landscape to her Christian beliefs. The evening before, she had found the scenery "picturesque," noting that the forests on the lake's distant shore were "a deep green color and blend imperceptibly with the blue and purple greys of lofty heights beyond." Now that the party was about to break camp, she regretted having to leave "this enchanting shore." To express the satisfaction and delight it had provided, she quoted from Paul's Epistle to the Philippians. "The pure, exhilarating atmosphere, its savage solitude, its scenery of varied, inexhaustible beauty, have given us a season of content and rest kin to the 'Peace that passeth understanding.'"[78]

Finally, as Mary and Jesse's journey drew to a close, she remarked upon a change they had found in themselves, which suggests that their adventure had achieved its goal. On August 13, their last Sunday in the park, Mary began her final letter by describing her party's adventures in the Upper Geyser Basin. They had visited many "Spouters" but had been most impressed by the "Grand Geyser of the World," which they had been lucky enough to see erupt twice in twenty-four hours, and by Old Faithful, which she found "the soul of punctuality." Concluding, she looked not outward at Yellowstone's landscape, but inward at its impact on her spirit. "We leave with genuine regret the National Park; where, added to the charm of its delicious air, the grandeur of its mountains and waterfalls, and the unique beauty of its geyser scenery, we have found the joy of absence from the 'vanities and cares that wither life and waste its little hour.' "[79] It had been a successful pilgrimage. As Mary Richards was about to leave sacred space and return to her normal life, she knew she had changed. She had satisfied her camping trip's goal of escaping the everyday world's "vanities and cares." Although she never returned to Yellowstone National Park, her satisfaction would be shared by many who would camp after her, whether in Yellowstone or elsewhere.

Decades after the publication of *Adventures in the Wilderness*, camping destinations rapidly expanded to include locations well beyond the Adirondacks, but no matter where campers went, their pursuit of spiritual and physical transformation, their efforts to recapitulate the frontier experience, the connections they made to national identity, and a variety of other elements demonstrate that they were on a pilgrimage to nature, albeit unconsciously on most occasions. At the same time, campers' disagreements about who should camp, what a camper should know and feel, and which techniques were most proper illustrate how camping's meaning was contested and recovered rather than monolithic and received. Disagreements about who was an authentic camper were common, and early in camping's history those who defended and practiced its roughest, most challenging techniques would dismiss as "tourists" anyone who followed smoother paths.[80]

All the basic camping techniques employed today—on foot, by horse, with a wheeled vehicle, in a canoe or other small boat—were in use from early on. As with other forms of pilgrimage, some techniques, such as backpacking, were relatively difficult and required a serious commitment, while others, such as wagon camping, were easier and called for little sacrifice, if more money. The published guidebooks and personal accounts of such authors as Bachelder, Gould, Kephart, and Richards provided useful information for novices, and they stimulated more interest among the uninitiated even as they shaped the rituals and practices of the many campers to come. Finally, camping equipment was bulky and often expensive, but it developed rapidly. Manufacturers and retailers discovered this new consumer market and began to invent gear that made camping more comfortable through improved ease of use and increased efficiency. This trend has continued and become more pronounced. By about 1915, as this formative period closed, camping was a firmly established American pastime, but it remained what it had been from the beginning—a largely middle- to upper-middle-class activity. The pool of campers, however, was about to expand dramatically.

CHAPTER THREE

LET'S HIT THE MOTOR-CAMPING TRAIL

The Automobile Transforms Camping

Between 1910 and 1940, each of camping's three primary techniques, plus canoe camping, grew increasingly popular, but one, auto camping, stands apart from the others. Canoe cruising continued to appeal, but only to a relatively small group. The expense was prohibitive, with a canoe alone costing approximately eighty dollars in the 1920s; and canoe camping continued to be centered in the Northeast and the Great Lakes region, where the physical conditions for it were most favorable. Backpacking's allure also remained narrow as a consequence of its weight limitations, pack designs, and the continuing bulk of equipment and supplies. Few backpackers wished to carry more than forty pounds, a limit that even the simplest of outfits for a short vacation could quickly reach. Moreover, packs were awkward, themselves quite heavy and uncomfortable to wear for a prolonged time (see chapter 7). Finally, pack-horse camping was popular, especially in the West, where stories by Mary Roberts Rinehart and promotions by the Santa Fe Railroad kept interest high; but the need for expertise constrained demand. As one well-known author put it, "unless . . . one is a veteran camper, and has also had experience in the handling of horses, it is unwise to venture upon an extended saddle and pack-horse trip without the assistance of a competent guide."[1] Of course, this professional aide added greatly to the already high cost.

Wagon camping, by contrast, expanded rapidly, but with a new source of motive power—the internal combustion engine. "Horseless carriages" had become available during the 1890s and within a few years were embraced by some of America's bolder campers. One of these early adopters, Hrolf Wisby, encouraged campers to embrace cars in a 1902 article in *Scientific American*. The latest auto designs included new "touring vehicles," which were "decidedly superior" to the speed-oriented models that had dominated the market only one year earlier. In spite of these improvements, the new models still carried less gear and supplies than a horse-drawn wagon. An automobile's engine and other mechanical devices occupied the space that in a wagon could hold a tent, a portable wood-burning stove, clothes, food, and other items. Nevertheless, Wisby insisted, campers should not resist this new form of transport, because "there is nothing impracticable about it, for when a soldier is able to carry on his back his entire camp outfit in addition to his weapons, the smallest automobile on the market ought to carry everything needed to make the passengers comfortable in camp."[2]

Despite Wisby's encouragement, the number of early automobile campers remained small, because only the most affluent of Americans could afford motor vehicles at first. The situation changed after Henry Ford successfully employed mass production, making it possible for his company to introduce a $600 "Model N" vehicle in 1906 when the average automobile cost $3,290. Two years later, Ford Motor Company released its "Model T" at a slightly higher $825, but as historian James Flink tells us, it nonetheless "became the low-priced car for the masses anticipated since the turn of the century," as the price rapidly declined. By 1916 a new Model T runabout sold for as little as $345. With incomes also rising in this period, sales exploded.[3]

Cars became increasingly common throughout America as many other manufacturers lowered their prices, the supply of new and used cars expanded, and as credit became available to working-class Americans. Automobile registrations soared nationally from 77,000 (or 1 vehicle per 1,089 Americans) in 1905 to 2,332,000 (1 per 43) in 1915, then to 17,481,000 (1 per 6.6) in 1925, and 27,466,000 (1 per 4.8) in 1940. The total of surfaced highways simultaneously increased from 190,476 miles in 1909 to 387,760 miles in 1921 and to 662,435 miles by 1930. These rapid and large-scale developments were so pervasive that they prompted "a lifelong resident and shrewd observer of the Middle West" to ask Robert S. Lynd and Helen Merrell Lynd, who at the time were conducting the interviews for *Middletown*, their pioneering 1929 study of American life, "Why on earth do you need to study what's changing this country? . . . I can tell you what's happening in just four letters: A-U-T-O!"[4]

The Motor-Camping Vacation

As a consequence of the automobile's growing ubiquity, the cost of a motor-camping vacation came within reach of many more Americans. In 1876, an upper-middle-class Fred Beverly had announced that a Florida camping trip was cheaper than staying home, but few were able to join him.

Now, people with less means could also embrace a long-distance camping trip. According to a 1924 article in *Sunset* magazine, "the total outlay" for a three-person, 2500-mile, thirty-day auto journey from Ohio to Puget Sound had come to only $142.96, or less than $1.50 per day per person. "It was," crowed the middle-class author, "cheaper than staying home. . . . The automobile and the municipal camps have so cheapened travel that the wonders of the West's national parks today are accessible to hundreds of thousands who ten years ago had as much chance to see them as Hobson has of becoming admiral of the Swiss navy."[5]

The exploding supply of inexpensive cars and expanding network of improved roads liberated America's variously named "motor campers," "auto campers," "auto gypsies," and "tin can tourists" from their previous dependence on spatially restricted railroads. "In the old days," recalled Elon Jessup in 1921's *The Motor Camping Book*, "none of us followed the open road in the carefree manner of the gypsy himself. . . . That was a thing we only wistfully dreamed about. . . . Our own open road was usually one hedged in by two steel rails which not a few times lead us to a country boarding house of uncertain quality. And as time, tides and through trains stop for no man, so we flashed by green beckoning hills that called in vain." At this time, Jessup was one of America's best known auto-camping promoters and "how to" or prescriptive authors, having written frequently about outdoor leisure in many forms. After college, Jessup had worked for the U.S. Forest Service, but he soon gave it up to become a freelance correspondent, then the assistant editor at *Adventure* magazine during 1916–1917, and finally the associate editor at *Outing* magazine from 1917 to 1921. During the 1920s, Jessup also wrote several popular auto-camping books. Born in 1885 and widely traveled, Jessup recognized how transportation had changed in recent decades as he declared the automobile to be "a modern miracle," which allowed the motor camper to "take along your own hotel and set it up by the roadside wherever night overtakes you. It is the real gypsy way."[6]

The growing availability of inexpensive automobiles not only attracted more campers; it increased camping's social diversity by heightening its appeal to families. "Some years ago when I went to the woods," observed Jessup, the campers whom he met "were almost invariably men." The automobile, however, had made it possible for motor campers to bring a wide array of equipment with which to set up "woods housekeeping" for the whole family (fig. 3.1). When he went camping now, Jessup noted, "the sight which not infrequently greets my eyes is a khaki clad mother seated in front of a tent holding a nursing baby on one arm and turning flapjacks with her free hand. Little Johnny and Susie are crouched beside the fire, expectant eyes glued upon the fast mounting pile of flapjacks. Father is setting the

W/*hen Good Appetites Get Together!*

It's strange how "Ol' Man Appetite" acts up when you're out in the open! Maybe at home you limit yourself to toast and tea. But when Mother Nature gets to flirting with you, a thick steak with all the "trimmin's" is just a teaser. You're ready for a meal that'll make you unhitch the belt a notch or two ... or groan in ecstasy.

A Coleman Camp Stove makes "Ol' Man Appetite" double up with joy! Eggs straight up and smiling! Bacon with that hickory flavor! Hot muffins. Fish ... browned to a tempting turn. Potatoes as you like 'em ... hashed brown, fried or baked! Coffee with that "come-hither" aroma! Real meals ... cooked as only a Coleman can cook 'em.

When good appetites get together, you'll hear "Coleman" mentioned. Good reason, too. It's the life of the party!

Coleman Camp Lanterns

—handiest lights for campers and tourists. Light up the whole camp. Brighter than 20 old style oil lanterns. Mica globes make them wind-proof, rain-proof, bug-proof.

Built of brass and other heavy metals to stand rough and ready use. Make and burn their own gas from clear, water-white, uncolored gasoline.

Instant-Lite Model 228 *(above)* No preheating. Has wide green porcelain Reflector Top, and Built-in Pump.

Quick-Lite Model L327 *(at left)* Match generating. Has nickeled top and separate pump.

Figure 3.1. The Coleman Company perceptively aimed its camp stove and lantern advertisements at the increasing number of auto-camping families that appeared during the 1920s. Courtesy of the Coleman Company.

table." Family camping, he concluded, had become "a perfectly practicable and surprisingly economical proposition."[7]

Car camping also grew more diverse as middle- to working-class Americans increasingly embraced it. The ready availability of cheap cars had certainly supported auto camping's class shift, but equally important was the advent of vacation time for many workers during the 1920s and 1930s. In 1900, paid holidays typically were given to managers, foremen, clerical staff, and senior craft workers and were a sign of white-collar status. They tended, however, to be denied to production workers, who being wage earners rather than salaried, were unable to make up at no cost to their employer the work that had accumulated while they were away. Moreover, since they were not "brain workers," their employers did not seem to think they would need any long stretches of free time. Consequently, only 5 percent of American wage workers benefited from a paid vacation in 1920. Some of the more skilled laborers were able to win this benefit during the decade, and the over-all number of production workers with paid vacations rose to 10 percent by 1930. It was, however, still small in comparison to the 85 percent of salaried, middle-class employees who enjoyed this benefit at the time. The 1930s, by contrast, were much better for wage laborers. After an initial decline in the number of workers with paid vacations, the percentage rose rapidly, with about 50 percent of wage earners receiving the benefit by 1940.[8]

The arrival of the working class on the camping scene was so notewor-thy that it became an object of fiction. One author, Emerson Hough, neatly captured the change in 1921's *Maw's Vacation*. Having borrowed a tent from "The Hickory Bend Outing Club," sixty-year-old Maw, husband Paw, and daughters Cynthy, Hattie, and Roweny packed their car and departed the farm for their first-ever vacation—a camping trip to distant Yellowstone National Park. They were not well-off like Mary and Jesse Richards who had visited the park in the 1880s, but instead were what Hough called "the new people of America, who never have been out like this before." For the past forty years they had been at home cooking, plowing, and paying taxes, but now Paw and Maw had decided that "they can at last read their title clear to a rest, and a car, and a vacation." Traveling west for days, the fam-ily crossed the prairies, came into the foothills, and "at last arrived among the great mountains of which Maw had dreamed [about] all her long life of cooking and washing and ironing."[9] Hough sometimes chuckled at his characters and revealed their foibles, but like many others he steadfastly supported motor camping's democratization of leisure.

The motor-camping tide rose rapidly and quickly flooded across the American landscape to campsites near and distant. Elon Jessup reported in a May 1921 article that Americans owned approximately nine million autos, and he surmised that "a surprisingly large percentage" of them would auto camp that summer. This large percentage even included the "Four Vaga-bonds" of John Burroughs, Thomas Edison, Harvey Firestone, and Henry Ford, who had begun to auto camp as a group in 1915 and would be joined by President Warren G. Harding that summer of 1921. Two years later, the Chicago Automobile Club agreed with Jessup's assessment but offered a more numerical forecast—ten million campers in two million cars during 1923—and Earl C. May of the *Saturday Evening Post* prophesied an extraordinary fifteen million campers riding in five million cars in 1924. At nearly the same time, Frank E. Brimmer declared that the country was suffering "National Vacationitis" and that the remedy was to "take your home and tour!" To illustrate the scope of the "disease," Brimmer also reported that over one million of the more than eight million motorists recreating in national forests "carried camping equipment and spent their nights in . . . camping parks maintained by the United States Forest Service." A Chicago radio personality and freelance writer like Elon Jessup, Brimmer previously had written three highly successful books—1923's *Autocamping* and *Motor Campcraft*, and 1924's *Autocamping Facts*—had contributed auto-camping articles to a wide variety of magazines, held the posts of managing editor and motor-camping editor of *Outers' Recreation*, and was motor-camping editor of the *Chicago Daily News*. In these jobs, Brimmer received six to ten thousand letters each year "from campers asking aid in selecting equipment, arranging itineraries, and telling of their delightful experiences." By 1924, he was among America's best recognized auto-camping promoters and prescriptive authors.[10]

The U.S. national parks experienced a similarly rapid growth in campers once they allowed automobiles onto their sites. Visitors increased by over 2,000 percent, from a total of 335,000 in 1915, the first year automobiles were allowed in all national parks, to 920,000 in 1920, 2,775,000 in 1930, and, despite the Great Depression, to 7,358,000 in 1940. Not every visitor camped in a park or even stayed overnight, but the percentage that arrived as motor campers increased dramatically, especially during the 1920s. At Yellowstone, for instance, a total of 51,820 visitors entered the national park during the 1915 season, but only about 5,500 of them camped, and of these, approximately only one-third had arrived in an automobile. Most Yellowstone visitors arrived by train at the time, and if they stayed overnight, they found accommodation either at a park hotel or in one of the permanent tent "villages." Eight years later, however, the situation had reversed. Yellowstone's superintendent, Horace Albright, reported that 138,352 visitors had entered the park during the 1923 season, with 91,224 coming by automobile. "It is estimated that each day between July 20th and August 15th, there was an average of 10,000 people in the park," he recounted to National Park Service director Stephen Mather. During this particularly heavy-use period, "practically two-thirds of the visitors to the park were motorists in their own cars, most of whom camped out and carried their own equipment." Over the next decade, auto campers would become an even greater percentage of overall national park visitors. By 1941, a National Park Service study called camping "one of the most popular forms of park recreation" in the United States, and their research ranked it only slightly less popular than sightseeing, fishing, picnicking, and swimming.[11]

The Auto-Camping Pilgrim

The growing attractiveness of auto camping resulted in an abundance of novice and intermediate campers who yearned for advice and insights. What type of tent provides the best shelter? asked many campers. How do

I prepare food at a campsite? Which shoes are most comfortable? Where should I camp? In response to these questions and many more, a prescriptive car-camping literature quickly emerged to introduce, encourage, reassure, and advise the "tenderfoot" on how to hit the motor-camping trail. Between 1910 and 1919, 214 auto-camping or general-camping articles appeared in *Scribner's Magazine, Sunset, Outing, Woman's Home Companion*, and dozens of other popular magazines, while publishers released fifty similarly directed books to a hungry public. The next decade, 1920 to 1929, produced even greater numbers, with 245 magazine articles and fifty-three books published, but the Great Depression that began late in 1929 truncated the expansion and resulted in a sharp decline in publications. The impoverished decade that began in 1930 produced a much reduced 104 auto-camping magazine articles and only twenty-eight books before 1940 began.[12]

Motor-camping publications mostly discussed the latest in equipment, well-liked destinations, and customary practices, but as they did so, they also flirted with its larger cultural meaning. Like the earlier camping literature, these publications indirectly suggested that this new camping technique was a pilgrimage to the wild. "Automobile camping," asserted Hrolf Wisby in 1905, "is modern man brought back to Nature on the latest vehicle of civilization." Like many Americans, he and succeeding auto campers were comfortable driving cars into the wilds because to them the former did not disturb the latter. To the contrary, their machines enhanced the camper's traditional relationship with wilderness. Auto camping, Wisby declared, "is closing in an embrace with mother earth, yet not locked with her in the compass of a day's slow tramp." The auto camper's relationship with sacred nature was as intimate as that of a parent and child or, as Wisby's choice of the word "tramp" reveals, that of a backpacker with nature. At the same time, the automobile liberated campers from old constraints, leaving them "free to roam, to camp, and to change your ground at will, to surmount the obstacles of the open country, to annihilate the wearying consideration of time and distance." Finally, in a burst of technological enthusiasm, Wisby linked the automobile to a desire as old as the tale of Icarus. Auto camping, he concluded, "is terrestrial man gifted by an almost aerial mobility—a gift of his own ingenious giving."[13]

Although Wisby assumed his readers would want to visit a wild place, other authors dwelled on why an auto camper might feel the need to do so. Almost always at the top of any list of reasons was a desire to escape urban life's travails, because in spite of their embrace of the automobile, motor campers remained skeptical toward cities. According to one 1913 author, car camping satisfied the desire of "all normal people" to get into nature and out of urban America's "closed-in houses and offices." Nor did that "closed-in" feeling develop only if one lived in a large city. In J. C. Long's opinion, "Probably every dweller in civilization, whether of Main Street or the metropolis,

dreams of breaking loose some time and getting back to 'fundamentals.'"
Auto-camping authors frequently referred to settlements large and small as
dirty, noisy, crowded, and ugly, with water and air badly polluted. In the
view of Wilborn Deason, "The irritating effects on our sensory nervous system of [a city's] excessively irritating sounds, the unpleasant odors, the dust
that irritates the eyes and sensative [sic] mucous membranes of our noses and
throats and the constant air vibrations which, while not noticed, continually
'pound' upon our sense reception organs really do much to produce a state
of 'nerves' or a chronic systemic irritation that has a powerful influence upon
the physiologic mechanism as a whole." Moreover, the problem was not simply the place itself, but also the way of life that prevailed there. "An ordinary
sort of chap leading an ordinary sort of life," insisted Long, was trapped
in "confining routine." An urban life, claimed another writer, made one "a
slave to a timetable" and "controlled by conventionalities of dress."[14]

It is easy to recognize that motor camping appealed most strongly to those
Americans who felt that their modern, urban lives were too fixed, regulated,
controlled, and contained. Writers like J. C. Long frequently described auto
camping in such dynamic terms as "free," "independent," "open," "convenient," and "easily available," suggesting how strongly he and his readers
felt just the opposite each day. Automobiles introduced a desirable modern
element into what had been a largely premodern activity—movement. In
America, movement has often meant freedom, and the automobile made it
more efficient, a dimension of McDonaldization, by amplifying a camper's
ability to change location rapidly and with relative ease. Ryland P. Madison
emphasized this point by foregrounding how the auto camper could "travel
where and as far as you will—thirty or one hundred fifty miles a day." Of
course, when auto campers established camp at the end of a day's travel, they,
like backpackers, canoe campers, or packhorse campers, might find the place
unappealing. Although the situation could be a problem for a backpacker, a
canoe camper, or a packhorse camper, Madison hinted, it would not challenge the auto camper. "If you dislike the neighborhood," he offered both fig-
uratively and literally, "a day's run will often place you in another state."[15] In
other publications, authors were sometimes even whimsical, referring to cars
as "magic carpets" or "yachts" and suggesting, as Hrolf Wisby had done, the
sort of spatial liberty associated with aircraft and ships.

Wisby had assumed that the automobile's utility made its appeal obvious to a camper, but many subsequent writers took the time to explain a
car's advantages. To some authors, like Robert Sloss, the motor camper was
responding to divine design. The automobile, Sloss wrote in 1910, could
"penetrate into the wilds" and bring the camper "into speedy touch with
primitive Nature." On the one hand, he could "sup royally," smoke his pipe,

sleep "as only men can . . . after a day in the open," and most deliciously, be idle at his campsite. The auto camper, Sloss concluded, could be "the outdoor man God made him." On the other hand, the automobile protected a camper from capitulating to the seductions of the wild. After he had been an outdoor man, the auto camper could return to the city "before he [had] dropped any of the necessary threads to our complex civilization."[16] Sacred wilderness was appropriately entered and exited in an automobile, but no pilgrim, Sloss implied, should remain there indefinitely.

A generation later, Dillon Wallace continued to share Sloss's view about the attractiveness of nature to the auto camper; but where the earlier writer had provided an explanation that fit within the romantic tradition, the more recent one offered a genetic connection. "It is natural that man, with the open road before him, should turn to camping as a means of relief from the humdrum routine of everyday life," declared Wallace. "There is something of the primitive in our nature, a harking back, perhaps, to a primordial ancestry. Man has an instinctive longing to get back close to the heart of Mother Earth, and to return to the elemental, both in nature and in his manner of living. He longs for freedom from the artificial, with which the conventions of congested humanity have surrounded him. . . . It is the desire to return to the primitive, and to Nature that sends him forth." Beneath the veneer of civilization, implied Wallace, was an innate need for wilderness, which meant that auto campers were simply responding to their own nature.[17]

The personal motivations of auto campers were also as varied as those of any sort of pilgrim. Along with spiritual satisfaction, they sought a range of material objectives, so auto camping's prescriptive writers mentioned a wide array of benefits to broaden their appeal. Many authors, including Sloss and Wallace, specifically mentioned the rest, relief, peace, and contentment that were also commonly noted by earlier camping writers. "Do you know that it is the most restful thing in the world to watch the stars on a desert night?" wrote J. W. Sutphen in "Desert Camps," a paean to auto camping in the Southwest's arid lands. Another writer similarly promised his deskbound readers that if they would motor camp frequently, it would provide them "refreshment and relaxation from the strain of an inactive position." He claimed that the hiking, swimming, fishing, and other activities that people commonly enjoyed on a camping trip, as well as the fresh air and water, also contributed to "better and sturdier physical development," making auto camping a beneficial pastime for the entire family. Still other writers, perhaps sensitive to auto camping's shifting class and family appeal, focused on its relatively low cost. In one author's view, not every motor camper could afford or wanted a tent, so he suggested that readers should save money by purchasing one of the many brands of collapsible cots that converted an auto's seats

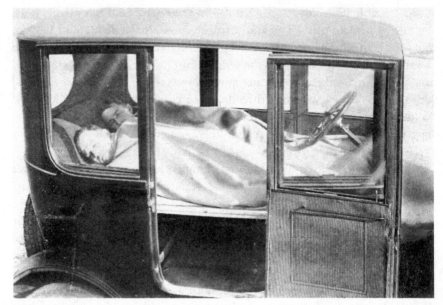

Figure 3.2. Camping with an auto bed. If a camper did not want a tent or could not afford one, many manufacturers sold kits that transformed a car into sleeping quarters. From J. C. Long and John D. Long, *Motor Camping* (New York: Dodd and Mead, 1923), opposite 32.

into a bed and then sleep there (fig. 3.2). "If you are in the habit of putting up at hotels," the article began, then you will realize that a vacation "can run into a lot of money." When an auto camper used one of these cots, however, he could beat this expense "by taking your hotel with you. Not only is it much more economical but it is a great deal more fun as well."[18]

Additionally, motor-camping advocates frequently mentioned that a feeling of rejuvenation accompanied the end of a trip and that it subsequently made urban life more appealing and more productive. In his 1916 account, J. W. Sutphen began by explaining how during his daily urban life, a "restless feeling" would steal over him from time to time, but most especially as spring arrived. He could not attribute it to anything specific, but it made his life dissatisfying; so he would auto camp in the desert. After a few days or perhaps a week of leisure, his attitude would change, and he would return to an urban life that no longer looked so bad. "You return to civilization," he admitted, "looking forward to a cool bath, and revel in the luxury of water free from alkali and flowing unaided from a faucet." Robert Sloss found his transformation to be even more dramatic. When an auto-camping trip came to a conclusion on Sunday, he informed his readers, "you make the swift run home at dusk for a dreamless sleep in your own bed, from which you go, clear eyed and invigorated, to work again on Monday."[19] Auto camping, it seemed, was more than just a break from life's routines. It was, promised Sloss, a wise investment in the camper's working future.

Prescriptive writers also praised auto camping for traditional reasons: as free from the class distinctions of conventional urban life, for its connection to American history and identity, and as a developer of individual self-sufficiency. A correspondent in the *Literary Digest* for August 30, 1924, was particularly taken by the democratic attitude and sense of social equality he encountered among the auto campers at Yellowstone National Park. Passing through a camping area, this writer described the scene. "Hub to hub stood parked the rattly old 'lizzie' of a sign-painter from Toledo, and the relatively shiny new seven-passenger touring car of a retired real estate man from Los Angeles." In town, the campers' homes would hardly have been adjacent, but here in the campground, and "just for to-night, they and their families were to be neighbors." Tomorrow, each would depart for some new destination, never to meet again, but now sharing the experience of having camped together in a sacred place. Instead of each of them ignoring the other, "their cheerful chatter passed across the supper tables, as between mouthfuls they compared notes on the day, the weather, the roads, the tour, Yellowstone park and the condition of the world in general."[20]

Continuing his stroll about the campground, the correspondent spotted another example of how motor camping reduced or eliminated life's customary social distinctions—a lawyer from Pittsburgh and a bricklayer from Kansas City were squared off in a horseshoe contest. "An interested gallery of sagebrushers from Iowa, Maine, Maryland, Texas, Florida, Montana, Missouri, British Columbia, Georgia and Ohio gathered to cheer one champion or the other. They were men of many molds, whose faces and clothes and manner of speech betokened differences among them; but just for tonight they were all neighbors under the Yellowstone's blue canopy, camp-mates and good fellows, all." Place differences, as much as class differences, also abated at a motor campground, intimated the writer, as these Yellowstone campers shared a national identity that superseded any state or regional one. Citing Stephen T. Mather, the correspondent noted that the first director of the National Park Service had called these parks "a great American melting-pot," and he felt that it was especially true of the motor campgrounds. Here "people from every section come together in a new friendliness, which grows out of the discovery that all these other folks, be they East or West or North or South, are pretty good people and, after all, Americans just like you and me."[21]

Such authors also associated auto camping with the frontier and the Americans who had struggled with it. "In the early pioneer days," began

Charles G. Percival in his 1927 guidebook, "a trip across the continent meant traveling in a 'prairie schooner' or 'covered wagon' with enough men in the party to repel the hostile Indians. Now it is possible to travel in the new 'covered wagon,' the motor car, and camp and live by the way as did our forefathers. 'Motor Camping' is the new recreation." J. C. Long also alluded to the frontier's national significance even as he gave it a direction when he noted that the urban resident who dreamt of an auto-camping trip did not wish to head just anywhere, but instead "wants to go 'out where the West begins.' "[22]

The author of "The Call of the Open Road" also saw connections between the premodern aspects of camping and early American virtues. The motor camper, he declared, "is returning to the days of his ancestors in being dependent solely on himself for his comfort and sustenance." He claimed that a camper could break from the everyday world because he was self-sufficient. "Having in his car everything that he needs for shelter and nourishment, [the auto camper] becomes a nomad, and casts off the last link with his ordinary routine." A decade later, Dillon Wallace again focused on the value of auto camping and self-sufficiency when he declared that it "develops initiative, self-reliance, and resourcefulness, and renews a man's confidence in himself, and his ability to stand alone." Wallace, however, provided a slightly different explanation, more biological and environmental than historical, for why auto camping was valuable. Away from urban life, he suggested, a camper recovers his own wild nature and learns "in contention with Nature and the elements, to use his brain, his eyes, and his hands. He must do for himself many things that in conventional life he depends upon others to do for him." This self-confident and resourceful camper, Wallace implied, was a more complete being and healthier than those who chose alternative forms of leisure.[23]

While motor-camping writers admitted that automobiles were central to this form of leisure, they nevertheless went out of their way to emphasize that it was the camping, not the driving, that made the experience transformative. Yes, announced the author of "The Call of the Open Road," motor touring could be interesting and fascinating, but it became something spiritual and more significant only after "the tourist became a camper. The tourist, expecting to spend every night under a roof, must keep to some sort of a schedule, and make his plans for the night on starting in the morning. Having wired ahead for reservations, he must keep to his estimated speed under penalty of missing his comfortable night, and all of the day is under that urge. Being in this 'hurry, hurry' frame of mind, which is not very different from that of his everyday life, his vacation does not always do him the good that is expected of it." The camper, by contrast, followed a "totally different . . . mental process," and so returned from vacation feeling refreshed and at peace. "No schedules are his; no boundaries nor limitations. He stops to absorb a view or to have a swim; he loafs or hurries as the road suggests; he explores; and as evening falls he finds a haven for the pitching of his tent, glorying in being his own cook and waiter and bell boy."[24] Self-reliant and with no pressure to be anywhere on time, the camper knew an "utter contentment" that the tourist could never experience.

Just Enough Comfort

Motor camping's promoters did not, however, follow their predecessors along every path. William H. H. Murray, Horace Kephart, and other early camping advocates often emphasized the distinction between camping's "rough" life and the ease of urban living, tying the rewards of camping—independence, freedom, self-reliance, rest, recuperation, and other spiritual and physical satisfactions—to its challenges. Auto camping's prescriptive writers and the sellers of its equipment instead frequently linked a trip's satisfaction to the equipment that reduced its challenges. "Modern science and invention have joined hands in smoothing the road to the enjoyment of outdoor life in a way that we seldom stop to understand," intoned one writer in the June 1913 issue of *Craftsman.* "Anything that makes for a greater opportunity to get close to Nature, to seek her out in all her beauty and vigor, is something to be appreciative of, and there are many of us who would lack the courage or the inspiration to get far out of doors if the way were not cleared, as it were, and made easy by the addition of comforts that belong essentially to civilization." The "smoothing the road" here points to the "McDonaldization" process discussed earlier, with the camping experience becoming more predictable and within a camper's control when he or she employed the prescribed equipment. At the same time, this equipment would, the author suggested, provide "courage" by allowing a camper to calculate in advance how much comfort and roughness would be a part of a camping trip.[25] These sorts of appeals became a permanent feature of auto camping.

McDonaldization offers powerful advantages to those who adopt it, but it can, like any rational system, generate irrationalities in terms of production, consumption, and management. For campers, the most likely site for such irrationality to emerge was her or his "gear," where no exact line separated too little from enough or too much. For example, the author of "The Call of the Open Road" encouraged the car campers of the 1920s to employ equipment that eased difficulties because doing so, he assured them, was pragmatic. "Motor camping is essentially practical, and each year becomes more so." However, he vaguely cautioned them that "the real success of such a venture rests largely with the perfection of the outfit." Other writers, by contrast, were blunter. Remember, Frank Brimmer emphasized, efficient and effective control was best. "The happiest auto-camper is the one who takes the least amount of equipment but has everything needed." New gadgets might be tempting, but avoid cumbersome and overly specialized equipment, he cautioned. "Test everything by two rules. (1) Is this article compact and portable? (2) Is this article so useful it serves more than just one purpose."[26] An excess of equipment offered no greater predictability of outcome yet would weigh down the camper. Employing a variety of terms like "roughing it deluxe," "the smooth way to rough it," or "the fallacies of roughing it," auto camping's promoters and equipment suppliers admitted that camping's difficulties were an essential part of its spiritual and physical satisfaction even as they implied that it was no compromise to soften its harshest edges and limit the most haphazard aspects. This process, of course, began with an automobile.

Motor camping's predecessor, wagon camping, had appealed to those urban dwellers who by choice or necessity sought an experience that was easier than backpacking, canoe camping, or packhorse camping. The appearance of the automobile greatly enhanced the appeal of this kind of camping, especially after cars had been around for about a decade and had become more powerful and better designed. "For perfect rest and healthful recreation," declared Thaddeus S. Dayton in 1911, "there is nothing like camping out. The most luxurious way of doing this is with an automobile." The earliest cars, however, were short on carrying space. Even as they increased in size and power, space continued to be at a premium if more than two people went camping, because additional campers had to sit in the rear seats where equipment would be carried. In response, the earliest auto-camping writers often emphasized the need for careful preparation and packing as well as the use of specialized storage features. In his 1905 *Outing* article, Hrolf Wisby urged readers to try auto camping but cautioned that it would be best only after "a little experience and a good deal of forethought." In particular, he prescribed a set of six "hampers" for carrying supplies and equipment on the outside of one's vehicle. The camper was unlikely to find these items at a store, he noted, "but any maker of wicker-ware and reed furniture . . . will build you any desired pattern for a slight extra charge, if you furnish dimensions and measurements." With these storage containers, campers could pack their "whole outfit in wickerwork and oilcloth—a decided advantage." A few years later, the situation became easier as autos grew larger and more powerful and as an assortment of equipment became available that fit easily onto a car's running boards or into commercially available luggage carriers fitted to the running boards.

Figure 3.3. Early automobiles rarely had much storage space for bulky camping gear and supplies. Many auto campers purchased or improvised devices to transport materials on fenders and running boards. Courtesy of National Park Service Historic Photograph Collection, Harpers Ferry (WV) Center for Media Services.

Alternatively, a camper could build his own running-board carriers based on designs reproduced in magazines and books (fig. 3.3). These innovations allowed campers to carry increasing amounts of gear on their cars, but by the 1930s the careful packing of a car was easing as an issue because cars were becoming larger.[27]

Even as automobiles' ability to carry equipment increased, manufacturers reduced the size and weight of many traditional camping items. Light aluminum or enameled steel cookware and dinnerware replaced heavy cast iron and ceramic items. In addition, a variety of manufacturers developed and promoted a wide range of new equipment to appeal to those campers seeking to make some practice simpler, more predictable or efficient, and thus to increase camping's ease. The Collis Company encouraged readers of June 1917's *Field and Stream* to "get ready *now* for vacation days." Their advertisement for an "improved folding camp grate-broiler combination" featured its compactness and durability as well as the ease it provided (fig. 3.4). According to an illustration, the implement could support multiple

Get Ready NOW
For Vacation Days
THE
Collis Improved Folding Camp Grate-Broiler Combination

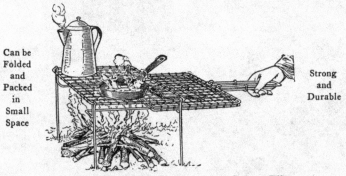

Can be Folded and Packed in Small Space

Strong and Durable

Cook the Whole Meal at the Same Time

A GRATE FOR THE COFFEE POT AND SKILLET AND A BROILER FOR STEAKS

Which Do You Prefer?

This   or   That

The Old Way   *The Collis Way*

Send for Booklet "S" Vacation Days

THE COLLIS COMPANY, Clinton, Iowa

Figure 3.4. The Collis Improved Folding Camp Grate-Broiler Combination promised the sort of comfort and convenience that typically drove the McDonaldization of auto-camping equipment. From *Field and Stream*, June 1917, 179.

pans and pots at once while sitting but a few inches above a wood fire, allowing the camper to "cook the whole meal at the same time." Moreover, another pair of illustrations promised that a camper using their product would suffer fewer spills and other cooking accidents.

A few years later, the Burlington Basket Company embedded its "Hawkeye Basket Refrigerator" in the same sort of romantic imagery that had presented camping as nature pilgrimage since the time of William H. H. Murray. "Still streams and quiet fragrant woods take on an added lure," whispered the advertisement, once you owned their device. An early version of the portable ice chest, this woven-reed and metal-lined food carrier suggested rural relaxation teamed with urban control and efficiency to produce contents as cold "as though just this minute taken from your own home refrigerator," and, they pledged, it would do so for thirty-six hours.[28]

The Abercrombie & Fitch Company, which sold a wide range of camping goods in its New York City store and through its catalog, recognized that many of the beginners who read Frank Brimmer, Elon Jessup, and other auto-camping enthusiasts would want to head out but would be uncertain about what to carry. Consequently, the company promoted a "Complete Auto Camping Outfit," which slipped into seven bags, weighed a modest 173 pounds, and was carried on a car's running boards. "Yes," began a full-page advertisement, "I know; used to feel that way myself. Every weekend we would fill the gas tank, oil up and start." According to the ad's narrator, he and his family or friends would then drive along the main highways to find services, but unfortunately, when they wanted to stop for dinner somewhere out of town, the restaurant's "good food" would have been "manhandled by a foreign-born chef." They would check into a local hotel, which generally was located on a town's main street, where entertainments would be poor or nonexistent. "Then, tired out, we returned to the office for another week's grind." The weekend motor camper, however, was free from these irritations. "He follows the highways and byways, enjoying the hills as they grow up to the sky [and] the brooks as they gurgle contentment." How was a motor camper able to be so free, implied the ad? Simple. "Equipped with auto tent, cooking outfits, bedding and food, the Auto Camper is not dependent on even the village store for his accommodation or food supplies." To become one of the liberated in a moment, the ad finished, purchase Abercrombie & Fitch's four-person outfit, albeit at the stiff price of $275.64. A complete package, it contained all the necessary basic equipment (outside of food and personal items), including tent, air mattresses, sleeping blankets, stools, table, gasoline stove, cookware, plates, bowls, cutlery, and dozens of other items. This gear made a wilderness journey possible, and, the advertisement claimed, it was "the best, lightest, most compact auto-campers' outfit ever assembled."[29] Such equipment innovation and promotion undoubtedly helped attract more Americans to the pastime and expand the market for producers.

Coleman Lights Up the Camp

Many of the new motor-camping products that appeared during the early twentieth century were developed by firms that sprang up to satisfy growing camper demands. The Tentobed Company of Chicago, for example, produced but one product, and it was clearly aimed at auto campers—a canvas tent that incorporated a bed inside itself. When a camper purchased a Tentobed, promised its manufacturer, he could depart on vacation without a cot or other form of portable bed. Moreover, a Tentobed was compact and efficient. It was designed to neatly ride on the running board of a car and was so arranged in a bag that one could "roll your blankets and extra clothing in with the tent, thus keeping [your] tonneau clear" to carry more equipment there. Other products pitched to auto campers were simply old products reconceived for the new market. The Carnation Milk Products Company, for instance, ran an advertisement in *Outing* magazine for canned milk. Although both evaporated and condensed milk had been available since the nineteenth century, a 1918 advertisement had "Campers! Be sure to take along Carnation Milk" emblazoned across its top to serve as a reminder, even though campers were but a small part of the company's customer base. The Lambert Pharmacal Company likewise advertised "Listerine for the Camp First Aid Kit" in a 1920 issue of *Literary Digest*, when the product's primary market was clearly elsewhere.[30] Carnation and Lambert were simply trying to extend their existing product lines into an emerging market that they likely recognized would never be central to them.

Other companies decided that camping offered them an opportunity to enter an expanding and potentially large market. One of these, the Coleman Company, stands out for its adaptation, innovation, and endurance, but at the outset it neither used its current name nor manufactured camping equipment. Instead, twenty-nine-year-old William Coffin Coleman founded the Hydro Carbon Company in January 1900 in Kingfisher County, Oklahoma (population 18,501), to sell light.[31] "W.C.," as he was universally known, had come to Kingfisher with a dozen gasoline-pressure lamps to offer an indoor lighting service to merchants. Businessmen increasingly wished to remain open in the evening so that customers could drop by after dinner, but shoppers were reluctant, because most lighting systems were so poor that they could barely see the items for sale. Coleman offered gasoline-pressure lamps as the solution.

Nonpressurized gasoline lighting had been perfected in 1869 and aimed at the many isolated homes and businesses that were not attached to municipal gas grids.[32] In one of these early systems, air was "forced" (blown) across the surface of a pool of gasoline resting in an enclosed tank, and the resulting mixture of fumes and air was piped to the building's lamps, which burned the "gas" openly. The equipment was complicated and relatively expensive, but once installed, the system was both convenient and easy to use.

For two decades, forced-air gasoline systems remained cutting edge, but in the 1890s "hollow wire" gasoline lighting emerged to compete with them. Unlike its predecessor, the new system required no moving parts except for a hand-operated bicycle pump to create pressure in a tank. Air pressure moved gasoline (not a fume-and-air mixture) from a storage tank through brass tubing (the "hollow wire") to a lighting fixture's "generator," where it was converted to a flammable vapor, which was burned within the "mantle." A small, chemically soaked fabric sack, a mantle contained the burning gas, and it, now a fragile ash, glowed as the vapor burned. The resulting light was much brighter than when the gas was burned openly, without a mantle. Hollow-wire lighting also cost about a third as much as an equivalent forced-air gasoline system and was easy to expand by laying tube to wherever it was wanted. Furthermore, after 1892, hollow-wire lighting used Welsbach incandescent mantles, which were woven of fabric and a rare metallic element (such as thorium) that glowed white hot, producing a bright, clear light that bested even the electric lights then available.[33]

Around the middle of the 1890s, inventors developed an independent, gasoline-pressure lamp based on the same principles as hollow-wire lighting. These hanging fixtures were typically about two feet in height, but even after being lit they could be moved easily from one ceiling hook to another, and they cost less than a full hollow-wire system. Coleman had come across a version of this lamp in 1899 and had been so impressed that he decided to quit selling typewriters and to take up lighting sales in Kingfisher. In a short time, the fruits of his new effort exceeded expectations, and in November 1901 Coleman decided to move his operation to Wichita, Kansas, which he felt was more central to the growing region he wished to service.[34]

When Coleman arrived, Wichita had a private electrical system, but like many early producers of electricity, the company often failed to satisfy its customers. The system sometimes broke down at night, which frustrated the shop owners who had extended their business hours; the grid was too small to cover the city thoroughly; and even though the price of the electricity was low, the cost of wiring a house was high. Consequently, Coleman felt he would find many customers in town, and within a few months he had hundreds. In addition, Wichita was surrounded by small towns, villages, and individual farms and houses, which lacked access to municipal electricity or gas, but which Coleman believed wanted the lighting that these suppliers provided. According to Herb Ebendorf, W. C. Coleman saw electricity as an ally rather than a foe. "The more the public accepted labor-saving and light-giving electrical appliances," Coleman believed, "the greater the demand became in non-electrified areas for gas from gasoline lights."[35]

During its first decade, the Hydro Carbon Company sold only hanging gasoline-pressure lamps and hollow-wire lighting systems, but Coleman set the company to developing a portable gasoline-pressure table lamp in 1907. In particular, he wanted this new lamp to be sturdy enough to withstand such common household accidents as falling off a table, and to not leak if it fell over, even if turned upside down. The first, second, third, and many more test models failed, but early in 1909, one finally passed W.C.'s personal test. According to Ebendorf, a lit prototype was placed on Coleman's desk. "He shook it, jarred it against the oak surface and held it upside down. The lamp burned brightly. He dropped it on the floor and the only damage was to the lamp's mantles. 'This lamp will do,' Coleman announced. 'We'll put it into production and I'll find salesmen to handle it.'" The company shipped its first portable table lamps in May 1910, released a second model in July 1911, and when 1911 closed, its table lamps had outsold all the company's other lamps by more than a third. Table lamp sales continued to increase dramatically for years as gasoline-pressure lights and stoves enjoyed their domestic heyday.[36] It was but a small step to a portable gasoline-pressure lantern for outdoors.

Shortly after his newly renamed Coleman Lamp Company began to manufacture its first table lamp, W.C. decided to develop a lantern, which was an outdoor version of this domestic convenience. First shipped in 1914, Coleman lanterns were an instant success. "All you've got to do is show it," commented a dealer who was deeply impressed by how quickly the lantern sold. "It's the most effective light maker on the market." Although campers were among the early adopters of the lantern, W.C. later recounted that he was thinking more about farmers and life-saving crews than recreationists when he pressed his staff to perfect a rugged and reliable outdoor light. Nevertheless, the lantern's durability and brightness appealed to anyone who had to be outside, so campers bought them too. The company soon became aware of this unintended use, likely through its dealer network, and ran its first camping advertisement in June 1917 to coincide with its introduction of the new "Quick-Lite" lantern. "For Campers," blazed the ad's headline.

This lantern was no ordinary, oil affair, the advertisement promised, but twenty times brighter, as well as "rain proof and fool proof." It was, in sum and without modesty, the "greatest lantern ever produced. No camping outfit complete without it." Sales of the new lantern rose so rapidly that by the end of the 1918 fiscal year, Quick-Lite lanterns alone had outsold the combined sales for every version of Coleman lanterns during 1917. Quick-Lite lantern sales continued to climb quickly for the next few years, especially to campers, exceeding ninety-one thousand units in 1922, which prompted the company to think about adding a line of camping stoves.[37]

Gasoline-pressure stoves, which employed the same principle as gasoline-pressure lamps and lanterns, had been in common household use for more than a decade when the American Gas Machine Company adapted this domestic technology in 1912 to offer the first camping stove. A simple, portable, and compact one-burner unit, it nonetheless appealed to many campers, who having come from cities, found its design and function familiar and therefore easy to control and use. With sales brisk and the cargo-carrying capacity of automobiles increasing, this same company introduced a two-burner stove, the "KampKook," in 1920. The Coleman Company noticed the success of the American Gas Machine Company's camp stove and introduced its own version early in 1923. Consisting of two burners with a built-in pump to pressurize the fuel and baffles to protect the flames from wind, as well as a complimentary fuel funnel and an attachable folding oven, Coleman's camp stove was a quick and solid success. The company shipped only 12 units in February, the month of its introduction, but over 4,000 units in December. Sales in 1924 were similarly vigorous, reaching a total of 33,652, and continued to rise through the decade, reaching an annual peak of nearly 50,000 units in 1928.[38]

Coleman products were efficient, predictable, durable, and easy to use, which made them popular with campers, but the company also promoted its products heavily. Richard P. Cole, a "stove expert" and the field representative for the magazine *Motor, Camper & Tourist*, traveled with his family through municipal, state, and national campgrounds across the country in 1925 to demonstrate Coleman Company lanterns and camp stoves. In 1926, the company went so far as to hire Frank Brimmer, who was then at the peak of his auto-camping reputation, to write them a guidebook—*Coleman Motor Campers Manual*. In a sixty-four-page guide to auto camping's basics, Brimmer blended useful information with Coleman product promotion. For instance, he told his readers that properly cooked food was necessary for an excellent camping vacation and that the way to transform campground cooking from a chore into something easy and "exactly like it is at home" was to employ a Coleman Camp Stove. The company would make repeated use of this formula—a blend of general information with product promotions—for decades to come. By the mid-1920s, Coleman regularly advertised in the *Saturday Evening Post, Country Gentleman, Outdoor America, Field & Stream, Outdoor Life,* and many other magazines. It also created a wide variety of promotional materials for retailers, including advertisements for placement in local newspapers, photographs, signs, calendars, and direct-mail pieces imprinted with the retailer's name and address. Additionally, company salesmen helped retailers with in-store and window displays using banners, decorations, and other materials.[39]

Like auto camping's how-to literature, the Coleman Company's promotional materials occasionally contrasted urban life with camping, implying that the latter was a pilgrimage to wild nature. One mid-1920s brochure, for instance, exclaimed, "Let's take a camping trip! That's the only answer to the 'Call of the Wild' or whatever it is that makes us long for the open country." The source of this "call," the promotion declared, was dissatisfaction caused by an urban life that was repressive and unnatural. "The Rush and clatter of crowded city pavements," it noted, "seems to stifle us." Consequently, "we yearn to be out where there's a smell of balsam in the air and the peace of the cool, deep woods is unbroken by man-made noises." On a camping trip, the brochure assured its readers, "we'll leave cares and worries behind and strike out for the 'Big Timber.'" Frank Brimmer took a different tack in his *Coleman Motor Campers Manual* when he focused on campsite selection. Do not choose a "remote camp where one must spend the night 'all by his lonesome.'" Campers like being around other campers, he insisted, and that makes sense in the United States. "The camaraderie of the motor camp is one of the best 'melting pots' of American Democracy— the one place where folks meet human beings in an informal and wholesome manner."[40] Like pilgrims elsewhere, a Coleman auto camper enjoyed the social equality that occurred at camping grounds and benefited by it.

Most promotional materials from the Coleman Company, however, focused on the comfort and ease its products would bring to auto camping. "The right outfit for motor camping will take out all the 'rough stuff,'" Brimmer promised in the *Coleman Motor Campers Manual.* The new camper should not listen "to some hard-boiled owl who loves nothing so much as misery, one of these 'rough it' kind" who thinks camping should be unpredictable and who makes one "believe that he ought to start out with nothing but a blanket, a pail and a spider." Recalling the sentiments of John M. Gould and other nineteenth-century defenders of horse-drawn wagons, Brimmer countered that comfort was "enjoyed by the women folks, and all those who do not care to make Spartans of themselves; as indeed most modern campers do not—most emphatically not." A brochure promoting the company's first camp stove announced that this product would not cause anyone any anxiety because it was a "Miniature Kitchen Range." The device, it implied, was not exotic but familiar in design, making its use obvious, predictable, and easy. A couple of years later, around 1926, Coleman began to advertise its camp stoves and lanterns under the heading "The Smooth Way to Rough It." According to one brochure, if a camper used a Coleman camp stove, she or he could "cook anything—anywhere." In the past, this brochure suggested, a camper in wild nature had to worry about finding firewood, starting a fire in stormy weather, and how long it would take to get a fire to cooking heat. With a Coleman camp stove, however, uncertainty disappeared, since a camper could "banish all old time cooking troubles. No more guessing about the 'eats.'" The modern camper did not have to rough it; he could instead satisfy his cravings "whenever Old Man Appetite says: 'Let's eat now.'"[41]

On the Motor-Camping Road

The swelling popularity of auto camping between 1910 and 1940 led to an abundance of prescriptive pronouncements, advertisements, brochures, and other promotional publications, but it also resulted in a variety of accounts detailing people's personal adventures along the motor-camping trail. The primary focus of these tales usually was the author's daily, often "rough" experiences. *Modern Gypsies*, Mary Crehore Bedell's description of a nine-month, twelve-thousand-mile motor-camping trip with her family in 1922, opened like many of these tales, with an account of its planning.

Bedell's husband, Fred, who was a professor at Cornell University in Ithaca, New York, had received a leave of absence, and they had decided to use the time trying something novel—an extended vacation around the perimeter of the United States (fig. 3.5). They had little if any auto-camping experience, so their long trip necessitated forethought, which Mary and Fred, who were in their fifties at the time, found challenging yet fun. "What outfit should we provide?" asked Mary Bedell. What clothes should we wear? Where would all the things be stored away to make room for the passengers?" Addressing these concerns, they became calculating, systematic, and deliberate. The Bedells decided that high-quality equipment would best endure wear and tear, be most efficient, and provide the greatest economy because it would allow them to skip hotels. Traveling from their upstate home to New York City, they visited "one of the best sporting-goods establishments," where they found nearly everything they wanted, including "tent, dufflebags, gasoline stove, Adirondack grate and a kit of aluminum kettles that nested, with coffee pot and enamel cups and saucers inside." (Oddly, other campers sometimes mistook the last for a hat box!) More

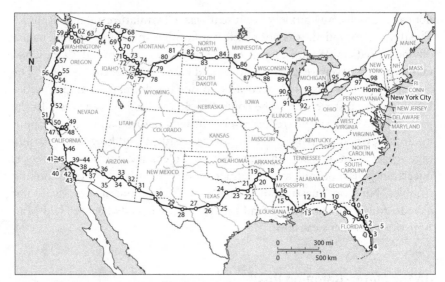

Figure 3.5. The stops along the Bedells' twelve-thousand-mile camping adventure. They departed by sea with their car from New York on February 1, 1922. Driving first southward then westward from Jacksonville, by April 1 they were at stop 30 (El Paso, Texas) and by June 1 at stop 45 (Santa Monica, California). They then visited Yosemite, Crater Lake, Mount Rainier, Glacier, and Yellowstone National Parks. They departed Yellowstone in early August and arrived home about September 1.

items were purchased, and after "hours of careful thought and experiment," their outfit was complete, weighing in at "four or five hundred pounds." Sheepishly, Mary Bedell admitted that upon reflection and "notwithstanding the warning of some of our friends, themselves experienced campers, we took too much."[42] The irrationality of McDonaldization is difficult to avoid.

Another book author, Frederic F. Van de Water, and his wife found it similarly challenging to plan for their 1926 motor-camping journey from New York City to San Francisco via Yellowstone National Park and the Columbia River valley. As recounted in *The Family Flivvers to Frisco*, they were able to agree on the car—the Ford "flivver" of the title—and on their camping equipment, but their clothing selection was their "first and worst problem." Initially, each had gathered all the clothing that she or he thought would be needed by themselves and their six-and-a-half-year-old son. "On the floor of the living room, we assembled a pile of raiment somewhat larger than a wartime munitions dump and across the top of this, we shouted protest and objection at each other." But, as is the case in many marriages, confrontation got them nowhere. "Eventually," Van de Water admitted, "we abandoned indictment for the more persuasive art of self-sacrifice." Each kept agreeing to remove an item from the pile until very few articles remained. To Van de Water's surprise, their final selection, achieved after hours of attrition, was "all we needed, and on the whole, served us well" during the entire thirty-seven-day adventure.[43]

Once beyond descriptions of initial planning, motor-camping accounts tended to accentuate issues related to automobiles, roads, and traveling through unfamiliar territory. Mary Bedell admitted that they encountered people struggling with inoperable automobiles "at rather frequent intervals all the way across the continent" for a total of "at least a dozen cars in more or less serious difficulty." On many of these occasions they stopped to provide assistance, and on one occasion two men, who happened to be mechanics, stopped and got them going again. She and Fred also frequently tangled with poor, often unpaved roads. As they traversed the southeastern states during the spring of 1922, heavy rains made many roads impassable, and even the open ones were tricky. On one occasion, between Hot Springs and Arkadelphia, Arkansas, mud holes and water up to the axle hubs limited their progress to only thirty miles in four hours. Frustrated by their slow advance, the Bedells asked local residents for travel advice, but to little avail. "Every road we took was described to us as 'good' no matter how bad we found it, if it was only navigable. Once upon inquiry we were told, 'That's a good road; a man got through there yesterday.'" About a month later and in the arid Southwest, the Bedells found that many roads ran through deep sands or were peppered with axle-shattering "chuck-holes." Moreover, whenever the Bedells traveled through relatively remote areas they also remained cautious about whom they might encounter. On one occasion they changed their morning departure time and route out of a small town because they thought they had been selected for a "hold up." On another occasion, Mary was frightened that a desperate desert hitchhiker was "insane, probably gone crazy over gold-hunting. . . . I felt that we might be knifed at any moment." Luckily, he was merely grizzled looking and "proved to be harmless."[44]

The campgrounds encountered by auto campers were also a popular topic in personal accounts, with opinions ranging from high praise to deep disgust. Mary Bedell and family were delighted by the Wawona campground in Yosemite National Park, where they pitched their tent "on a wooded slope near a rushing torrent" that was so attractive they decided to remain several extra days. A municipal auto campground they approached in Spokane, Washington, by contrast, was so "dry and dusty" that they chose to stay in a hotel instead. Another couple, Jan and Cora Gordon, who were English tourists auto camping across New England for the first time, were generally unimpressed with municipal campgrounds and even less taken by the towns that created them:

These towns are blots of transition, naturally. No race of human beings could bear to imagine its descendants living permanently in such places. They are ugly, as the first lumps of clay which a sculptor sets up for his statue are ugly. Chamber of Commerce signs are not really welcomes; they are warnings. They should read:

> THIS IS SAPBURG. WE ARE JUST AS UGLY AS EVERY OTHER CITY ALONG THE ROAD AND NO MORE REMARKABLE. BUT, IF YOU WANT TO BUY SOMETHING, WE WILL BE OVERJOYED TO GET YOUR MONEY. THAT IS WHAT WE ARE HERE FOR.
> SAPBURG CHAMBER OF COMMERCE

If some town did determine to adopt that sign for a change? What a kick that would be for the motorists! At last a Chamber would have found something which would be remembered.

Frederic Van de Water, who had no previous camping experience, frequently discussed his family's experiences with municipal auto campgrounds, because, as he related, an arriving motor camper often had no idea what he might confront. From his perspective, the quality of these camps, which were generally established by a local chamber of commerce to attract travelers to their town, varied "from atrocious to excellent." Auto camping was still a new recreation, he reasoned, and since campers traveled "with the expectation of roughing it," they tolerated many unpleasant elements. Nonetheless, "the gossip of the road has branded certain camps with disapproval and endorsed others and wanderers absorb this gossip about campfires of evenings and govern themselves accordingly." As a consequence, Van de Water felt certain that the poor camps, which were generally free, would soon disappear, while the better facilities, which usually charged, would flourish.[45]

Another common challenge for motor campers was injury or illness. The Bedells unexpectedly had to transport a man injured in an automobile accident the sixty miles to Deming, New Mexico, where the nearest physician lived. A few weeks later, Mary was herself sick with "ptomaine poisoning" near Blythe, California, for nearly a week. Unfortunately, little could be done for her, because the Bedells had no medicine with them, no local physician was available, and she felt too sick to travel. Instead, she had to suffer through a high fever and severe discomfort. Charles E. S. Wood, a lawyer and author from the San Francisco Bay area, went camping with his children and grandchildren in central Oregon in June 1928 and recounted a similar tale in his personal journal. He and his family had been enjoying a long stay at several, slightly separated campsites when a number of people at his daughter's campsite came down with "ptomaine poisoning" from the mutton they had eaten at a restaurant. Wood, who had not visited the restaurant, had to drop by the sufferers' campsite to give each a dose of milk of magnesia and light broth, which helped, but they remained so ill that he stayed overnight to continue to minister to them.[46]

The trial of living with an uncontrollable natural world was also a frequent topic in auto campers' personal accounts. Mosquitoes, fleas, snakes, and other bothersome creatures often entered these pages, as well as the authors' tents. As Maud Keck, a novice camper observed, until she went camping in 1921, she "had forgotten about crawling things," which she quickly rediscovered "went with Nature too." Fierce winds could also be a hardship, pummeling the Bedell and Van de Water families on repeated occasions, as well as Keck. She and her friend, neither of whom had camped previously, decided to establish camp on a Southern California beach on their first day out. Alone, they struggled to find a suitable spot, but ultimately erected the tent and were feeling somewhat smug when Keck "discovered why a tent should not be set up facing the wind. A puff entered the doorway; the tent suddenly billowed out like a balloon; and the pegs began flying out of the sand."[47] Luckily, they were able to grab the tent before it was carried away, but thereafter decided to sleep in the open.

In contrast, the Van de Waters had been camping for weeks when they pulled into the motor camp in Omaha. They had learned many lessons on camping technique, but they had not yet experienced a punishing prairie wind. Blissfully ignorant, they erected their tent on the crest of an available hill and slept peacefully until "the gale struck." Then they "received a further education in camp craft," which is best described by Van de Water.

> The wind came with the deep-throated roar of a dozen express trains. Its noise and the boom and creak of straining canvas dragged the Engineer [Van de Water] back from a bottomless pit of slumber. A spurt of gravel rattled against the tent wall. An iron waste can fell over and bounded away into the middle distance with diminishing thunder. Outside in the furious darkness, some one began frantic hammering upon his tent pegs. There was a crash and a yell of dismay downhill. Thereafter, for several minutes, we had no concern for external noises. . . . A heavier gust of wind smote us. Above, we heard a smart crack and our tent, our sole habitation, folded itself up and sat down upon us.

After some anxious moments spent finding his pants and determining that his wife and son were fine, Van de Water exited the collapsed tent, only to find other campers stumbling around in the darkness to repair damage and to drive their tent pegs deeper into the ground. He managed to jury-rig the tent pole together again and would replace it in a few days, but after that experience, any "gentle soughing of the mildest zephyr was sufficient to bring [him] leaping from his air bed to cling frantically to the tent pole."[48] The Bedells, by contrast, had endured several brushes with blustery conditions, so they knew that it was difficult to sleep in a tent during a strong wind. Consequently, they decided to sleep in their car at the El Paso auto campground when the wind began to blow. The next day, they were particularly happy with their decision, because they had gotten a good night's rest while at least one nearby tent had come down and several others had threatened to do so during the night.

The possibility of wind, insects, illness, and myriad other challenges were a raison d'être for new equipment manufacturers. Campers' fears that they might find nature too unpredictable and rough became a fertile field plowed in advertisements for pest repellents, gasoline-pressure stoves, ice chests, air mattresses, and other comfort-enhancing devices. Motor campers' personal accounts indicate that they generally embraced these new products. Maud Keck packed "Indian blankets, camp chairs, cots, kitchen utensils, folding gasoline stove, electric lantern, and a 'one woman' tent" in her car. With such an array of equipment she felt that she "could pass the night almost anywhere." The Van de Waters similarly carried along an umbrella tent, inflatable mattresses and pillows, nine blankets, a gasoline stove, a "portable refrigerator" (ice chest), a nest of pots, dishes and cutlery, a frying pan, an electric torch (flashlight), and a medicine kit. The Bedells were equally prepared for their adventure, although Mary recognized the contradiction involved. "It may not seem so romantic" to use the latest equipment, she told her readers, "but remember, we were *modern* Gypsies, and found some recent improvements of great advantage in a life such as we were leading."[49]

However, the auto campers' experiences with gasoline-pressure stoves, ice chests, and such indicate that these devices did not always smooth away camping's roughness. Frederic Van de Water was thankful that they had a gasoline stove, because some campsites did not allow open fires, and so they would have been unable to cook anything without it. At the same time, these stoves could be a challenge to operate. Van de Water's wife found it "a stubborn and resentful devil," which led her to approach it "with the expression of an early Christian martyr." Van de Water described similarly ambiguous relationships with nearly all their comfort devices. He volunteered that he would buy the same tent again, but only with a single, solid tent pole. The air mattresses became "the most comfortable of couches," but the need to inflate them daily using only his lungs left him wondering more than once "whether he would ever breathe naturally again." The ice chest was equally problematic. It had been advertised as "an ideal article of camp equipment," but he and his family found it to be "a first-class nuisance." Van de Water and Charles Wood both complained about another item that nearby campers had brought along for their amusement—the phonograph. Wood allowed that phonographs were "fashionable," but he nevertheless rejected them as "the noise and games of the city" rather than a part of the "quiet wilderness." For the Van de Waters, their musical distress arrived early in the journey. On their first night away from New York they camped at Gettysburg, Pennsylvania. No sooner had they "crept into our blankets" and "had done with the cares of the day" than a carload of campers from Indiana pulled into the campsite next to theirs and began "filling the night with song from the most stentorian portable phonograph yet invented by man. They had only four records along, but they spent hours playing these over and over." And for some campers, most often the wives and mothers on whom auto camping's domestic burdens fell most heavily, no combination of innovative equipment made it attractive. As one immigrant woman in a New England motor campground told Jan and Cora Gordon, "Dot kemping. Dot ain't no holidays for us vomans. It's yoost vash and cook yoost like de vay ve do it at home. Yoost de same." Such comments did not appear in auto camping's promotional literature for many years, and when they finally did, they came out under such humorous titles as 1973's *The I Hate to Camp Book* by Charmaine Severson.[50]

Furthermore, auto camping's prescriptive authors and equipment advertisements frequently failed to recognize its rapidly shifting gender composition. They focused on nuclear families, extended families, and groups of men camping, but only rarely mentioned women camping without men. The reality, according to the personal accounts of motor campers, was much closer to the picture sketched by historian Virginia Scharff, of "women moving into and away from, through and around the shifting ground of the American West." Maud Keck described her two-week adventure through Southern California in 1921 as "a true tale of how two totally inexperienced women set out to camp and what they learned of that popular pastime by first-hand experience." The next year, Mary and Fred Bedell encountered two women camping alone at Fort Stockton, Texas, but unlike Keck and her friend, these campers were not on a local adventure. Instead, they were auto camping their way across America from Florida to Oregon. The Bedells were so impressed with their new acquaintances they agreed to have the two cars travel together through the desert to El Paso so that all would be safer. A few years later, in 1926, Frederic Van de Water and his family came upon numerous women motor campers as they traveled west from New

York. "Frequently we camped besides parties of young women, touring the country alone, with only the most elementary knowledge of Campcraft or motor lore." At Yellowstone National Park alone they met a camping party composed of two recently retired teachers from Massachusetts and then another made up of three young women from Salt Lake City. In addition, park superintendent Horace Albright told Van de Water that shortly before the latter arrived, "a party of eight women in two motor cars had been welcomed. . . . None of them was young. The eldest was seventy four. They had traveled several thousand miles without mishap already and were going on to Glacier Park and Banff after leaving Yellowstone." In the end, Van de Water admitted begrudgingly that it was "possible that women who motor-camp have a better time in general than a male or mixed party." Despite the silence of other media, these personal motor-camping accounts make it clear that women took quickly to camping without men (see fig. 3.6). At the same time, they did so for the same general reason as men, couples, and family groups—to make a pilgrimage to wild nature; but since any pilgrimage is an arena of competing discourses, not all campers recovered the same meaning from their travels.[51]

Figure 3.6. Early auto-camping guidebooks and advertisements rarely featured women campers without men or families, but a rapidly growing number of women enjoyed camping, including this group preparing breakfast in July 1932 at Two Medicine Campground, Glacier National Park. Courtesy of National Park Service Historic Photograph Collection, Harpers Ferry (WV) Center for Media Services; photographer George A. Grant.

Maud Keck decided to try camping with a friend because she had found her life in Pasadena, California, unsatisfying. "Things like houses, husbands and clothes had made me wonder if there was any romance left in the world." Auto camping, she decided, was the remedy to restore her sagging spirits, so Keck and her friend consciously abandoned their everyday lives by driving to the coast and then south along the Pacific shore toward San Diego. Motor camping, she declared, allowed them "to run away from home cares for a while and live the wild, free existence of the gypsy, with no more cares or worries . . . to taste to the full the joy of the nomad on the open road."[52]

Mary Bedell and Charles Wood also sought romance as auto campers, most especially in the form of natural beauty. Wood's diary records numerous events, conversations, poems, and personal interactions both on the journey and at camp, but his descriptions of the natural landscapes, which were rich in the sort of romantic imagery that stretched back to William H. H. Murray, stand out. "We swiftly clear the flashing Mackenzie River bordered by glittering leaved cottonwoods perfuming the air," he wrote as they traveled to their campsite. He noted "meadows alternating with groves of the cottonwoods through which show flashes of the river—and on the left hand high hills covered with evergreen pines, firs—hemlocks, tamarack." At the summit of a high pass along the way, he regarded the twisted forms around him. "The long reach of lava—dark—stormy contorted areas. The agony of the earth. Here and there a small pine tree made desolation more desolate. Ridges, pillars, peaks, valleys, gorges, bowls as the thick lava had spewed out and flowed and curled and poured down and piled up in the fiery birth and cooled to the very shapes before us." Mary Bedell, less a poet than Wood, nevertheless revealed her romantic side in more prosaic language. She had departed her urban home and camped around America with "the idea of . . . gaining a more intimate knowledge of the wonderful things with which this beautiful earth of ours is endowed." Frederic Van de Water, by contrast, appeared less influenced by any romantic inclination, but equally skeptical about his urban life. He referred to his family's forty-five-hundred-mile camping trip as "our pilgrimage," and he allowed that it was only after they left New York City that he discovered "the real America." New Yorkers thought that Americans were "perfectly awful," "rowdies," and "thieves" who would "lack of manners and all decency." Instead, the many other campers the Van de Waters met were, "to New Yorkers, strangely kind and friendly people," and he came to enjoy their company.[53]

Another element of normal life—a schedule—was dropped by some campers as they moved toward a sense of time shaped by their journey. Maud Keck was pleased that when she and her friend departed from Pasadena they were not traveling to a specific destination and did not have a planned arrival time. Some travelers might have found their lack of planning to be an error, but Keck trusted that "romance would beckon us on and lead us to the right places." The Van de Waters, in contrast, did not share Keck's attitude when they set out for the West Coast. They departed with a strict itinerary and "scorned" those auto campers who did not know where they were going each day. "To us it seemed shiftless not to have some definite port in mind." But soon the rhythm of camping penetrated their consciousness, and they changed their tune. Instead of aiming at a target, Frederic Van de Water recounted, they began to accept whatever campsite appeared at the end of a day's travel. "Only by such fatalism," he declared, could an auto camper "enjoy to the fullest the country through which he travels." Van de Water came to realize what the author of "The Call of the Open Road" had warned against—that if he identified a destination at a day's outset, he would feel obliged to reach it by whatever "rushing" and "striving" was necessary.[54]

At the same time, Van de Water felt that auto camping's freedom should occur only within some relatively clear and brief time limit; a journey should not continue indefinitely. If one did, Van de Water changed his attitude toward that auto camper, no longer treating him as an equal. At one point he comments that the better municipal auto camps were the ones that charged for the privilege to camp. He declared the fifty-cents-a-night fee "a protective tax," which kept a camp free from "undesirables." West of the Mississippi River, he explained, the "roads swarm with auto tramps, folk who have started out motor camping and have not been able to stop. They are a sinister, frowzy, none too honest lot."[55] To succumb to an auto-camping siren and remain in the other world of wildness for the foreseeable future was clearly a personal failing and the sort of distinction that separated the true camper who sought a material or spiritual reward from the simple wanderer who lacked goals and direction.

Frederic Van de Water's personal account and those of other auto campers reveal that they, like any sort of pilgrim, had set out on their journeys from a variety of motives. Mary Bedell pursued twin goals, to "gain . . . more physical vigor" and to "expand . . . the soul." Van de Water began his family motor camping with the expectation that it would be an adventure, which it was, but it turned out to be more. He was pleasantly surprised to discover that it had "therapeutic" value, which he was happy to find many others also felt. At one campsite, the Van de Waters met a "Dakota farmer" who "had had a long and serious illness that had shattered him nervously." However, the man "was recovering stability and strength" as he motor camped around the West. Elsewhere, they encountered a teacher who had been "threatened with tuberculosis," accompanied by her mother.

Unsurprisingly, the young woman's physicians had prescribed a therapy well known since the nineteenth century—being outside as much as possible in fresh air—so the pair had hit the motor trail. To both women's delight, "the ominous cough was vanishing under the touch of Wyoming sunlight." Finally, Van de Water mentioned their crossing the path of a young girl who had been smitten by "Infantile Paralysis," but who, "after six weeks of motor camping," had become "brown and vigorous." These accounts reveal that many auto campers expected the extraordinary to occur on their journey, which sometimes included the physical restoration first mentioned by William H. H. Murray in 1869 and by many camping advocates since him.[56]

In a similar fashion, some motor-camping accounts reveal that their authors felt the social leveling or *communitas* that can occur among pilgrims. Jan and Cora Gordon, who had come from England to auto tour and camp around the eastern United States, were particularly struck by the social equality of American campgrounds.

> This easy, good natured democracy ruled the camps. The possession of a car was enough to frank you into camp society. A camper bowed and greeted any other camper; and equality included the well-to-do in his Packard, with a trailer, and the pair of lads cutting loose on a 1918 flivver. To enter a camp was to accept camp conditions; so that at the basins, Jo, washing her head, might find [herself] alongside a man shaving and explaining to her through the lather the influence of the automobile on road graft; while a woman, rinsing her children's underclothes on the other side, was discussing the relative duties and pleasures of the male and the female in this camping business, or even discussing the subject of comparative religions with some signs of study. You never knew what you might hear at the wash basins or other places where campers congregated.[57]

Mary Bedell, who with her family was driving north from San Diego, reported a similar experience as they camped near "several fishermen" one night along the Southern California coast. Each party might have stayed in its own space, but, she reported, all were campers, "and as is the custom in this part of the country, we soon made their acquaintance." It was not, however, at just this one place that Bedell and her family found that a sense of equality prevailed among campers. A few days later they were camping at Wawona in Yosemite National Park when Mary realized how much it was the camping rather than the location that transformed social relations. "We met some pleasant people who were camping near by, and several of us sat around the campfire that first night telling stories of our individual

experiences. It is remarkable how quickly friendships spring up in such surroundings. With all the conveniences of civilization reduced to a minimum,
how much easier it is to estimate the real character of a person met casually
in this way."[58] Whatever social distinctions may have been apparent, Bedell
never mentioned them, instead preferring to focus on the similarities she
recognized among her fellow motor campers.

The Van de Waters also found that during their stays at automobile campgrounds "the easy, pleasant, completely democratic life of the camp flowed
around" everyone, more or less. But, Frederic reported, limits existed. In
particular, social mechanisms had emerged to contain and isolate any motor
camper who had the temerity to display his or her higher class and wealth.
"The democracy of 'tin can touring' is a jealous and sensitive thing," he
declared, and when his wife slipped, "she felt the weight of its disapproval."
On one occasion, in a communal camp laundry, she became dismayed about
her inability to keep her family's clothes clean. In an unguarded moment
and in front of other women campers she sighed, "Oh dear . . . I don't
know what my laundress would say if she were to see our clothes." The
consequences were immediate and sharp. "Silence fell, a silence as heavily disapproving as though she had uttered some highly colored obscenity.
The comradeship in which she and her fellow toilers had chatted a moment
before was broken off and never resumed." His wife, Frederic noted, had
so strongly felt the other campers' disapproval that she never made that
mistake again. "The old independent self-helping spirit," he surmised, "still
pervades the road which parallels the trails the covered wagons followed."[59]

Throughout his account, Van de Water alluded to covered wagons, the
frontier, and pioneer life. At journey's outset, he predicted that his six-and-
a-half-year-old son's auto-camping experiences in the West would set him
apart from other children his age. When the family's motor camping travels
were complete, Van de Water declared, his young son would have seen the
Rocky Mountains and the Mississippi River, smelled the Wyoming sagebrush, and experienced bears at Yellowstone National Park, while the other
children would have just read or heard about them. "If by the time he studies school history, values have been recast and the westward march of the
backwoodsmen and later of the covered wagons, receives an attention equal
to that now expended upon Plymouth Rock, he would thrill a little, too, for
he has seen much that the pioneers saw." A few weeks later, as the family
traveled along the Platte River in Nebraska, Frederic and his wife realized
that they were "on the ancient highway into the Old West." As do many
campers, they felt nostalgia for the past and so were thrilled to discover
that they could not only camp in those places where pioneers had struggled,

but could follow their predecessors' routes. "Covered wagons had creaked and lumbered along its banks and before the first of these came, the trappers' moccasins had padded westward beside it and its frugal current had borne the traders bateaux down to the Missouri." A decade later, Leo Borah described his travels from Washington, D.C., to the Shenandoah and Great Smoky Mountains National Parks along the Eastern Park-to-Park Highway in much the same way. "To commune in spirit with the makers of the Nation, to recapture the poignancy of outstanding events in American history on the scenes where they were enacted, to trace again the path of Daniel Boone and the plodding ox teams that bore the pioneers to the winning of the West, and to refresh mind and body in three glorious national recreation areas, motor over the new Eastern National Park-to-Park Highway."[60] Although Borah's and the Van de Waters' modes of transport and equipment were modern, they felt strongly linked to the mythic, nation-forming frontier because they could camp along routes used by earlier Americans.

From the beginning, the Van de Waters had found the other campers to be friendly both in the auto campgrounds and along the road. However, Frederic eventually recognized that their fellow motor campers were becoming friendlier and more hospitable as the family went farther west and as their car and equipment became dustier and more "disreputable" looking. They always enjoyed this friendliness, whatever its degree, but Frederic also admitted that "it was baffling and alarming at first." Moreover, the other campers' pleasant demeanors were a clue to how different motor camping was from everyday life. The Van de Waters felt, Frederic confided, that they "had been transported into a world differing in many things from that to which [we] are accustomed."[61] This sense of having entered another world would reach a peak at Yellowstone National Park, which he treated as a sacred place.

Frederic Van de Water gave his chapter on Yellowstone a title that recalled the sacred—"Place of Peace." He and the family spent six days in the park, which left him feeling that "Paradise . . . will be only an adventure repeated, now." He attributed the attraction of the park to three principal elements, with beauty being its first. They visited the usual sites, such as the geysers, and saw the usual attractions, for instance the bears, but he did not feel that these extraordinary elements made the park unique. "Rather, it is the bright, unspoiled, eternal beauty of the land itself." The auto campers' freedom also set the place apart for Frederic. The Yellowstone camper enjoyed temporal freedom, being able to move "when he pleases and as he pleases. No one directs him." Furthermore, he had spatial freedom on several scales. "He sets up his tent where his fancy directs. . . . He is not compelled, ever, to camp at any special place. Save for a few localities where signs proclaim that camping is forbidden, the entire reservation is open to him." Only one sensible rule is applied to campers, Van de Water allows, "that he leave his camping place policed and orderly when he departs." Finally, "rangers who were eager to advise and help us, [and] camp employes who, however overworked, were willing to go out of their way to do us favors" also set the national park apart from the ordinary world.[62]

Something about Yellowstone, nonetheless, gnawed at Frederic and his wife, because they sensed that the place's beauty, freedom, and the helpful attitude of its people did not quite capture its character. "There is something heartening and comforting in the atmosphere of Yellowstone; something rarer and more intimate than its great beauty; something cheering and pleasant that three wanderers found hard to identify." They apparently discussed this issue on several occasions, and it was Frederic's wife, whom he called "the Commodore" throughout the book, who put her finger on the answer. " 'You feel,' she diagnosed, 'as if you were at home. It's as if the place belonged to you.'" Motor camping in Yellowstone, they concluded, was not a journey away from home, but to it. In Yellowstone's sacred space, the Van de Waters found a central and intimate place—home.[63]

Once Van de Water started to think of Yellowstone as home, he began to see it as intricately tied to his American identity and sense of connectedness. "You became conscious that nationality means something," he admitted. "The campers from almost every state in the Union who pitch their tents near yours are transformed into relatives." One was no longer an anonymous individual in a mass society, but a participant in a better future. "In the auto camps of Yellowstone you get a faint, far-flown echo of the brotherhood that some day may be. You are an American. This is your land. These are your friends."

Auto camping's ability to reinforce identity did not necessarily work at the national scale alone. Mary Bedell also had her identity and sense of belonging confirmed, but it was not so much as an American than as a New Yorker. As she and her husband traveled farther west, New York State license plates became so rare on cars that often when they passed someone in a campground or elsewhere, they were "almost always greeted with much cordiality by our neighbors, who seemed so pleased that any one had taken the trouble to come way from New York to see them." As other automobiles passed them on the road, she recounted, they would often be hailed, " 'Hello, New York!' a greeting that gave us a pleasurable sense of pride for our home state." Charles E. S. Wood likewise found his sense of identity and belonging confirmed on an auto-camping trip. While quietly resting near his campsite, he recalled not nation or state, but his own family. The landscape stretching away was not just beautiful, he recorded, but filled with memories, "the meadow covered with red top [grass] as when baby Judy," his now adult daughter, "used to be lost to sight in it."[64] For Wood, his personal roots grew deep into this place.

With goals met and sense of belonging affirmed, many motor-camping accounts dwelled on the bittersweet quality of journey's end. Frederic Van de Water, reflecting on the just-completed trip, clearly placed himself and his family with other pilgrims whose travels have necessarily concluded. They had been, in his opinion, transformed by the experience. "We will never again be quite the same people whose images we last saw in New York. . . . No month, no year in our lives has accomplished as much in enlightenment, education, broadened comprehension, as those thirty-seven days we spent on a Ford's quarterdeck, bound for San Francisco. . . . We know America and Americans as only those who go motor camping can learn to know them. We have discovered a people and land whose existence the average New Yorker never even suspects."[65]

His wife was also different because of their travels. When they first returned home, she had told friends that one auto-camping trip was enough for a lifetime, but when the next spring arrived and she was looking at a photograph of western mountains, she remarked wistfully to Frederic, "Doesn't it make you *homesick*?" Mary Bedell was similarly pleased when her twelve-thousand-mile, nine-month auto-camping trip concluded, but she was willing to go again after "an interval of quiet enjoyment of home comforts and friends." Having been enlightened and transformed like Frederic Van de Water, she realized from her motor-camping journey that Americans had a desire "for right living and right thinking," which she had not known before her voyage. Subsequently, she was willing to go auto camping again and to encourage others to do so as well because "there is no better way of discovering the fine traits of our fellow countrymen than by packing up a kit and going a-gypsying."[66]

The Motor-Camping Trail

Between 1910 and 1940, one form of camping—with a car—grew dramatically in comparison to backpacking, packhorse camping, and boat camping. The primary impetus for the growth of motor camping was the rapid change in the cost, financing, and availability of automobiles. Fewer than one hundred thousand cars were registered in 1905, but by 1940 over twenty-seven million were on the road. Inexpensive automobiles drew many more families and working-class Americans to the growing number of campgrounds scattered through the country's local, state, and federal protected areas. Soon camping was one of Americans' favorite pastimes.

This wave of new auto campers sparked a large prescriptive literature to assist novices. Like their predecessors, these "how to" authors described motor camping in the language of pilgrimage. In particular, they suggested that urban life was hard on Americans because it was hierarchical, overregulated, impersonal, ugly, and polluted, and that the best cure was a camping trip into sacred nature. The automobile was praised for its ability to provide social equality, mobility, and freedom even as it eased a camper's ability to carry such new equipment as ice chests and gasoline-pressure lanterns.

A wide range of new equipment arose during this era, which sets motor campers apart from their predecessors. Manufacturers developed and produced improved equipment, while camping advocates promoted it in order to smooth some of the more challenging aspects of "roughing it." Many existing forms of equipment, such as cookware, were reduced in size and weight to improve portability, while other items brought domestic conveniences into the wild. One producer that excelled at this domestication was the Coleman Company, which produced highly successful lines of gasoline-pressure lanterns and camp stoves. Its products sold well because of their high quality, but Coleman also relied on other strategies to boost sales. The company developed outdoor versions of items already common in American homes, while its advertisements and other promotional material portrayed urban life negatively and camping as an adventure into the wild even as they extolled the ease, comfort, and convenience provided by Coleman products.

The popularity of motor camping also led to short and long accounts about campers' adventures along the motor trail. Some of these campers traveled great distances, while others stayed closer to home, but all shared some common characteristics. Cars were a new luxury to most Americans, so these tales focused often on the pleasures and trials of being on the road and in the campgrounds that had recently sprung up around the country. Readers presumably had had little contact with Americans from other regions, or even with the natural world, so authors frequently discussed their interactions with people and nature during their travels. Generally, these personal accounts were positive or humorous, and they correlated closely with prescriptive authors' and manufacturers' depiction of camping as a form of pilgrimage. Motor campers found their urban lives dissatisfying and wild nature appealing and restorative. Freedom, social equality, and a sense of identity swelled when camping. The sense of having entered a new world, one that was really the camper's home, was palpable. These moving, deeply emotional, and positive accounts kept drawing campers out of America's cities for many decades, but as the next chapters will demonstrate, the growing number of motor campers soon meant that their environmental impacts would have to be managed and that their increasing social diversity would generate controversy.

CHAPTER FOUR

THE GARAGE IN THE FOREST

E. P. Meinecke and the Development of the Modern Auto Campground

As the number of motor campers skyrocketed during the 1910s and 1920s, many were pleased to escape for a weekend to some easily accessible destination near their residences. Lakes, woods, seashores, and deserts within a few hours' drive generally satisfied these campers' desire to escape their everyday world, but some found these sites' ability to renew and transform to be limited. Urban dissatisfaction, they felt, reappeared too soon. A solution, however, was complicated. When a camper sought greater restoration, he had to travel to spaces more sacred, but to do so was geographically challenging, because most Americans lived in the East, and the most sacred and desirable destinations—Yellowstone, Yosemite, and the other national parks—were in the distant West. Consequently, the demand for campsites was not just strong near campers' homes, but also along the most popular western routes that carried these travelers to their ultimate objectives.[1] In response, a variety of automobile campgrounds emerged.

Municipal Auto Campgrounds

Both private and public automobile campgrounds initially appeared before World War I, but only in its aftermath did their numbers, like those of the campers, mushroom. Unfortunately, no source provides a reliable count of the camping facilities operated between 1918 and 1930 or the ratio between private and public facilities, but approximately three thousand to six thousand auto campgrounds, many of which were free, flourished during the

1920s as campers traveled widely across the nation. Municipal governments often supported the creation of free automobile campgrounds in their towns for at least two reasons. On the one hand, unregulated auto campers were considered a nuisance, so cities supported auto campgrounds to reduce the number of "promiscuous" or "gypsy" campers who "squatted" along roadways when night overtook them. On the other hand, the cities hoped to cash in on the potential traveler dollars.[2]

As noted in the last chapter, many municipal campgrounds were small and haphazard, encompassing but a few acres while offering virtually no amenities. Some, however, were thoughtfully laid out by professional designers like John W. Gregg, a professor of landscape gardening and floriculture at the University of California, Berkeley. He developed a comprehensive campground design for the city of Marysville, California, as early as 1919 that aimed to be both aesthetically and socially attractive to auto campers. Situated in a city park, the campground he created was designed to be seamless with the larger park through "the use of a reasonable amount of ornamental plantings and the utilization of materials of construction which are similar to those used elsewhere in the park." Gregg incorporated individualized campsites, each with an "attractive little shelter house," roads and walkways that were "well built and maintained," cooking facilities, drinking water, sewers, bathing and toilet facilities, playgrounds, and electric lighting. At the same time, he included "a proper mass planting of trees and shrubs" to provide visual privacy between campsites.[3]

Professionally designed or not, a typical small town's motor campground during the 1920s was situated on ten to fifteen acres at the outskirts of the municipality and laid out to provide each camping group with a recognizable space. In addition, it would provide drinking water, restrooms (often outhouses), electric lighting, a shared kitchen with stoves (wood- or gasburning), a "lounge," showers (usually cold), and laundry tubs. A larger, more elaborate facility might also include a dance room with piano, writing desks in the lounge, a complete self-service laundry (including irons), a radio, daily newspapers, and police protection. Municipal auto campgrounds could be found in many American towns and cities, but above them all stood Denver's Overland Park. Sometimes called "the Manhattan of autocamp cities," it sprawled across 160 acres and could accommodate over two thousand campers on its eight hundred campsites, with each 25-by-30-foot site lighted, and none more than 150 feet from clean, piped water. Moreover, this comprehensive campground sported a central, three-story structure that contained a grocery, kitchen and grill, steam table, lunch counter, barbershop, and restrooms. Conveniently located near Rocky Mountain National Park, Overland Park was an ideal starting point for the many easterners who came to Denver to motor camp around the new National Park-to-Park Highway loop. As a consequence, Overland Park attracted more than six hundred thousand auto campers during the summer of 1923.[4]

Although many municipalities established free auto campgrounds, the majority of them disappeared by 1930 for economic and social reasons. Increasingly disturbed by "gypsy automobilists" and "undesirables" who might camp for indeterminate periods, cities imposed fees, mandatory registration, police patrols, and limits on length of stay. Fees were especially favored by the critics of free campgrounds, because "no service is to be expected without some fair return." All these changes discouraged this particular class of campers, but the fees in particular opened the door to private businessmen, and municipal campgrounds subsequently dwindled in number. In Colorado, for instance, a mere nine of sixty-four auto camps were privately operated in 1925, but by 1928, only twenty of eighty-five remained in the hands of public agencies. Many private campgrounds, however, provided little natural scenery and recreational space and were simply a place to stop overnight, often being attached to such unattractive features as gas stations and roadside stands. As a consequence, nearby state and national parks and forests increasingly drew auto campers, and the demand for these campgrounds rapidly swelled. In response, the states expanded their park facilities to serve both local and long-distance auto campers. Although only 194 camping areas were designated in twenty-five states' parks in 1923, the number of campgrounds swelled to 1,335 areas with 21,577 campsites in forty-seven states by 1941.[5]

Forest Service Auto Campgrounds

The U.S. Forest Service (USFS) also reacted to the growing popularity of automobile camping. As early as 1912, the Forest Service chief forester's annual report had noted that "more people are visiting the forests for recreation purposes and there is a growing demand." Although the report did not specifically mention auto camping in any region, it was already common throughout California's national forests. As an aid to these visitors, in 1915 the USFS issued *A Handbook for Campers in the National Forests of California*, which for the first time offered advice about clothing and equipment for the inexperienced, reported on the new roads and trails that provided improved access for auto campers, and noted that the telephone lines installed to fire lookout stations now made it possible for campers to send and receive messages. Nevertheless, it is clear that camper-caused fires were foremost in the mind of the booklet's author. People were permitted to camp more or less anywhere in a national forest, the *Handbook* allowed, but they were "urged to use fireplaces prepared by the rangers in attractive camping sites" wherever the fire threat was great.[6]

The following year, 1916, was a USFS milestone, as the Oregon National Forest constructed an auto campground at Eagle Creek, the first developed anywhere by the Forest Service. Although no professional assisted with its design, the Eagle Creek camping area included features that would soon become typical—camp tables, outhouses, a check-in station, and a ranger station. Located about forty miles east of Portland and easily accessible by car, the campground sat on a beautiful spot overlooking the Columbia River Gorge and attracted nearly 150,000 campers annually within a few years of its opening. At the same time, demand was escalating at other national forests around the country. According to Frank Waugh, a landscape architect and professor at the Massachusetts Agricultural College who consulted for the Forest Service during 1917, national forest campgrounds in many locations were highly popular, especially along roads. Campers, he observed, preferred to pitch their tents and cook around campfires to spending their nights in a hotel or farmhouse. When located near water and equipped with a source of firewood, simple sanitation provisions, and fireplaces of some sort, "such camps," Waugh concluded, "are extensively used by travelers."[7] The number of motor campers headed to national forests, however, had not yet peaked and would greatly increase soon.

As World War I drew to a close in late 1918, the USFS reviewed the recreational situation in the nation's forests and concluded that campground demand was likely to expand, especially in California and the Rocky Mountains. With growth on the horizon, the Forest Service realized that it could no longer rely on makeshift amenities but instead would need professionally designed automobile campgrounds to increase its ability to calculate, predict, and control campers and their impacts. In other words, the USFS was moving toward the McDonaldization of its camping policies and practices. The Forest Service's Rocky Mountain District was the first to move toward professionalization, and after a short search it hired Arthur Carhart, who had graduated in landscape architecture from Iowa State University in 1916 and had recently mustered out of the army. In short order, Carhart began traveling around the district to visit popular recreation areas and assess their conditions; his report was not optimistic. The district contained few usable campgrounds, warned Carhart, and the forests would become less secure if developed camping areas were not provided, because "there are some who will invade the territory anyway." Of course, campgrounds with amenities would likely attract even more forest visitors, he admitted, but the new facilities would also contain and control them. If nothing was done, the few but uncontrolled campers, he cautioned, would cause greater damage and be worse for the forest than the many that were controlled. It was "safer," Carhart advised, to create campgrounds and to direct auto campers to them in order "to see that sanitary measures are practiced efficiently." Carhart's argument carried the day, and with his supervisor's support he began to plan the district's new campgrounds and other recreation facilities in May 1919.[8]

   Arthur Carhart was the first USFS professional to design the agency's campgrounds, but the dearth of developed camping areas in the Rocky Mountains had already moved camping proponents to action elsewhere. In one of the district's forests, the San Isabel, the Commerce Club (Chamber of Commerce) of Pueblo, Colorado, a small industrial town nearby, had brought the matter to a head in 1918 when it asked the Forest Service to build a campground in the Wet Mountains just west of town. In his reply to this appeal, San Isabel National Forest's sympathetic supervisor, Albin G. Hamel, admitted the need for such a facility, but he also had to inform the Commerce Club that he had no funds for the project because Congress had never appropriated money for national forest campgrounds. Not to be stopped, the club raised $7,200 between 1918 and 1920, got the state to donate six hundred acres adjacent to the national forest, and, with the encouragement of Carhart and the cooperation of the Forest Service and the city of Pueblo, hired Carhart's teacher, Frank H. Culley, the head of the Department of Landscape Design at Iowa State University, to plan and supervise the construction of two automobile campgrounds along Squirrel Creek, another on South Hardscrabble Creek, and a fourth on North Creek. Each of these campgrounds had a shelter and included dozens of campsites, each with its own fireplace. The campsites were arranged in clusters of three to six, and all clusters were provided with pit toilets, a garbage pit, and wells with hand pumps. Furthermore, the campsites in each cluster were never more than forty feet apart, which was relatively close together, and no intervening vegetation was planted between sites, which left them open to the view of nearby campers. Cars were parked in widened areas along the roads rather than indiscriminately within the campgrounds. According to historian Robert Cermak, these four campgrounds "may have been the first designed and built by a landscape architect in the national forests."[9]

   In 1922, after repeated requests, the Forest Service finally received its first congressional funding to support camping—an appropriation of $10,000 for "sanitation and fire prevention, to be spent on the development of campgrounds." Satisfied with the service's use of the initial funds, Congress expanded the campground appropriation to over $37,000 in 1925. Although the funding was modest (forest fire prevention and fighting, by contrast, received nearly $2 million in 1925), the Forest Service accomplished much with it because development was inexpensive. According to the chief forester, it cost the USFS only $200 to improve an average campground in 1925. In following years, congressional funding continued to flow, which allowed the number of developed camping areas in national forests to swell from a paltry 138 in 1920 to more than 1,700 in 1930, and then to over 4,200 by 1940.[10]

Auto Campgrounds in the National Parks

Camping facilities in the national parks also expanded during the early twentieth century, especially after the National Park Service (NPS) was created in 1916. Campground development received solid support under the NPS because its first director, Stephen T. Mather, envisioned the parks as tourist destinations and justified their development and management on that basis. He and his top staff, however, did not view tourism as simply an economic generator. Instead, according to historical geographer Lary Dilsaver, they "firmly believed in the recreation mandate as proper and democratic." To promote these nationalist ends, which fit neatly with the goals of contemporary campers, Mather labored to make national parks both popular and accessible. In particular, he worked with automobile associations that encouraged auto tourism, including camping. In 1915, for instance, even before he became head of the new Park Service, Mather had helped found the National Park-to-Park Highway Association, which lobbied for highway improvements to connect the major western national parks. In 1920, this six-thousand-mile route was formally dedicated.[11]

At the same time that NPS director Mather was persuading automobile associations to support national park visits, he encouraged the agency to increase automobile tourism and camping in the parks through the development of "such imperative necessities as new roads, improved roads, trails, bridges, public camping facilities, and water supply and sewerage systems." Mather considered the existing facilities to be "entirely inadequate" and feared that if the parks did not develop their amenities, then the political threat facing the national parks—attracting too few visitors to maintain the support of Congress—might come to pass. Mather's superior, Interior Secretary Franklin K. Lane, also seems to have shared the new director's political anxiety and so supported the effort to attract automobile campers to the national parks. In a 1918 letter to Mather, Lane expressed his positive regard for the private "low-priced camps" supplied by park concessionaires, but he clearly signaled his even stronger backing for public automobile campgrounds. "In each reservation [i.e., national park], as funds are available," Lane ordered Mather, the director was to create "a system of free camp sites . . . and these grounds will be equipped with adequate water and sanitation facilities." Mather followed the secretary's directions, and as campgrounds appeared, the public responded immediately and enthusiastically. Forty thousand campers visited Yellowstone in ten thousand cars in 1919, and three years later all but fifteen hundred of the park's more than fifty-one hundred visitors stayed in its campgrounds. To the west, Sequoia National Park showed a similar trend, receiving only 766 cars in 1918, but the number swelled to nearly 21,000 by 1930, and nearly all these visitors camped. Similarly, at Yosemite National Park, it was common during the 1920s for Yosemite Valley's public camping areas to accommodate between five thousand and seven thousand campers each night.[12]

Despite crowds, Mary Crehore Bedell, who camped with her husband near Yosemite's Camp Curry in the summer of 1923, found the experience exceptional. "The camp-grounds are kept in good order being inspected daily by Rangers who ride continually around the Park on beautiful horses. It was one of the cleanest camps we had encountered anywhere, and we thoroughly enjoyed our two weeks stay in this lovely spot." One reason the Bedells took pleasure in their camping experience was that the Park Service recently had begun to manage its camping visitors. Not long before, auto campers had been free to set up equipment at nearly any attractive park location that they could access. If a campground existed in a park, campers might be required to use it, but oftentimes they were not obliged to do so. This libertarian management approach mirrored the outlook of the campers, who generally chafed at the constraints in their urban lives. Having a "go as you please" attitude, they found the national parks' spatial freedom appealing. One of them, Frederic Van de Water, latched on to this lack of restraints to explain why he and his family so enjoyed themselves while camping in Yellowstone National Park during the summer of 1925. A camper, he noted, enjoyed temporal freedom, being able to move "when he pleases and as he pleases. No one directs him." Furthermore, a camper took pleasure in his spatial freedom on several scales. "He sets up his tent where his fancy directs. . . . He is not compelled, ever, to camp at any special place. Save for a few localities where signs proclaim that camping is forbidden, the entire reservation is open to him."[13]

Yosemite National Park, where the Bedells camped, had once been managed much like Yellowstone. According to historical geographer Stanford Demars, campers who visited Yosemite before 1916 "pitched their tents practically everywhere in the valley but concentrated mainly in the meadows" near its eastern end. After the NPS was created, however, the Park Service diligently pursued Mather's goals, so Yosemite and the other national parks became progressively more developed and organized both to attract and to manage campers. An early leader of this McDonaldizing effort was Charles P. Punchard, the Park Service's first "landscape engineer." A landscape architect by training, Punchard had been working in the Office of Public Buildings and Grounds in Washington, D.C., when he moved to the National Park Service in 1918. As he settled into his new post, the number of auto campers visiting the national parks was increasing rapidly. Initially focused on the Yellowstone Park, where automobile camping was especially fast growing, Punchard spent his time locating and developing new, attractive campgrounds or rehabilitating existing ones to a higher standard so that campers could be easily directed into them and would not use other portions of the park's landscape. As he worked on one location after another, Punchard, reports historian Linda McClelland, "worked out the basic requirements for national park campgrounds" by the end of 1919. Drinking water and sanitary facilities were foremost, but he also recognized that auto campgrounds were more practical and attractive when they were screened from roadways, provided with parking space in forested areas, and equipped with fireplaces and seats and tables. Within a few years, these amenities became common at Yellowstone's campgrounds and also began to appear in other national parks, including Yosemite where the Bedells camped.[14]

Deteriorating Auto Campgrounds

The rapid development of campgrounds and other recreational amenities in the national parks achieved Mather's primary goal—they attracted growing crowds of fun seekers to the nation's "playgrounds," which reduced the political threat to the parks. These same throngs of campers, however, also became an environmental threat to the parks, because the Park Service's wildland protection and preservation policies and practices were developing more slowly than the size of the crowds. Park administrators had not wished to be too overt, so they had adopted a "hands-off" approach to visitor control and relied primarily on indirect manipulation to influence or modify behavior.[15] Through the 1920s, for instance, the NPS was reluctant to install signs indicating where visitors could not venture. Instead it constructed roads, restrooms, campgrounds, and other infrastructure to act as the magnets that would draw visitors to approved locations. This management approach, when combined with the auto campers' independent attitude, unfortunately resulted in a variety of negative impacts on park landscapes and ecosystems.

From the national parks' earliest years, campers often had dumped trash and damaged vegetation, especially shrubs and small trees, by crushing them with their vehicles, cutting them for firewood and tent poles, or accidentally setting them ablaze. During her 1882 visit to Yellowstone National Park, Mary Bradshaw Richards was dismayed by the "blackened logs, tin cans, and bits of pasteboard or paper lying about" the otherwise "charmingly smooth" campground at Elk Park. This all-too-common debris, she sadly noted, "told the tale of former and recent campers." The situation, unfortunately, did not improve as campers and guides gained experience. Ten years later, Interior Secretary John W. Noble expressed his support for "camping parties" at Yellowstone, but he also recommended that they be kept "under surveillance" by park personnel because "they make much litter and permit the escape of fires." A decade later, during the summer of 1908, First Lieutenant Henry F. Lincoln of the U.S. Medical Reserve Corps made a ten-day inspection tour of the campgrounds of General Grant (now Kings Canyon) National Park. Campsites, he reported to the park's superintendent, were "easily determined" because they were generally "near a stream or spring and are well marked by the lack of policing and the consequent presence of camp and kitchen refuse. . . . There may be found manure from animals and practically always within a few feet of the evident camp site—so that there occurs this offal with that of human negligence—soiled linen, empty cans, paste board and wooden boxes, bones, etc., etc. This condition is the prevailing one on all trails and roads." As the number of national park campers increased, the hazards spread, with Yosemite's streams rather than its trees or rubbish becoming a focus of environmental concern in 1913. According to R. B. Dole, a water-resources chemist who had been sent by the Department of the Interior to inspect the sanitary condition of the Merced River and one of its tributaries, Yosemite Creek, both streams were badly polluted by contaminated surface and groundwater flows. This public health threat had developed because auto campers arriving in Yosemite Valley were directed to camping areas along the Merced River that had no individually designated campsites within them. Wanting to be near the water, auto campers established themselves anywhere they could squeeze in a car, tent, and gear. When they were packed together like this near water, their wastes tended to migrate into the streams. Declaring the situation to be "questionable," Dole reported that "no practicable measures of inspection or policing can keep this water safe to drink"; some additional actions would be needed. Furthermore, he reminded his supervisors darkly, "Some of the most disastrous epidemics of typhoid fever in this country have occurred because of stream pollution under similar conditions."[16]

In addition to stream pollution, campers' pursuit of the ideal site caused severe damage to park plant life. As they drove cars randomly across meadows' struggling grasses and forbs and among trees and shrubs along water, they crushed, broke, and barked vegetation while generally degrading the landscape.

This unregulated movement and crowding also produced frequent social dramas, especially over holidays like July Fourth. "On such occasions," reports Stanford Demars, "it was not uncommon for one camper to awaken in the morning and find that another camper had moved in and set up his tent in the middle of the first camper's campsite, often 'sharing' his tent stakes and support ropes."[17] Under such conditions, the most crowded, noisy, and environmentally degraded portion of Yosemite Valley became its camping areas, which by the 1920s were sometimes derided as "canvas jungles" (fig. 4.1).

Sequoia National Park's Big Trees

As the years passed, Yosemite Valley's camping areas continued to degrade, but the problem was not confined to them alone or even to Yosemite National Park. By the 1920s, public campgrounds nationwide were deteriorating and being abandoned as marred and unappealing. In *The People's Forest*, Robert Marshall described the developing situation starkly. Many once-beautiful camping areas, he observed, had become "deserts, with the few remaining trees all sickly, with the undergrowth and reproduction virtually extinct, and with the surface of the camp ground merely bare soil which in wet weather becomes a slimy mud and in dry weather gives off a constant cloud of dust."[18]

Some locations were particularly hard hit, including California's Sequoia National Park, which had suffered from inadequate management. By the outset of the 1920s, Sequoia's most popular camping areas had degraded into a snarl of "temporary" camp structures, scattered and messy campsites, degenerated vegetation, and underdeveloped waste, water, and sewage-treatment systems. On one 1920 visit, Charles Punchard found the park heavily used and its camping areas in poor condition, especially around "Giant Forest," where the famous "Big Trees" (*Sequoia gigantea*) grew thick and dramatically close together. Until that time, vegetation management in the park had been largely aesthetic and emotional rather than scientific, with an emphasis on fire suppression and little interest in natural regeneration or systematic planting of replacements for any trees damaged by campers. As a consequence, Punchard was forced to report that intense usage had led to the "gradual destruction of the undergrowth, leaving the ground bare and dusty" in Giant Forest. When the park's new superintendent, John R. White, arrived that same year, he was also struck by the stark and miserable scene. "It was barely possible to see Round Meadow [in the center of Giant Forest] because of the tents which surrounded it. The very choicest

Figure 4.1. These and many more haphazardly situated auto campers in Stoneman Meadow, Yosemite National Park, caused clear and persistent environmental damage. Courtesy of National Park Service Historic Photograph Collection, Harpers Ferry (WV) Center for Media Services.

places were pre-empted by public campers and by those who had permits to establish little cabins at Giant Forest. The whole of the Hazelwood, Firwood, Nob Hill, and other central camp areas were given over to camping and in every direction there were pit toilets, cess pits, and a criss-cross of water lines under the Big Trees." The previous superintendent, Walter Fry, had improved sanitation by having a sewer system installed, but contrary to his expectations, it had also encouraged more visits and a greater density of campsites. Even worse, many of Giant Forest's campers placed their tents adjacent to the Big Trees, using them as rope braces, and thus brought their destructive impacts hard against the park's famous namesakes (fig. 4.2).[19]

Superintendent White, who was a pragmatist as well as someone with some romantic sensibilities, was a leading advocate for what he called "atmosphere preservation" in the national parks. He saw the parks as "inspirational tableaux" for the public, and shortly after his arrival at Sequoia he had decided to renovate Giant Forest's natural environment in order to reinstate the exhilarating beauty of the park's premier attraction and namesake. Clearly the park needed attractive, alternative camping areas, if only to draw visitors away from their traditional sites in Giant Forest. To this end, the Park Service designed and built several new campgrounds and expanded others between 1921 and 1928—Lodgepole, which was well away from Giant Forest, plus Firwood, Highland, Paradise, and Sunset Rock, which were nearer Giant Forest but along the edge of the park's central belt of Big Trees rather than among them. As the first of the new campgrounds opened in 1924, White cheerfully reported to NPS director Mather that the plan was moving forward and that his office had been able "to close additional public auto camps in the heart of Giant Forest."[20] Nonetheless, many visitors continued to camp in Giant Forest, and the condition of its vegetation, including the "indestructible" Big Trees, remained poor. To address this issue, Superintendent White instituted a revegetation effort.

In October 1925, the Sequoia Park inaugurated its "Landscape Department," to replant "a considerable area of denuded camp grounds at Giant Forest." To begin, auto and foot traffic were excluded from that section of the park, while rangers Lawrence Cook, Irvin Kerr, and others planted 2,057 young fir, pine, and cedar trees and prepared a *Sequoia gigantea* seedbed to produce seedlings for the following year's planting. At the same time, Superintendent White wrote to William Taylor, chief of the U.S. Department of Agriculture's Bureau of Plant Industry in Washington, D.C., to request grass seed and information on which trees and shrubs the bureau might supply to support the park's revegetation effort. Taylor responded quickly, but the letter came not with supplies and instructions, but as an apology. He no longer had grass seed for distribution or any California species native to

Figure 4.2. Campers cheerfully erected tents, enjoyed meals, and parked cars around the base of the Big Trees at the Firwood camping area in Sequoia National Park, circa 1935. From RG 79, entry 187, U.S. National Archives, College Park, MD, box 25.

the park's area. As a consolation perhaps, Taylor instead offered to provide a variety of species collected from "the mountains of southern China at altitudes ranging from 5,000, to 10,000 to 12,000, feet." Unsurprisingly, White did not respond to Taylor's offer and apparently never requested any of these exotic species for the national park.[21]

The effort to restore Sequoia's Giant Forest was spearheaded by White, but NPS director Mather also supported it. Mather had been keenly concerned about the park's Big Trees since at least 1920, when his report to the secretary of the interior had singled out the park and praised the environmental protection work being done there. Nevertheless, trees continued to die in the park, especially in the Lodgepole campground. The rangers suspected that the loss was caused by some sort of root disease but were uncertain, so they asked the Washington headquarters for professional assistance. Mather, who preferred to consult with specialists employed by other federal agencies rather than to hire such specialists into the NPS, decided to approach the Forest Service. On November 4, 1925, he contacted Paul G. Redington, the USFS's California District forester. In particular, Mather asked Redington to help the NPS with the damage that "intensive camping and heavy foot traffic" was causing to Sequoia's Big Trees.[22] Redington considered Mather's request and decided that the expert who could best assist the NPS would be a colleague at the San Francisco office of the Bureau of Plant Industry.

E. P. Meinecke

Emilio Pepe Michael Meinecke was born in Alameda, California, on July 26, 1869. His German parents and grandparents had been early arrivals to American California and had also quickly prospered. Meinecke's maternal grandfather opened San Francisco's first bookstore about 1850, while his father ran an importing business and later also served as the German consul general at the port of San Francisco. "Invalidism" in the family necessitated Meinecke's moving to Germany when he was a boy, but his parents decided to keep him there for his education, which eventually included studies in botany, especially mycology, at Freiburg, Leipzig, and Bonn universities, and a doctorate from Germany's oldest university, Heidelberg, in 1893. Meinecke's interest in botany may have had its immediate source in his mother, who was an active gardener and leader of the California Floral Society in San Francisco, but it was also fed by a deeper family interest in plants. His maternal great-uncle had been none other than Matthias J. Schleiden, a professor of botany at Friedrich Schiller University in Jena, Germany, and a principal developer of the cell theory in plants. Following graduation, Meinecke worked as a researcher in several German universities (including a turn as assistant to Robert Hartig, who was one of the first researchers to apply scientific methodologies to forest pathology), but he changed direction in 1907 when he accepted a teaching post at the Universidad de la Plata in Argentina. A fluent speaker of Spanish, German, English, French, and Danish, Meinecke taught a variety of courses and enjoyed field trips into the Andes, but he nevertheless left for California in 1909 because he found the university too conservative.[23]

Shortly after he arrived in the San Francisco Bay Area, Meinecke developed a serious eye infection, which prompted him to travel into the Sierra Nevada Mountains to speed his recovery. As he prepared for this sojourn, Meinecke learned that a USFS ranger school would shortly be held at California Hot Springs in the mountain foothills of Tulare County. According to one account, Meinecke was intrigued and decided to attend the school to "get acquainted with budding American forestry." Once there, he met many foresters, and they persuaded him to present a few lessons, which left a very favorable impression among the foresters. A short time later, Meinecke was asked to join the San Francisco office of the U.S. Department of Agriculture's Bureau of Plant Industry (BPI) as a consulting forest pathologist to District 5 (California) of the U.S. Forest Service.[24]

Figure 4.3. E. P. Meinecke, circa 1928. Courtesy of National Park Service Historic Photograph Collection, Harpers Ferry (WV) Center for Media Services.

In the years that followed, "Doc" Meinecke, as he was almost universally known, earned renown for his many contributions to the field of forestry, especially concerning the diseases of incense cedar (*Calocedrus decurrens*), white fir (*Abies concolor*), western yellow pine (*Pinus ponderosa*), and sugar pine (*Pinus lambertiana*), which are coniferous trees common to the Sierra Nevada. At the same time, Meinecke developed a reputation as "a colorful personality" (fig. 4.3). Professionally he was "never a man to let his position be misunderstood," asserted a close colleague, Frederick Baker, and someone who had been "more heartily cussed out as [a] stiff-necked perfectionist" than other foresters. Nevertheless, Meinecke's peers respected his research, his analytic and applied field methods, and his well-trained assistants, even as they (generally) accepted his even-tempered but forthright manner. According to Baker, Meinecke was a professional who "stood persistently for something foreign to the current American forestry development—for a brand of forestry concerned more with biology than economics, silvics rather than politics, and for a professional society dedicated to such forestry." An active and respected pathologist, Meinecke regularly participated in the Society of American Foresters, the American Phytopathological Association, the California Academy of Sciences, the American Association for the Advancement of Science, and others. He was not, however, a narrowly focused, uninteresting drudge. He was instead a man of great talent with a wide range of interests. A skilled illustrator (he created the drawings for his own publications), Meinecke painted in oils and watercolors as well as collected fine art. His love of music was well known—he wrote for and played both the piano and the pipe organ "extremely well"—and he was an avid reader of literature. In addition, Meinecke enjoyed entertaining guests at his home, who must have relished these invitations because he was a gourmand and frequently praised as a superb chef. Outdoors Meinecke was equally comfortable. He enjoyed riding horses, albeit primarily during fieldwork, and was considered an accomplished skier and figure skater. These interests led him to join San Francisco's Commonwealth Club, the Society of California Pioneers, Pro Musica, the Sierra Ski Club, and the Wilderness Society. A man with a sharp and inquisitive mind, plus talent, taste, and energy, Meinecke nonetheless felt that he had an important weakness. According to Frederick Baker, "the 'one thing,' [Meinecke] said to me, 'I have never been able to learn—how to be bored.'"[25]

A Prescription for Sequoia

As early as 1915, Meinecke demonstrated his interest in forestry issues in the national parks when he attended (but did not speak at) the National Parks Conference in Berkeley, California. Organized by future NPS director

Stephen Mather, the meeting attracted a wide range of national park experts on such subjects as engineering, landscape design, construction, biology, entomology, and forestry. It was not, however, until sometime shortly before August 1925 that Meinecke began to focus on the effects of heavy and unrestricted human activity on trees and other forest vegetation in recreational settings. At about that time, he and another Bureau of Plant Industry pathologist, Carl Hartley, began exchanging correspondence and publications about the management of these vulnerable landscapes. An avid outdoorsman, Meinecke suspected that the increasing public access to wooded sites might ultimately destroy the latter unless properly regulated. It was in the midst of these exchanges that Mather, now NPS director, approached Paul Redington for the Forest Service's assistance with Sequoia National Park. Redington subsequently referred Mather's request to his district's forest pathologist, "Doc" Meinecke, who visited the park in mid-May 1926. During his four-day inspection, Meinecke also counseled the park staff on how to protect the Big Trees, especially General Sherman, the largest tree, and about the planting of young trees. They immediately began to implement his recommendations, even as Superintendent White, in his monthly report to NPS director Mather, praised Meinecke's advice as "invaluable."[26]

The following month, Meinecke presented a more formal, nineteen-page "memorandum" to the park that summarized his findings and clearly laid out a series of recommended actions. The problem, he assured the NPS, was clear—the public was loving Sequoia's Big Trees to death, with the largest and oldest ones attracting the greatest attention. "The bigger the tree," Meinecke quipped, "the greater is the desire of the tourist to make its acquaintance, whether he enters the grove from curiosity or is moved by deeper feelings of admiration and reverence." Moreover, as he observed in a follow-up piece, the public generally was not satisfied to view these giants from a distance. Instead, people preferred "to come up close to the trees and to touch them with their hands. There is," Meinecke admitted, "a peculiar attraction in camping under the shade and protection of huge trees 2,000 or 3,000 years old." Unfortunately, Meinecke cautioned, the Big Trees could not withstand their suitors' constant attentions. "It must be remembered that the very trees which make for the beauty of the Park are not the young and vigorous saplings and poles or even younger standards," which could be found throughout the park. Instead, people came to experience "that class of large and picturesque trees which are approaching the end of a long life," and thus "their recuperative power is not what it was in the time of their youth." Centuries of fires, heavy storms, lightning, fungal diseases, and insects had injured the largest trees at many points, but most especially at ground level, where the trunk met the roots. As an example, Meinecke noted that only 36 percent of the General Sherman tree's trunk remained "effectively connected" to any roots.

In such a state, the tree was handicapped in one of its most vital points," and, Meinecke stated, "any additional burden may prove fatal." The old trees' sensitivity to even slight disturbances meant that the NPS had to carefully manage the environment surrounding each tree. Unfortunately, under current park practice, that environment was often a shambles. "One of the deplorable consequences of camping and long continued milling of tourists around selected favorites," continued Meinecke, "is the almost complete eradication of undergrowth." The obliteration of these plants made areas around Big Trees less attractive, but the loss was not primarily an aesthetic issue. The missing vegetation was key to the park's future because it included the young Big Trees that one day would replace the current ones. Moreover, in the zone where undergrowth had been demolished, Meinecke explained, the soil had become compacted, which threatened the living trees. The roots of Big Trees, he pointed out, are shallow and can extend 40 to 50 feet from a tree's base, "always keeping relatively close to the surface. It is a general rule that such roots are very sensitive to any change in the surface level and in the depth and character of the soil which covers them." The loss of undergrowth and the soil's compaction had caused the most important and active roots to be compressed to the point of destruction. Furthermore, "the chemistry of the soil had been influenced by the accumulated ashes from countless camp fires . . . the slow penetration of [these] salt solutions into the deeper soil must finally affect the roots of the Big Trees," which normally grew in acidic soils.[27]

Without changes in current practice and the advent of remedial actions, Meinecke warned, the oldest Big Trees would die. Park authorities had to adopt measures that would minimize and counteract past injuries and degradations as well as prevent new ones. These measures, Meinecke urged, should not be "direct" ones, because "the basic constitution of the parks more or less precludes" them. Moreover, Meinecke recognized, either consciously or unconsciously, that visitors primarily came from cities to escape urban life's regimentation and to immerse themselves in nature as an act of devotion. As a consequence, "both remedial and preventive action," he counseled, "must be predominantly indirect." Direct measures would remind visitors too much of the world that they had recently escaped when setting out for the park. With "indirection" as a guiding principle, Meinecke recommended that the compacted zones be reforested with *Sequoia gigantea* and the other plant species that had been destroyed by visitors, and that any camping areas situated under the Big Trees be abandoned. A burst of sunlight onto a shadowy and threatening situation, Meinecke's report supported Superintendent White's efforts and expanded on them. Sequoia's authorities, insisted the pathologist, had to restore the battered vegetation of Giant Forest. Nonetheless, the process would be contentious and take nearly eighty years to complete.[28]

California State Redwood Parks and Beyond

E. P. Meinecke produced his Big Trees report for the national park, but other agencies read it too. Early in 1927, California's deputy state forester, W. B. Rider, approached Meinecke for similar advice. California was expanding its park holdings, and Rider, impressed with the pathologist's report for Sequoia, had decided to ask Meinecke for his analysis of the ailing coast redwoods (*Sequoia sempervirens*) at Big Basin Redwood Park near Santa Cruz and at several coastal redwood groves under consideration for inclusion in the budding state park system. Visiting the several sites, Meinecke found a situation remarkably similar to that at Sequoia National Park—people "attracted by the largest trees and by the finest and most beautiful spots" were causing environmental degradation from an "excessive concentration of traffic."[29] Consequently, Meinecke's observations in his California report were similar to what he had related to the NPS. The older coast redwoods, like their Big Tree cousins, have surface roots that are particularly sensitive to the ongoing soil compaction caused by trampling underfoot and motor vehicles. In addition, young vegetation was being physically damaged and destroyed by the same agents, and campfires were degrading soil chemistry.

Unsurprisingly, Meinecke's recommendations for the state of California were similar to what he had offered to Sequoia, but before he offered them in his report, the pathologist entered terrain he had avoided before. In the conclusion that preceded his recommendations, Meinecke stepped away from the biological sciences and into the social ones to suggest that park policies had to take into account the attitudes of the public toward the giant trees. Individual redwoods were not everyday objects or their groves everyday spaces to visitors; instead, they were viewed as special and outside the realm of the ordinary. "To some," Meinecke offered, "they are objects of wonder and amazement, unique in size and age. To others they offer ideal surroundings for a pleasant outing and camping. To a third group the rare beauty of the parks will make the strongest appeal. Still others will find spiritual uplift and emotion." These views, of course, could overlap, and since they arose "from cultural sources," they had to be acknowledged "in any well reasoned policy." Meinecke recognized that the redwood parks were sacred space—an escape from urban life for the campers and others who visited. Consequently, they had to be guarded as "austere temples" of nature. "The legitimate demands of those who desire to carry the pleasures of the city life into the country are best taken care of by the many summer resorts along the highway. They are out of place in the Parks themselves." Without directly stating it, Meinecke recognized that the campers who came to California's state parks were pilgrims seeking connections they could not make in ordinary places.[30]

Meinecke's recommendations for managing the state parks were no less expansive than his characterization of their meaning. First, he focused on the parks' sacred qualities by pointing out how some conflicting uses were spatially intermingled when they should be discrete. Inappropriate "heavy uses," such as campgrounds, stores, and parking areas, were permitted within visually attractive redwood groves, but they should not be. Instead, he suggested, a "segregation of areas" was needed to isolate mismatched activities from each other. The redwood groves that provided the impetus for the existing and proposed parks, in particular, needed to be functionally separate from other, less valuable areas. Once a park's land survey was complete, the heavy uses needed to be directed onto lesser lands. This change would bring an enhanced sense of place to the parks. After spatial reorganization, "the main groups of Redwoods," Meinecke declared, would "thereby resume the rank they held before a heavy and uncontrollable invasion tended to cheapen their prodigious beauty in the eyes of the public." Next, he turned to the primary cause of the redwoods' decline—camping. Since camping areas suffered the heaviest trampling and soil compaction, this recreation should be "absolutely banned from the main [redwood groves] and concentrated in the marginal areas." If it was not, the environment would only degrade further. Third, Meinecke addressed the management of traffic in the parks' sacred spaces. "If soil conditions are to be brought back to normal," he warned, "the public can not be permitted as heretofore to use the main part of the groves indiscriminately." Instead, trails and paths had to be established, and the public trained to stay on them. On this last point, Meinecke offered a caveat that again illustrates his understanding of the cultural role of these emerging state parks. In city parks, signs and fences were used to constrain and direct movement, but he warned, "Both are distinctively objectionable in the atmosphere of the Redwood parks," where they smacked of urban order and control, "and should be used only as an ultimate resort." Instead, he indicated, the "public can be guided through suggestion." The typical camper or tourist, "coming from city or town, neither feels perfectly at home in the forest nor is he inclined to exert himself unduly. He follows the beaten path." Consequently, visitor management could be subtle and nonurban in character. A carefully placed log, fallen limb, or rock, or a thoughtfully planted shrub "serves as well as a solid fence. . . . The best trail is the one which leads through green undergrowth" rather than between fences or on a constructed walkway. An optimally designed trail system would cover the least amount of space while simultaneously providing public access. Finally, Meinecke recommended how the parks' trampled and barren areas could be restored. Physically aerating the soil with a light harrow or a handheld spading fork were effective interventions, and the long-term exclusion of people would most facilitate recovery, but the planting of indigenous species should also be a part of any restoration. The reintroduction of ferns and flowering plants would "contribute strongly to the desired end," but he once again raised the specter of urban life and cautioned that "unless this is done with great skill the effect will be one of artificiality and consequently undesirable." If planners were not careful, a wild redwood grove could end up looking like a city park.[31]

Meinecke's reports for the Sequoia National Park and California's state forester shook both concerned and complacent park managers throughout the state and beyond and brought widespread attention to the problem of vegetation damage from excessive tourist traffic, especially by campers. One reader, NPS director Mather, was so impressed that he asked Meinecke to again assist the Park Service through an investigation of the Big Trees situation at Yosemite National Park's Mariposa Grove, which was heavily visited by tourists and filled with campers, and which Mather feared was deteriorating. After an examination of the site during the summer of 1927, Meinecke moved on to reexamine Sequoia's Giant Forest and then traveled to "a series of camping grounds in Inyo, Los Angeles, San Bernardino and San Diego Counties" to investigate their environmental conditions. True to his reputation, Meinecke was blunt and unequivocal in his September report for the NPS director. The situation at the Mariposa Grove was similar to what he had found at Giant Forest the previous year, and if the Park Service wished to preserve the redwoods, "camping should be banned altogether from the immediate vicinity of Big Trees. . . . The farther removed the camping grounds are from the trees the safer will be the latter from injury. Even at a distance of 150 to 200 feet from camp a large specimen exerts a strong attraction, and attraction inevitably means visiting and trampling. . . . My unqualified recommendation is to prohibit camping in or near Big Trees."[32]

As Meinecke's reports were read by U.S. park and forest managers, the negative impacts caused by the swelling number of forest visitors in general and campers in particular were becoming increasingly apparent throughout the western United States. Soon administrators were contacting Meinecke for his assistance. He agreed in April 1929, for instance, to consult on fir pathology at Glacier National Park, a place he had not previously visited. At about the same time, Meinecke's superiors recognized the high quality and usefulness of the pathologist's work. In July 1929, Meinecke was promoted to the Bureau of Plant Industry's principal pathologist post and placed in charge of research planning for the entire country. Moreover, his responsibilities expanded in other areas as well—he was named consulting pathologist to the entire national park system, which caused his park visits to skyrocket. During 1930 and 1931, for instance, Meinecke consulted on forest disease issues at Mesa Verde, Crater Lake, Mount Rainier, Sequoia,

Hawaii Volcanoes, Grand Teton, Rocky Mountains, and Glacier National Parks, and he spoke at a variety of local, regional, and national meetings on protected-area forestry and campgrounds. The latter, he generally argued, tended to become run down and then were abandoned for new ones, which subsequently suffered the same fate. A well-considered policy on camp-grounds and a system for their rotation rather than abandonment was his prescription for this wasteful practice.[33]

Respect for Meinecke and his analyses rapidly grew within the NPS, and on April 1, 1931, its director, Horace M. Albright, mailed a copy of Meinecke's California redwood parks report to every national park super-intendent with a letter declaring it to be of "vital interest" because the principles it espoused could be applied widely to the problem of campground degradation in the national parks. One month later, Albright further cemented the relationship between his agency and the pathologist when he signed off on a forestry policy that formalized the growing role of the BPI in general and Meinecke in particular for the Park Service. The Bureau of Plant Industry, Albright announced, "is the agency designated to furnish techni-cal advice relative to fungus diseases and pathological conditions affecting the park trees and forests." Furthermore, should a park need to approach the bureau about these or other issues, "Dr. E. P. Meinecke . . . has been designated as general advisor to the National Park Service in matters of for-est pathology." Continuing, Albright turned to the issue of "Camp Ground Protection" because these camps were generally "located within timber." Paraphrasing Meinecke's earlier reports about the environmental impacts of compaction on tree roots, Albright again directed park superintendents to seek "the advice of the forest pathologists of the Bureau of Plant Industry," which meant they were to contact Meinecke.[34]

"A Camp Ground Policy"

Meinecke's 1926 and 1927 reports, as well as his subsequent analyses for western national parks and forests, clearly indicate that he was inclined to use spatial strategies to control and mitigate camping's environmental dam-age while simultaneously maintaining the appeal of sites for campers and other visitors. It was not until early 1932, however, that he fully embraced the possibilities offered by a spatial approach and produced the automo-bile campground plan that soon became, and long remained, the model for parks and forests throughout the United States.

The genesis for Meinecke's auto campground plan apparently occurred during the summer and fall of 1931. His park and forest consultations con-tinued to focus primarily on forest pathology issues, but increasingly he was

also asked his views toward campground damage. The problem was growing starker, and those supervisors responsible for dealing with it hungered
for his recommendations. The eastern Sierra Nevada, where the mountains
are remarkably steep and relatively dry, was an environment particularly
susceptible to degradation and a vexing problem for the Forest Service. In
early July, Meinecke traveled with L. A. Barrett, the California District's
assistant forester in charge of lands and recreation, on an inspection of the
region's campgrounds to ascertain what might be done to remedy the situation. The destinations visited on that trip and any discussions about what
the two men saw went unrecorded, but Meinecke's interest in the subject was
clearly enhanced. Before the month was out, he informed his Washington
supervisor, Haven Metcalf, that he would be making still another inspection
tour "through Park Service, Forest Service and Municipal Camp Grounds"
in November to learn more about how they were being managed. Neither
Meinecke nor Barrett left accounts of their campground inspections, but the
assistant forester must have asked the pathologist for a formal statement of
his views, because Meinecke worked up an analysis of the situation over the
winter of 1931–1932. This product he presented at a USFS conference in the
late winter / early spring of 1932. Meinecke then revised and expanded this
talk into his most momentous report, "A Camp Ground Policy," which he
handed over to the Forest Service on April 2, 1932.[35]

Meinecke's newest analysis built upon his previous explanations and recommendations, but with some notable changes in emphases. Where people
on foot had once been the peak concern, "A Camp Ground Policy" now
fastened onto the greater impacts of automobiles. Unlike pedestrians, cars
rapidly and thoroughly compacted soil, frequently broke large branches, and
barked many trees, even as they poisoned the ground by leaking gasoline
and motor oil. This combination of shocks, Meinecke declared, led inevitably to a severe loss of vegetation. "A single invasion of a new camp site by
an automobile would soon be repaired," he admitted, but such was not the
situation at many public campgrounds. Instead, "it is the constant repetition
of the injurious action, day after day, year after year, that ends in disaster,
and the final result is the destruction of the elements that make a certain
locality suitable for camping." Using his own drawings to illustrate the analysis, Meinecke argued that unregulated or "self-made" campsites tended to
sprawl and waste space as they became increasingly degraded as campers'
cars kept striking and crushing vegetation in vulnerable locations. Of course,
it was not just campers and their cars that were responsible for the damage.
The Forest Service unwittingly fostered damage through its libertarian policies; it needed to regulate camping through design and management changes.
Looking forward to new campgrounds, Meinecke encouraged the USFS to
reduce the randomness of camper movement and trampling. To achieve this

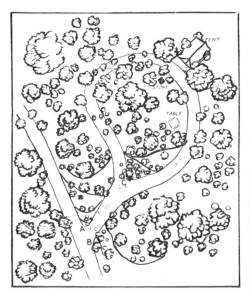

Figure 4.4a. An unregulated, "self-made" campsite. According to E. P. Meinecke, these sites wasted space and resulted in the "steady whittling away" of the vegetation at points A, B, and C, which were most likely to be struck and crushed by automobiles. From E. P. Meinecke, *A Camp Ground Policy* (U.S. Forest Service, 1932), 6.

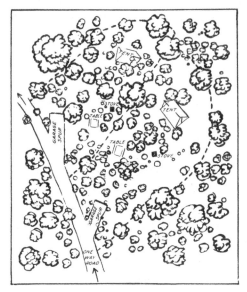

Figure 4.4b. Plan of the regulated development in a Meinecke campground, including "garage" spurs, tables, stoves, and tents. These two campsites cover the same amount of space as the one unregulated campsite, and a minimum of vegetation has been removed. From E. P. Meinecke, *A Camp Ground Policy* (U.S. Forest Service, 1932), 13.

end, the USFS should no longer allow campers "to do their own haphazard planning" but should instead first identify a potential campground, analyze the ground, and then divide it up "into individual camp sites of legitimate size, each offering approximately as much privacy, shade and other advantages as the other, based on the vegetation on the ground and on the preservation of its essential features" (fig. 4.4a and fig. 4.4b).[36]

Concentrating on the individual campsite, Meinecke emphasized that his approach was premised "on the definite fixation of certain essential camp features," namely the automobile, the fireplace, and the camp table. For environmental damage to be controlled, these elements had to be placed in a permanent arrangement that would foster several outcomes. First, they had to be "comfortable and convenient" so that the average camper would not attempt to alter the site. Second, these features clearly had to appear as an integrated unit so "that there can be no doubt in the mind of the visitor newly arriving" that this indeed was a campsite. Third, "the ground plan of the temporary home," that is, the campsite, had to be "logical and practical" so that a camper "will have no incentive for a rearrangement." The advantage of his approach, Meinecke felt, was obvious. "Natural and permanent trails [will] develop between car, fire place, tent, and table. The disorderly and destructive tramping about, that characterizes the unregulated camp, is obviated since there is no need for it." Of course, a raw site might include an excess of vegetation before it was developed for camping, so Meinecke recommended that personnel should identify which shrubs and trees would make a site less comfortable and convenient, and then remove them before the campground was opened. Employing domestic imagery, Meinecke suggested that "the task is much like furnishing a home overcrowded with all kinds of furniture. It consists in the wise elimination of the encumbering surplus."[37]

The best campsite, however, would be of little value if it was not conveniently accessible. Therefore, Meinecke insisted that the automobile traffic within a campground also needed to be planned in order to minimize negative impacts and maximize campers' positive experiences. "The regulated camp ground," Meinecke insisted, "should be provided with roads, laid out and made, instead of being mere tracks resulting from the chance driving of tourist cars." The latter sort of roads tended to be wide and chaotic, which wasted space, produced more mud or dust, led to increased vegetation losses, and resulted in a less pleasant camping experience. Consequently, Meinecke recommended that "in the interests of space economy . . . they be one-way roads," which he again illustrated with his own hand.[38]

Meinecke primarily recommended one-way roads because they use a minimum of space, but he identified three related advantages as well. First, since the road was narrow, it offered less chance that a driver could "break out" into undamaged vegetation. When a road was slim and designed to facilitate forward movement alone, then a driver found it difficult to turn sharply to the left or right. Second, a campground composed of one-way loop roads could be readily expanded as demand grew, because "new roads leading into the older ones can be added [easily]." Finally, planned one-way roads made possible "an essential feature" of his plan—"the fixation of the automobile" (fig. 4.5)[39]

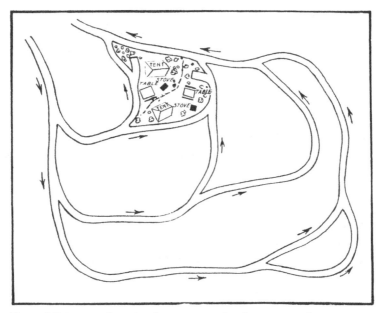

Figure 4.5. Layout of a Meinecke campground with its system of one-way roads. Only two campsites are illustrated, each with its fixed table, stove, and garage spur. The road system can be easily expanded with new loops, which allow for more campsites. From E. P. Meinecke, *A Camp Ground Policy* (U.S. Forest Service, 1932), 10.

A moving automobile that wound among the trees was, in Meinecke's view, camping's "most destructive element." As a consequence, campers could not, he declared, be allowed to use cars freely. Instead their autos had to be "fixed at the entrance to the camp site and not permitted to enter the latter at all." Again employing a domestic image, Meinecke insisted that this control could be "easily accomplished by providing for each site a definite garage in the shape of a short spur leading off at a suitable angle from the one-way road." However, Meinecke warned, a campground planner should not attempt to be subtle when laying one out. Each "garage spur" had to be "cleared of vegetation," "plainly marked," and "immediately recognized as such" so that campers would use them. Of course, Meinecke recognized, campers might try to move their cars off the garage spur and into a camp-site or beyond, which was unacceptable. Signs and fences could be used to prevent such movement, but Meinecke was no more in favor of them now than he had been when he recommended against their use in California's redwood parks. The camper, he explained, did not simply pursue beautiful natural scenery. In language that reveals how much Meinecke perceived camping's romantic antimodernism, he declared that the camper also "seeks release from the restrictions of town and city life. He wants a certain amount of freedom, and in this mood he resents too obvious directions such as sign boards with prohibitions and demands." Furthermore, Meinecke's frequent interactions with NPS personnel would have reinforced his aversion to urban methods, since the national parks had been pursuing a policy of "atmosphere preservation" and "landscape harmonization" for nearly two decades. That is, wherever possible, the NPS attempted to maintain the natural aesthetic by blending its developments with the surroundings and thus shielding the public from human intrusions into the landscape. So instead of signs, Meinecke recommended an indirect control method that was less likely to disturb a site's sacred feeling for the camper who had come to escape the city and be rejuvenated in nature. "Use the tourist's desire to protect his property," Meinecke declared, "particularly his car, from injury." At strategic points along a campground road and around a campsite's spur, obstacles, preferably rocks, "sufficiently heavy so as not to invite moving by the average camper, are placed in such a way that, in self-preservation, the camper will not drive over them. . . . They keep the car in place" and consequently reduced the destruction of vegetation.[40]

Having identified the key elements for planning new campgrounds, Meinecke named his guiding principles—regulation, economic use of space, and permanency—and provided an illustration of two improved campsites. Contrasting his controlled approach with unregulated camping, he promised less environmental damage, greater privacy, and a doubling of carrying capacity because the "track space" (i.e., the de-vegetated areas where cars had repeatedly traveled) that had been created by the formerly unregulated auto would never appear, which would allow two well-vegetated campsites to occupy the same area formerly used by one degraded site.[41]

Turning from the creation of new campgrounds to the restoration of existing but damaged ones, Meinecke admitted that it was "far more difficult to make over old and run-down camps, to repair the damage done and to convert them into permanently useful units." An administrator would need to decide site by site whether enough vegetation remained and how far he was willing and able to commit to restoration. If the situation was not hopeless, then Meinecke recommended that the guiding principles during reconstruction should be the same ones underlying a new site's development—"the introduction of made one-way roads, of the fixed garage spurs and the fixed fireplaces together with the protection of the key trees." The rate of recovery, he warned, could be slow and would vary depending on the soil type, the degree of degradation, and the climate. To speed along the process, soil could be "loosened carefully with the aid of a spading fork" and replanted with "native trees at strategic points." However, he again cautioned that, "landscaping in the usual sense," that is, like a domestic garden or an urban park, "has no place . . . where the visitor seeks at least the illusion of wilderness."[42] Plantings that followed straight lines or that introduced species commonly used in cities would be rejected because they would express the urban order that campers had traveled to escape. Even landscaping, Meinecke hinted, could too strongly resemble a campers' life at home. Finally, in recognition of the dismal state of most Forest Service camping areas, Meinecke recommended that new grounds be opened as older ones were closed so that the latter could recover, be redesigned, and then rotated with the newer ones.

Meinecke's auto campground proposals became U.S. Forest Service policy in California in short order. The number of auto campers visiting the state's national forests had continued to climb despite the economic depression, so a management plan that could mitigate camper damage and enhance the camping experience while increasing campground capacity strongly appealed to the district's top administrators. To get the word out, they rapidly distributed mimeographed copies, but these were followed by printed copies after October 1932, because demand was high both in California and around the country. Field personnel soon began to implement Meinecke's recommendations—sometimes, if they were lucky, after taking a training course with Meinecke himself.[43]

"A Camp Ground Policy" grew out of E. P. Meinecke's campground tour with the USFS's L. A. Barrett, but it was the National Park Service's support for Meinecke's proposals that prompted him to complete this document on April 2. NPS director Horace Albright knew that Meinecke had been working on campground policy "for some time" when he asked the pathologist for a fuller, more formal, and typed version on April 1. Overnight and "under high pressure," Meinecke revised and expanded the policy paper he had recently presented to Forest Service supervisors so that it could be read aloud at an NPS superintendents' conference in Arkansas from April 4 to 6. Meinecke presented mimeographed copies of this second and more complete version of his proposals to both the Park and Forest Services on April 2, and within days he was receiving requests for copies "from a number of men all over the country."[44]

Transforming Sequoia

NPS administrators were no less impressed with "A Camp Ground Policy" than their peers at the USFS. By June 1932, numerous copies of the report had been distributed to Park Service personnel, and Meinecke quickly began to receive requests for his services from throughout the NPS. "The demands for advice and visits are coming fast and furious," wrote an exasperated Meinecke to his supervisor in Washington, D.C. "The Yosemite is howling, the Sequoia Park bombards me with letters and the Mesa Verde is putting all its new 6-year camp ground plans off until I come to help them. . . . I almost wish I had never written that 'Camp Ground Policy.'" Despite his momentary frustration, Meinecke visited numerous national parks, and soon "major changes began to appear in the[ir] campgrounds."[45]

The first and among the most notable of Meinecke's national park consultations was Sequoia, which was where the practicality of his ideas were initially put to the test. In early May Meinecke took the time to mail a copy of "A Camp Ground Policy" directly to Superintendent John R. White. The report, Meinecke told White in his cover letter, "expresses a number of things which I have, in the past, had occasion to discuss with you and culminates in definite proposals for the treatment of camps and for a definite policy." These earlier discussions clearly had left Meinecke with a strongly positive impression of both White and the park, because he told the superintendent that he "would be very grateful to have your reactions" to the report. Meinecke previously had not solicited such feedback from any national park personnel, and he would not have to wait long for a reply. White's response came before the month was out. The report, the superintendent declared, was "splendid." He then offered a variety of observations, asked for twelve additional copies for his rangers, and requested that Meinecke visit the park in September 1932. Meinecke thanked White for his comments, sent him the copies, and agreed to a consultation in mid-September. On the same day that White wrote to Meinecke, Sequoia's superintendent also forwarded his copy of the report to his campground construction foreman with a note. "There is no more important work ahead of us this season than that of systematizing our campgrounds, restoration of areas already injured and protection in areas already developed or to be developed." As a consequence, White told his foreman, you will make a "careful study of the report of Dr. E. P. Meinecke of the Forest Service [because] his ideas and suggestions will be followed."[46] In short order, Meinecke's proposals were being applied to the park.

During the summer of 1932, Sequoia personnel began to transform one of the park's older and most heavily used camping areas—Lodgepole—into "an example of . . . a protected campground." By the end of June, ranger Irvin Kerr could report that about three-quarters of a mile of one-way, rock-lined roads with 110 "short parking spurs" leading to accompanying campsites had been developed. These new features, testified Kerr to Chief Ranger Cook, would achieve the design's principal purpose—"protect the [campground's] trees and other vegetation" from the destructive movements of cars. In addition, he assured Cook, the new campsites also had the park's campers in mind. Each site had been situated "to give everyone plenty of room and have natural barriers between camps where possible." Finally, Kerr reported that thirty-five new campsite fireplaces would be completed by July 1 and that they would "do a great deal towards preserving the campgrounds as [they] will reduce the damage to trees and other plants as well as tend to keep fires in one place." Moving beyond the immediate campground, Kerr had boulders placed twenty feet to a hundred feet from the edge of the nearby Kaweah River to keep automobiles away from the water, even as he ordered the remains of "old camps, fireplaces and other rubbish" removed from between the line of boulders and the river. The result was an open and attractive shore area where visitors could "stroll without stumbling through camps." Superintendent White was so pleased with his rangers' efforts that he wrote Horace Albright on July 5 to emphasize that when the director visited Sequoia at the end of that month, he had to see the "good work" at Lodgepole campground. The water system had been completed, adequate pit toilets created, and new camp tables, garbage racks, and fireplaces installed. Moreover, White emphasized, "above all we have laid out the campgrounds scientifically along the lines of Dr. Meinecke's suggestions, having in view the protection of foliage and trees for all time." In light of the summer's developments and with Meinecke's visit almost upon them, Chief Ranger Cook took the next step in early September. For a year, he had been advocating for defined roads and definite campsites at Sequoia's second most heavily used campground—Firwood—and he now sketched out a plan to modify it in the manner suggested by Meinecke.[47] By the time the pathologist arrived for his consultation on September 24, 1932, many of his proposals had become reality.

Among the many rangers at Sequoia who would work with Meinecke during his September visit was twenty-nine-year-old Lemuel L. Garrison. "Lon," as the ranger was generally known, was enjoying the first of what would become forty years with the National Park Service when, in his words, Meinecke came to Sequoia "to provide professional oversight and control as we tested his philosophies and plans." According to the young Garrison's account of his 1932 summer at Sequoia, he spent much of his time on Lodgepole campground's reconstruction and with Meinecke when he visited that September. The pathologist, Garrison related, "was fascinated with my psychology degree and my belief that it was a proper background for a park ranger." For his part, the young ranger enjoyed the time he spent with Meinecke. Like many others, Garrison found the park's consultant to be "a rigid and precise scientist but also a lively and inquisitive fellow." In particular, Garrison was charmed by Meinecke's fascination with "the philosophy which lends to the creation of this new land management and park protection agency" as well as the park service's interpretive programs. Meinecke was clearly concerned about the future of the national parks as both nature reserves and as sacred destinations, because he confronted Garrison with the contradiction captured by these two issues. According to the ranger, Meinecke "challenged me as to which direction [the NPS] might be going in the apparent conflict between preservation and public use." The pathologist had developed "A Camp Ground Policy" and come to Sequoia because this conflict was undermining the park service's mission to preserve the natural environment. Garrison, nevertheless, was optimistic. He was keeping his eyes open, the ranger insisted, because he "could not see why we could not follow both directions."[48] As it turned out, preservation and public use did come into a better balance, but not because Garrison was an optimist. Instead, Meinecke and other experts developed techniques to contain and control the environmental damage caused by campers and other national park visitors, which park personnel then effectively implemented.

The importance of garage spurs, fixed campsite tables, tent sites, and fireplaces became clear to Sequoia's engineer Jack Diehl, its landscape architect Tom Carpenter, and work crew chief Irvin Kerr as they pursued the reconstruction of Lodgepole Campground. They came to recognize how each component in Meinecke's plan played its part in remedying the campground's environmental degradation. Nevertheless, the critical feature for them was the new roads, because it was the roads that would exert the greatest control over automobiles and so most reduce vegetation damage. Practical concerns, however, confronted them from the beginning as they struggled to merge Meinecke's prescription with the campground's landscape. They had no precise maps for Lodgepole, which had developed haphazardly, so they were forced to survey and sketch the grounds as best they could before building "to fit the topography." Armed with new maps, they developed "a series of interconnected one-way loops," with river stones of four hundred to six hundred pounds along them as barriers. Luckily, rocks were abundant, but transporting them proved a challenge. After trying a number of approaches, they ultimately chose to move the boulders on "a stone boat which was just a heavy wood or metal sled we towed around with a truck." Once a section of road and its garage spurs were complete, the rangers would "test" each one in their pickup truck to see if it was functional. Practice, they quickly discovered, was different from theory. Some of the first roads, Garrison explained in his autobiography, "were too narrow and the curves too tight. In our zeal to keep them strictly one-way we were aggressively restrictive." Early garage spurs also worked poorly because the rangers sometimes made "the angle of approach too abrupt." Moreover, they learned that most of them "had difficulty reversing their cars to get out of a parking spur and into a loop road" during these tests. Nevertheless, the rangers and crew persevered, adapting Meinecke's proposals as best they could while looking forward to the inauguration of their efforts. It turned out to be a disappointment. According to Garrison, "when we opened the new roads and spurs to the public, there was very little public acclaim. We were surprised at the resentment of restrictions on driving. We were amazed in particular by the power and ingenuity of a little old lady in digging out and moving a six hundred-pound barrier rock! She wanted to come in from a different direction and park two automobiles." The park rangers nonetheless understood why the use of cars had to be restricted to the roads and garage spurs, so they "built by trial and error until we got it done." At the end of the day, the rangers recognized that control was not that difficult to achieve. To keep campers from defying them, they simply had to "just put in bigger stones."[49]

Beyond Sequoia

The early enthusiasm of Superintendent White, his Sequoia staff, and NPS director Albright for Meinecke's approach to visitor management, campground design, and land use encouraged other national parks and forests to embrace the proposals. In March 1933, for instance, the California Region of the Forest Service distributed an updated version of its "Camp Ground Improvement Manual," which built upon Meinecke's program and was aimed at eliminating "the '57 Varieties' of improvements on our camps." In the five years since the manual's previous version, L. A. Barrett wrote in the preface, public use of the region's campgrounds had increased "enormously," so a revision had become necessary. At the same time, the USFS wanted greater standardization, and Meinecke's approach would be the basis for it. "In making the plan for development of a camp," reminded the manual, "be sure and consider the suggestions in Dr. Meinecke's Camp Ground Policy bulletin." Meanwhile, Meinecke traveled to Salt Lake City in June 1933 to attend the American Association for the Advancement of Science meeting and then to consult with local Forest Service people about their campgrounds. At the conclusion of this consultation, Meinecke was pleased to report to Haven Metcalf that "all the campgrounds in this region are reorganized and newer ones established on the basis of A Camp Ground Policy. That's encouraging." Later that summer, Meinecke visited Crater

Lake National Park to consult with administrators on the redevelopment of
the park's Rim Campground. He suggested general changes, as well as specific ones at individual campsites, and he directed park officials to restrict
automobile parking but to allow cars to drive through the campground.
Meinecke's suggestions were followed, and by September of that year the
park's superintendent could report that sufficient alterations had been made
"so that automobile driving and camp fire burning cannot occur indiscriminately and destroy the forests."[50]

Not everyone, however, immediately found Meinecke's approach attractive. Many Forest Service officers at the local level and even some at the
regional level considered the public-use restrictions in "A Camp Ground
Policy" to be unnecessary or worse. They were concerned that many
national forest campers would reject such "regimentation" in an area
dedicated to nonurban recreation. Without criticizing urban life directly,
these foresters feared that campers would feel that a quality they sought as
pilgrims—spatial liberty—was being reduced and subsequently revolt. As a
consequence, the Forest Service expended little effort to control automobile
traffic in campgrounds before 1935. At those locations where Meinecke's
proposals were tried and campers resisted, rebellions typically took the form
of broken, removed, or in other ways disrespected barriers, especially when
they were small or inconspicuous. Nevertheless, the USFS slowly became
aware that barriers were sometimes useful, and more Forest Service officers
came to embrace Meinecke's proposals.[51]

From the outset, NPS managers were generally more accepting of "A
Camp Ground Policy" than were their Forest Service colleagues, but not
every park immediately put Meinecke's proposals into practice. Yosemite
National Park, in particular, developed no plans to convert the valley's
campgrounds until 1935. The Yosemite Advisory Board, which consisted
of three non-NPS advisers recognized for their contributions to the parks,
was initially skeptical about the use of the Meinecke system throughout
Yosemite Valley. The board slowly came around, but then, before any con-
versions could begin, a December 1937 storm brought devastation and
extensive flood damage to the park, including the submergence of six valley
campgrounds under a rising Merced River. It was not until 1940 that a
Civilian Conservation Corps unit began to reconstruct the valley's Campground 11, using a modified Meinecke approach. As at most national parks,
Yosemite's managers sought to eliminate the vegetation damage caused by
unregulated campers and the overcrowding that was especially common
in the valley. Nonetheless, they were in no hurry to embrace Meinecke's
approach, and the park's campgrounds were not completely transformed
until the late 1960s.[52]

The Modern Auto Campground

Despite some resistance to E. P. Meinecke's approach to auto campgrounds, the three years following the release of "A Camp Ground Policy" were exceptionally busy for the pathologist. Thousands of printed copies of his program were distributed to national forest, national park, and state park administrators and field personnel, who readily adopted it and adapted its prescriptions to their local situations. At the same time, Meinecke himself visited innumerable campgrounds from Hawaii to the East Coast to provide advice on how best to tailor the policy to a site. He was also, however, learning better ways to plan new campgrounds and to reconstruct existing ones.

The enhanced understanding that Meinecke gained during this period of frenzied activity led directly to his most comprehensive publication on campgrounds, 1934's "Camp Planning and Camp Reconstruction." As he had in previous publications, Meinecke stressed that planned campgrounds were preferable to unregulated ones because they best eliminated camper-caused threats to the natural environment even as they provided "permanent protection of the woodland character of the camp ground." In particular, planned campgrounds lessened the likelihood of soil and water pollution and wildfires even as they maximized the environmental and social value of existing vegetation and reduced the loss of the grasses, forbs, shrubs, and trees that made camping destinations attractive. But in contrast to earlier prescriptions, this one also emphasized the need to fully utilize the space within bounded campgrounds while planning for camper convenience and comfort. While keeping this last pair of outcomes in mind, Meinecke insisted, a planner must be careful to correctly design a campground's key elements—the roads and the campsites. The first of these he treated much as before. They should be one-way, lined with rocks or other obstacles, and provide easy access to each campsite. Autos remained the greatest threat to vegetation, so they had to be controlled. Campsites, by contrast, were given a new emphasis, with Meinecke highlighting the importance of creature comforts and privacy. "People," Meinecke declared,

> go camping in order to enjoy certain pleasures they do not find at home, and they are willing to pay for them, up to a certain degree, the price of inconvenience. They want, above all, shady trees and green shrubs, reasonable protection from dust and wind, and fairly level ground to pitch their tent on, and to go about their simple housekeeping. They want water near by, but object to being located too close as well as too far from garbage pits and comfort stations. They desire a certain degree of privacy obtained either by a screen of

shrubs or young timber against neighboring campsites and the road
or by a broader belt of unoccupied ground.

Meinecke expanded upon this prescription and revealed the inspiration for his approach—the suburban development. Campers, he disclosed,
occupied a "roofless cabin" in a forest campground subdivided into "lots or
individual campsites." According to Meinecke, an ideal campsite included
many of the same "essential commodities" that were found in a suburban
home—"the garage, the kitchen stove, the dining table and the sleeping
quarters, with enough space to move around without inconvenience. The
trees and shrubs surrounding it form the walls." It was even possible to
hang "pictures on the wall" if the campground planner was careful. As a
new campground was subdivided, some unused or unusable space would
tend to occur. These open spaces, Meinecke offered, might be "covered with
a tangle of vegetation, small patches and groups of reproduction, or picturesque outcrops of rock with some green." Such openings were "decorative"
and tended "to break the monotony and [add] to the feeling of living in
the woods, away from the restrictions of civilization." However Meinecke
came to see campsites as "cabins," and however much he thought the "pictures" would push away distasteful civilization, it remains ironic that he
was inspired by the suburban developments that were springing up across
America, because many campers were seeking to escape this sort of urban
regulation and control. The response by campers to the first attempts to
develop Meinecke campgrounds at Sequoia National Park—rejection and
disobedience—suggest how negatively they felt about the new roads, garage
spurs, and ordered campsites. Nonetheless, the creation of new campgrounds
along these lines and the reconstruction of existing ones proceeded rapidly.[53]
Park and forest administrators readily implemented Meinecke's designs
for multiple reasons. First, his approach reduced the environmental damage
caused by libertarian camping policies. Campers could no longer damage
soil, water, and vegetation by camping wherever they wished within a park
or forest and by wandering in their autos within any established camping
areas. Second, and relatedly, Meinecke's plan spatially concentrated campers into a bounded tract, which reduced the total amount of area impacted
by their actions. Last, Meinecke unitized the campground, which made it
possible for management to declare a campground "full." Before Meinecke,
auto campgrounds were generally amorphous spaces with no obvious internal boundaries or campsite distinctions, which left an administrator with
no unambiguous measure for determining whether a campground was currently underused or at capacity. One consequence, especially during holiday
periods, was the overcrowding that degraded both the natural environment and the camping experience. A Meinecke campground, however, was

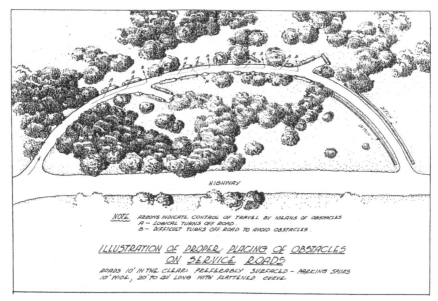

Figure 4.6. The California Region of the Forest Service rapidly transformed the updated campground system described in E. P. Meinecke's "Camp Planning and Camp Reconstruction" of 1934 into serviceable plans. Here the proper use of roadway obstacles is illustrated. From *Public Camp Manual* (San Francisco: U.S. Forest Service, Region 5, 1935), 14.

neatly subdivided into individual campsites, each with its own number or "address." When a facility had campers occupying every "lot" or "unit," an administrator could declare that it had reached capacity. As a management tool, the Meinecke plan had strong appeal because it neatly solved the immediate dilemma that faced authorities—how to contain and sharply reduce environmental degradation without declaring a park or a featured attraction off limits.

Meinecke's approach to campgrounds quickly influenced landscape architects and other professional designers, as well as campground administrators. T. G. Taylor, a professor at Utah State Agricultural College, and W. L. Hansen, a forest recreation instructor at the college, produced "Public Campground Planning" in 1934 to "offer some of the guiding principles in the planning of public campgrounds." They cited Meinecke's publications and like him emphasized the importance of vegetation protection, one-way roads, camper comforts, and privacy. The Forest Service's California Region revised and updated its 1933 publication, "Camp Ground Improvement Manual," to take into account Meinecke's additional prescriptions. The "Public Camp Manual" of 1935 specifically referred the Forest Service's rangers to Meinecke's most recent publication and transformed his policy proposals into detailed designs (fig. 4.6).

In late 1934, the Park Service's Herbert Maier, whom historian Ethan Carr described as "perhaps the most accomplished park architect of the day," also recognized Meinecke's novel approach in a handbook produced to train other park designers. By the mid-1930s, the National Park Service was engaged in a systemwide expansion and reconstruction of its facilities funded by the Federal Unemployment Relief Act of 1933, even as it became involved in the nationwide creation of dozens of state parks with hundreds of campgrounds being built by the Civilian Conservation Corps (CCC). The NPS could not directly train the hundreds of professionals employed on these projects, so it published standards handbooks instead. Maier's handbook included examples, descriptions, and photographs of guard walls, shelters, bridges, and many other typical park features, including a campground plan based on Meinecke's proposals. So rapid and universal was the adoption of Meinecke's approach that by 1935, NPS architect Albert Good referred to it simply as the "Meinecke Plan" in his standards book, *Park Structures and Facilities*. Furthermore, the term "Meineckeizing campgrounds" became commonplace for the implementation of the plan among CCC and NPS landscape architects and supervisors during the 1930s and could still be heard among camping authorities into the 1950s. Today a large percentage of America's public campgrounds are designed according to Meinecke's proposals, and his approach has been disseminated internationally by the Park Service (fig. 4.7).[54]

The Meinecke system protected the natural environment by spatially constraining campers within designated campgrounds and by reducing the number of people who could simultaneously occupy a campground. At the same time that this system was being implemented, however, the number of campers was increasing nationwide. If the growing ranks of campers were to be accommodated, additional changes would be needed. The NPS and the USFS, for instance, both added campgrounds, but the NPS also embraced a novel strategy—the time limit. Most national park campgrounds prior to the 1930s had placed no limit on how long one could remain at a campsite, and in consequence some campers had taken to erecting semipermanent structures and to staying for the entire summer. As Stanford Demars noted, the NPS initially had viewed such open-ended stays "as a symbol of Yosemite's growing success," but they were a serious problem by the 1930s. The most desirable locations—among the Big Trees at Sequoia, for instance—were continuously occupied, often badly crowded, and consequently suffered severe environmental damage. Moreover, long-term campers tended to develop a proprietary attitude toward the places they occupied, which sometimes led to confrontations when Park Service rangers had to enforce regulations.[55] These campground conditions had led directly to the Meinecke

Figure 4.7. The "Meinecke Plan" quickly became common in parks and forests around the country, including Flamingo Campground at Everglades National Park in the 1950s. Courtesy of National Park Service Historic Photograph Collection, Harpers Ferry (WV) Center for Media Services.

system, but an embrace of his solution also meant that an auto campground could easily end up being full for much of a summer if an unlimited number of open-ended stays were allowed.

An answer to the problem of slow turnover emerged from several sources. In the private sector, auto campgrounds in cities and along the highways began to charge fees and to set time limits by the mid-1920s in order to keep "undesirables" from staying indefinitely. In the public sector, Platt National Park, a relatively small park (approximately 925 acres) in Oklahoma, became the first national park to restrict the length of stays, establishing a thirty-day camping limit in 1926. This new policy undoubtedly arose from pressure to open campsites in the increasingly popular park, which had never had many sites. While the thirty-day limit appeared to work well for Platt, it was not immediately embraced by other national parks, many of which did not experience the same degree of popular demand. However, when the tool was next employed, it unsurprisingly occurred where similar conditions had arisen. Both Hot Springs, another small and crowded national park in Arkansas, and Sequoia, where the Meinecke system was first adopted, imposed thirty-day limits by the fall of 1933. At the latter location, the impetus for change may have been Meinecke himself, who in October 1932 had provided Sequoia Park's chief ranger, Lawrence F. Cook, with a list of "camp development" suggestions that noted how Canadian parks limited camping privileges to thirty days per year. This point apparently stuck with Cook, and one year later he requested and received permission to apply a thirty-day limit to the park's Giant Forest campgrounds. The summer of 1934 brought the first real test of the limit at Sequoia, and although a few disagreements arose, chief ranger Ford E. Spigelmyre judged it a success at the end of the season and recommended continuation to the park's superintendent. Moreover, Daniel J. Tobin, Sequoia's second-in-command, recommended the limit to C. G. Thompson, Yosemite's superintendent, who was considering adopting the measure at his park. A few months later, in the fall of 1934, the Park Service's superintendents and field officers gathered in Washington, D.C., for a conference on pressing park issues, and again the subject came up. Meinecke, whose "Camp Planning and Camp Reconstruction" had recently begun distribution throughout the NPS, addressed the group on the value of camping and on the need to regulate it, which prompted a lively discussion on time limits. The superintendents at the smaller parks (Platt and Hot Springs) and the parks closest to major population centers (Mount Rainier, Sequoia, and Yosemite) unequivocally supported the thirty-day limit as a useful tool for controlling the crowding they regularly faced. Some of the other superintendents, however, supported only selective imposition of the rule, on a park-by-park basis, not to the system as a whole. Many expressed no opinion. As a consequence of these discussions, the thirty-day camping limit became an official service regulation in June 1935 but was applied only to Hot Springs, Platt, "The Central Giant Forest Area" in Sequoia, and to the floor of the valley in Yosemite. The summer of 1935 passed with few public complaints lodged in any of the four parks and with the staffs feeling that the rule generally worked to improve camping conditions for all. Subsequently, Interior Secretary Harold L. Ickes approved application of the rule to the entire national park system in June 1936. By 1938, the rule was working effectively at all the parks, with Yosemite reporting that a systematic survey had revealed that of the ninety thousand campers who stayed in the valley between May 1 and September 30, 1938, the average stay was only seven days.[56] The modern auto campground had arrived.

"Doc" Meinecke never again expanded on his basic campground system after 1934's "Camp Planning and Camp Reconstruction," but he continued to work along these lines. In March 1935, he and Thomas C. Vint, chief architect for the NPS, released a short report on stove and fireplace designs for campgrounds, which aimed to provide plans for a useful cooking device that controlled fire and ashes and harmonized with the natural landscape. Late the following year, at the Foresters' Conference of the National Park Service, Meinecke gave a presentation on the issue of recreation, which was published in December 1937 as "Recreation Planning: A Discussion." Unsurprisingly, he praised the value of recreation, but also cautioned against losing sight of its limits. If recreational development in parks was not restrained and balanced with the landscape, he warned, both the physical contents of a park and its social value could be damaged.[57]

During the latter half of the 1930s, Meinecke also continued to consult with the NPS and the USFS about campgrounds and their issues. He and J. D. Coffman, the Park Service's chief forester, intensively discussed campground plantings and campground rehabilitation, especially at Grand Canyon, Mesa Verde, Glacier, Yellowstone, and Yosemite National Parks. The last was of special concern to the pathologist, who considered its campgrounds to be in the worst shape, calling them "utterly hopeless" and a "mess." In the spring of 1938, the Forest Service also tapped Meinecke for a chapter on "The Need for Non-urban Outdoor Recreation" and another on camp and picnic grounds for an agency report on recreation. In the former, which was something of a philosophical treatise, Meinecke again made clear his view that camping was an escape from the humdrum urban life into a timeless place of freedom and social equality. Campers sought this temporary escape, he argued, in order to return to their urban life refreshed, renewed, and prepared "to plunge again into the current" of daily life. Camp life remained, in effect, a pilgrimage for Meinecke.[58]

Emilio P. Meinecke retired in 1939 at the age of seventy, but for a few years he continued to give public presentations on outdoor recreation and to consult for the National Park Service on campground issues. Fittingly, his last professional consultation was on the developments in Sequoia National Park. NPS director Newton B. Drury had asked Meinecke for his "impressions and conclusions concerning the proposed relocations" of the park's facilities. Reliably consistent, Meinecke recommended changes that would protect the physical integrity of the forest, especially the Big Trees, and others that would eliminate or minimize the visual invasion of the park by inappropriately urban structures. A post office, grocery store, and souvenir shop needed to be relocated away from the Big Trees because, as he so aptly put it, "a forest of Sequoias does not tolerate architectural sophistication."[59] During his last dozen years, Meinecke led an active social life in and around San Francisco and was an avid gardener like his mother before him. He died in his home city at the age of eighty-seven in February 1957.

By carefully regulating automobile movement and by offering preposi-
tioned, comfortable domestic elements only in designated campgrounds,
Meinecke spatially structured nature and thus sharply reduced the negative
environmental impacts that had resulted when auto camping's popularity
boomed after World War I. Additionally, Meinecke's approach established
individual campsites, what the Park Service termed "unitization," each with
its own distinct "address." When the NPS combined unitization with a limit
on how many days a party could occupy a campsite, it created a powerful
management tool—a McDonaldized nature that made more efficient use of
campground space and time than had been possible previously; provided a
calculable basis upon which to measure a campground's carrying capacity
and to declare it "full"; assured that campground services were predictably
the same in all campgrounds; and exerted control over any campers who
entered the campground. Ironically, this new auto-campground approach
was structured according to the same spatial and temporal principles that
were shaping the physical and social forms of modern urban life. Nevertheless, the tool effectively reduced environmental damage and enhanced the
experience for the growing diversity of campers who flocked to the nation's
parks and forests. One example of the social conflict that followed closely
on the advent of the auto camper and the modern auto campground is the
subject of the next chapter.

CHAPTER FIVE

LIBERALIZING
THE CAMPGROUND

W. J. Trent Jr. and the Struggle against
National Park Segregation

Environmental degradation was not the only issue to emerge as campers poured across America's natural landscapes in the years before World War II. Some had hit the road because camping offered them an escape from the mounting class and ethnic diversity that had begun to appear at fashionable resorts. As one early convert to auto camping remarked, "Why stick in one place at fifty a week . . . listen to the old and young maids ladle out the current scandals, observe Mrs. O'Goldburg try to out-dress Mrs. Sullivanstein, etc., etc.?" Auto camping once had been an escape for such enthusiasts, but now that its social diversity was increasing, camping rubbed some of these same people the wrong way. Frank Brimmer, the noted author, wrote in 1926's *Coleman Motor Campers Manual* that "obnoxious" auto campers were a problem that needed to be controlled. According to him, many of the municipal campgrounds, especially "the best ones, have gate keepers who do not allow undesirables." These new pay camps, where people who could not pay a daily fee would be turned away, were spreading quickly, "not because the camp managers need to raise any more money, but to keep out the 'cheap camper,' called by the Forest Service men a 'white gypsy.'" R. L. Duffus similarly reported in the *New York Times Sunday Magazine* for September 1, 1929, that the growing number of middle- and working-class campers and other tourists was grating on some of the wealthier ones. "The increasing numbers who go on vacations must go somewhere. Naturally they go to places they have heard of" like Yosemite, the Garden of the Gods, and the Adirondacks. Their arrival, however, did not generate paeans about democracy, but rather sneers of disdain from some of those who had once dominated these destinations. "Vacationing having ceased to be aristocratic and exclusive," his informants told Duffus, "it becomes more difficult to find an aristocratic and exclusive place in which to practice it."[1]

It was not, however, just motor camping's growing class differences that generated negative responses; race was also an issue, especially where African Americans were involved. During the 1920s, some African Americans, like their white counterparts, had grown wealthier and embraced a variety of short and extended recreations, including such nature-based activities as relaxing at the beach, swimming, picnicking, fishing, hiking, participating in the Boy Scouts and Camp Fire Girls, enrolling at summer camps, and family camping. One black recreationist called these "ideal forms of recreation for city people," while another argued that urban African Americans, again like their white counterparts, needed such diverting leisure activities "if ill health and crime are not to result." Often these activities were enjoyed at private resorts located in or near the participants' hometowns, but popular destinations could also be in such distant places as Port Monmouth, New Jersey; Idlewild, Michigan; or near Denver, Colorado. By contrast, when African Americans wished to engage in outdoor activities at the public facilities supported by their taxes, they frequently found them to be segregated and generally inadequate. Efforts were made to change these situations; for instance, individuals and groups attempted to use the public beaches of Fort Lauderdale, Florida, in the summer of 1927, but such challenges were typically blocked by white authorities and the participants directed elsewhere.[2]

Two Southern National Parks

This recreational inequity was further extended into the public arena and became the basis for a prolonged dispute when two new national parks, Great Smoky Mountains astride the North Carolina–Tennessee border and Shenandoah National Park in Virginia, were opened respectively during 1934 and 1935 in order to realize the National Park Service's long-term goal of eastern national parks nearer the centers of national population (fig. 5.1).[3]

Before 1934, most national parks were in the West, and until the new parks appeared, national park racism had generally consisted of the ejection of indigenous peoples from such places as Yellowstone and a conscious but unpublicized policy of discouraging visits by African Americans. Black visitors and campers were, in the opinion of administration, "conspicuous . . . objected to by other visitors . . . [and] impossible to serve." As a consequence, the NPS superintendents had decided at their 1922 conference that "we cannot openly discriminate against them, [but] they should be told that the parks have no facilities for taking care of them."[4] This policy changed when two national parks were formed in the South.

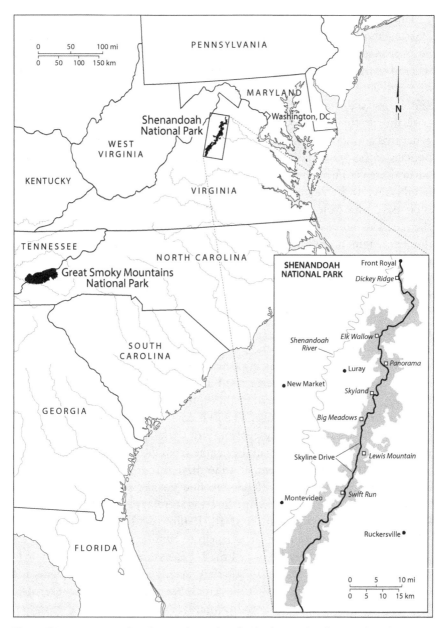

Figure 5.1. Most national parks were located in the thinly populated West when the Great Smoky Mountains and Shenandoah National Parks were created in the early 1930s. They emerged from a variety of efforts to place national parks closer to where the majority of Americans lived.

Unlike the western national parks, which had been carved from existing federal holdings, the lands for the new southern parks had to be purchased from individuals and businesses. Unprepared to buy land where possible and to condemn it where necessary, the Park Service had negotiated an arrangement where the states of Virginia, North Carolina, and Tennessee would acquire the land and then donate it to the federal government for the parks. A radical and time-consuming approach, it generated numerous confrontations and lengthy deliberations about the policies to be practiced in the new parks. In particular, the NPS wanted natural areas to be as wild as possible, which meant hundreds of residents would have to be relocated; but the states acquiesced on this point. For their part, the states wanted local regulations and laws to apply inside the parks where appropriate, to which the NPS agreed, since it had similar arrangements with other states. This accord, however, meant that the Shenandoah and Great Smokies parks would have to include racially segregated facilities, since Jim Crow was the law in Virginia, North Carolina, and Tennessee.[5]

With auto travel and camping expanding rapidly across America during the 1930s, picnic areas and auto campgrounds were among the first facilities constructed in the new national parks. Popular with both black and white Americans, such facilities quickly became the sites for race-related controversies as the NPS created segregated amenities. The correspondence that the agency received about these facilities, nearly all of which was negative, can be divided into two groups. The first consisted of complaints focusing on the extension of racial segregation into parks controlled by the federal government. Some of these critiques came from citizens like L. E. Wilson, who on an "enjoyable" September 1936 drive through the "beautiful" new Shenandoah Park had been offended to find racially segregated restrooms. "This is a National Park," he wrote Interior Secretary Harold L. Ickes, "and should show no race separation at all. I think we have a right to know whether we may expect your Department to condone this practice or not." Responding for Secretary Ickes and the NPS, Associate Director Arthur E. Demaray attempted to assure Wilson that racially segregated restrooms and other facilities did not mean that the remainder of the park was segregated. "Under no consideration," offered Demaray, "does the National Park Service regard such separate facilities as any evidence of or intention towards race separation in the park." Moreover, the quality of the separate facilities was to be the same for both races, and, he noted, the Park Service was not doing anything unusual but simply providing for "white and colored people to the extent only as is necessary to conform with the generally accepted customs long established in Virginia."[6]

Despite Demaray's assurances, a similar complaint was soon lodged by a political colleague of Ickes, Walter White, secretary of the National Association for the Advancement of Colored People. Founded in 1909, the NAACP at first had focused its efforts on a national campaign to stamp out lynching, but during the 1920s it had begun to struggle against segregation in education and for the right of African Americans to vote in political primaries. The organization had not, until this time, taken a position on any national park policy, but the extension of racial segregation into the parks crossed a line that could not pass without a response. In a January 1937 letter, White advised the interior secretary that newspapers were reporting that six "recreational colonies" were to be built for whites in Shenandoah National Park and one for African Americans. "We are writing," White stated, "to inquire if these accounts, which indicate the establishment of a Jim-crow project on Federal territory, are correct." Racial segregation was widespread and legal in southern states, which is where the NAACP most often fought it, but not at the federal level, with major exceptions being the military and the District of Columbia. If the news accounts were true, White declared, the NAACP did not wish simply to complain, but to also "go on record as most vigorously protesting against the inauguration of such a policy." Any additional embrace of racial segregation by the national government was anathema to the organization and would only set back the NAACP's efforts to end it.[7]

Out of respect for Walter White and his position, Ickes himself responded, but he did not directly address White's complaint. Instead, he opened his reply by first noting that "everyone, regardless of creed, color, or race, who conforms to the rules and regulations, is invited to visit the national parks and monuments." At the same time, he informed White, "it has long been the policy" of the national parks "to conform generally to the State customs with regard to accommodation of visitors." In keeping with this policy, yes, he admitted, the plans for Shenandoah National Park did include racially separate facilities, because that was the custom of Virginia, the state where the park was located. This dissatisfying letter would not be the last exchange about racial segregation between the NAACP, the NPS, and the Department of the Interior.[8]

Segregated Campgrounds

The second group of complaints received by the NPS was less general, focusing specifically on the segregation surrounding park amenities, especially campgrounds. Great Smoky Mountains National Park opened officially in June 1934, but even before its inauguration, Superintendent J. Ross Eakin had received a request for a meeting from an African American camping enthusiast who wished to ascertain whether he and his fellow campers would have a place to camp. Writing in September 1933, William P. Gamble of Knoxville, Tennessee, informed Eakin that he and a "delegation of colored men" wanted to discuss the construction of an auto campground for "colored people" in the rapidly developing park. Undoubtedly concerned that the southern national park might end up like many municipal, regional, and state parks in the South—for whites only—Gamble and his colleagues sought to ensure that the new park would be open to African Americans too, even if the campgrounds were racially segregated. Eakin, however, rebuffed their visit as premature and unnecessary. "You may rest assured that this will be provided for at some future time," he soothed, "but plans for the park at this time are so indefinite nothing would come of a conference."[9]

Although William Gamble apparently never responded to Eakin's dismissive letter, T. Arnold Hill, acting executive secretary of the National Urban League, again raised the issue of national park campgrounds and other recreational facilities for African Americans in a June 1935 letter to an old but influential acquaintance and one of Eakin's superiors, Secretary Ickes. "Few needs of the great mass of Southern Negroes are so completely underserviced as those of recreation," Hill informed Ickes. Nearly everywhere in the South they were unable to enjoy municipal, regional, and other parks. The federal government, however, was now creating recreational opportunities, so Hill proposed that "park projects [be] planned for states in the deep South that will definitely take care of the needs of Negroes—which will offer camping, hiking and picnicking sites." Moreover, federal provision for these activities was justified, because they would give African Americans much-needed opportunities to counteract the evils of urban life. "The masses in such cities as Atlanta, Birmingham, Montgomery, New Orleans and similar localities," he asserted, would finally have "a chance to build themselves physically and to enjoy the natural beauties of their states to a degree which is now denied them."[10]

Hill had known Ickes professionally for many years when he mailed this missive, since he had taken a post in 1917 with the Urban League in Chicago, where Ickes had lived and worked as a progressive lawyer. Moreover, Ickes was a member of the NAACP and had been president of its Chicago chapter from 1922 to 1924. Undoubtedly the men's paths had crossed many times, and Hill must have felt that he would receive a sympathetic hearing by the secretary. Before the month was out, Theodore A. Walters, an Ickes assistant who was acting secretary while his superior traveled, responded to Hill. On the one hand, he began, "the recreational needs of the negroes in Southern States . . . is a social problem which has my sympathy." On the

Figure 5.2. National Park Service associate director Arno B. Cammerer in January 1933. He became director in August of that year. Courtesy of National Park Service Historic Photograph Collection, Harpers Ferry (WV) Center for Media Services.

other hand, Walters continued, there was little the federal government could do for the problem as a whole. Nonetheless, he promised to refer the matter to Arno B. Cammerer, director of the National Park Service, "who will give it proper consideration and write you at a later date" (fig. 5.2).[11] Although Walters's reply was copied to an assistant park service director, Conrad Wirth, no evidence indicates that the NPS director ever contacted Hill.

During this same period, criticisms about the dearth of camping facilities for African Americans also rolled in from Interior Department staffers, most notably Robert C. Weaver, Secretary Ickes's "Adviser on Negro Affairs." In a July 1, 1936, memorandum to the NPS's Cammerer, Weaver asked that the Park Service "take some definite stand" about its failure "to include camping facilities for Negroes in National Parks." Weaver recently had received a letter from a man in Memphis, Tennessee, who had complained about the lack of campgrounds for African Americans. Moreover, "the same issue has been raised in Georgia," where "requests have come in for the opening of said facilities to Negroes in that State." Deflecting Weaver's pointed critique, Cammerer replied that the Tennessee complaint was not really about a national park but a recreational demonstration area (RDA) near Memphis. However, he admitted, since the project was under the supervision of the NPS, "I will have it looked into." Six weeks later, Cammerer had not gotten back to Weaver, and the latter conveyed his frustration with the NPS to Secretary Ickes. While talking with "the men in charge" of campground construction, Weaver informed the secretary in a memorandum, he had learned that the National Park Service was no longer building the camping facilities it had planned for blacks at the RDAs. Apparently the "topographic nature" of some sites had prevented "an expansion of facilities to include Negro participation," but more importantly, the NPS claimed it had run out of money before any campgrounds could be built. Weaver was told that campground construction funds had been cut, and he concluded that the "proposed Negro camp facilities seemed to have borne the brunt of the reduction, and they were eliminated." It was a flimsy excuse but not surprising, since NPS director Cammerer was neither a progressive nor welcoming to African Americans. Instead, on repeated occasions when the subject of African American campgrounds was broached, he would insist that demand should drive the provision of black facilities, even when his immediate subordinates recognized the opposite—that the presence of campgrounds would stimulate demand.[12] According to Cammerer's mean-spirited and unrealistic logic, once African American campers began to arrive at national parks but had to be turned away because no segregated campground existed for their use—or, much less likely, once they began to use whites-only campgrounds—the Park Service would build them facilities.

The following spring, Charles S. Johnson crossed a critical line, confronting the NPS about the undemocratic and socially inequitable nature of camper segregation itself. A sociologist and director of the Social Science Department at Fisk University, Johnson wrote to Cammerer on April 23, 1937, to inquire what the Park Service's policy would be concerning camping and other recreational activities by African Americans at Great Smoky Mountains National Park. Does the agency, he asked, "feel it within the scope of its authority to insist upon the participation of all elements of the population?" After consultations both among and with his principal assistants—Arthur E. Demaray, Julian H. Salomon, Thomas Vint, and Conrad Wirth—Cammerer replied to Johnson on May 27 that "we have attempted to provide park facilities for all people on exactly the same basis, regardless of race." In practice, he admitted, this policy had led so far to only one designated, but unbuilt, campground for African Americans at Shenandoah National Park, as well as a "probable" and similar arrangement at Great Smokies. However, Cammerer assured Johnson, the construction of such facilities would follow "the demand of people for them." Johnson must have found Cammerer's bland yet condescending letter profoundly irritating, but his response was a model of diplomacy and insistence. He thanked the director for his reply and assured him that he understood the Park Service's policies, but he added that "it is our hope and expectation that the National [Park] Service can render an important aid to the people by strongly suggesting the desirability of the inclusion of groups which are frequently neglected." In July 1937, one month after the receipt of Johnson's second letter, Cammerer finally ordered construction of the first black picnic ground and auto campground at Lewis Mountain in Shenandoah National Park. Although Cammerer seems to have inferred Johnson's larger point, the director was unwilling to follow through. Rather than approaching Secretary Ickes about the issue and supporting Johnson's plea that it was the "duty of a benevolent government" to recognize the social impediments that left African American campers excluded, Cammerer embraced segregation. "There will be some criticism by colored people against segregation," Cammerer admitted to his principal assistant, Arthur E. Demaray. "But I think we would be subject to more criticism by the colored people as well as the white people if we put them in with the white people."[13]

William J. Trent Jr.

The Lewis Mountain campground in Shenandoah National Park, the only such facility for blacks in all the southern national parks, was still undergoing development when a young William J. Trent Jr. (1910–1993) became Secretary Ickes's new adviser on Negro affairs in July 1938. A 1932 graduate of the Wharton School at the University of Pennsylvania, Trent had been born in Asheville, North Carolina, and had grown up in Atlanta. The son of a college president, he earned a bachelor's degree in 1930 from Livingstone College in Salisbury, North Carolina, and then proceeded to the University of Pennsylvania. According to Trent, he had dreamed of working for the North Carolina Mutual Life Insurance Company in Durham while earning his master's degree in business administration, but when he graduated, no openings were available. "The only job I ever went looking for was the only job I didn't get," he once joked with a reporter. Instead, he went to teach at Bennett College in Greensboro, North Carolina, and was there when Robert C. Weaver tapped him to be his successor in the Interior Department adviser's post. Longtime friends and associates, both men held advanced degrees in economics, and they had married into the same family. In 1936, Trent had served as an assistant administrator on a national employment survey run by Weaver. When Weaver was preparing to move from Ickes's office to the federal housing department, he recommended that Trent take over his post.[14] Trent readily accepted the offer when it arrived and immediately jumped into the work of his new position, recommending speaking engagements for Ickes, arranging the secretary's travel to national parks and other Interior Department sites across the country, and coordinating with his counterparts at other agencies.

Prominent among Trent's new Washington peers was Mary McLeod Bethune at the National Youth Administration. A friend of Eleanor Roosevelt, she would work repeatedly with Trent on recreation issues in national parks and elsewhere (fig. 5.3). Bethune had been the impetus behind the creation of Washington's "black cabinet" in 1935, an unofficial group of approximately forty-five African American professionals, many of whom were "racial advisers" in the federal government. The cabinet kept no minutes and met irregularly, but nonetheless provided a forum where race problems could be addressed and potential solutions suggested.[15] Robert Weaver was a charter member of the black cabinet, and he welcomed Trent into the group.

Trent's position in Ickes's office was a broad one that drew on his economics training and educational experience. According to Trent, his primary responsibility was "securing maximum Negro participation in the programs under the jurisdiction of the Department of the Interior and the Public Works Administration. This involves integration of Negroes into the activities conducted by these two governmental agencies," which covered employment financed by the agencies, services provided by them, and the agency employees themselves. He was not hired to focus narrowly on national parks, recreation, or camping. Moreover, he did not enter the post with a "special interest in the outdoors," even though he was a member of the NAACP and the Urban League, both of which had recently expressed displeasure about segregated parks, and even though he and his father enjoyed hunting together.[16] Nevertheless, Trent's interest, understanding, and efforts to support African American camping and related recreational activities would increase dramatically over the next three years.

William Trent Jr.'s involvement with outdoor recreation and parks began shortly after he started his new post. Within his first month, he met with the Park Service's Julian Salomon, who worked on youth camps and state parks, and Herb Evison, who worked with the states on parks. At about the same time, Ickes also engendered Trent's engagement with parks, and camping in particular, when he directed him "to make a thorough study of the camping needs of Negroes and make recommendations to him." Initially, the primary focus of Trent's research was organized camping for young people, but the work fostered a deeper look into the relationship between youth, American ideals, and spending time in a natural environment. In the end, Trent came

Figure 5.3. Eleanor Roosevelt strongly supported antisegregationist Mary McLeod Bethune (*left*). As director of Negro affairs at the National Youth Administration and chair of Washington's unofficial "black cabinet," Bethune encouraged W. J. Trent Jr. (*center*) in his budding interest in outdoor recreation for African Americans. Courtesy of Judy Scales-Trent.

away from these investigations with a richer understanding of camping and related activities and a firmly positive attitude toward them. In an article he composed about African American camps for the magazine *National Educational Outlook among Negroes*, Trent sounded like many other camping advocates when he linked camping to education and the development of Americans. "Formerly education and recreation were considered separate and distinct phases of a child's development," he wrote. Now, however, they were known to reinforce each other, and it was clear that "in the field of recreation, there is no agency more stimulating to adolescent development than organized camping."[17]

The Battle Is Engaged

In December 1938, during the same week that Trent mailed his manuscript to *National Educational Outlook*, he also sent Mary McLeod Bethune a reply to one of her communications. Back in 1937, her federal agency, the National Youth Administration, had sponsored a "National Conference on the Problems of the Negro and Negro Youth," and she had sent its recommendations to President Roosevelt. Forwarded to the Interior Department for a response, most of the recommendations related to equal access to jobs, project funding, and federal support for hospitals for African Americans. One recommendation, however, dealt with an issue of increasing importance to Trent: "that all facilities, services, and privileges in national parks, forests and other centers be made available to Negroes without discrimination." Trent's communication informed Bethune that he had read the conference's recommendations and subsequently had undertaken "a comprehensive study" of the issue in order to make his own recommendations.[18]

Then, around New Year's 1939, just as he was considering the recommendation to eliminate discrimination in national parks and forests, Trent discovered that the National Park Service's superintendents would be meeting January 5–10 near his Washington office. Without hesitation, he decided that he had to address them. On January 3, Trent fired off a memorandum to Ickes, requesting his permission to attend the conference to raise the issue of racial segregation in the national parks. "It is urgent," Trent argued, "that the question of the participation of Negro citizens in all of the benefits of the National Park Program be discussed fully and frankly." At the time, camping opportunities for black Americans ranged from limited to nonexistent in many national parks. A change in policy, he recognized, might mean "separate but equal facilities" in some sections of the country and "full use . . . without hindrance" in others, but it was, he concluded, "fundamental that citizens regardless of color shall participate in all of the benefits and accept all the responsibilities of any governmental program." His request to attend and to discuss the issue of racial segregation was quickly approved by Ickes and by the Park Service itself.[19]

On Saturday, January 7, Trent delivered an impassioned presentation to the assembled superintendents. First, he prefaced his talk with a statement—"the main job now [is] to establish policies with regard to Negro inclusion in National Parks and to see that they [are] carried out as established." Then, having made this point distinct, Trent turned to his appeal for equal recreational opportunities for African Americans by relating to his listeners that he understood how "the National Park [Service] has a dual function to perform." Referring to the mission outlined in the 1916 Organic Act, he noted with little interpretation that the Park Service was charged first to conserve the natural features of a national park. When he turned to its second charge, however, he neatly interpreted the act's original "provide for the enjoyment" of the parks as making the park system "accessible to and comfortable for the visiting public." This second function, built on the assumption that the parks were for everyone, "is my primary focus," he declared. Turning to his topic, Trent noted that any facilities in a park had to be inexpensive or they would be unavailable to the poor, among whom, he pointed out, were the largest percentage of African Americans. They could little afford expensive recreation, and Trent the educator and youth supporter knew that they needed recreation; national park facilities, he announced, could be "just the solution to their recreational problems," but for the fact that "some very important difficulties [stand] in the way."[20]

In order that the superintendents not misunderstand, he made it clear that several of these difficulties were under their control. First, Trent pointed out that African Americans initially had been excluded from the Park Service's recreational demonstration areas and therefore had not obtained the organized camping areas that he had so recently praised in a magazine article. Luckily, Secretary Ickes and his staff had become aware of the exclusion and countermanded it. Clearly, Trent told the superintendents, "we must be continually alert in order that the program as laid down will be carried out." Second, the NPS had started to plan its facilities at the emerging Cape Hatteras National Seashore in North Carolina and at other recreation-oriented areas around the South. Trent believed that these protected areas could provide all of the region's urban dwellers with relief, and since the NPS was soliciting the public's thoughts, he stressed that it was "essential that all groups of peoples be included in the program." When properly carried out, he suggested, broad participation "will result in the establishment of a policy of providing the same facilities for Negroes in all National Parks." Third,

Trent moved his discussion beyond the South to illustrate that the problem was not confined to that region. A group of African American campers, he revealed, recently had applied for a permit to stay at Yellowstone, but a "National Park official" did not wish to grant it. Of course, Trent noted, "no individual group can be denied certain types of privileges in parks on account of race, creed or color." However, "subterfuge" could be used. Since the official could not overtly discriminate, he simply "filled up the entire summer schedule of the park with dummy groups [to] shut out this Negro applicant." Was this official later embarrassed or remorseful for his act of discrimination? Hardly, related Trent; he "had considered it a fine joke."[21]

Finally, Trent rejected NPS director Cammerer's approach toward the construction of black recreational facilities in the segregated southern parks. Usually, Trent noted, when it was suggested that the Park Service needed to build campgrounds and other amenities for African Americans, "the first reply is—'when there is sufficient demand by Negroes for facilities in these areas, then they will be provided.' By implication the following statement might be added—'Meanwhile we will continue to construct various types of facilities for the use of white citizens because we know that the demand will be increased once the facilities are provided.' A better example of inconsistency cannot be imagined!" thundered Trent. And yet, despite his frustration with this hypocrisy, Trent's goal was not to support separate but equal campgrounds. Instead, he pointed toward social equality and racial integration by suggesting that the "white only" signs come down in the southern parks. If the agency wanted proof that blacks wished to camp and picnic, he declared, "I say open the facilities—the demand will be there." Furthermore, he argued, discriminatory practices in national parks only lent themselves to "the continued oppression of minority groups." "The Federal Government should not lend itself to discriminating against or segregating any race or religious group. To do such," he offered, "allows a contradiction in democratic government." Instead of supporting discrimination, he urged, the Park Service should take the lead and "insist that local social patterns be continually liberalized." This positive social change, he concluded, would occur if only the Park Service embraced "a policy of non-discrimination and non-segregation in federal park areas." In addition, he promised, "if such policies be put into practice faithfully and with sincerity of effort . . . interracial relations might be improved" and an American identity, rather than a black or a white one, might emerge.[22]

Despite the truth, fairness, and passion of Trent's appeal for nondiscrimination and nonsegregation in national parks, the superintendents retained their conservative policy. In the ensuing dialogue, Director Cammerer ignored Trent's critique and once again maintained that demand had to precede supply. "Projects," he insisted, "could not be established until the demand grew for them." He knew that little would therefore happen, because Great Smoky Mountains National Park, the one southern park that had reported racial statistics to him in the last year, had received only 1,109 African American visitors, or approximately 0.15 percent of its annual total. J. Ralph Lassiter, superintendent of Shenandoah National Park and a Virginia native, further cemented Cammerer's unwelcoming stance when he declared that the statistics his park had gathered (and apparently not shared with the director's office) indicated that during the last three years only one-half of 1 percent of Shenandoah's visitors had been African American. Like Cammerer, Lassiter implied that these visitor numbers demonstrated it was pointless to build segregated facilities for African Americans at this time. On the heels of this discussion, and with no voices raised in opposition, the superintendents decided against the elimination of segregation. Instead, they recommended that when "providing accommodation for Negroes in National Park Service areas, the control, type and extent of accommodations conform to existing State laws, established customs of adjacent communities, and Negro travel demands."[23] Nevertheless, their conformist policy would soon be challenged from another quarter.

The Interior Department Weighs In

A few days after Trent's ardent plea to the superintendents, a legal analysis of the racial segregation policy at Shenandoah National Park was completed for Nathan Margold, the Interior Department's solicitor. Margold's request for this analysis is unsurprising, because before he was hired by Ickes, Margold had been the author of the NAACP's landmark 1933 study detailing the inequality of "separate but equal" educational resources, which had become the foundation for the long fight against segregation laws. The legal analysis, which was developed by Phineas Indritz, a recent graduate of the University of Chicago's law school and a newly hired lawyer at the Interior Department, called the National Park Service's response to the racial complaints received from such individuals as L. E. Wilson "evasive," and it highlighted the fact that Shenandoah National Park was "not maintained by funds of the State of Virginia but by Congressional appropriations derived from the taxation of all the people of the United States." Moreover, Indritz was concerned about the long-term impact of the policy. "Once segregation is established in any service or accommodation, it may become increasingly difficult to eradicate it." His recommendation consequently fell in line with that of Trent—racial segregation in the national parks should be "completely abandoned."[24]

Margold reviewed Indritz's provocative memorandum and then consulted "with various leaders of thought in such matters," including Trent. Subsequent to these deliberations, Margold informed Ickes that although segregation was legal and constitutional when facilities were equal, according to the reports he had received, they were not so at Shenandoah. "It appears that the facilities for colored people are not as numerous, as adequate, as appealing or as well cared for as are those available for whites." More importantly, however, Margold argued that Shenandoah National Park need not be segregated at all. "The United States has exclusive jurisdiction over the Park and, in its management of that Park, is not bound by either laws or customs of the State of Virginia. Likewise, it would be legal and proper under existing concession contracts to require by appropriate rule or regulation, that park operators remove all traces of race segregation." Margold recommended to Ickes that the practice of racial segregation be eliminated "even though the National Park Service feels strongly" that the policy should continue.[25]

Ickes, however, was uncomfortable with both Trent's and Margold's recommendations. A cabinet member in a Democratic administration that was reluctant to support civil rights matters actively, he had to think about the political repercussions from such a policy change. Congressional seniority rules had made southern Democrats the chairmen or strategically located members of most Senate and House committees, so proposals for civil rights legislation made the White House nervous. As President Roosevelt explained to the NAACP's Walter White in 1935 after White had asked the president to support proposed anti-lynching legislation, "If I come out for the . . . bill now, [the southerners] will block every [subsequent] bill I ask Congress to pass to keep America from collapsing. I just can't take that risk." Given this political climate, Ickes pursued two approaches. First, he notified NPS associate director Arthur Demaray that the Park Service "must insist upon early provision for Negro Accommodations equal to facilities for white persons." If segregation was to be park policy, the facilities had to be made racially equitable as quickly as possible. At the same time, Ickes decided to broach the subject of integration with Virginia's senators, but was cautious because of his recent tangles over racial and other issues with one of them, Carter Glass. The senator was a deeply conservative Democrat who, in contrast to Ickes, supported racial segregation. Their differences had simmered for years but had come to a boil when Ickes had given a speech at the NAACP's 1936 convention in Baltimore advocating "a fair deal for everyone, regardless of race, creed or color, and educational opportunities on the same basis." This controversial presentation was followed by another in March 1936 at Raleigh, North Carolina, where Ickes questioned why one

Figure 5.4. E. K. Burlew (*left*) and Interior Secretary Harold Ickes at the swearing in of Burlew as assistant interior secretary in April 1938. Courtesy of National Park Service Historic Photograph Collection, Harpers Ferry (WV) Center for Media Services; photographer Allan Rinehart.

of Maryland's U.S. senators, Millard Tydings, was holding up the appointment of two African Americans to high posts in the U.S. Virgin Islands. This pair of critiques ignited Glass, who denounced Ickes during a volatile radio broadcast on March 29, 1937, saying the secretary had "openly advocated . . . the repeal of all segregation laws."[26]

Although Ickes dismissed Glass's radio address as ineffective, he still must have been thinking about the senator's animosity when he ordered the assistant interior secretary, E. K. Burlew, to contact Glass and Virginia's other Democratic senator, Harry F. Byrd, to ask for their responses to the complaints lodged against segregation at Shenandoah National Park and the proposal to eliminate all forms of segregation in the park (fig. 5.4).[27]

Letters were mailed on March 6, 1939, and on March 7 Senator Glass sent his brief and dark response. "It is obvious you are familiar with the segregation laws," he cautioned Burlew. "I completely approve these laws; and if the Interior Department desires to disregard them . . . it will have to take full responsibility for any such remarkable proceeding." Two days later, Byrd's equally adamant reply arrived. "I have had no complaints . . . with regard to the segregation of negro visitors in the Shenandoah National Park," he declared. Suggesting that any complaints were from suspicious individuals and that he would deal with them, Byrd asked the assistant secretary to tell him "the source of the numerous and well formulated protests that you state have been made to you."[28] Taken aback by these two responses, Burlew consulted with Trent, who recommended that the assistant secretary not limit his queries to the two Virginia senators. Instead, Trent encouraged Burlew to seek a greater diversity of white opinions, and he gave him a list of "informed Virginians" to question about the issue. The assistant secretary, however, decided that the discussion had caused disturbance enough and so recommended an early meeting between Secretary Ickes and NPS associate director Demaray to settle the issue. One was scheduled for March 24, but before it occurred, William Trent would once more weigh in to the interior secretary about national park discrimination.

Segregation Begins, but with an Exception

As an advocate of equity and opportunity for African Americans, Trent steadily worked to ensure that the Interior Department's actions were even-handed and that the public understood the programs and services it made available to them. After his January 7, 1939, presentation, where he had argued against segregation and for more recreational opportunities for African Americans in the national parks, Trent again supported two related issues of growing importance to him—African American summer camps and youth recreation. Beginning on January 12, Trent participated in the second "Conference on the Problems of the Negro and Negro Youth," where he expressed his deep concern about the need to support education and recreation for young people. Once again organized by his colleague at the National Youth Administration, Mary McLeod Bethune, this conference prompted Trent to think more about the general value of recreation.

Then, a month later, Trent completed the manuscript for a second article about African American camps. In this piece, he did not advocate for non-discrimination and nonsegregation, but for the more immediately available goal of enhanced opportunities. In particular, he described to his readers, especially those in the South, how they could create campgrounds for their children. African American groups, he explained, had a chance to organize youth summer camps through a cooperative project with the National Park Service. The agency's RDAs were intended to develop sites "to meet one of the pressing recreational needs of the day"—inexpensive camps for youths. The Park Service would purchase the land and build the camping facilities, Trent continued, so the expense of construction was not an issue, but the NPS would do so only when an organized group sponsored one. Since campgrounds of every sort were segregated in the South, "It is up to Negro groups," he encouraged readers, "to do so organize that they can meet the minimum standards required of sponsoring agencies" and thus win one of these camps for their community. In his previous article, Trent had argued that camping was valuable, so in the body of this one he laid out the conditions for a group's success and a clear set of procedures for securing a camp. When he came to the conclusion, however, Trent must have been thinking about NPS director Arno Cammerer, whom he knew to be reluctant to provide black facilities without "sufficient demand." "Within the next few years," Trent explained, "two national parks and two parkways will be completely developed by the National Park Service in the Southern section of the United States. . . . In all of these sites recreational areas are proposed. . . . It is important in this connection that groups interested in this phase of the National Park program make plans to utilize these areas and make recommendations as to how best the Negro citizen might be served by these areas." Local and state agencies, Trent warned, were not going to treat African Americans equitably until studies established that they would use recreational facilities. Consequently, Trent informed readers, the federal government was creating the RDAs as an attempt "to stimulate interest in and show the need for recreational facilities for all citizens regardless of color." African Americans, he urged, should organize and sponsor an RDA summer camp to "provide the necessary local pressure so that Negroes . . . will have adequate recreational facilities" at all scales.[29]

On March 17, 1939, approximately one month after Trent completed the manuscript for his second article and one week before Secretary Ickes was set to meet with Associate Park Director Demaray, he sent a memorandum about national park equity to Ickes. Trent had learned that subsequent to his January presentation, the NPS superintendents had agreed to establish racially segregated campgrounds, picnic areas, and other facilities wherever it was the local practice. Trent undoubtedly felt disappointed, and his memorandum made it clear that he strongly opposed this decision, again calling it "contrary to general democratic principles." If the National Park Service followed southern customs, he argued, it would become involved "in serious discriminatory practices." In step with Solicitor Margold's argument, Trent noted that wherever racially separate facilities were required, it was also the law that they be equal facilities. "It is obvious," he stated unequivocally, "that no such equality obtains" in the national parks. As an alternative, Trent suggested that public reaction to a change in social policy "can never

Figure 5.5. Norma E. Boyd of the Alpha Kappa Alpha Society sent this photograph to E. K. Burlew, asking him to remove this sign and all other segregationist signs from Shenandoah National Park because such signs were "fundamentally opposed to the spirit of constitutional democracy. The horror aroused by the medieval practices of Nazi Germany is eloquent evidence of American disapproval of governmental distinctions based on race, creed or color." From N. E. Boyd, letter to E. K. Burlew, April 1, 1941, folder "Shenandoah, Lands (General), Camp Sites," box 1650, RG 79, appendix 2, U.S. National Archives, College Park, MD.

be ascertained *a priori.*" National park visitors might not be upset or even care that nonsegregated restrooms, campgrounds, and other facilities were the rule. Therefore, he recommended that all picnic areas and campgrounds at Shenandoah National Park be "undesignated; i.e., open to all persons who desire to use them" and that every "Negroes Only" and "White Only" sign be eliminated from the park (fig. 5.5 and fig. 5.6). If his recommendations were followed, Trent concluded, the National Park Service would move closer to its "ultimate aim"—"to provide for all citizens, without segregation or discrimination, use of all facilities."[30]

Respecting Trent's analysis and concerned about national park segregation, Ickes invited his adviser to the March 24 meeting with the NPS's Demaray. At the meeting, Demaray and Trent each presented his plan, but to the surprise of both men, Ickes chose to follow a third path. On the one hand, the secretary did not wish to make a radical move, so he ordered that racial segregation be "generally" enforced in national parks throughout the southern states. On the other hand, Ickes supported the liberalizing notion

Figure 5.6. Shenandoah National Park initially included four areas with campgrounds, but only Lewis Mountain was racially segregated for African Americans alone. From "Photo Gallery: Segregated Facilities 1939–1950," Shenandoah National Park, https://www.nps.gov/media/photo/gallery.htm?id=20B61590–155D-451F-6786CFBCF8DF232B.

espoused by Trent, and therefore ordered that one "large . . . most conveniently located" picnic area become nonsegregated and "open to all comers" at Shenandoah National Park. "No signs indicating race segregation within the picnic grounds or in the comfort stations are to be permitted within this area," so that it would act as a demonstration of racial integration to visitors. Finally, Ickes, who in December had told Cammerer that "he was a misfit in the job" and that he, Ickes, "had no confidence in his ability," made it clear to Demaray that he "sharply and distinctly disapproved" of Cammerer's directive that facilities for African Americans should be built only after demand was apparent. Instead, Ickes "emphatically stated" that the NPS "must provide equal facilities proportionate to [current] travel and that Negro facilities must be increased as use increased."[31]

Within two weeks, Ickes's instructions had brought a variety of changes to Shenandoah National Park. The Lewis Mountain area, which already had been designated as the one site exclusively for African Americans, but which still only included automobile parking spaces and fireplaces, not tables or campsites, had been upgraded to "a complete picnic ground," which meant it eventually would include a campground and other amenities. As a consequence of that change in status, the park's concessionaire "soon will begin construction of a building similar to the ones built at [white-only facilities] where foods, soft drinks, and confections will be sold." At the same time, the previously white-only Sexton Knoll area had all its racial segregation signs removed, was thrown open to all visitors, and was renamed "Pinnacles Picnic Ground." As ordered, the park's other racial signs remained in place. However, another indicator of the segregation that dominated Shenandoah's management—one that neither Ickes nor the other meeting participants had considered—was about to emerge as an issue.[32]

Mapping Segregation

On April 5, 1939, Edwin B. Henderson, head of the Health and Physical Education Department at Dunbar High School in Washington, D.C., sent a letter of complaint to the interior secretary. Henderson enjoyed trips to Shenandoah National Park, he explained to Ickes, and found the park's Skyline Drive to be "mentally and physically healthful," but he was "tremendously humiliated and depressed" to find that the park guide map he recently had received at the entrance indicated that "Negroes would have a special reservation [area] for lunch, picnic or stopover privileges." No such discrimination had been indicated on the park's earlier guide map, and its inclusion now, he argued, would discourage many African Americans who needed the recreation. "That the Federal Government has once more set an example or copied a practice of the German government in its segregation of its 'hated' minority is to thousands of self-respecting Negro citizens intolerable." Continuing, Henderson made it clear that he did not regard the Park Service as a reliably progressive institution. He "knew" that Ickes did not support such practices, but "many of your subordinates are believers in this sort of segregation and discrimination." Furthermore, he warned the secretary, "unless a more liberal group gets in control, those who hold over will go even further."[33]

Henderson's letter was quickly forwarded to the Park Service, but before the NPS could react, Ickes received a similar complaint from Secretary Walter White of the NAACP. "A well known Negro physician of New York and his wife" had recently driven to Shenandoah National Park, began White. When they entered the park, they were handed a guide map that, "to their great amazement," indicated that picnicking African Americans were to use the facilities at Lewis Mountain rather than at Dickey Ridge or anywhere else. When they returned home, the couple shared the guide map with White, who "was as surprised as they." A long-term, political colleague of Ickes, White gained the couple's permission to contact the interior secretary for them and to send this letter requesting him to "immediately abolish this discriminating regulation and practice."[34]

In the face of these pointed complaints and with the integrated Pinnacles Picnic Ground undergoing development for the 1939 season, Ickes had his staff confer with the Park Service, but while the NPS was formulating a response, its management situation shifted. On April 30, NPS director Cammerer suffered a severe heart attack that would keep him convalescing at home until late summer. Ickes, who admitted in his diary that he found Cammerer to be "fatuous, blundering and inefficient," temporarily replaced him with the associate director, Demaray, whom Ickes considered a man of "integrity" and "ability." This modification in the Park Service's leadership likely eased the changes that were about to unfold. The NPS, which initially took the lead in responding to the complaints, prepared Ickes a rambling, two-page draft reply to Walter White, but Ickes apparently found it unsatisfactory and forwarded it to William Trent for review and revision. While Trent was reducing the letter to one page and focusing on its policy implications, Harry Slattery, under secretary of the interior, heard about the complaints and told Ickes that "the language of the Park Service map should be changed."[35] Ickes, however, withheld his decision until he had heard from Trent.

On May 9, Trent sent his version of the draft letter and a covering memorandum to Assistant Secretary E. K. Burlew. In the memo, Trent informed Burlew that he had considered including in the draft "a statement to the effect that the wording on the [guide map] for Shenandoah National Park might be revised in order to eliminate any mention of race," but had not done so because neither Ickes nor any of his staff had made any official move in that direction. Seizing the opportunity to reduce discrimination and create more equity, Trent recommended to Burlew that "if the Secretary thinks it feasible, that the National Park Service be instructed to call in this objectionable literature and revise it." Even though many of the park's facilities would remain segregated, Trent regarded this advertising as "unfortunate" and its elimination to be an improvement. Burlew, who had come to respect Trent's views, shared this recommendation with Ickes, whose one-word decision was, "approved."[36]

Embracing Trent's draft letter as his own, Ickes now replied to the NAACP secretary. The National Park Service, he began, had not stumbled into this situation, but had given "very serious consideration" to the question of recreational facilities in its parks in segregated states. In light of these reflections and "in the interest of all the people," Ickes had concluded that the parks should not disregard local practice and custom to create "jurisdictional islands" in the states. Moreover, he was of the opinion that "the history of discrimination . . . cannot be changed at once by an order of the Secretary of the Interior." Nevertheless, Ickes felt that the NPS could be progressive and take steps "to demonstrate the possibilities of non-segregated areas." To do so, he informed White, Shenandoah's Pinnacles Picnic Ground had been officially desegregated and was now open to all users. However, the park's other picnic and camping grounds would remain segregated "for the present." Replying on May 15, Walter White thanked Ickes for his efforts and expressed his wish for a positive outcome. "We sincerely hope that the opening and operation of the Pinnacles Picnic Ground for use by all Americans, without discrimination, may prove to be so successful that it will demonstrate how silly are most of the notions about the necessity of separation."[37]

Now that Ickes had replied to Walter White, and the NAACP secretary had offered a supportive response, Assistant Secretary Burlew turned to the issue of the Shenandoah Park's guide map. Starting at the top, he quickly shot a memorandum to the Park Service's new acting director. Secretary Ickes, Burlew notified Arthur Demaray, had approved the recall and revision of Shenandoah's objectionable guide map, so the acting director was instructed to "have this matter handled as promptly as possible." Demaray swiftly ordered the revision, but several painful missteps would occur before all the discriminatory language would disappear.[38]

To initiate the process, Demaray passed Burlew's instructions to John R. White, the new acting associate director. White, who had been promoted into Demaray's former post while the latter was filling Cammerer's shoes, first ordered all of Shenandoah's existing guide maps destroyed, and then he arranged for a meeting with William Trent so that the two men could agree on the new publication's language. They easily reached an accord. Instead of telling African Americans that they were to use the Lewis Mountain facilities, the new guide-map pamphlet, they decided, would only identify the park's picnic and campground areas in alphabetical order. This approach struck White as "the sensible thing to do" and was "agreeable to Mr. Trent." Demaray accepted this format, and two days later he notified Burlew that the text of the revised Shenandoah pamphlet would no longer include any discriminatory language and that the new wording had been finalized with Trent's concurrence. However, Demaray also revealingly admitted that none of the guide maps that Acting Associate Director White had just ordered destroyed had ever been distributed at the Shenandoah Park. Apparently, they never had left their warehouse in Washington.

Instead, Demaray sheepishly conceded, the discriminatory statement that had prompted Edwin Henderson's and Walter White's complaint letters had "unfortunately" been added "in the park before distribution" to a previous version of the guide maps that did not include any racial designations. Moreover, we can conclude that this addition of racial language must have been occurring in the park for approximately six months to a year. Edwin Henderson, who had visited the park in the past with friends, had been surprised to find segregationist language on the guide map he had received while visiting the park sometime during 1938. Demaray did not identify who had inserted the discriminatory statement or why, but he assured the assistant secretary that he had ordered the park's superintendent, J. Ralph Lassiter, "to discontinue this practice immediately."[39] Burlew offered no further comment, but ultimately it would take more than one order to bring this practice to a halt at Shenandoah.

Confident that the situation was under control, Demaray now replied to Edwin Henderson's April 5 letter. However, his May 25 letter did not begin by addressing Henderson's complaint about the guide map's language. Instead, Demaray offered a paraphrasing of the letter that Secretary Ickes recently had sent to Walter White. "Serious consideration" had been given to the issue of racially segregated national parks in the South, and "in the interest of all the people the parks should not become jurisdictional islands in those states." However, Demaray informed Henderson, the NPS was taking a step "to demonstrate the possibilities of non-segregated areas"—throwing open the Pinnacles Picnic Ground "for use by all without discrimination." Then, turning to the issue that had prompted Henderson to write, Demaray simply quoted the new Shenandoah pamphlet's list of racially undesignated camping and picnicking facilities. He offered Henderson no explanation or apology for his experience, which he could have done, since the inserted language had not been authorized by Demaray's office, but closed by stating that "the National Park Service is doing everything possible to extend a friendly welcome to all visitors." It is hard to imagine that this reply satisfied Henderson.[40]

Three weeks later, Trent again demonstrated his now enhanced interest in the national parks and his confidence that the NPS would listen to his views. On June 19, 1939, Trent advised Assistant Secretary Burlew that the problem with the Shenandoah pamphlet had not been completely resolved. In its haste to revise the new pamphlet's wording, the Park Service had neglected to revise the *map*, which as before read "Lewis Mtn. Picnic Ground for Colored People." This omission, Trent patiently observed, "defeats the purpose of the [text] revision," and he called for a correction. Burlew readily agreed and passed along Trent's memorandum to Demaray, who wrote back in two days. "The change on the map for Shenandoah National Park, suggested by Mr. Trent, has already been made."[41] No additional printing errors cropped up on the Shenandoah pamphlet during the remainder of the 1939 season, but during the next year an old twist would return to revive the controversy.

An End to Discrimination?

Soon after the Shenandoah map was fully revised, Trent's employment situation changed. In July 1939, having worked in the secretary of the interior's office for one year, Trent transferred to the Federal Works Agency to become the adviser on Negro affairs at the Federal Emergency Administration of Public Works. In his new position, Trent was responsible for the monitoring and enforcement of racial equity in the construction and use of the many houses, schools, and hospitals being built under federal contracts. In addition, his new post eliminated Trent's direct ties to the national parks and camping, but the change diminished neither the positive impression he had created among African Americans nor his own fervor to end segregation in America's parks. For example, in October 1939, Trent was invited by the Colored Professional and Business Men's Club to assist the black community of Greenville, South Carolina, in obtaining land for an RDA. Clemson College had some surplus land available, and the club was spearheading an effort to claim it for a park. Although supporting black groups seeking to develop RDAs was no longer among his official duties, Trent replied that he would be pleased to speak with them when he was next in the area. More letters were exchanged, and a plan was emerging when the effort collapsed during November as the Ku Klux Klan "took over control" of the city and began persecuting African Americans.[42] Although Trent would lose the opportunity to assist the Greenville community with their RDA, another opening would soon arise.

In February 1940, the NAACP's Walter White contacted Trent at the Federal Works Agency "regarding discrimination against Negroes" in the national parks. Secretary Ickes, he reminded Trent, had indicated in his May 1939 letter to White that segregation would be eliminated from Shenandoah and the other parks "as speedily as possible." Since Skyline Drive, a parkway along the spine of Shenandoah, would soon open for the summer, White wondered "if there will be any further relaxation or removal of discriminatory practices during the coming season." Even though White knew that Trent no longer worked in the interior secretary's office and no longer had interactions with National Park Service personnel, he must have trusted Trent and felt that Ickes trusted him, too. Moved by White's inquiry,

Trent forwarded the letter to Ickes, along with a three-page memorandum recounting the developments that had led to the creation of the nonsegregated Pinnacles Picnic area at Shenandoah National Park. In particular, Trent noted that it had been his impression during the March 1939 meeting, when this policy had been decided, that the transformation of the one picnic area "was being taken to determine whether or not there would be any serious friction between the groups using the area. I was of the opinion, also, that if the reaction to this step was favorable, more of the restricted areas would be made available to all people regardless of race." Furthermore, he continued, the possibility that the policy might be expanded to additional areas had been implied in a May 1939 letter from the secretary to Walter White of the NAACP. Ickes had informed the latter that other areas in the park would not necessarily have to remain segregated, but would be so only *"for the present"* (emphasis in the original). "To date," concluded Trent, "I have heard of no untoward incidents resulting from the opening of the Pinnacles Picnic Ground to all groups." Perhaps, he suggested, the time had come to integrate some additional picnicking and camping areas in the park. He admitted that the superintendent of Shenandoah would have to be consulted to confirm his impression, but if there had been no incidents, "I hope that it will be possible to remove other restrictions" before the park opened for the 1940 season. If the secretary would take this next step, Trent assured Ickes, he would not be alone. "I am sure," confided Trent, "that Negroes would be grateful to you for any action that you might take to relieve them of the disabilities imposed by racial barriers and restrictions." In response, Ickes contacted the superintendent about conditions at Shenandoah, but after reading his discouraging reply, decided against any change at the park. "The situation," he recounted to Trent, "requires careful and tactful handling." Consequently, "until the present plan is tried out for a longer period, it will be unwise to make any change in the present authorization."[43]

A Second Pamphlet Controversy

Meanwhile, the campground at the black-only Lewis Mountain area of Shenandoah National Park was completed in time for the 1940 season, and the racial situation seemed calm to the NPS when another controversy erupted. As before, it began with William Trent. In July, Trent visited Shenandoah National Park to see for himself if the park's staff were violating policy. Trent was well known for the watch he continued to keep on the Park Service's racial policies, and a number of African Americans had complained to him about Shenandoah's pamphlets. Pulling up to the park's

Front Royal entrance, Trent was shocked at what he discovered in the pamphlet a ranger handed him, and he soon sent a letter to E. K. Burlew. The letter began by pointing out that last year "it was agreed that it would be undesirable to make specific mention of race in [Shenandoah's] literature." It then referred to the enclosed pamphlet, in which "on the map on the inside someone has inserted [at Lewis Mountain] the words 'For Colored People Only' and on the back a section [of the text describing Lewis Mountain] is encircled and labeled 'For Colored People Only.'" These red-pencil "write-ins," Trent noted, contradicted the "express desires" of Secretary Ickes and Burlew. Furthermore, they distorted the truth, because the Pinnacles Picnic Ground was open to all without discrimination. Trent concluded that he hoped Burlew could have the pamphlet alteration stopped. At the same time, since he was discussing a reduction in national park discrimination, Trent inquired if it might be possible to remove Shenandoah's "large, blatant, yellow signs designating areas by racial groups." Their overwhelming presence, he confided, was "especially disheartening" for African Americans, and they were not necessary, because the park was staffed. Should the signs be removed, people could still "depend on the rangers to direct parties to the proper areas." If, however, they could not be eliminated, "then surely these signs might be made less obnoxious." Clearly irritated by this policy violation, Burlew ordered the NPS's Demaray to carry out an investigation "to ascertain who in the park has taken it upon himself to discriminate in this way." Furthermore, he continued, "I have a great deal of sympathy with Mr. Trent's request to use smaller and less conspicuous signs." He requested that the acting director provide him with a report on the feasibility of changing them.[44] Demaray quickly ordered a response from the park.

On August 14, 1940, J. Ralph Lassiter, Shenandoah's superintendent, offered a rejoinder to "Trent's criticism." He reported that the penciled insertions were an accident, done "on instructions from the Chief Ranger, who had no knowledge of the ruling . . . that no mention was to be made of racial segregation." Lassiter, however, offered no explanation for Chief Ranger Stephens's ignorance, which was a red flag, considering that the latter worked for the superintendent. It is unclear if the chief ranger also had been involved in the insertion of similar language on the guide maps that had offended Edwin Henderson and Walter White the previous year, but it is reasonable to conclude that Lassiter should have informed Stephens about the current prohibition on such language. The superintendent also could have accepted responsibility himself, but instead he defended the chief ranger. Stephens, Lassiter wrote in his report, considered the lack of discriminatory language in the park's pamphlet to be "an omission of very important information," which "could be corrected and brought to the attention of those most interested." Moreover, the altered pamphlets were not handed out to everyone, he assured Demaray, just to African Americans, so that they would know "that there was an area in the park expressly set aside for their use." Lassiter did not acknowledge that everyone was allowed to enjoy the Pinnacles Picnic Ground, and he implied that inserting the information was helpful, because when African Americans were informed, they would not use the white-only areas and upset white visitors. Lassiter also twisted Trent's words when he suggested that the discriminatory insertions were exactly what had been requested. When "For Colored People Only" was penciled onto the pamphlet, he asserted, "we accomplish in a simple and most effective means the very object that Trent wanted when he states—'Depend on the rangers to direct parties to the proper areas.' "[45]

Demaray was not pleased with the superintendent's response. "Your memorandum," he warned Lassiter, "does not cover the situation adequately," and if it were forwarded to Assistant Secretary Burlew, Lassiter could be criticized for the chief ranger's ignorance of official policy. "We do not understand why Chief Ranger Stephens and the other members of your ranger organization were not advised in regard to that ruling." In light of Lassiter's failure to accept responsibility for the practice or to provide an adequate explanation of it, Demaray ordered him to produce another report, and he cautioned him to make it informative, comprehensive, and objective, because, unlike the previous report, it would be forwarded to Burlew. Then, in a biting postscript, Demaray curtly instructed the superintendent to have his rangers presume nothing until African American visitors asked for information about where they might camp or picnic. When such an inquiry occurred, rangers could then tell the visitors where they should go and "simply underline with red pencil, or by the use of a red arrow, the areas available for their use."[46]

Superintendent Lassiter's second report, which arrived in early September, again failed to cover the ground sought by Demaray. The superintendent explained that the practice of red-penciling "For Colored Only" on the pamphlets had developed that spring after Chief Ranger Stephens and one of his subordinates decided that they needed to do something about "the number of Negroes who were using the [white only] Dickey Ridge and Elk Wallow Picnic Grounds." In order both to inform African Americans about where they were supposed to go and to "not . . . hold up other traffic," a quantity of pamphlets were pre-marked with pencil and "held for issuance to Negroes." Again, Lassiter neither took responsibility for the practice, nor did he explain why the chief ranger had been unaware of national parks policy. He had, however, ordered an end to the practice. Nevertheless, Demaray was true to his word, and he forwarded Lassiter's report to Assistant Secretary Burlew under cover of his own memorandum. Surprisingly, Demaray's memo largely paraphrased Lassiter's report, which provided some cover for the superintendent, but he also offered no additional explanation for the chief ranger's ignorance, which Burlew was likely to notice.[47]

In his brief reply, Burlew angrily declared Shenandoah's superintendent "negligent" for his failure to inform his staff about the NPS policy of not including any racial references in park literature. If he had informed his staff, Burlew pronounced, "this incident would not then have occurred." Furthermore, Burlew stated, the report was incomplete. It included no response to Trent's proposal that the park's racial designation signs be made "less conspicuous." No longer requesting, Burlew bluntly told Demaray to let him know "when this change has been made." Demaray immediately forwarded this order to Lassiter. On the same day that Burlew responded to Demaray, September 10, he finally could reply to Trent's July 31 letter that had initiated the investigation. In his letter, Burlew enclosed a copy of Demaray's last memorandum, but not his own angry response, and he declared the Park Service's insertions in Shenandoah's pamphlets to be "most ill advised, especially since we had removed any such reference in reprinting the circulars." He made no mention of the park's signs.[48]

On September 16, Superintendent Lassiter sent the NPS director his response to the proposal to make the racial-designation signs less conspicuous. To date he had made no changes because "here we have two opposing viewpoints." On the one side, the concession operator of the white-only Skyland and Big Meadows areas wanted the signs to be larger because "many visitors to the park go by the entrance" to these areas without stopping. On the other side is "Mr. [handwritten into the typed memo] Trent [who] wishes to have the signs designating an area for Negroes made smaller." Throwing his support behind the concessionaire, Lassiter announced that "if the signs are made any smaller than they are at present, they will not serve their purpose." Nor, he informed the director, could a ranger remain at each developed area "to direct parties to their proper areas." The park's appropriation was too small to provide such services. Only signs could handle the task, and they had to be "large enough and conspicuous enough to accomplish the purpose." In the face of this response, Burlew threw up his hands and informed Trent that he was "at a loss as to what the next step should be." Apparently Trent was also stymied and offered no reply.[49]

Lassiter's failure to take responsibility for the red-penciled park pamphlets and to explain his chief ranger's ignorance of NPS policy, as well as his resistance to the proposal to make the park's racial-designation signs smaller, should surprise no one, because they were consistent with views he had expressed just six weeks earlier. In July, Acting Director Demaray had asked Lassiter to respond to a proposal to change the "For White Only" signs to "White." Lassiter strongly rejected the proposed modification. The park did not need shorter signs, he argued; "what we need [are] more and bigger 'For White Only' signs." Lassiter wanted enhanced signage because the park was "continually having Negroes in the white picnic grounds," and the Negroes were sometimes confrontational when told to move. On one recent occasion, he related, a black physician and a florist had "a discussion" with Chief Ranger Stephens when they made use of a white-only picnic area. At the conclusion of the exchange, the two African Americans rejected the park's segregation policy and made it clear that "they were going to take the matter up with the [Interior] Secretary." Moreover, Lassiter continued, the nonsegregation of the Pinnacles Picnic Ground was not a success. "The mingling of the races has only bought criticism from the white, and the separation has brought criticism from the black." Tension was building between the races in Lassiter's view and would soon, he declared, result in "a small local disturbance to put it mildly." To head off such a disturbance, Lassiter recommended that "the best policy to pursue is definite segregation." Such an approach, he admitted, would be rejected by some African Americans, but he held a poor opinion of these critics. They were the ones "who are not content with a gradual and steady improvement in the interracial relations but must have their millennium at once." The Park Service, he concluded, should slow down and quit "making a mountain out of a mole hill . . . every time a high-toned Negro files a complaint about segregation of races." Instead, the NPS should reconsider its policy of nonsegregation, which might be fine for some people elsewhere in the country, but, he added darkly, "will work to the disadvantage of the southern Negro, although it might be to the advantage of the rare Negro tourist."[50]

An End to Segregation

Thus, the situation in the southern national parks remained largely static for a year. William J. Trent Jr. continued to work at the Federal Works Agency, where he occasionally received requests from the public to end national park segregation or inquiries about national park segregation from Interior Department staff, even as he intermittently fired off his own missives against it to Secretary Ickes and his staff. Even so, a larger lesson was being learned—Trent had been correct about the unpredictability of social change. Frequent, numerous complaints were lodged about the continuing racial segregation at most of the Shenandoah National Park facilities, including from one writer who, like Trent, denounced it as "an inexcusable violation of the letter and spirit of democracy," but no one complained about the nonsegregated Pinnacles Picnic Ground. Ickes, however, remained cautious, generally sticking to his policy. Nonetheless, he said nothing when Assistant Secretary Burlew, with Trent's support, persuaded Cammerer's permanent successor at the National Park Service, Newton B. Drury, to extend the nonsegregation "experiment" to all of Shenandoah's picnic grounds in the spring of 1941. Burlew was able to persuade Drury to change the park's policy because a January 1941 study had revealed that only about 1 percent of Shenandoah National Park's visitors during 1939 and 1940 had been African American and that only a handful of complaints had been lodged during the 1940 season when the various white-only picnic areas occasionally had been used by African Americans. Despite this positive move, Drury and Burlew (and undoubtedly Ickes as well) retained some wariness. Shenandoah's two campgrounds and its other accommodations, they decided, were to remain segregated, and fearing a public backlash, they ordered that "no publicity or statements will be given out locally regarding this decision."[51] As before, no written complaints were received by the Park Service about the elimination of the segregated picnic areas or the creation of nonsegregated ones.

This progressive change in policy might have continued to expand slowly over the next several years, but as with so many other social issues, World War II overwhelmed racial segregation in the national parks. In early April 1942, as the United States marshaled its natural and human resources for a prolonged fight, Archibald MacLeish, director of the U.S. government's Office of Facts and Figures, sent Ickes a confidential memorandum about "Negro morale." A recent report by his department's Bureau of Intelligence had revealed a poor situation, which he and the other members of the Committee on War Information viewed as one of "extreme seriousness." MacLeish was therefore contacting Ickes and other high-ranking federal officials in the hope that "such action as can be taken within the federal government to alleviate existing tensions may be taken as rapidly as possible." The committee recommended a variety of informational steps to be pursued by the federal government, but, MacLeish reported, "words should be supplemented by action." In particular, he declared, "Every effort should be made to advance as far as possible, under war conditions, the Negro's aspirations to be freed from discriminatory restrictions." Eliminating inequity would be more difficult than issuing propaganda, he admitted, but doing so "is clearly the most effective" action to be taken. In conclusion, MacLeish asked Ickes to "send me your views as to what steps, if any, your department feels it can take, or has already taken, with respect to this problem."[52]

Unsurprisingly, Ickes had E. K. Burlew meet with William J. Trent Jr. to discuss the Interior Department's response to MacLeish's inquiry. On May 19, 1942, Trent sent Burlew his thoughts in a memorandum that called for a variety of actions, including "improving employment opportunities for Negroes" and for the secretary to speak more frequently before African American organizations. Trent, however, had not lost his interest in camping and outdoor recreation, and so he also insisted that national park segregation had to end. "You will recall," Trent reminded Burlew, that during earlier meetings on the subject "the Secretary was of the opinion . . . that he was not inclined to want to set up 'jurisdictional islands' in the various states." African Americans, however, feel differently, he insisted. They believe "the Federal Government does have a responsibility in such matters and should exert its authority to destroy racial barriers within the confines of its jurisdiction." Trent recommended that the secretary "issue a directive to all National Park Superintendents in the south and southeast informing them that hereafter there are to be no segregated areas in National Parks." Such a change would be exactly the type of action that MacLeish had suggested would achieve the greatest improvement in African American opinion about the war.[53]

Two days later, on May 21, Ickes replied to MacLeish's April letter. In it he discussed his hiring of three "Advisers on Negro Affairs," including Trent, and several other efforts his office had made to improve the condition of African American life. Prominent among the latter were steps taken concerning national park discrimination. "For several years," offered Ickes, "I have been working with leaders of the Negro race in Washington to open up national park and monument areas in the Southern States to Negroes. In the Shenandoah National Park we experimented with several picnic areas and have had no serious complaint." As a result, Ickes informed MacLeish, he had decided to embrace Trent's recommendations. "I expect to extend this non-discriminatory policy to other areas as rapidly as possible." Although Ickes did not commit to a timetable for the policy change, he had Burlew send a copy of Trent's recommendations and his own reply to the MacLeish letter to NPS director Drury, with a memorandum asking the latter to "have a review made at an early date with reference to national parks and monuments in the Southern States to extend the non-discriminatory practice which we inaugurated in the Shenandoah National Park." Within a week, Drury contacted the regional director for the southern national parks, the superintendent of the Blue Ridge Parkway (authorized in 1936), and the national park superintendents at Shenandoah, Great Smoky Mountains, and Mammoth Cave (authorized in 1941) to ascertain their views on the situation. What, he asked each, are "your observations on this general subject of extending non-segregation practices to [Park] Service areas in the southern states?"[54] Drury soon had an answer for the secretary.

On June 12, 1942, Drury personally handed Assistant Secretary Burlew a memorandum stating that nonsegregation was close to being de facto policy in national park campgrounds and recreational facilities throughout the South. "The signs designating picnic and campgrounds for Negroes and whites have been removed" at the Shenandoah Park. At Mammoth Cave in Kentucky, "the campground and picnic area are open to whites and Negroes alike," and all personnel and concessionaire employees had been instructed that "Negro visitors were not to be segregated" in any way. Again, Trent's insight proved correct, and Drury could note that "this arrangement has resulted in no criticism." No segregation signs were located at the picnic or campground areas at Great Smoky Mountains, and although restrooms at the park's Newfound Gap and Forney Ridge areas "have separate toilets designated for Negroes inside the building," they have "a common entrance" on the outside. The only site where any segregation appeared was along the Blue Ridge Parkway. No segregation signs were present at any of the picnic areas or campgrounds, but paradoxically, three new picnic areas were under construction at Bluff Park (later Doughton Park), North Carolina, with one being for whites, one for blacks, and one for joint use. Also, at Pine Spur near Roanoke, Virginia, a "special campground" was being constructed for "the large Negro population" that lived nearby. Tying up these loose ends, Drury sent a final memorandum on the subject on June 15, 1942, to the regional director for southern national parks to inform him that it was his task "to make certain that the policy of the Department on the non-segregation of Negroes is carried out in the southern areas administered by the National Park Service." He was responsible, Drury implied, for eliminating the segregated parkway facilities rapidly because racial segregation had finally come to an end in the parks.[55]

At the same time, Drury cautioned the regional director to say nothing to the public and to let their superiors make any announcements. If the nonsegregation of national park campgrounds was to become news, that news would come out of the Department of the Interior. Four days later, however, the Interior Department's director of information, Walter Onslow, recommended to Burlew that no announcement about the policy change be made. In Onslow's view, a press release "might give the impression that we are going out of our way to raise an issue." Instead, he suggested that it was possible to "find a better opportunity for issuing a bona fide release which will be of interest to the Negro press regarding the Park Service." After a few days, Secretary Ickes approved Onslow's recommendation, yet no release was ever made. The first federal agency had officially eliminated racial segregation from within its jurisdiction, but the opportunity was lost to inform the nation that this instance of official discrimination had fallen.[56]

Nonetheless, the end of national park segregation was good news to William J. Trent Jr., who had spent years encouraging African Americans to organize and support recreational demonstration areas, promoting camps for black youths, and pushing back racial discrimination and segregation in the campgrounds of southern national parks. Trent continued to work in Washington as a race relations officer in the Federal Works Agency until 1944, when he debarked for New York City to become the first executive director of the newly formed United Negro College Fund. He remained in that position for twenty years, during which time the fund raised about $78 million. In 1964, Trent was hired away from the fund by James Linen, the president of Time Life Inc. Linen was unhappy with the small number of black employees at the firm, and he was able to persuade Trent to become the company's assistant personnel director with an emphasis on affirmative action. According to Trent, "Percentages didn't increase drastically the first year or so, but after that they started moving along."[57] Trent retired in 1975 to return to Greensboro, North Carolina, where he lived and remained active for the rest of his life. At various times during his New York and Greensboro years, Trent volunteered to serve on a wide range of community organizations, including the boards of Livingstone College, Johnson C. Smithy University, New York Community Trust, the National Council of Philanthropy, and the National Foundation for the Improvement of Education. After a lifetime of service, he passed away in 1993.

William J. Trent Jr. did not consciously begin his campground odyssey, but he embraced it as its importance became clear. During his lifetime, Trent never took up camping himself, but his lack of personal interest did not prevent him from being at the forefront of the successful fight to make it more available to African Americans. In contrast to the many advocates for camping, for Trent the issue was never whether people should camp, but their right to do so. As a consequence of this struggle to liberalize national park campgrounds, African Americans could, should they wish, make a pilgrimage to wild nature along with white Americans, and together they could attempt to reinforce their common American values and identity.

CHAPTER SIX

A CLEARER PICTURE
OF THIS COUNTRY

Trailer Camping to Discover America

In August 1971, President Richard Nixon honored Carolyn Bennett Patterson for her public service efforts on behalf of the Wally Byam Foundation, which she chaired. "It was a pleasure to learn recently of the outstanding contributions which you have made to promoting international goodwill and to increasing foreign tourism to this country." The foundation, which was named after the founder of the Airstream Trailer Company, had been supporting international cooperation programs since the early 1960s, but Nixon especially wished to praise "Caravan America," the cooperative program that it had developed with the U.S. Department of State. Using Airstream trailers and automobiles arranged by the foundation, the State Department had been able to send many groups of foreign visitors on camping trips into America's rural and wild lands. "Your imaginative caravan trips," Nixon declared, "have given hundreds of distinguished foreign families, including those of diplomats, a clearer picture of this country and of the American people."[1] According to the president, if not for the camping trips, these foreign visitors would have seen little but the country's cities and necessarily come away with a misimpression of America's true character (fig. 6.1).

The president also applauded the foundation's support for America's diplomatic corps. State Department staff and their families normally were cycled through the United States as their posts changed from one foreign land to another. During this hiatus, they were given extended vacations before they again went abroad to become America's face. Nixon was particularly pleased with the Wally Byam Foundation because it had been providing

Figure 6.1. Carolyn Bennett Patterson accepted a U.S. State Department "Tribute of Appreciation" in early August 1971 for the cooperative programs organized by the Wally Byam Foundation. Two weeks later, the White House commended her personal efforts. From Carolyn Bennett Patterson Collection, Manuscripts Division, Special Collections Department, Mississippi State University Libraries. Photo by Vardell C. Nesbitt / U.S. State Department.

these staffers with a camping opportunity that reinforced their connections to America. "You have been most generous," he thanked Chairman Patterson, "in making it possible for American Foreign Service Officers and their families to travel throughout the country [with Airstream trailers] on their leaves." The Rediscover America program, Nixon continued, "has proven to be a particularly enjoyable way for our diplomats to renew their appreciation for the country they represent."[2] Again Nixon seems to have felt that a trailer camping vacation provided a more authentic and vital experience of America than would one spent in any of its cities.

Nixon's perception of trailer camping as truer and more renewing than any form of urban leisure fits comfortably within the historic arc of camping's development. From the outset, campers of all sorts had regarded cities with suspicion, and the camping diaries they filled, the guidebooks they thumbed, and the other camping literature they read commonly resonated with this dissatisfaction. The solution, of course, was clear. Trailer campers could escape from the routine and restrictions of ordinary life by temporarily stepping out of their urban lives, into the world of nature, and then returning to everyday life both physically and spiritually renewed and refreshed. Trailer campers, like other campers, were pilgrims taking a turn through sacred space.

The First Recreational Vehicles

As detailed in the first two chapters, nineteenth-century campers had backpacked, horse packed, canoe camped, or horse-and-wagon camped, but early in the twentieth century they began to embrace cars. The inexpensive automobile had appeared before World War I, and by 1918 many middle-class campers were using it to camp in tents. At about the same time, they also began to use motor vehicles to power or pull a variety of recreational vehicles (RVs), but it is uncertain when the earliest trailers and motor homes appeared. During the late nineteenth century, urban residents seeking nature recreation had begun to travel in horse-drawn wagons along rural and wildland roads. Many of them camped, but some, imitating "Gypsies," went so far as to transform their vehicles into colorful wagons. Motor-home historian Roger B. White argues that these vehicles may have been the first RVs, but Americans did not in fact own large numbers of camping vehicles until automobiles began to be mass produced.[3]

Even though automobiles rapidly became inexpensive, the enhanced efficiency, calculability, predictability, and control of McDonaldization was slow to take hold among RV manufacturers, who generally failed to provide the earliest RV campers with the specialized equipment that might enhance their comfort and convenience. Nonetheless, such equipment quickly appeared among RV campers, as they, like tent campers, happily invented, constructed, and modified a wide array of devices to fit their visions and to smooth RV camping's roughness. They cheerfully embraced this "tinkering" approach to RV camping because they were embedded in a cultural discourse that regarded technology positively and a society that praised those with the knowledge to adopt and adapt it. According to historian Kathleen Franz, the source of this "almost unqualified enthusiasm" was the recent and widespread appearance of electricity, telephones, radio, and many other devices in middle-class homes, workplaces, schools, and other public settings. Some critics questioned these technological changes, but popular culture endorsed and fostered this American ardor, with magazines like *Popular Science* and *Popular Mechanics*.[4] Early trailer and motor-home campers in particular directed their technological enthusiasm toward creating RVs that would temper the challenges of natural environments by introducing the comfort, regularity, and familiarity they associated with home.

Loosely defined, a motor home is a self-propelled RV that provides living accommodations, and handcrafted ones appeared on America's roads shortly after the turn of the twentieth century as the middle classes embraced camping. One of the first was constructed in 1905 by Roy A. Faye and

Freeman N. Young, who, in the words of Roger B. White, "built a special sleeping body and installed it on an automobile chassis." Technologically sophisticated, it slept four adults on bunks, was lit by incandescent lights, and included an icebox and radio. During the following decades, other well-off tinkerers adapted a variety of automobiles and truck chassis as they sought to create more spacious and comfortable vehicles. A watershed was crossed in 1915, however, when Roland and Mary Conklin leapt up in design and scale. Unlike their predecessors, the wealthy Conklins modified a bus into a fully furnished, double-deck motor home that they called the Gypsy Van. Strikingly equipped—some might say overequipped—with an electrical generator and incandescent lighting, a full kitchen, Pullman-style sleeping berths, a folding table and desk, a concealed bookcase, a phonograph, convertible sofas with throw pillows, a variety of small appliances, and even a "roof garden," this RV was a marvel of technology and brio. The *New York Times*, which published several articles about the vehicle, was not sure what to call it, suggesting that it was a "sublimated English caravan, land-yacht, or what you will," but was certain that it had "all the conveniences of a country house, plus the advantages of unrestricted mobility and independence of schedule." Of course, the vehicle might have remained nothing more than a local oddity, but, according to White, it "influenced the design of camping vehicles for decades" because the family journey in it from New York to the Panama-Pacific Exposition in California was "widely publicized" in American newspapers and magazines.[5]

The Conklins were not the only wealthy Americans to be attracted to camping in motor homes, but the others usually purchased their vehicles ready-made. During the 1920s, for instance, Pierce-Arrow manufactured touring landau cars and modified delivery trucks (including one for T. Coleman du Pont) for wealthy customers who wished to camp. By the middle of the decade and with the economy booming, several additional automobile and truck manufacturers also offered a limited number of fully complete motor homes, including REO's "speed wagon bungalow" and Hudson-Essex's "Pullman Coach."[6]

For any camper who sought (and could afford) to smooth the roughness of an adventure, the appeal of motor homes was simple and clear: the ease of camp establishment and an enhanced sense of freedom. An auto camper had to erect a tent, prepare bedding, unpack clothes, and establish a kitchen and dining area, which could take hours. The motor-home camper could avoid much of this effort. According to one 1920s observer, a motor home enthusiast simply "let down the back steps and the thing was done." And departure was just as simple. After breakfast, "he pulled up the steps and drove away while his wife washed the dishes." Motor-home campers, this observer admitted, could not travel as fast as other vehicles, but their freedom to depart quickly and to stay on the road later than other campers allowed them to "cover as much ground as the best of them."[7] By the middle of the 1920s, many Americans of more average means were converting vehicles into small motor homes or, if they heartily embraced tinkering, building their own motor homes along the lines identified by the Conklins.

Motor homes might have remained the only motorized alternative to auto camping with a tent, but they came with two distinct limitations. According to our 1920s observer, who owned a camping trailer, motor homes possessed "a bulk that sometimes proved troublesome, and an inappropriateness for sight-seeing purposes." The motor-home camper could not, like a trailer camper, disconnect the latter and drive the automobile alone to shop at a nearby store, swim in a lake, or reach a remote trailhead for a hike. Moreover, many motor homes were large and could travel only on an automobile-friendly road after a serious (and sometimes alarming) effort. According to our observer, he and his family met a motor-home camper "who told us he had been obliged to cut some timbers from an overhead railroad bridge before he could manage to squeeze beneath it"! As a consequence of these limitations and their relatively high cost, motor homes remained a marginal choice among recreational vehicle campers before 1965.[8] Trailers, in contrast, found considerable favor among campers.

Any unpowered, wheeled device pulled by a separate power source can be called a trailer, and many such devices have been used to haul goods and materials. Trailers were first pulled by horse-drawn vehicles and thus predate the development of the automobile by millennia, but have become common since the latter's appearance. The recreational-vehicle form of a trailer, which is organized around the idea of a bedroom on wheels and is sometimes called a "travel trailer," is a specialized device designed for camping and other sorts of touring. Trailer historian David A. Thornburg reports that the first camping trailers appeared not in the United States, but in southern England by 1906. Typically called "motor caravans" throughout the United Kingdom, they included minimal conveniences—a stove and bunks—and were often modeled on the colorful, horse-drawn caravans used by the Roma people, or Gypsies, but with two wheels instead of four, and towed by a car. Happily embraced by the English, stripped-down versions of these camping trailers quickly crossed the Atlantic and were reported in the United States during the 1910s.[9]

The earliest American trailers were even more spartan than those of their English cousins. Instead of being a form of mobile housing that recalled some sort of romantic past, they were a plain device for carrying tents, sleeping bags, coolers, and other camping equipment. A few of these initial trailers were commercially manufactured by mid-decade, but most were tinkered together by the same sort of campers who modified the running boards on their cars. Sometimes campers converted the back half of an automobile or truck into a trailer, or they might assemble one from motor-vehicle components, many of which were readily available through mail-order catalogs. Still others, perhaps concerned about reliability and safety, purchased a complete basic trailer from a firm like Sears, Roebuck & Company. In its fall 1918 catalog, the company offered a forty-by-fifty-six-inch trailer for $62.50 that, when assembled, could carry up to eight hundred pounds and attached easily to a Ford car. Furthermore, truly motivated campers were not restricted to simply carrying equipment in their trailer. They could attach such features as tent canvas and a frame for shelter, cots for sleeping, cupboards for cooking equipment, and anything else that struck their fancy and that could be accommodated. These customized trailers were frequently eccentric because, as historian Warren James Belasco observed, "campers loved gadgets." Whether homemade or purchased and assembled, collapsible equipment of all sorts held a strong attraction for campers, especially when it could transform basic trailers into "trim wagons that miraculously mushroomed into bungalows with beds, stove, table and screened windows." Nevertheless, some of these early trailers performed poorly on the road, no matter how comfortable, convenient, and attractive they may have been. In Melville F. Ferguson's 1925 account of his family's camping adventures, he reports that they occasionally came across homemade trailers for sale by owners who were far from home but disgusted with their towed burden and wished to be rid of it quickly.[10]

Tent Trailers

For campers who could not or did not want to construct a trailer, it became possible to purchase a fully equipped one by the mid-1910s. A September 1916 article in the popular magazine *Outing* recommended "camp trailering" to its readers and informed them that they did not have to build one themselves. "Several firms," it announced, "have recently taken up the manufacture of camping trailers [which] is proof of their increasing popularity." These companies produced the first travel trailers in a collapsible form, what today is referred to as a "tent trailer." When being pulled, a tent trailer was folded into a compact form with a tight exterior that was generally either a low "A" shape or smoothed down flat. When erected at a campsite, however, it opened into an expanse of canvas that rested on or over the trailer. The unfolding process was, according to *Outing*, simple and straightforward.

Figure 6.2. The Los Angeles Trailer Company was among the first to manufacture tent trailers, in 1916. As with other new, modern camping equipment, the company's advertisement emphasized enjoyment and comfort. From *Sunset* magazine, July 1916, 76.

"First the two large bed frames that close in the top of the trailer are opened out on either side and propped in place by means of attached uprights. They are each large enough to form a double bed. Then the framework of the tent is set up. This consists of three-sided rectangular frames of ash forming the ridgepole and the side-supports, which slant upward from the body of the trailer. Then the tent, which is a double-filled, army khaki duck affair, is drawn over them and fitted into place. Between the beds, on the floor of the trailer, there is room enough to set up a folding table on which meals may be served. Compartments to serve as icebox and 'pantry' are also provided."[11]

None of these companies, however, constructed camp trailers in large quantities. Instead, they produced them in small numbers along with other camping products, but the market would soon change.

From its outset, trailer camping appealed to people from a variety of social backgrounds. The first mass producer of travel trailers was the Curtiss Aeroplane and Motor Company of Buffalo and Hammondsport, New York, whose products were anything but working class. Beginning in 1917, aviation pioneer Glenn Curtiss built a fifth-wheel "Motor Bungalow" that David A. Thornburg called "a clever combination of airplane and boat design." The Motor Bungalow, however, was not a tent trailer, but a sleek plywood container over six feet high and six feet wide inside, with a rounded roof. The design skillfully integrated canvas-covered tilt-out beds into each side, which when unfolded nearly tripled the width of the trailer. Subsequent Curtiss trailers were generally smaller but nonetheless attractive, well-appointed, easy to tow (although the fifth-wheel design required a special hitching arrangement), and even easier and faster to set up than tent trailers. They were not, however, a commercial success. Costing as much as $3,000 when a Ford Model T could be purchased for about $400, Curtiss trailers were unaffordable for the middle and working classes yet not to the tastes of the wealthy. As a consequence, the Curtiss Company ceased trailer production in 1922 but not before demonstrating that a market existed for such mass-produced but lower-priced vehicles as the Chenango Camp Trailer, which had begun production in 1920.[12]

Chenango and other tent-trailer companies were successful during the 1920s because trailer camping, like auto camping, grew rapidly, although the former never reached the scale of the latter. Unfortunately, no reliable data exist to indicate the true scale of trailer camping. Nevertheless, we can sense the size of it from the decade's "how-to-camp" literature. The principal guidebooks from the period, including F. E. Brimmer's *Auto Camping*, J. C. Long and J. D. Long's *Motor Camping*, and Elon Jessup's *Roughing It Smoothly*, each provided at least one chapter on trailer camping, while articles in popular magazines like *Sunset* and *Popular Mechanics* regularly mentioned trailer camping. In all these publications, trailer camping was typically held in a positive light. In addition, popular sources indicate that the number of trailer manufacturers was increasing, which strongly suggests a growing market. In his 1921 publication *The Motor Camping Book*, Jessup devoted a chapter to camping with a trailer because, he asserted, "the motor camping trailer is more or less in a class by itself." A tent camper had to be cautious about his selection of bedding and tent because these items had to fit into a camper's auto while leaving enough room for the campers themselves. If, however, every camper used a trailer, suggested Jessup, the point would be moot, and "there would be few problems left to discuss." At the same time, he admitted there had been criticism of trailers, but he dismissed it as old news and no longer relevant. "For several years, trailers were in an experimental stage," but no more. Manufacturers had made significant improvements, "with the result that the trailer is much more of an established working proposition than it was a few years ago." Nor was Jessup alone in his conclusion that trailer camping was "established." According to *Automotive Industries*, a trade magazine, "about a dozen makes of camping trailers" were on the market in the summer of 1922.[13]

Trailer camping grew in popularity for at least two reasons. First, like other modes of camping, it supported campers' desire to head out of their mundane urban lives and enter nature's uplifting, refreshing space. In 1923's *Motor Camping*, J. C. Long and J. D. Long made no distinction between auto camping with a tent versus with a trailer when they declared that urban

Americans were "hemmed in by the restrictions of modern business life" but were "possessed of the desire to be somewhere else." Consequently they have found "a new and increasing way of satisfying this desire for recreation and adventure"—motor camping. Millions traveled to campsites each year, and "the immense popularity of motor camping is easy to understand when one realizes that this pastime is romantic, healthful, [and] educative."[14]

Trailer camping also increased in popularity because it appealed to those families who wished to have their equipment ready for quick use, to be off the ground at their campsite, and to be able to cook and eat under cover when the weather was inclement. This mode of camping provided its practitioners with greater calculability, predictability, control, and efficiency than did auto camping with a tent. Using "home" as a principal point of reference and generally promoted in terms of "comfort," "convenience," "ease," and "economy," trailers obviously expressed the ongoing McDonaldization of camping. "Your camping trip will be made doubly enjoyable by using a BRINTNALL CONVERTIBLE CAMPING TRAILER," blared an advertisement by the Los Angeles Trailer Company (fig. 6.2). The trailer was "light," incorporated "comfortable exclusive folding bed features," and had a "roomy" storage compartment for luggage, which left the car free to be "used for passengers." In the same vein, the Chenango Equipment Company noted in a brochure for its trailer that its mass-production method meant "standard units," which provided control and eliminated "all the element of chance." They also quoted the letters of satisfied owners that reveal the aspects of trailer camping most important to prospective buyers. "The Chenango Camp Trailer is all that you claim for it," wrote S. K. Simon of Rockville Center, New York. "I have never slept any more comfortably—even at home. The whole design and outfit cannot be improved upon for camping with the entire family with safety, ease and comfort." It was like being at home; the camper did not need to fear that a trailer was uncomfortable, unsafe, or difficult to use. The *New York Times* also addressed similar concerns about the common fears and annoyances of roughing it. A 1916 article, with the subtitle "Latest Devices Promote Comfort and Add Little to the Ardent Motorist's Expenses," reviewed a range of the latest equipment for smoothing camping's roughness. One item, however, stood out for the author—the trailer. "The most complete device for an extended camping trip is a two-wheeled trailer," which "embraces a waterproof tent with two full-size beds, and a complete equipment for enjoying all the comforts of home for any length of time, regardless of weather conditions. This trailer . . . can be readily attached to any car and operated without annoyance to car or trailer." At the same time, some authors cautioned campers that trailers had limits and could be difficult. In 1923's *Motor Camping*, authors Long and Long warned readers that when campers employed a trailer, they had to either stick to "wide roadways and easy grades" or be well trained at backing down steep and curving mountain roads.[15]

The Fergusons' Long Adventure

The Longs' caveat about trailers did not deter Melville F. Ferguson, whose family odyssey neatly captures the trailer camper's tempering of the roughness that accompanies pilgrimage with the McDonaldization that smooths and comforts. A contemporary of the long-distance tent campers Mary Crehore Bedell and her husband (see chapter 3), Ferguson became known for his *Motor Camping on Western Trails*, his account of an eighteen-thousand-mile journey from June 1923 to June 1924 as he trailer camped across the West and around Hawaii with his wife, three college-age daughters, parents-in-law, and seventy-eight-year-old mother. Starting in his book's preface, Ferguson made it clear that he had trailer camped as a pilgrim and hoped his story would inspire others to do so as well. The book's object, he asserted, was "to present in faithful outlines a picture of the every-day routine of a mode of travel that is yearly taking a stronger hold upon the fancy of the vacationist who is weary of sticking to conventional ruts and who feels that life owes him a new thrill." It was a thrill, Ferguson would imply, that could not be found in an exclusively urban life.[16]

For Ferguson, who at age forty-eight was a reporter for the *Philadelphia Record*, the adventure began a year before departure when he read a magazine article that contrasted urban strictures with camping's freedom. "The eye of a jaded city-dweller" fell on the appealing article, began Ferguson. It described "the care-free existence of those nomads [i.e., campers] that one meets on the country roads on a summer's day," and to Ferguson it "drew an alluring sketch of the joys which those only who are willing to foreswear soft creature comforts may taste." In other words, Ferguson understood that campers had to rough it in order to feel the joy. Camping appealed to Ferguson, he admitted, because he was tired of his daily life. Speaking of himself in the third person, he wrote: "He had been looking at brick walls, the asphalt pavement, the hard, narrow cañon of cut stone, for forty-eight years." But it was not just the physical place that repulsed him; it was also the routine. "He hated alarm clocks, the cellar heater, and the face of the conductor who twice daily punched his ticket on the suburban train." When he read the camping article, the solution to his angst became clear to him. He must retreat into nature. "He longed for the open spaces, the scent of the moist forest, the wide sweep of the wind across the stark prairie, the gurgle of meadow rivulets, the roar of the mountain torrent, the acrid tang of burning wood. He knew he must go." Ferguson discussed the idea with his family, which concurred, and these eight people, who were "habituated to an easy routine that is carelessly called solid comfort," settled on a twelve-month camping adventure.[17]

As the family set about planning their travels, they realized that other campers might dispense with many conveniences when going only for a week, but that they did not care to be so spartan when going for a year. "In view of the length of the expedition," Ferguson related, they understood that "a way must be found of roughing it smoothly." With eight on the voyage, they decided to auto camp with both of their cars and then identified all the gear they would need. However, when they realized how much equipment, clothing, and other items they collectively claimed were necessary, "it dawned on us that we were about to essay the impossible. It was then that we determined upon trailers."[18]

No one in the Ferguson household had trailer camped before, so they began to systematically peruse catalogs, study brochures, and correspond with manufacturers before settling on two of the "bungalow types." These included such typical comfort-enhancing features as "double spring-beds, with mattresses" that were attached to the inner surface of the trailers' sides. "When the sides were lowered to a horizontal position, extending four feet outward from the line of the body, the roof automatically rose two feet. Behold a cunning little cottage with sleeping room for four persons, amply ventilated by screened and curtained windows, and sheltered by a roof" (fig. 6.3). It was waterproof, dividable with a canvas curtain, included a "kitchenette" of shelving and an icebox, a wardrobe, a folding table, and six-volt lighting. As much as they appreciated the kitchenette, they did not think it alone would be able to provide them with "the accustomed wholesome fare of home life," which they considered essential on their long voyage. Consequently, they built a custom food and cookware storage box with shelves and two hinged doors, which rode on one car's running board.[19]

Despite the author's pointed link between camping's "joy" and "roughing it," on the family's second day of travel, Ferguson noted the comfort provided by the tent trailer. It was raining, and they "pitied poor campers whose footing was the muddy earth while we perched high and dry . . . in our bungalow" trailer. Eight months later he still felt this way. In contrast to the paeans of some camping advocates, Ferguson never mentioned feelings of personal "uplift" or "rejuvenation" while camping conditions were rough (for example, when it was very hot and water scarce in the Mojave Desert), but he did remark readily upon the benefits of the tent trailer and their equipment. At the Grand Canyon it was so cold that snow lay on the ground. "Happily," he smiled, "while the interiors of our bungalows were

Figure 6.3. The Fergusons prepare breakfast around their tent trailer in Milford, Illinois, during the summer of 1925. From M. R. Ferguson, *Motor Camping on Western Trails* (New York: Century, 1925), opposite 33.

not exactly comfortable dressing-rooms when the thermometer hovered near the freezing-point, we slept under thick layers of blankets, and, clad in flannelette pajamas with the legs tucked into heavy woolen bedsocks, we suffered but trifling inconvenience."[20]

As the year unfolded, Ferguson commented positively on the social aspects of trailer camping. He and the family stayed in many private auto campgrounds, as well as municipal, state, and federal campgrounds along the way. They met many people in these facilities, and like other types of campers came away feeling better for the interactions. About midway through the year, while traveling along the Pacific Coast, Ferguson became aware of the social diversity in campgrounds. "All sorts and conditions of people are on the road: the business man on vacation; the farmer whose crops have been harvested and who seeks relaxation gadding about; the migrant removing from one section of the country to another . . . and the hobo whose only worldly goods are the clothes on his back, a ragged blanket, and the dilapidated vehicle, resurrected from a boneyard, in which he travels." Ferguson did not condemn or disparage these campground conditions or the social mixing in them. Quite the contrary, he described them as valuably "eye-opening" for himself and his family as well as just plain "interesting."[21]

On another occasion, at a national forest campground on Lake Tahoe, Ferguson remarked on the spotlessness of the camping area, which stood in contrast to many private and municipal campgrounds the family had visited. He felt the neatness was a response to how the campers were treated.

The rangers treated the campers "decently," and the latter subsequently kept the place clean. "Would that all camps were presided over by these efficient, courteous young men," he proclaimed. Other camp managers varied widely in their policies and practices, and some on occasion had treated the Fergusons and other families poorly, as if they were unwanted and untrustworthy. Forest Service rangers, in contrast, "have a knack of making the tourist feel that he is neither a mendicant nor an intruder, but a stockholder visiting his own property to inspect the investment." In these public camping areas, *communitas* prevailed, and everyone appeared to Ferguson to be equal in the eyes of the government. Moreover, social equalization and group identity were heightened at these forest and park camping areas by their policy of campfires. "There was a spirit of sociability," observed Ferguson while they camped at Lake Tahoe, "fostered by the community camp-fire, not to be found so highly developed elsewhere."[22] Camping with a tent trailer did not prevent the Fergusons from feeling sociable and equal to the other campers, most of whom were likely using tents, and vice versa. Everyone was part of the larger community. Trailers, however, were about to change.

Solid-Body Trailers

In the summer of 1928, just four years after Melville Ferguson and his family tent-trailer camped about America, Arthur G. Sherman and his family headed out from their Detroit home on a more modest camping trip to upper Michigan. A bacteriologist and the president of Sherman Laboratories, a pharmaceutical company, Sherman departed with a newly purchased tent trailer that the manufacturer had claimed could be opened into a waterproof cabin in five minutes. Apparently Sherman had never tested this claim, so that when he and his family went to set it up for the first time during a rainstorm, they "couldn't master it after an hour's wrestling," and everyone got soaked. The experience so disgusted Sherman—who recalled having read about "houses on wheels," which struck him as a better approach than a canvas trailer—that he decided to create his own trailer. According to David A. Thornburg, the initial design for Sherman's travel or camping trailer was "a little masonite bungalow on wheels," which stood six feet wide by nine feet long and no taller than the family's car. On each side was a small window for ventilation, and two more up front. Inside, Sherman placed cupboards, an icebox, a stove, built-in furniture, and storage to either side of a narrow central aisle. "It was ugly and cramped," admitted Thornburg, "but it had a solid, waterproof roof, and you didn't have to unfold it." Sherman

Figure 6.4. The Covered Wagon Trailer Company's catalog for 1937 featured seventeen-, nineteen-, and twenty-two-foot "all steel" trailers. Courtesy of the Wisconsin Historical Society.

had a carpenter build it for him for about $500, and the family took their new "Covered Wagon" (named by the children) on a camping trip the following summer of 1929. It had some problems—principally that it was too low inside—but the trailer "aroused interest wherever it went," and many campers offered to buy it from him.[23] An idea, as they say, was born.

That fall, Sherman built two additional Covered Wagons. One was for a friend, but the other one he kept and displayed as a model at the Detroit Auto Show in January 1930. He set the price at $400, which was expensive, and although few people came by his display, those who did were "fanatically interested." By the end of the show, Sherman had sold 118 units, and the Covered Wagon Company was born. Over the next decade the trailer company grew rapidly, and to meet demand, Covered Wagon built its trailers on an assembly line modeled on the auto industry. Parts came down from above or moved in from the sides as the unit traveled on its own wheels from one end of the line to the other. At its peak, the company could complete thirty-five units per day, and it offered several models, from basic to deluxe, at prices ranging from $395 to over $1,200 (fig. 6.4).

In 1936, Covered Wagon was the largest trailer producer in an expanding American industry, selling approximately six thousand units (about one of six commercially produced trailers), with gross sales of $3 million.[24]

Arthur Sherman's solid-body trailer quickly gained acceptance, and his company succeeded for a range of reasons. First, Sherman was in the right place, at the right time, with the right idea. Detroit was at the center of the Great Lakes states, which were the source of most of the period's auto campers headed south and west. Furthermore, it was the hub of the automobile industry, so a wide range of parts and skills was available, especially once the Depression dampened demand for new automobiles. Second, the homemade construction and alteration of automobiles and trailers that had been an integral part of the era's fascination with "tinkering" was in decline. According to Kathleen Franz, the manufacturers of automobiles and their accessories made "a concerted effort to consolidate innovation in the hands of professional designers and engineers," which made their products easier for amateurs to use but more difficult to modify. Third, a solid-body trailer took another step along the path of McDonaldization by providing space that was usable at any time. Unlike a tent trailer, no folding or unfolding of canvas and packing or unpacking of equipment was necessary, and since clothing and supplies were kept in closets, cupboards, and drawers, they were ready for use whenever wanted. A hard-body trailer was clearly more comfortable and convenient than a tent trailer. Finally, some campers became disillusioned with canvas tents and tent trailers as they became associated increasingly with the population of unemployed and underemployed in America's "Hoovervilles." These squatter settlements sprang up on the edges of cites and in rural areas as the Depression unfolded. Housing in them was often constructed of any scavenged materials, but canvas tents were a common sight, too. A travel trailer priced beyond the reach of poor tent dwellers appealed to many campers. The embrace of these trailer lovers was so intense that the media covered them closely. As historian Warren Belasco neatly put it, "As several hundred thousand Americans invested up to a thousand dollars each in streamlined [trailers], gypsying and tin-can tourists became respectable again."[25]

From the late 1920s through the mid-1930s, many Americans still chose to tinker together a hard-body trailer, but commercial manufacturers of this new type of travel trailer emerged rapidly and expanded around the country in spite of the ravages of the Great Depression. By mid-decade, commercially produced hard-body travel trailers were as common as homemade ones, and tent trailers had largely disappeared. In 1937, *Fortune* estimated that approximately 160,000 to 200,000 travel trailers roamed about America. Despite the tremendous increase in the number of trailers, from this magazine's perspective, factory-built trailers were still "a luxury" for the average American family. Yes, the authors admitted, trailers could be purchased for as little as $450, but the industry emphasized their $800 to $1,200 models, which meant "they are aiming for the well-to-do." The industry, *Fortune* estimated, included approximately four hundred manufacturers nationwide, including Curtiss Aerocar of Coral Gables, Florida. The exploding popularity of the travel trailer had prompted the Curtiss Company to reenter the trailer field, and in the view of *Fortune*, they had "gone after the carriage trade," since the cheapest model they sold cost approximately $3,000, while customized ones ran as high as $25,000. Nevertheless, four Great Lakes companies dominated the travel trailer business—Covered Wagon (Detroit), Silver Dome (Detroit), Palace Travel Coach (Flint, Michigan), and Schult Trailers (Elkhart, Indiana). Together they sold about ten thousand units in 1936. By the end of the 1930s, the entire industry was producing more than twenty thousand units per year.[26]

The Trailer in Print

In concert with this expansion in trailer sales came a flowering of travel-trailer-oriented articles in popular magazines and the emergence of specialized trailer publications. This surge in trailer popularity during the 1930s is demonstrated clearly by the number of publications that addressed the topic. While automobile trailers were the subject of only three articles in widely read national magazine between 1920 and 1930, the next decade witnessed more than a hundred articles. Topics ranged from the prosaic (the quality of trailer hitches) through the fearful (trailer squatters as "menace") to the practical (a school that taught both trailer driving and trailer housekeeping). Meanwhile, the first trailer-focused periodical appeared in 1936 with the publication of *Automobile and Trailer Travel*. Within one year it was the leading specialized periodical, had changed its title to simply *Trailer Travel*, and had achieved a circulation of fifty thousand. Four additional trailering magazines were launched that same year as well.[27]

Manufacturers and advocates of travel trailers, in contrast to those of tent trailers, promoted the increasing array of products to campers with an even greater emphasis on home and the ability of their products to provide the comfort, convenience, and control characteristic of McDonaldization. The increased emphasis came about because the market for travel trailers was different from that for tent trailers. The latter appealed primarily to campers and other vacationists; few non-campers owned them, and so the market remained relatively small and promotion stayed focused on this group's sense of the balance between camping's challenges and domestic ease. From their first appearance, however, travel trailers appealed to a larger and more complex market. Campers and other vacationists were a significant segment of the market during the 1930s and beyond, but in short order travel trailers were also being purchased by sales people and others who wanted mobile housing (what came to be called house trailers) and by those seeking an alternative form of permanent housing (what today is known as a mobile home). During the 1930s, all three markets were expanding, and the distinctions between them were unclear to trailer producers and promoters. Customers from every market segment sought domesticity, comfort, and convenience in their new travel trailer, so these issues were generally foregrounded in ads targeted at campers. According to a 1930s advertisement titled " 'Home Sweet Home' Wherever You Roam," Kozy Koach trailer campers "go in comfort, and economically— minus the sacrifices to hardship and inconveniences . . . and everybody can, easily." *Popular Mechanics* hit the same notes in an article aimed at readers concerned with the latest devices—"Hitting the Trail—1935 Style." "Structurally the trailer is like a modern home," declared the author, and therefore easy to live in. In particular, it is "insulated against summer's heat and winter's cold, and [has] practically every convenience which makes for good and comfortable living." The level of convenience varied, of course, according to the price a camper was willing to pay. A 1937 Covered Wagon advertisement emphasized these optional levels by contrasting the company's different models. The lowest-priced one, the "Master," was "streamlined," which was the latest in design styles, and provided similarly contemporary amenities. This model, promised the ad, "matches the modern trend of automotive design to serve the prideful owner with permanent travel luxury." Of course, the manufacturer needed to justify a higher price for the larger "DeLuxe," which it did by comparing it with the Master in terms of domesticity and pleasantness. The more expensive trailer was not merely contemporary; it "provides an entirely new degree of travel luxury, a home-like comfort coupled with matchless interior appointments to rival the most modern home." Nothing was mentioned about either trailer's ability to carry its owners out of the city and into the wild, to generate a stronger sense of American identity, or any of the other outcomes typically mentioned by campers. Perhaps the inclusion of the "Custom Coach" in the ad is a clue that Covered Wagon was trying to appeal to all three emerging markets. In contrast to the other two models, this last one was called a "travel home" that was "the last word in privacy, year 'round livableness and spaciousness." These last qualities seem far more appropriate for the home than for the campsite.[28]

Despite any emphasis on comfort, convenience, control, and domesticity, travel trailers and trailer camping were often promoted and praised as connections to the wild and to the generative and transformative qualities sought there. The same 1930s Kozy Koach advertisement mentioned above began by questioning the workaday world. "Is there anything finer than to 'get away from it all' now and then?" asked the ad. Weekends, holidays, and vacations spent camping with a Kozy Koach trailer, it assured readers, would allow them to escape dulling routine—by traveling to the out-of-doors. Of course, work-ethic concerns might arise, leading one to feel that such leisure was inappropriate, so the ad reassured readers that such relaxation is "not only enjoyable but necessary for healthful, zestful reserve on the job." Camping in a Kozy Koach, promised its manufacturer, was not time wasted, but a marshaling of energies for production.[29]

In the same vein, a desire to "get away from it all" was perfectly natural in the view of author Freeman Marsh. In his 1937 book, *Trailers*, he announced that trailers were a step in national progress because they satisfied "a basic need or needs of a large number of people." What was it that all Americans needed? "Escape," declared Marsh. "No matter how fortunate our lot in life, there are always some things from which we would like to flee, some responsibilities we would avoid." The American national identity had its origin in acts of fleeing for freedom, Marsh noted. From the Atlantic coast where they first came ashore, "these pioneers ventured north, south and west." For Marsh, they traveled in their era's equivalent of a trailer; today a trailer gave Americans the freedom to escape the habitual. With such freedom, Marsh observed, a trailer camper could temporarily imitate the pioneers and "live in close communities," such as in a trailer camp or public campground, "or wander away to the wilderness, miles from your fellow man." Nor was Marsh the only author who saw a direct connection between pioneer wagons on the frontier and trailer camping in the wild. Charles Edgar Nash clearly felt this way when he reprinted Gene Lindberg's poem, "New Covered Wagon," in his 1937 book, *Trailer Ahoy!*

> Across the far horizons of the west
>   The covered wagon rides the trail again.
> No oxen pull it now. This wagon keeps
>   The swifter, smoother pace of modern men.
>
> . . . .
>
> The methods change, their purpose is the same,
>   And turning wheels can still make history.
> To go—to see the mountains and the plains;
>   To leave the noise of cities far behind;

> To seek a fairer fate; at least, to flee
> The dull monotony of daily grind—
> Time has not dulled the urge. The wanderlust
> Lives on forever in the hearts of men.
> Trails have grown smooth and comfort goes along
> As covered wagons travel west again.

Travel trailers may have been promoted broadly for their homelike qualities, but when the audience was campers, the desire to escape routine, to find connections to the nation's formative past, and to be renewed and restored were likely a part of the discussion and would remain so for decades to come.[30]

Wally Byam's Airstream Trailer

As the number of commercial trailer producers expanded rapidly during the early 1930s, one of the more original and enduring manufacturers from this period was the Airstream Trailer Company, formed by Wally Byam (fig. 6.5).

Described by contemporary newspapers as "jolly," "indefatigable," and "a man in motion," Byam was one of the most creative and iconic figures in the history of trailer camping. Wallace Merle Byam was born on July 4, 1896, in Baker City in far eastern Oregon. The child of divorced parents, "Wally" primarily grew up with his mother and stepfather in Astoria and then Portland, Oregon. Always adventurous, Byam revealed a love of travel early on, when during his fourteenth summer he shipped out as a cabin boy aboard an Alaskan fishing boat. He was also very bright, generally earning A's in high school and graduating in 1921 from Stanford University with honors and a bachelor's degree in history. Then, saying he had "to get out of the place," Byam headed south to Hollywood to work in the film industry. He was unable to land a position with a movie studio, but with his experience as a commissioned advertising salesman for Stanford's daily newspaper, he did find work as an advertising copywriter. He soon moved to a tabloid newspaper and then to the *Los Angeles Times*. He left this last, relatively reliable position to strike out on his own as the publisher of several trade, sports, and other magazines. By the late 1920s he owned and published seven magazines, and with his businesses flourishing, he married Marion James. But then came the 1929 stock-market crash, and his publishing days came to an end.[31]

After the loss of his magazine business, Byam decided to use his newly available free time to build a small tent trailer for himself and his wife.

Figure 6.5. Wallace "Wally" Byam and Stella Byam on 1956's European caravan. Courtesy of Dale Schwamborn.

Wally was an avid outdoorsman and long had enjoyed camping, but Marion had disliked her time in the wild. With the comfort and convenience of the trailer, Byam hoped he could change her opinion. As it turned out, neither Wally nor Marion was pleased with the tent trailer, so Byam built a small, "teardrop"-shaped hard-body trailer that slept two inside and incorporated an ice chest and gasoline-pressure stove. According to Byam, "My wife and I took a trip [through] Oregon with it; it was very easy to tow with a four-cylinder Dodge. . . . When I got back with this thing, it had caused so much comment along the way that I began to think this might be a pretty good business to get into. So I wrote a story for *Popular Mechanics* on how to build one." Byam's article, "How to Build a Trailer for One Hundred Dollars," was an immediate hit, prompting readers to write to the magazine for more information. Seizing the opportunity, Byam placed an ad in *Popular Mechanics* offering a booklet with detailed drawings for one dollar. A wave of orders followed, earning the author more than $15,000. Around the same time that he was selling these plans, a neighbor asked him to build one of the teardrop trailers for him, too. Keen to profit from the trailer business where possible, Byam settled with the neighbor on a price, hired a handyman to construct it, and fabrication began in the Byams' backyard. Soon, yet another neighbor asked Byam to build him a trailer, but this was too much for Byam's immediate neighbors, who started to complain about the noise. Consequently, Byam decided to open a small factory in Los Angeles, and his first trailers went on sale in 1932. He dubbed them "Airstreams" because, he said, they moved along the road "like a stream of air."[32]

The first Airstream trailers were attractive, colorful, and interesting in appearance because of their "humps and bulges," but they also were relatively expensive. Nevertheless, the company rapidly built and sold over one thousand units by the spring of 1932. Riding the crest of the travel-trailer craze, Byam's business steadily expanded, and in 1934 he decided to augment his income by also selling another brand of trailer, the Bowlus-Teller, which had recently been developed by William Hawley Bowlus, the aeronautical engineer who had supervised construction of Charles Lindbergh's *Spirit of St. Louis*. By using the monocoque construction technique then common in Southern California's aircraft industry and manufacturing with "duralumi-num" (aluminum with copper and magnesium), Bowlus had developed an attractive, streamlined trailer that weighed a mere eleven hundred pounds and could be pulled by hand. Unfortunately for this creative designer, he and his partner were poor businessmen, and their firm soon went bankrupt. Byam, who knew and liked the trailers, felt that he could run the company profitably, so he bought it at auction in 1935. On the heels of this move, Byam also hired several Bowlus-Teller employees, smartly redesigned the original trailer, and in 1936 began production of the first aluminum Airstream trailer—the Clipper—a name intended to recall the streamlined Pan American Airways Clipper aircraft.[33]

From the beginning, Byam capitalized on the unusual look, light weight, and solid construction of his aluminum trailers. Early advertising for the Clipper emphasized beauty, safety, and low operating costs. Calling the trailer "Sleek-dashing-svelt-daringly new, modern in the extreme," a company advertisement declared the Clipper "the ultimate picturization of the streamlined age." Furthermore, the Clipper was exceedingly well built and "all metal," so it was secure to ride in. "It is the safest thing on wheels," assured the advertisement. "There is little to splinter and it will withstand a tremendous impact." Finally, pulling a Clipper would not break the bank. With its design "determined by the laws of physics," its streamlining was so efficient and its weight so low that "at speeds above 50 miles an hour the car that tows it uses no more gasoline than it does without the trailer." Calling the Clipper "America's Finest," Airstream built nineteen-foot to twenty-six-foot versions and finished every trailer's exterior to resemble cutting-edge aircraft, while its interior—as expected with McDonaldization—was appointed to provide above-average trailer comforts. Such conveniences as a self-contained water supply, an enclosed galley, wood-lined walls, electric lights, insulation (in all walls plus the floor and ceiling), "air conditioning," and "shower, and tub baths" were typical. Moreover, these features had been arranged and appointed as carefully and as thoughtfully as they would be in a home. "To perfect a livable and comfortable interior," promised the company's advertising, "Airstream has employed the best designers and interior decorators available." In an Airstream trailer, prompted the company, "you feel that you are in your own living room or a train club car, not living in a kitchen or cooped up in a closet." At the same time, these appeals to convenience, comfort, and domesticity did not signal that an Airstream trailer was aimed only at salesmen or as alternative housing. Instead, the overall combination of engineering and design explained why, in the words of a 1937 advertisement, "Airstreams are so preferred by hunters and fishermen who go 'way back beyond.' "[34]

The Clipper was an immediate hit with campers, despite a $1,500 to $5,000 price tag that made it anywhere from two to ten times as expensive as the other Airstream models. During 1936, the company struggled to fill all its orders, including ones for Mexican president Lázaro Cárdenas and a variety of "Hollywood luminaries," but this boom was short-lived. During 1937 the trailer industry suffered a sharp downturn that would not dissipate until the 1950s. Although Airstream would survive, the company had to relocate to smaller quarters in 1938 and again in 1940 while Byam "barely kept the company alive." At the same time, the use of trailers by working-class campers and others had been viewed skeptically for decades, but as the poor economic conditions persisted, trailers became increasingly viewed as inexpensive housing rather than as travel amenities. As this perceptual shift developed, popular attitudes toward trailers and trailer camping slipped, prompting more negative comments than in the recent past. One early critic, Emilio P. Meinecke (see chapter 4), condemned trailers as "a highly objectionable and dangerous feature" in forest and park campgrounds because they used an exceptionally large amount of space, were more likely than tents to damage vegetation, and introduced "city and town life" into places designed to protect "simplicity" and "the camp spirit." In particular, Meinecke warned, if trailer camping was not regulated, there would remain little left of "the state of nature," and "a new type of city slum or suburban village with a floating population" would become established in parks and forests. Even more pointedly, conservationist Aldo Leopold (see chapter 7) denounced trailers as the "cap" on a "pyramid of banalities" that was powering "the retreat of wilderness."[35]

However, a sharp change came beginning in December 1941, when the American entry into World War II halted trailer production for the war's duration. Factory space, machinery, materials, and labor were needed to support the war effort, but once the conflict ended, many trailer manufacturers, including the Airstream Company, resumed production. Forced savings and a shortage of consumer goods during the war led to mass buying afterward. Initially, most companies emphasized house trailers to satisfy the pent-up demand for general housing, the shortage of housing that followed a wave of new marriages, the lack of student housing as universities welcomed their largest classes ever, and other market demands. In these taxing yet constrained times, camping's affordability made it popular even as advancing technologies, including camping trailers, made it increasingly attractive to those families who sought domestic comforts and less "roughing it" in the wild. As the war's impacts faded, America's economy grew rapidly with the 1950s. Soon a swelling number of affluent vacationers with powerful automobiles prompted a new round of demand for luxurious travel trailers. Increasingly, buyers sought "self-contained" trailers with all such "essential" comforts as hot and cold water, bath, toilet, refrigerator, and more. Airstream, of course, had built for this market throughout its existence, and under these conditions it became a leader and prospered.[36]

Wally Byam formally restarted Airstream Trailers Inc. in 1948 at a new factory in Los Angeles, and by 1951 the company was profitable and its trailers were in growing demand. Byam, who was then fifty-five, had begun in 1950 to hold meetings with Airstream trailer owners to identify defects and complaints. Inspired by these meetings, his own trailer camping, and perhaps by his knowledge of earlier trailering events, Byam felt that he and a group of Airstream owners ought to travel in their trailers on a "caravan" to Mexico and Central America. Byam himself had previously trailer camped in Mexico and around Europe, but early in 1951 he suggested to an Airstream trailer friend that they caravan together to Mexico City. He and this friend had enjoyed trailer camping to Baja California, Mexico, the year before, and they were thinking that a "more ambitious tour" might be more fun, especially if they invited a few additional friends to join them. A trailer magazine caught wind of their plan, mentioned it in an article, and several readers wrote to Byam to see if they could come along. Taken by these inquiries, Byam ran an ad announcing his "first annual Inter-American Caravan" in the June 24, 1951, edition of the *Los Angeles Times*. Byam's announcement was followed by a flurry of articles in the *Times* about the upcoming adventure, which anyone with a trailer could join for a fee. By November, applications to join the caravan were no longer being accepted, and fifty-two trailers were expected to gather at the starting point. To everyone's surprise, sixty-three trailers appeared for the caravan, which departed from El Paso, Texas, on December 1, 1951. Four months later, only fourteen of the original trailers had made it to Managua, Nicaragua, and back because of many broken axles, failed transmissions, inclement weather, and more. By the time he returned to Los Angeles, Byam had lost twenty-seven pounds, and he vowed that he would lead no more trailer caravans; but the experience turned out to be more enticing upon reflection, and it had expanded his view of trailer camping. The caravan idea had become lodged in Byam's mind, and he led his next one in 1953.[37]

Trailer Camping as International Doorway

Byam, like other camping advocates, promoted trailer camping as a way to escape daily routines. In his 1953 book, *Fifth Avenue on Wheels*, he promised that trailer camping allowed you "to lose yourself mentally," to slow down, and to be free of time constraints. Harking back to the sentiments of William H. H. Murray, Horace Kephart, and the many advocates who had unconsciously fit camping inside a pilgrimage frame, Byam asserted that trailer campers were "freed from the fetters of schedules and reservations and where to sleep and eat." In this new mental and physical state, he explained, "you find yourself in a mood to see and to absorb and to enjoy the new land and the new people to the full." In this mental state, trailer campers could readily reconnect to the wild and to the nation even as they restored themselves. At the same time, Byam embraced the idea of home, convenience, and ease expressed in the ongoing McDonaldization of camping. According to the Wally Byam Creed—a poem he composed to promote trailer camping—it was his "dream" and the Airstream Company's goal "to place the great wide world at your doorstep for you who yearn to travel with all the comforts of home."[38]

Like many of his trailer camping contemporaries, Byam neatly linked the roughness of wildland adventures with the smoothness of domestic ease. His personal communications, publications, and company advertisements regularly presented Airstream trailers as the perfect balance between these contending cultural forces. Byam, however, went further than other advocates when he extended the freedom and connectivity of trailer camping beyond the bounds of the American nation. According to *Fifth Avenue on Wheels*, trailer camping was not just an outstanding method for connecting to America; it was also the best way "to get the low-down" in foreign countries. Unlike other travelers, a trailer camper met foreigners "on their own ground." The camper could visit locals, a local could visit trailer campers, "and when you have finished your leisurely journey through that land, you know more about the real thoughts and conditions of the people than any congressional junket that ever went on an investigating mission." The following year, Byam reaffirmed his assertion that the best way to develop an understanding of foreign cultures was through trailer camping. In June 1954, the Airstream Company launched the *Caravanner,* a publication dedicated to trailer caravans, and in a page 1 editorial, Byam touted the benefits of trailer camping overseas. Not only was foreign trailering romantic, leisurely, and convenient, but "in new countries," Byam declared, "you stop by the wayside and get acquainted with the people who live there. They are always glad to meet the trailer traveler, and whether you speak their language or not, you soon become friendly with them. You learn what they are thinking about, what their problems are, what their hopes are, what makes them tick. You get close to the people and close to the soil."[39] For the rest of his life, Byam remained committed to this notion of a truer, more honest understanding of identity and place through trailer camping and travel, whether in the United States or abroad. Soon he would lead a caravan into new regions.

By the mid-1950s, Wally Byam, his second wife, Stella, and a variety of friends had repeatedly trailer camped outside the United States, including in Europe, and Byam had led several Airstream trailer caravans to Mexico and Canada. In 1956, however, he chose to organize and direct the first Airstream trailer caravan to Europe. Recounted in the *National Geographic Magazine* by Norma Miller, one of eighty-six participants, the caravan began in April at Rotterdam and wound its way through sixteen countries over the next six months. According to Miller, these travels reinforced the campers' sense of being American through regular "town meetings" of all trailer travelers and group decisions based on one trailer, one vote. Like many pilgrims, they came to see each other as social equals as they moved together through the landscapes of Europe. At the same time, Miller related that trailering gave campers a special insight into the places and people they met: "There may be a better, more flexible, more economical, more comfortable way for a family to see a country and to know its people. But if so, we haven't yet seen it come down the pike!" Carolyn Bennett Patterson, who was a *National Geographic* editor at the time and whose memoir recalled this caravan, recounted that the locals flocked to campgrounds to see the Americans in their trailers. Typically, these visitors would be invited inside the trailers to look around and would then reciprocate by inviting the Americans to visit local homes. "From these exchanges, as among neighbor-to-neighbor,"

wrote Patterson, "Wally became convinced that international trailer caravans did much to promote understanding between peoples—and peace."
According to Patterson, Byam was so pleased with *National Geographic*'s
coverage of the European caravan that he visited the magazine's headquarters in Washington, D.C., where he met Patterson for the first time. She
found him to be "a valuable American original . . . completely himself," and
they became fast friends.[40]

Wally Byam Foundation

Byam led several more international caravans, to Mexico, Canada, and,
most famously, from Cape Town, South Africa, to Cairo, Egypt; but in
July 1962, at age sixty-six, he fell ill of brain cancer and died in Southern
California. To honor him, friends and associates at the Airstream Company
established the Wally Byam Foundation, a nonprofit, volunteer organization
dedicated, in the words of one of the founders, "to promote international
understanding through trailer caravanning." At the first board of trustees
meeting in the winter of 1962, Carolyn Bennett Patterson was elected the
foundation's first (and ultimately only) chair. Mary Carolyn Bennett was
born in Kosciusko, Mississippi, in April 1922, but her family soon moved to
Jackson and then to Yazoo, Mississippi. A child of college-educated parents,
she followed in their footsteps when she entered Blue Mountain College
upon graduating from high school. She was, however, determined to become
a professional writer, so she transferred to several other universities before
finishing her education at Louisiana State University's School of Journalism.
During World War II, she worked for the *New Orleans States* newspaper
as a police reporter and then for the Red Cross in Miami Beach, Florida,
where she met her future husband. At the end of the war, she and Frederick
Gillis "Pat" Patterson married, and the two soon moved to Washington,
D.C., where, on the advice of a friend who worked for *Kiplinger Newsletter*,
she landed a job with the *National Geographic Magazine* in 1949. Hardworking, talented, and driven, Patterson rose to become the magazine's first
female editor in 1962. She held this post when she was elected chair of the
Wally Byam Foundation.[41]

In addition to Patterson's election, the first board settled on what would
become the foundation's three mission objectives: "1. To expand and deepen
the basic purpose and concept of travel by trailer, both national and international; 2. To participate through travel in projects of a humanitarian nature
which take advantage of the travel trailer's mobility and flexibility; 3. To
contribute wherever possible to international understanding and good will."

A number of possible projects were considered, but with an annual budget of only $25,000, the foundation was limited to small humanitarian activities. Nonetheless, just such an opportunity presented itself in early 1963.[42]

Rediscover America

Edward R. Murrow, the head of the U.S. Information Agency (USIA), had hit on the idea of sending the U.S. Foreign Service officers who were back in America for vacations on bus trips across the United States so that they would better understand and represent their own country when abroad. The officers were generally away at their foreign posts for extended periods, and their vacations between assignments were usually a matter of weeks. Most officers could not afford to travel widely while on their vacations, and the USIA could barely manage to support them either. Murrow had come up with long-distance bus trips as a low-cost mode of travel, but these arrangements could not include spouses or families, making them far less attractive to the officers. One of Murrow's subordinates, Sanford S. Marlowe, approached Patterson about the USIA's proposed program, and following discussions, Patterson recommended to the board that the Wally Byam Foundation and the Airstream Company provide the agency with a trailer or two for a "pilot project" that would, as Murrow phrased it, help the agency people and their families "reacquaint themselves with the United States." "I could sympathize with the problem, as could any American who wishes to see our nation represented overseas by persons who know America and Americans at every level," explained Patterson about her response. "I could also understand the problem from the point of view of the USIA and its officers." Moreover, the idea of trailer camping as an outstanding method for refamiliarizing these personnel with the country made sense to Patterson because of her extended friendship with Airstream's founder. "Wally Byam had so often extolled the trailer as the best way for people to travel in a country and to learn to know that country well. He was speaking mostly of foreign travel but his beliefs applied just as well to this country." The board cheerfully funded her proposal, the Airstream Company provided three fully provisioned trailers, and the Ford Motor Company supplied cars to pull them, launching the Wally Byam Foundation's "Rediscover America" program. When Murrow accepted the trailers and vehicles, he made it clear that he considered trailer camping an outstanding tool for affirming and restoring a faded American identity. The alternatives of traveling the country by bus, staying in the vicinity of Washington, D.C., or traveling to some other U.S. city would not have offered returning foreign service officers the same opportunity for contact with nature and the authenticity of non-urban life in America. "I would like you to know," Murrow wrote Carolyn Patterson, "that I believe the Wally Byam Foundation and the Airstream Corporation are performing a very useful public service by making these trips possible. The more our officers know about our country, the better they are able to represent it abroad." Patterson shared Murrow's opinion; not only would trailer camping benefit the USIA families, she noted in her autobiography, but it would be good for "the country as a whole, since the more informed our representatives abroad were, the better they might perform in the nation's behalf."[43]

The pilot project got under way in June 1963 when two USIA officers and their families departed Washington on three-week trailer-camping travels through the nation's small towns, countryside, and wildlands. The first of the two families to depart consisted of Irving S. Lewis, his wife, five children, and Plato, their dog. Lewis and his family were recently returned from El Salvador and were soon likely headed for somewhere in South America to begin a thirteenth year of service in Latin America. The Lewises likely were trailer camping novices, so it made sense that their "break-in" journey took them only sixty miles, to the Crow's Nest Campground near Thurmont, Maryland, where they participated in an event quite novel for them—a regional "rally" of the Wally Byam Caravan Club (WBCC). A camping organization formed in 1955, the WBCC planned numerous local, regional, national, and international rallies that could attract hundreds and sometimes more than a thousand Airstream and other trailers to a prearranged location for a mass form of social camping. These events typically included such nature recreations as hiking, fishing, boating, and swimming, but they could also involve ad hoc parades, musical revues, communal campfires, and other, more urban-oriented entertainments. In support of the Wally Byam Foundation, the WBCC had agreed to assist the pilot project's participants before departure and to host them occasionally during their travels. When the Lewises departed from Thurmont, they made the much longer drive to Bemidji, Minnesota, to again attend a WBCC event—the first international rally held in the United States. After staying for a few days, they departed to trailer camp alone at national parks and historic sites in the Dakotas, Wyoming, and Colorado.[44] Other USIA personnel and their families would similarly trailer camp around America that summer, and the pilot project, everyone agreed, was a success.

For the summer of 1964, the program moved from pilot to permanent status, received a formal title—Rediscover America—and expanded beyond USIA to include a wide array of foreign service officers in the U.S. Department of State. According to one reporter, these travels were designed to be both a vacation and "to expose [the campers] to various aspects of American life and thought, particularly as expressed by everyday Americans at work and play." For Rediscover America's organizers and sponsors, trailer camping emerged as the optimal mode for reengaging with America and for affirming national identity. Rediscover America was not, however, merely a tool to propagandize State Department personnel; individual participants generally found the same virtues in the program as its promoters. One of these, William F. Keyes, had applied to participate in the program because he and his family were hoping to "'Go West' as our pioneer ancestors did not so long ago." Accepted into the program, the Keyeses covered nearly ten thousand miles during the winter of 1965. Keyes, who was on leave from duty in South Africa, reported that they saw "parts of America we would never have been able to under other circumstances." They visited historic sites like the Alamo, natural features such as the Grand Canyon, and tourist sites like Disneyland as they camped their way from Washington, D.C., to San Francisco. The trip was, declared Keyes, "memorable and rewarding . . . the best possible reorientation after years abroad, reawakening memories and exciting the imagination." Like pilgrims in general and other campers specifically, William Keyes returned from his journey into sacred space restored and ready for a reinvigorated reentry into his everyday work life.

At the same time, the McDonaldization expressed by the trailer found its supporters. One of the other participants, John Alden Mason Jr., who had no experience with trailers, had expected this form of camping to be "rather uncomfortable and spartan." To his and his family's delight, they found it to be quite the opposite—"relaxed, easy and almost 'plush,' with all the amenities of home." As a result, he planned to recommend trailer camping "as the finest possible way to experience our great country."[45]

Caravan America

Rediscover America was such a solid success with its organizers and participants that the State Department had more than twenty applicants for future openings by the end of March 1965. And it might have continued as the only camping program to be organized by the Wally Byam Foundation and the U.S. government. State Department officials were pleased, the Airstream and Ford Motor Companies felt they were providing a valuable public service, and the foundation was satisfied with the outcomes. But in February 1965, President Lyndon Johnson and the U.S. Congress asked the nation "to invite citizens of the other lands to discover and enjoy the scenic, historic, and recreational attractions of the United States."[46] This proposal "sparked" the Wally Byam Foundation, and a new effort, "Caravan America," was launched. In contrast to Rediscover America, which was aimed at Americans, the new program would introduce influential foreigners to America through trailer camping. Planning for the new program, however, was complex and would take at least a year, which meant the foundation could offer nothing before the summer of 1966. In the meantime, the foundation took advantage of an opportunity that arose that spring.

In April 1965, the White House contacted the National Geographic Society to see if it might be interested in publishing an article about a trailer camping trip by the president's daughter Lynda Bird Johnson, through the wild and scenic lands of the American West that summer. The society's senior staff, including Patterson, assented to the proposal and turned to the Wally Byam Foundation to obtain three Airstream trailers for a three-week trip. The planning rapidly came together, and when Johnson, who provided an account of her travels for the December 1965 issue of *National Geographic*, wrote about her and her friends' adventure, she employed the sort of imagery that solidly tied them to past and present generations of campers and camping advocates. "Our ancestors saw the West in a covered wagon," she opened. "I saw it in the covered wagon's successor, the travel trailer." Working their way through the Grand Canyon, Monument Valley, Yellowstone National Park, and along the Snake River, Johnson repeatedly linked her camping experience to the national identity. "We applauded Old Faithful," she announced, camped for the night "among tombstones where Custer, his men of the 7th Cavalry, and his stubborn foes . . . died at the Little Bighorn River, and paused in homage at Theodore Roosevelt's crude cabin in his memorial park." At no point did Johnson suggest that the comfort of trailer camping ever threatened the renewal of her sense of being American.[47]

At the same time that Lynda Bird Johnson was traveling in her Airstream Trailer through the West, members of the Wally Byam Foundation were developing their plans for Caravan America. In the foundation's continuing program, Rediscover America, families trailer camped alone around the country. Each had a prepared itinerary, but mostly the families were on their own. Caravan America, by contrast, was intended to be larger, substantially more organized, and to incorporate two phases each summer. During the first phase, as many as twenty fully outfitted trailers with tow cars would be provided to foreign families so that they could travel together from coast to coast as a caravan. These families would be selected from trailer camping clubs in their home countries and would not travel alone but be escorted across the United States by knowledgeable members of the Wally Byam Caravan Club. This phase, which would consist of one westbound caravan followed immediately by one headed east, was intended to "prime the pump of foreign travel" and enhance "international understanding and friendship" through "cultural exchange and person-to-person recommendation" while trailer camping. It was hoped that these travelers would return home to encourage their friends and acquaintances to visit America. Once the second set of foreign families had departed for home, phase two of Caravan America would begin. Again a caravan of trailers would camp across America, but this time the campers would be Washington, D.C.–based foreign diplomats, along with their families. In this phase, the foundation would not so much be attempting to stimulate tourism as employing trailer camping to promote "an understanding of our country" and "better international relations."[48]

The two groups to participate in the initial phase of Caravan America consisted of twenty families drawn from the Caravan Club of Great Britain and twenty families from the Caravan Club of France. The initial forty-seven British participants began their adventure as soon as their plane landed at Dulles International Airport in Washington on June 3, 1967. Upon disembarking they were greeted by John Black of the U.S. Tourist Service and introduced to their neatly arranged Pontiac automobiles and Airstream trailers (fig. 6.6).

For three days the British visitors camped at nearby Bull Run Regional Park to prepare for their cross-country journey to San Francisco, as well as to sightsee around the national capital. During this time the novice campers were met by Agriculture Secretary Orville L. Freeman, who "presented them with pictures of famous U.S. national parks and wilderness areas"; by Senator Alan Bible of Nevada, who "spoke to them of what they would see in the western United States"; and by the First Lady, Lady Bird Johnson, who "wished them well" and gave them autographed copies of daughter Lynda Bird Johnson's account of her recent trailer-camping travels that had appeared in *National Geographic*. After departing from the Washington area on June 6, the British and their WBCC hosts camped for one night at nearby Gettysburg, Pennsylvania, where they received an informal evening presentation by former president Dwight D. Eisenhower, who had retired to a farm near the town. The next morning the caravan recommenced its monthlong travel toward the West Coast. Along the way they camped in the Black Hills, the Grand Tetons, Yellowstone, and many other parks and forests. In addition, they traveled through many small towns and visited a variety of commercial destinations, including Disneyland. According to the *Caravanner*, an Airstream company publication, "everywhere, as advance word of their coming appeared in local newspapers and on TV, the British families were greeted by local families. Immediately there were exchange 'home' visits in which the American families would enter the trailers and stay long enough to overcome their shyness. Then they would invite their

Figure 6.6. Upon their arrival at Dulles International Airport outside Washington, D.C., on June 3, 1967, the Caravan Club of Great Britain is welcomed by John Black, U.S. Tourist Service, to the first Caravan America tour. Carolyn Bennett Patterson (in white in the left foreground) listened with her back to the camera. Courtesy of Dale Schwamborn.

foreign guests to their homes in the area." For their part, the British campers were "marvelously impressed" by America's parks and recreation areas, and they chose to travel "by way of meandering state roads" instead of the national highways, because the latter were viewed as impersonal and artificial, while the former "took them through America's 'villages,' where the 'stout fellow,' the ordinary American could be found." The British campers, like many American campers, apparently found the country's wildlands and its small towns to be most authentically American.[49]

The British caravanners rolled into their final destination, the WBCC's Tenth International Rally near Santa Rosa, California, on July 4, 1967. The following day, the twenty automobiles and trailers were emptied, cleaned, and handed over to seventy-seven French trailer campers who had flown into San Francisco in order to caravan eastward to Washington, D.C. Following roughly the same route, in reverse, as the British, the French caravanners visited eleven national parks and monuments, eleven national forests, reservations of the Sioux and Navajo nations, and a variety of commercial theme parks. Even more than the British, the French "wanted to get beyond the bustle of the cities into the hills and forests." They particularly enjoyed nature walks with their children, and they "got a great kick out of the bears that amble through some of the national parks." Being novices to American nature and thinking that the descriptions of many of these places were "wild exaggerations," the French campers "had to be warned repeatedly by the forest rangers that the bears were dangerous." At the farewell party held on August 5, the French trailer campers frequently expressed a heightened sense of awareness about America and Americans. Most had never visited the United States, but now described its landscapes as "beautiful," "vast," "diversified," and "splendid," while its people were "friendly and welcoming." As hoped for by Caravan America's promoters, these French travelers went away feeling that they better understood America because they had trailer camped through it.[50]

Once the French campers had returned to Washington, phase two of Caravan America began. Since the Wally Byam Foundation had its own contacts with British and French caravan clubs, it had had no need to cooperate with any other agencies or organizations to find appropriate participants for phase one. Phase two, however, aimed to introduce "a grass-roots genuine" America to foreign officials who were not known to the foundation. Consequently, Carolyn Bennett Patterson and her staff co-organized this phase with another Washington–based nonprofit, the Travel Program for Foreign Diplomats, which previously had taken approximately twelve hundred foreign diplomats on trips. To inaugurate this phase of Caravan America, fourteen foreign consuls, UN delegates, and other diplomats, along with their families, "hitched up their rigs" and hit the road for San Francisco.[51]

Following nearly the same westward route as the British caravanners of phase one, these sixty-two campers spent five weeks visiting national parks, monuments, and forests, as well as Native American reservations and small towns. Along the way, they felt crowded in their trailers, challenged by twisting, steep roads, were bruised on hikes and bitten by mosquitoes, yet the outcome was as planned—they gained a sense that they had seen a truer America and met authentic Americans. Recalling his and his family's experience for the *New York Times*, Pedro Olarte of Colombia recommended that all foreign diplomats in Washington and New York make the trip "to see the 'other' United States." Outside these big cities, he declared, "people are neighborly and courteous and if you ask a question, they don't snarl." The Olarte family's experience was mirrored by that of Argentina's chief UN delegate, José Maria Ruda, and his family. "I learned more about America in that one month than I had in six years living in New York," volunteered the delegate's wife. She and her family had enjoyed the Grand Tetons and Yellowstone, but the people had made the strongest impression on her. Being involved with the United Nations, she noted, was "like living at a club." One

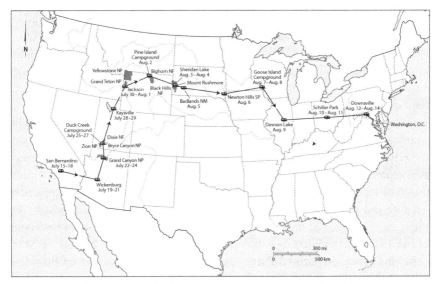

Figure 6.7. The route followed by the West German Parliament Tour of July 15–August 14, 1972, was typical of Caravan America. The cars and trailers the Germans picked up in San Bernardino, California, had been left by an earlier tour of diplomats from sixteen countries that had departed Washington, D.C., on June 8.

met and talked to the same people repeatedly. When, however, she and the family trailer camped, they met many different people "in their own natural surroundings. . . . It was then that we really got to know the people and it was enlightening. We found them less brassy, less sophisticated and more real than most city people." Trailer camping, it seems, was able to connect even foreigners to authentic America, which is exactly what the Wally Byam Foundation wanted.[52]

Rediscover America continued into the mid-1970s, ultimately providing trailer camping adventures for hundreds of State Department families, while Caravan America, which was renamed "Open House USA" in 1973, lasted until the bicentennial summer of 1976. The latter program continued to entertain camping families from foreign trailer clubs and foreign diplomats, sometimes more than one hundred at a time, who were often new to America and trailer camping. Over the years, travel itineraries changed and specialized groups of diplomats, such as members of the West German parliament in the summer of 1972 (fig. 6.7), occasionally participated, but the program remained largely the same until 1974, when its focus expanded to create caravans of foreign correspondents and their families. The experiences of the correspondents would, it was hoped, infuse and inform their writings about the "true" character of America and Americans. The caravans were generally positive adventures for the participants, as demonstrated by reports and interviews, but they were not without their challenges. On a tour in the summer of 1976 from Petaluma, California, to Dayton, Ohio, for instance, automobiles had to be repaired, trailer closet and cupboard doors repeatedly had to be rehung, windows broke, water pumps failed, tires went flat, and reservations mysteriously vanished.[53]

Despite minor irritations and setbacks, Carolyn Bennett Patterson, who oversaw all these productions, considered Rediscover America, Caravan American, and Open House America to be great successes. She found every participating foreign group to have been interesting, but the ones composed of diplomats and their families were "the most rewarding experiences because most of them had never met the kind of ordinary Americans who filled campgrounds and visited state and national parks." Looking back, one of the 1972 participants in a diplomatic Caravan America, Hélène de Margerie of France, confirmed Patterson's recollection and validated President Nixon's honoring of the Wally Byam Foundation and its chair. According to de Margerie, trailer camping across the United States had allowed her to see the country in "a unique way." Before this journey, she and her husband had only met diplomats and other Washington people in their daily routines, but as they camped, they found themselves developing that clear picture of America that Nixon had praised. On Caravan America, de Margerie discovered "the basic kindness and friendliness of the American people. 'They yearn for understanding,' she said, 'as we all do.' "[54]

The Wally Byam Foundation launched its final Caravan America tour during the bicentennial summer of 1976. The buildup and delivery of this "enormous and important effort" had drained the foundation's resources and left it in debt to the Airstream Company. Moreover, the source of its income was a fee on every Airstream trailer sold, and that revenue had diminished "due to the uncertainties of the national energy crisis" that had begun early in the 1970s. "In the face of it all," admitted Patterson in a June 1978 letter to Airstream's president, "the Foundation trimmed its expenses to the bone, closing the office and releasing for other employment . . . our Executive Secretary." For more than a year, the foundation had been "operationally shut down," and she felt it was time that the organization should officially cease. The board of directors agreed with her judgment, and the Wally Byam Foundation ended on June 30, 1978.[55] Patterson, however, continued her career with *National Geographic* magazine until her retirement in 1986. Afterward she traveled widely while continuing to work and live in Washington. In 1998, she published her memoir, *Of Lands, Legends, and Laughter: The Search for Adventure with National Geographic,* and contributed her personal papers to Mississippi State University in 1999. She passed away quietly in 2003.

The experiences of Carolyn Bennett Patterson and the many participants in the trailer camping adventures organized by the Wally Byam Foundation suggest that trailer camping fits within the arc of camping's development. From its beginning, trailer campers reported that they felt improved by their voyages out of America's profane cities and into the sacred spaces of its more rural and wildland areas. At the same time, trailer camping's comfort, convenience, and other domestic qualities allowed both Americans and foreigners, most of whom had no camping experience, to temporarily step out of their conventional urban lives, visit the "real" America, and then return to their daily world both renewed and better connected to the nation. They were, in other words, pilgrims to America's true sources. Trailer camping was not, however, the only mode for accessing the wild. As we shall see in the next chapter, backpacking provided a satisfying alternative and prompted the creation of special places for its proponents and practitioners.

CHAPTER SEVEN

A RENEWAL OF OUR
FAITH AND IDEALS

The Development of Backpacking
and Long-Distance Trails

In late 1968, even as Caravan America and Rediscover America were enjoying their second summer of trailer-camping excursions (see previous chapter), the Pacific Crest Trail (PCT) was officially launched as a part of the newly created U.S. National Trails System. Building on the passage of the Wilderness Act of 1964 and the Land and Water Conservation Fund Act of 1965, President Lyndon B. Johnson had called for the development of a national system of trails in his February 8, 1965, "Natural Beauty" message to the nation. "The forgotten outdoorsmen of today are those who like to walk, hike, ride horseback or bicycle. For them we must have trails." In response, a study was organized by Interior Secretary Stewart L. Udall with representation from the federal government's major outdoor management agencies—the Bureau of Outdoor Recreation, the U.S. Forest Service, the National Park Service, and the Bureau of Land Management. Their 1966 report, *Trails for America*, became the basis for the National Trail Systems Act of 1968. According to the enabling legislation, the system was established "in order to provide for the ever-increasing outdoor recreation needs of an expanding population and in order to promote the preservation of, public access to, travel within, and enjoyment and appreciation of the open-air, outdoor areas and historic resources of the Nation." The act declared that the trails "may contain campsites, shelters and related-public-use facilities" but that "the use of motorized vehicles by the general public . . . shall be prohibited." Identifying the Pacific Crest Trail as one of the two initial components in the system (the other was the Appalachian Trail), the law authorized an appropriation of up to $500,000 "for the acquisition of lands or interests in lands" for the PCT. Over the next twenty-five years, nearly 1,000 miles of trails were constructed in Washington State, Oregon, and California to extend and link several preexisting regional trails into a single, 2,650-mile trail extending from the Mexican border to Canada. In June 1993, Interior Secretary Bruce Babbitt and other dignitaries participated in a "golden spike" ceremony near Soledad Canyon in Southern California's Angeles National Forest, and the Pacific Crest Trail was declared officially complete.[1]

Backpacking as Pilgrimage

During recent decades the Pacific Crest Trail has been enjoyed by many day hikers, horse riders, and packhorse campers, but its primary users are the thousands of backpackers who thread the route each year. Like the other forms of camping examined in this book, backpacking has been described by its advocates, including those promoting or using the PCT, in terms that illustrate its pilgrimage character. For example, in 1969's *The Complete Walker: The Joys and Techniques of Hiking and Backpacking*, Colin Fletcher contrasted his occasional backpacking experiences with the routine urban life that many campers, no matter their technique, found questionable. "By walking out alone into wilderness I can elude the pressures of the pounding modern world, and in the sanctity of silence and solitude—the solitude seems to be a very important part of it—I can after a while begin to see and to hear and to think and in the end to feel with a new and exciting accuracy." The everyday, Fletcher implies, dulls the senses and the mind, but wilderness backpacking restores and refreshes. Twenty-five years later, Charles Cook reiterated Fletcher's sentiment in *The Essential Guide to Wilderness Camping and Backpacking in the United States*. Backpacking, he insisted, was enjoyed by many people because it provided a "feeling of adventure" and "exploration." Wild nature was "endlessly varied," and it had "rules (mostly unwritten) unlike those we normally live under." Backpackers felt socially and psychologically "liberated" once free of "routines" and "the countless encumbrances we surround ourselves with in daily life." Moreover, the body improved, too, as backpackers left "the world of 'clock time'" and found their "own natural rhythms and [got] in sync with the rhythms and cycles of life" around them.[2]

The pursuit of adventure and the idea of exploration have long been common tropes among backpackers, but each backpacker generally also pursues some personal goal, which may or may not have relevance for another backpacker. Nevertheless, they can end up on the same trail together. Christopher

McCandless, a backpacker who ultimately gained fame after he died in the Alaskan wilderness, sought to re-create himself as "Alexander Supertramp" through a form of environmental purging that would eliminate the negative impacts of urban life and allow his "true" nature to emerge. On May 22, 1992, along Alaska's historic "Stampede Trail" and near the banks of the Teklanika River, McCandless carved a poetic "manifesto" that detailed what he hoped to achieve in the wilderness:

> And now after two rambling years
> Comes the final and greatest adventure.
> The climactic battle to kill the false being within
> And victoriously conclude the spiritual revolution!
> Ten days and nights of freight trains and hitching
> Bring him to the Great White North.
> No longer to be poisoned by civilization
> He flees, and walks alone up the land
> To become
> LOST IN THE WILD[3]

Hiking the entire two-thousand-plus miles of the PCT in the 1970s, David Green began his "journey" expecting "to be swept away by the spirit of adventure," but it did not occur. Instead, he found himself "placidly adapting to the rhythm of the trail." Over time, he came to look forward to that rhythm. "The trail," he declared, "had become my life, my sustenance, my joy." Cindy Ross, by contrast, sought to "experience, change, grow," as well as find the liberation described by Charles Cook, as she described in her 1987 account, *Journey on the Crest: Walking 2600 Miles from Mexico to Canada*. She was tired of working as a waitress, a position she felt "reduced to," and wished to break free. The solution, she decided, would be a "long-distance hike." When people asked her why she didn't just settle down and marry, she responded, "I dream of a rustic home in the mountains, a loving husband. They aren't found in bars. Neither is adventure or freedom. To walk in the wilderness is freedom. To work a routine, in a subservient situation, is death. In this environment, people merely maintain their existence. I want to live deeper." But then, when they would ask her, "Why hike the Pacific Crest Trail, Mexico to Canada?" she would always respond, "How can I not?" More recently, Cheryl Strayed recounted in her best-selling memoir, *Wild: From Lost to Found on the Pacific Crest Trail*, that her life had gone "over the edge" before she backpacked eleven hundred miles on the PCT. Her beloved mother had died unexpectedly, then her siblings had drifted apart, and finally her marriage had broken up, all despite her best efforts to keep everything intact. Uprooted in space, society, and family, Strayed had "ranged and roamed and railed . . . until at last I found myself . . . in the summer of 1995, not so much loose in the world as bound to it."

> It was a world I'd never been to and yet had known was there all along, one I'd staggered to in sorrow and confusion and fear and hope. A world I thought would both make me into the woman I knew I could become and turn me back into the girl I'd once been. A world that measured two feet wide and 2,663 miles long.
> A world called the Pacific Crest Trail.

Her life, Strayed admitted, had been a wreck, and she had decided to backpack alone on the Pacific Crest Trail "to save myself."[4]

Despite variations in pilgrims' goals, they tend to return to their daily lives "with a difference" that may or may not be tangible. For Colin Fletcher, restoration and reinvigoration were the desired outcome. "When you get back at last from the simple things to the complexities of the outside world, you find that you are once more eager to grapple with them. For a while you even detect a meaning behind all the complexity." However, the "eagerness" would fade, because normal life would ultimately diminish the transformation. "The simple life's not a substitute," admitted Fletcher, "only a corrective." For others, however, the transformation could be more subtle and durable. At the completion of his journey, David Green wrote the last entry into his diary. "The full moon rises, luminous, golden. A harvest moon. The journey's been six moons growing, growing in the fertile soil of a soul left city-fallow. The yield has been abundant." Green had set out backpacking to have an adventure but instead discovered something more numinous—personal growth. Cindy Ross, in contrast, had sought personal change and growth, which were hers when she returned home. Her father died of cancer six months after her return, but her journey on the PCT had helped. "Living so close to the natural world helped me understand the life cycles of all living things, that we are directly connected to the earth and one another, and that death is an important and precious part of our existence." On the trail, she recalled, one had to handle stress, difficulties, and dangers. "Life wasn't easy out there, so when life isn't easy here, back home, we can cope much better." Ross's difference endured well past her return from the journey. Finally, Cheryl Strayed returned to her daily life with the most robust change. She had made her PCT backpack trip during the summer of 1995, but she did not recount it until 2012. Looking back across those years, she admitted that when she had completed her hike, she had had no idea how her life would unfold. Everything going forward was unknown.

> Everything except the fact that I didn't have to know. That it was enough to trust that what I'd done was true. To understand its meaning without yet being able to say precisely what it was. . . . To believe that I didn't need to reach with my bare hands anymore. To know that seeing the fish beneath the surface of the water was enough. That it was everything. It was my life—like all lives, mysterious and irrevocable and sacred. So very close, so very present, so very belonging to me.
>
> How wild it was, to let it be.

For Strayed, backpacking the Pacific Crest Trail had resulted in an ability to accept life. As these excerpts indicate, backpacking is a form of pilgrimage, but it has not always been known by this name.[5]

Tramping

The term "backpacking"—when a camper walks and carries her or his own supplies and equipment—is of recent origin. Before the mid-twentieth century, this mode of camping had been known as "tramping," "knapsacking," and a variety of other names. Despite these name changes, backpacking initially became popular at the same time as the other forms of camping—as the nation urbanized after the Civil War.[6]

Recreational outdoor walking was a relatively rare activity during the first fifty years of the American republic because few people found anything attractive in the wilder lands of the country. A notable exception to this rule was a Vermonter, Alden Partridge, who walked widely throughout his region on hikes that sometimes lasted more than a week. Many of these walks were through "trackless" areas, since few trails existed anywhere in the country before the 1850s. An instructor at several schools, including West Point, Partridge took male students on multiday, cross-country field trips because he thought it strengthened them and taught lessons that could not be learned in a classroom. These excursions were not, however, backpacking, because Partridge and his students usually spent their evenings on farms or in small settlements. Nevertheless, they did wear knapsacks to carry their clothing.[7]

One of the few areas with trails in the early nineteenth century was Mount Washington in New Hampshire's White Mountains, which is where an important first occurred. Three sisters, Eliza, Harriet, and Abigail Austin, began to recreationally hike this mountain with male friends in 1821. Most of these outings were day trips, but sometimes they were multiday adventures. Like Partridge and his students, however, they stayed overnight in homes and inns, so they were not actually backpacking. Nevertheless, the Austins were pathbreakers, and soon families with children were also to be found on the trails. By the 1830s, women were no longer a rarity on New Hampshire trails.[8]

During the 1840s and 1850s a growing number of Americans in the Northeast became increasingly passionate about their mountains and backwoods areas. Previously these landscapes had been viewed as difficult, hostile, and of low utility, but attitudes began to change as the wild retreated and as romantic antimodern ideas arose. As views shifted, the 1850s witnessed an escalation in the number of hikers in New England, although the total number remained relatively small. Romantic attachment to American nature was largely scenic and passive. Multisensory, active engagement with nature held little appeal at this time; mountains and wildlands appealed primarily because they appeared sublime or picturesque. As a consequence, mountain hotels sprang up at "vacation centers" in the White Mountains and elsewhere around New England. From verandas, guests were satisfied to gaze upon the landscape from their rockers or to take a short walk or horseback ride along the handful of trails that might radiate from a hotel to nearby peaks. Guests remained in the hotels' domestic spaces and treated the surrounding wilds as a garden for viewing, sketching, strolling, and picnicking. Even the few adventurous spirits who took to the wilder Adirondack Mountains rarely selected and carried their own equipment and supplies. Accounts by Joel T. Headley, T. Addison Richards, and others reveal that the participants were the products of a comfortable urban society. They may have been physically fit and educated, but, as Philip G. Terrie noted, "hunting, fishing and wilderness camping were as foreign to urban men of the nineteenth century as they are to most twentieth [and twenty-first] century men—perhaps even more so." Consequently, they hired guides who arranged for all the necessary gear, established the camp, prepared the food, and provided the knowledge and experience necessary for an extended trip into wild nature. Moreover, hiking rarely occurred in the Adirondacks, because the complex system of lakes, streams, and portages provided easier access to wilderness than by foot.[9]

The American Civil War of 1861 to 1865 interrupted mountain and backcountry vacationing, and by the time people's interest in the wild began to recover toward the end of the 1860s, the romance and appeal of gazing upon natural scenery had declined, even as people became more interested in entering wilderness. Postwar economic growth, urban expansion, and a preoccupation with material wealth steadily eroded transcendentalism's goal of spiritual renewal. Wilderness lovers no longer simply wished to view natural landscape from the comfort of a hotel; more and more of them wanted to leave their mundane urban lives to enter nature as campers.

Bachelder on "Pedestrianism"

The first book to promote the merits of the various camping techniques, including backpacking, was 1875's *Popular Resorts and How to Reach Them* by John B. Bachelder. Bachelder followed in the footsteps of William H. H. Murray by extolling the virtues of camping. "Beyond all question," he began, "the most delightful and healthful way to spend one's summer vacation is in 'camping out,'" and then he identified the three principal camping techniques employed today—with a wheeled vehicle, on horseback, and afoot with a pack (see chapter 2). Drawing on a popular pastime of his era, he termed the last "pedestrianism."[10]

Virtually forgotten today, pedestrianism referred, during the mid-nineteenth century, to both pleasure and competitive walking, with interest in it being similar to today's fascination with running and marathons. Pedestrianism had been mildly popular in America for decades before *Popular Resorts* was published, but its allure had surged across the national scene after the Civil War. A key stimulus to the rise in postwar attention to the pastime was Edward Payson Weston's 1867 feat of walking 1,136 miles from Portland, Maine, to Chicago in thirty days. Competing for a prize of $10,000, Weston generated national and international attention with his walk, as well as a host of bets by gamblers. Departing on October 29 and arriving on November 28, the twenty-eight-year-old Weston transfixed the public with his adventure; the *New York Times* published twenty-five articles about his progress, as well as his daily efforts and challenges. Moreover, Weston gave public lectures on the health benefits of walking during his effort. In the wake of Weston's accomplishment, the *Times* observed that "a kind of pedestrian mania seems to afflict this country just now." Nor did the affliction retreat; it only intensified. By 1870, American men and women could be found strolling about their cities, vacationers were pacing on "pedestrian tours" through the countryside, both college and nonstudent groups were organizing clubs, and national figures were recounting pedestrianism's virtues.[11]

It should come as no surprise that Bachelder attempted to situate camping on foot within the widespread national phenomena of pedestrianism.

Few people camped at all in the 1870s, so Bachelder was trying to provide them with some sense of the technique and the experience. Nevertheless, he admitted that pedestrian camping was not for everyone, but only those "physically able to endure it." Associating the three camping techniques or methods with the age cycle, he surmised that pedestrian camping would most appeal to youths. "There is a certain age," he observed, "when young men glory in pedestrianism, and see in it as a source of great pleasure."[12]

Beyond possessing strength and youth, a pedestrian camper also had to be thoughtful about his choice of equipment and supplies. A pedestrian camper was expected to cover "eight or ten miles per day," so Bachelder emphasized a warning that has been repeated to every succeeding generation of backpackers. "It is of the greatest importance to reduce the stock of clothing and equipment to actual necessities," he cautioned, "for 'every ounce becomes a pound' at the end of a long jaunt." Since Bachelder wrote for novices who knew little if anything about camping, he felt it important to warn them that "a frequent error of the novice in tramping tours, is to choose new and elaborately equipped knapsacks, heavy rifles [and more] . . . the accumulation of which soon becomes burdensome, and the pleasure of the excursion is spoiled." Despite this important and enduring caveat, Bachelder merely sketched out the makings of an ideal pedestrian "kit." Include, he recommended, "strong shoes and clothing . . . a rubber and woolen blanket . . . a shelter tent . . . drinking cups . . . a light game-bag or haversack, in place of the heavier knapsack . . . [and] a cape." In addition, he reminded readers, it was not necessary to carry everything for the entire excursion. Many food items could be obtained during travels, for instance. "Milk, bread, &c., can always be purchased from farmers; coffee and crackers at the stores." In addition, he suggested, a change of clothing could be packed in a valise and "forwarded from point to point." At the same time, Bachelder recognized that he could only begin to identify which equipment to include, so he offered a suggestion to address the anxiety that preparation and planning might induce in a newcomer. Pedestrian campers with practical concerns should draw upon a resource that increases after every war, including the recently ended Civil War—veterans. "Fortunately," promised Bachelder, whatever questions may arise, "nearly every one can get valuable hints on the subject of out-of-door life from men of army experience."[13]

Despite these admonitions, if a camper was reasonably healthy, cautious when choosing gear, and properly supplied, pedestrianism was the *premier* form of camping, and it would, Bachelder promised, "be found a source of great enjoyment, particularly if an interesting country be selected." Backpacking was superior to packhorse camping ("equestrianism") and horse-wagon camping ("wagon riding") for several reasons. In the scheme

Bachelder laid out, all three modes were pilgrimage, because each provided the benefits of "the camp." No matter which mode was employed, the campsite was outside the ordinary. All campers temporarily lived in a natural setting away from "the stiff formalities of conventional life . . . [with] the mind . . . in constant and cheery repose. . . . [In camp,] health comes to the invalid . . . and the strong feel an electric energy, daily renewed, unknown in the great cities and marts of trade." In other words, all campers were transformed by the experience and would return home positively changed. Horse-wagon camping, however, was the best choice only when a party's campsite was going to be permanent. A fixed site and a horse with wagon allowed campers to bring a large amount of equipment, food, and hired help, which translated into greater ease and comfort. At the same time, both equestrian and pedestrian camping were superior to wagon riding because they combined "the advantage[s] of tour and camp." Equestrian camping allowed a camper to bring along enough "clothing and equipments" to elevate "the comforts and pleasures of an excursion" above those experienced by someone afoot. And without the encumbrance of a wagon, an equestrian could "tour" more easily and therefore experience shifting scenery and an assortment of campsites. A variety of scenes meant one was more likely to have a romantic antimodern moment and thus be mentally refreshed and spiritually uplifted. Nevertheless, Bachelder implied that camping's greatest value lay not in its comforts or its shifting scenery, but in pedestrianism's ability to provide "romantic novelty" and adventure. When touring through the wilds, a pedestrian camper could better pause to contemplate a sublime or picturesque scene than even could someone on horseback. Moreover, only a pedestrian had opportunities to closely examine and ponder wild plants and animals, making it possible for her or him to be morally educated in the fashion of Susan Fenimore Cooper. Finally, Bachelder argued that a tramping trip's "novelty" was not only an opportunity for mental recuperation and a spiritual journey, but also a chance for adventure. It was true that romantic elements could be explored in the domestic setting of a hotel or home, but a pedestrian camping trip meant that one had the most immersive encounter with nature and could best experience "a sort of woodman's or frontier life."[14] Pedestrian camping, in short, was the superior mode for recapitulating an earlier and rougher way of life that was widely revered among Americans. It best linked a contemporary activity—camping—with the historical experience of frontier life. Furthermore, since pedestrian camping was the simplest and most primitive mode, it provided the most transformative experience.

In the decades following the publication of *Popular Resorts*, Bachelder's ranking of the three camping techniques continued. "Tramping" remained most authentic, with packhorse camping a steady second, and wagon camping growing ever more inauthentic as it became motorized and its practitioners embraced an expanding array of equipment to smooth out camping's roughness.[15]

In addition to ranking camping's three basic modes or techniques, Bachelder revealed the multiple types of natural spaces that could be worthy of reverence. Horse-wagon campers generally traveled to fixed campsites, which suggest that these locations were in or adjacent to the sort of nature that a camper deemed sacred. After temporarily residing at one of these sites, he or she could return to daily life "refreshed." Yet transformative sacred space did not have to be so geographically constrained; it might extend across a relatively large area. Indirectly, Bachelder was implying that the sacredness of the extensive nature that walking and horseback campers moved through was equal to that experienced by the horse-wagon camper. A foot or horseback camper could wander from place to place within a large region and become as "refreshed" as the horse-wagon camper who remained at a specific destination.

Gould on Tramping

A variety of camping articles and books followed in the wake of the publication of *Popular Resorts and How to Reach Them*, but the first how-to manual to focus primarily on what had now become known as tramping was John M. Gould's *Hints for Camping and Walking*, which appeared in 1877. John Mead Gould (1839–1930) was born and raised in Portland, Maine. An outdoor enthusiast from an early age, he recounted that he had experienced "pleasant days" when, in his teens, he had "climbed the mountains of Oxford County, or sailed through Casco Bay." When he was only twenty-two, the Civil War broke out, and he volunteered for service in the Union army, where he rose to the rank of major and served until the spring of 1866. Returning to Maine the next year, Gould soon found a growing interest in camping, and in the mid-1870s he decided "to collect the subject-matter for a book of this kind" because he was frequently being asked for camping advice by "young friends" who wished to tramp but were uncertain as to how. His small, lightly illustrated handbook of only 134 pages was aimed at this audience, but he also thought "it contains much, I trust, that will prove valuable to campers-out in general." From the outset, Gould made few attempts to persuade people to take up camping. He launched no direct attacks on urban life, nor did he present wild nature as some sort of urban antidote. Gould assumed that his readers wished to tramp, and he offered only hints as to why they should do so. Nevertheless, these hints were largely antimodern. Tramping, he described, was slow rather than "fast," inexpensive rather than costly, and, in the manner of Susan Fenimore Cooper, a romantic opportunity "to see every separate detail of the glory of the world."[16] *Hints for Camping and Walking* was a simple technical and procedural guide that lacked the extensive philosophical and ideological underpinnings detailed by William H. H. Murray but included far more practical advice than had been provided in John B. Bachelder's *Popular Resorts and How to Reach Them.*

In thirteen brief, conversational chapters, Gould addressed a tramper's primary concerns, many of which remain at the forefront today: planning a trip; clothing; food and cooking; "marching"; the campsite; tents; hygiene; the keeping of a diary (strongly recommended, for "the act of writing will help you remember these good times"); and various other tidbits of "general advice." Like Bachelder before him and nearly every backpacking advocate since, Gould emphasized the need to carefully select one's equipment for fit, durability, and practicality and to limit the weight of everything carried. "Let me caution you first of all about overloading," he began. A novice tramper will tell himself that he can easily carry twenty pounds, since soldiers sometimes have to carry forty of fifty pounds. "Take twenty pounds, then, and carry it around for an hour, and see how you like it. Very few young men who read this book will find it possible to *enjoy* themselves, and carry more than twenty pounds a greater distance than ten miles a day, for a week." As a consequence, much of the first section of the book pursues this simple adage: "Let us cut down our burden to the minimum, and see how much it will be." Working through a list of commonly considered items, Gould accepted some, for instance a woolen blanket, and then would press for the most effective type for a tramper—"a good stout one, rather than the light or flimsy one you may think of taking." During the same review, Gould rejected other items, such as a tent and its poles, with a pointed explanation why. "If you take tent-poles" for a standard sort of tent, he warned, you will find they are heavy, large, and difficult to maneuver, and they "will vex you sorely, and tempt you to throw them away." Instead, he recommended, use a light "shelter" style tent, "as poles for this can be easily cut" at a campsite and therefore did not need to be carried.[17]

At the conclusion of this review, Gould presented his recommended list of items to be carried and their weights (fig. 7.1). Some substitutions and alterations were possible, but it was clear that it would be difficult (even impossible) to reduce the weight below twenty pounds. Pondering the situation, Gould observed, "You see, therefore, that you have the prospect of hard work." At this point, no rigid-frame packs existed, only soft leather

Rubber blanket	2½ pounds
Stout woollen blanket and lining	4½ "
Knapsack, haversack, and canteen	4 "
Drawers, spare shirt, socks, and collars	2 "
Half a shelter-tent and ropes	2 "
Toilet articles, stationery, and small wares	2 "
Food for one day	3 "
Total	20 pounds

You may be able to reduce the weight here given by taking a lighter blanket and no knapsack or canteen; but most likely the food that you actually put in your haversack will weigh more than three pounds. You must also carry your share of the following things:

Frying pan, coffeepot, and pail	3 pounds
Hatchet, sheath knife, case, and belt	3 "
Company property named on last page	3 "

Figure 7.1. John Mead Gould's recommended equipment and supplies for the typical tramper of 1877. From J. M. Gould, *Hints for Camping and Walking* (New York: Scriber, Armstrong, 1877), 22.

and canvas knapsacks, which Gould did not endorse. As a "work"-saving alternative, he recommended tightly rolling everything except the food into the woolen blanket, folding this roll lengthwise to make its ends meet, and then wearing it diagonally across the body (fig. 7.2). With this arrangement, it was possible to eliminate the knapsack and thus save some weight. For the next fifty years, tramping advocates would debate the virtues of blanket rolls versus knapsacks, baskets, and the like.[18]

Wearing his blanket roll and haversack, a tramper was now ready to depart, but Gould did not endorse any specific destinations. He did, however, praise a type of terrain—"the roads of a settled country." He labeled tramping along the paths and roads of some rural area as "rational" and "a fine way" to travel, but countryside was not Gould's favorite landscape. Like many who would succeed him, Gould preferred to "start into wild and uninhabited regions," but he did not commend it to his readers because there were few trails through the forests of Maine, where he lived, or in wilderness areas elsewhere in America. Tramping through trackless areas was "*very* hard work . . . and, although it sounds romantic . . . if [trampers] meet with a reverse, have much rainy weather, or lose their way . . . all sport will end." A shortage of trails would continue to inhibit tramping through wild areas for decades, but the situation would slowly improve.[19]

Figure 7.2. A tramper wearing his blanket roll and haversack. From J. M. Gould, *Hints for Camping and Walking* (New York: Scribner, Armstrong, 1877), 17.

Hints for Camping and Walking was written for trampers, and the vast majority of the book covered this technique, but Gould also addressed horse-wagon camping, packhorse camping, and canoe camping, giving us a sense of how he ranked them. The last two modes he praised in a sentence or two but offered little more, hardly distinguishing between them. The mere length of discussion suggests that Gould considered them less worthy than tramping. Horse-wagon camping, however, earned nearly a chapter's discussion, but his equivocal treatment of it appears to have been meant to discourage its practice. As noted in chapter 2, Gould admitted that camping with a horse and wagon allowed campers to bring additional equipment and to carry a mixed party of campers (not just young men). Nevertheless, it had a major drawback—"the expense"—which was not just monetary. The

United States was still an agrarian nation in 1877, which meant that "the time for camping out is when horses are in greatest demand for farming purposes; and you will find it difficult to hire of any one except livery-stable men, whose charges are so high you cannot afford to deal with them." As a consequence, "You will have to hunt a long time, and in many places, before you find your animal." Nonetheless, all was not lost. "You can overcome [the expense] in part by adding members to your company," which would distribute the costs and the searching for a horse among a larger group and thus result in a lower cost per camper. But, Gould wondered aloud, was it worth it? You could add more campers, "but then you meet what is perhaps a still more serious difficulty,—management of a large party."[20] Clearly, Gould ranked horse-wagon camping at the bottom of any camping hierarchy.

In the decades following the publication of *Hints for Camping and Walking*, tramping continued to appeal to campers around the country. Interest remained sufficiently strong that Gould's book was reprinted in 1880, and tramping articles about attractions from New England to California appeared from time to time in such magazines as *Outing*, *Country Life in America*, *Outlook*, *Ladies' Home Journal*, and more. Of note, one of the best enduring guides to tramping and canoe camping appeared during this era, *Woodcraft* by "Nessmuk" (George Washington Sears). Packed with practical information that had been obtained through experience, but written in a personal, often anecdotal style, 1884's *Woodcraft* sold widely, was reprinted frequently, and remains in print today. In contrast to Gould, Sears wished every reader to know the antimodern reason why someone would camp, incorporating an opening chapter titled "Overwork and Recreation.—Outing and Outers. How to Do It, and Why They Miss It." Quoting Herbert Spencer, Sears noted the frequency of men who had "suffered from nervous collapse due to stress of business, or . . . who had either killed themselves by overwork, or had been permanently incapacitated." Such "prostration" was not necessary, at least not for middle- to upper-middle-class men, because a camping trip could relieve their suffering. "There are hundreds of thousands of practical, useful men, many of them far from being rich; mechanics, artists, writers, merchants, clerks, business men—workers, so to speak—who sorely need and well deserve a season of rest and relaxation at least once a year. To these, and for these, I write." Like other campers, a tramper needed only to head out of his everyday life and into nature in order to be transformed and again able to engage modern life.[21]

Unsurprisingly, reliable statistics do not exist concerning the number of trampers, the frequency of their travels, or the places most visited. Nonetheless, it seems likely that the numbers were never large, either absolutely or in comparison to other camping techniques. In the 1910s, for instance, the ratio of advertisements for tramping equipment to auto-camping equipment was approximately 1 to 5 or less, which suggests a smaller group of participants.[22] It also reflects the differences in technological change between the camping modes.

Comfort through Control

The process of McDonaldization unfolded on a more limited scale and with a different focus among trampers than among horse-wagon campers or their successors, automobile campers. The latter were enticed by a stream of products that extended domestic and urban comforts into the experience of camping. However, the tents, mattresses, ice chests, stoves, and myriad other items being promoted to auto campers were far too heavy to be carried by a tramper. Instead, the McDonaldization of early tramping emphasized comfort through personal control rather than the comfort, convenience, and predictability offered through consumption. Indeed, William Hobbs discouraged his 1895 readers from taking along unneeded or "unsuited" items on a tramping trip. A decade later, the widely read author Stewart Edward White similarly warned readers away from novel camping equipment. "Every once in a while an enthusiast writes me of some new and handy kink he is ready to swear by. It is indeed handy; and if one could pluck it from the nearest bush when occasion for its use arose, it would be a joy and a delight. But carrying it four hundred miles to that occasion for its use is a very different matter. The sporting catalogues are full of very handy kinks . . . but when you pack your duffle bag, you'd better put them on a shelf."[23]

Tramping's technology did not change much during its earliest decades because comfort for trampers did not result from new gadgets but from simplicity and personal skill. "Comfort means minimum equipment," offered Stewart Edward White, and "bodily ease." The first concerns for a tramper were a "proper" outfit, that is, the equipment and supplies needed (not desired) and a manageable weight. Of course, authors varied in their prescriptions, which resulted in loads ranging from about twenty to fifty pounds, depending on the season and the length of the trip. If a trip was to be only for a few days, then a blanket roll and a small bag would suffice to carry a light load. In an account of his first tramping trip during the summer of 1914, Paul M. Fink related that three of the four members relied on blanket rolls. They were the novices; only the fourth man had previous experience and owned a knapsack. When a tramping trip was to extend for a week or longer, the weight would increase, a knapsack would be the better choice, and its packing became of paramount concern. On the one hand, "If a pack is not properly laid out to begin with, if the strap is not properly adjusted, if the pack as a whole does not sit the back at the proper place between neck and buttocks, so that it will distribute the weight to the best advantage," warned W. S. Harwood in 1902, "then there is trouble ahead for the bearer of the burden." On the other hand, Dan Beard announced, when packing was done properly and straps were adjusted properly, a tramper could carry up to fifty pounds in continuing comfort.[24]

The tramping relationship to the physical environment also remained one of exploitation during these early decades. Trampers often cut trees, polluted streams, and killed wildlife without a second thought, because these activities generally contributed to their comfort and convenience. In "Outfit for a Tramping and Camping Trip," William H. Hobbs identified four instances where a tramper could interact with the environment to improve the camping experience, but he never expressed any awareness that these actions might degrade the physical world. First, when preparing one's bed, a "shake down" of tree branches should be used underneath the blankets. "Fir boughs are the best, but either spruce or hemlock will answer well." Second, when preparing one's outfit, a light but effective hand ax (or hatchet) should be selected, its principal use being to cut wood. "One is apt to be surprised when he sees how much can be accomplished with one of these little axes." Third, the choice of cooking utensils was critical, because they had to function in unusual circumstances. Since acceptable items were difficult to find and purchase, he suggested that a tramper simply customize one article. "A suitable fry pan is obtained by cutting all but about three inches from the handle of the common type of long handled fry pan. On the top of that portion of the handle which remains is firmly riveted an iron socket of square cross section, into which the squared end of a green stick is thrust as a temporary handle." The advantages of this design were several, including not having to carry the handle. Instead, one simply constructed it at a campsite. Lastly, Hobbs was not concerned about water pollution when he recommended a personal kit that included "simple toilet articles and soap."[25]

Many guidebook authors and trampers shared Hobbs's attitude. Stewart Edward White concurred with Hobbs about standard axes—they were too heavy. Instead, "a light hatchet is every bit as good for the purpose of [cutting] firewood and better when it is a question of tent poles or pegs." In the same vein, Horace Kephart emphasized the value of a hatchet and noted that he had used one to cut "young trees eight or more inches thick, often laying in a winter night's wood with it." Moreover, environmental damage by trampers was not always a result of practical utility; sometimes it was destructive entertainment. Paul M. Fink related how he and his companions went for a swim in a lake, and "then some time was devoted to snake hunting, both with rifle and by hand." In particular, the trampers overturned the rocks where brown watersnakes hid, grabbed the snakes by their tails, and then cracked their heads against the rocks. "So plentiful they were we must have killed a score." Sadly, they did not eat the snakes, which are harmless, or make use of them in any way; their killing seems simply to have been for fun.[26]

Tramping practice in these early decades might have resulted in environmental regulation had its impacts been anywhere near as cumulative and damaging as those in America's national parks. As early as 1892, the situation was so poor where horse-wagon campers congregated in Yellowstone National Park that the park's management had established surveillance over them because "they make much litter and permit the escape of fires." By the summer of 1896, formal campground rules also were being enforced because more than twenty-five hundred visitors had camped in the same several locations in Yellowstone that year.[27] In contrast, the small number of trampers was spread so thinly across America's natural landscapes that the tree boughs they cut, the water they polluted, and the other degradation they caused were soon absorbed and mitigated by natural systems. Furthermore, they largely failed to perceive their impacts as problematic. This change in perception would have to wait until the second half of the twentieth century.

Antimodern Tramping

Trampers did not cut trees and damage the physical environment only to be comfortable and to reduce the weight they carried. They also exploited nature in order to recapitulate the "frontier experience" that they idealized (see chapter 2). Just as tramping was becoming a popular form of camping, Americans were realizing that many of the forces that had forged the national character, including the frontier, were disappearing. At the same time, urban life with all its social disruptions grew increasingly common. Trampers, like other campers, wished to enter "wild" nature in imitation of earlier explorers and pioneers, to reenact their formative way of life. Tramping would, they believed, foster the self-reliance and other admirable American qualities that purportedly had developed when the original pioneers engaged primitive wilderness. According to one tramper, the consequence of his recapitulation of the frontier experience would be that "no matter what obstacles Nature and the weather used in an attempt to defeat us, we [would know] we had what it took to win through." In 1904's "The Wilderness near Home," Robert Dunn suggested that tramping had a recognizable geography that did not occur just anywhere. Authentic tramping took place only once the tramper had taken up the mantle of the frontiersman and traveled beyond the sights and sounds of ordinary life. Go, Dunn ordered, to the edge of civilization, to where the lumbermen disappear. "Then you are ready to plunge for a day or so on beyond the line of the ax's desolation, following no trail, on the hunt for the tiny pond you have marked on the map; straight over the mountains, not to stop till the rumble of the night freight on the railroad no longer reaches you—alone as a voyageur in the heart of Athabasca." Paul M. Fink was even more explicit when explaining why he took to tramping. Yes, he admitted, he had "inherited" his affection for the out-of-doors from his father, who had been "a great camper, hunter and fisherman," but he really was motivated more by the romantic antimodernism of "woodcraft, the way of living in the woods," than by the pursuit of game. Reminiscent of John Ruskin, Fink called for competence with the complex set of traditional (not industrial) skills that his predecessors had employed. "I had read the accounts of the Long Hunters and others of the old frontiersmen; how they lived comfortably in the wilderness making do with what little they carried on their backs and the much they had in their heads. I craved to do likewise, insofar as present-day conditions permitted."

Blending the flowery descriptive language of romanticism with the transformational experience of pioneering, Harriet Monroe reveled in her summer 1908 tramp through Yosemite Valley and the Sierra Nevada beyond. Spending a week in the valley, she explained, "We grew aware as never before of [nature's] splendor and joy; we saw it in the green of the meadows and woods, in the sparkling white of the granite domes; and we heard it in the race of cascades, in the tumult of an hundred waterfalls." Of course, woods, rocks, and waterfalls presented challenges, which made her tramping trip "rough"; but difficulty, she indicated, was the path to satisfaction now and in the past. "Something will be lost, no doubt, when many pilgrims follow the mountain trails—when this wilderness, like Switzerland, is smoothed and carved for the foot of man, and dotted with lodges for his comfort. It must be, and on the whole it is best; but the facile tourists of the future will be less happy than we adventurers, who found nature virgin and inviolate, and braved her beauty and terror in the mood and manner of the pioneers."[28]

In addition to relishing wild scenery and recapitulating the frontier experience, early trampers often sought relief from their modern urban lives. "Towns were purgatory," wrote one tramper who projected his antimodern feelings onto the city's physical characteristics. "What torture is worse," asked Robert Dunn in 1904, "than that abysmal fear you get, prisoned between brick walls in June, that all instincts of plant and creature in the wilderness . . . will be all weary and fading by the time vacation sets you among them." For others, the city was not so much a physical environment as a social one. In the daily routine, groaned William H. Hobbs, the urban resident was categorized and ranked, unavoidably dependent upon others, and forced to submerge his true qualities. A tramping trip into wilderness, by contrast, "begets a spirit of freedom and independence. The ratings of society quickly disappear and a man's real character comes to the fore." And, for middle-class women, tramping offered the glimmerings of a social liberation unavailable at home. While gender inequality generally continued while on a tramping trip, sometimes class differences weakened as everyone's activities became constrained. According to Harriet Monroe, women trampers "learned, or thought we did, to wear our short skirts and high hob-nailed boots with an air, as though we had been born to the joy of them; . . . We knew literally the emancipation of having 'only one dress to put on,' and the difficulty of keeping that one dress unspotted; and we found it no hardship to wash our washable clothes in the running stream and dry them in the sun and wear them unironed, like Homer's ladies of long ago."[29] In the wild, the material differences between a woman of the house and her staff shrank, leaving all, as on many a pilgrimage, more socially alike.

During the interwar years of 1918 to 1941, the motivations of trampers would remain more or less the same as before: modern urban life was physically, psychologically, and socially debilitating, but tramping through scenic, wild landscapes, with its echo of the woodsman, the explorer, and the pioneer, could restore and rejuvenate a camper before his or her return to everyday life. The quantity of trampers likely increased as a consequence of social and technological changes, though again the numbers are uncertain, because no one gathered tramping statistics. Alternative measures are available, however, and they suggest the pattern of tramping's increase. Between 1917 and 1941, for example, the number of recreational visitors to national parks rose by 1,633 percent, while those to the national forests climbed 286 percent between 1924 and 1941. Undoubtedly, very few of these visitors were trampers, but if the proportions of various outdoor recreationists held anywhere near steady over these years, then the overall number increased notably.[30]

Tramping's Shifting Technology

As explored in chapter 3, the arrival of inexpensive automobiles during the 1910s converted horse-wagon camping into auto camping, and the number of such practitioners exploded, especially after World War I. With an enhanced capacity to easily carry equipment, supplies, and people, auto camping began to appeal to people who previously had been unable or unwilling to try it. Less obviously, the appearance of the automobile also supported an increase in the number of trampers during these same years. Trampers did not need an auto to transport themselves, or require increasing amounts of gear, but inexpensive cars and an expanding network of passable to excellent roads did enhance their ability to access distant wild areas and reduce the time needed to do so. Many more people began to enjoy weekend tramps because they could quickly drive to and from backcountry entry points. Trampers also began to take more multiday trips as automobiles brought new, previously inaccessible areas within range.

In addition to autos and roads, some other technological changes enhanced tramping's appeal. Bedding consisting of blankets and conifer boughs persisted among trampers, but sleeping bags became increasingly widespread and advertised. "Sleep in comfort in an O Joy Sleeping Bag," offered Leibold & Company, the bag's manufacturer. No matter what sort of camper you were, an O Joy Sleeping Bag would improve comfort and convenience, because it was "warm, compact . . . and absolutely waterproof," declared the advertisement. Nonetheless, the manufacturer was clearly targeting trampers in particular when its ad declared the bag to be "lightweight (weighs only 8 pounds)" and "easily carried on a hike." Serious trampers were also now more likely to use a pack of some sort rather than a blanket roll. Most often a simple canvas bag with straps sufficed for a trip. Sometimes a pack might be World War I surplus, but many companies that produced canvas products also sold a line of sacks. Some trampers preferred pack baskets, especially in the Adirondack region, while others embraced the "Trapper Nelson" packboard, which appeared in the mid-1920s and consisted of a wood frame with a cloth sack attached (fig. 7.3).

A decade later, Jack Van Coevering, in the magazine *Popular Science*, published the instructions for making an "Alaskan back pack." Unlike the Trapper Nelson packboard, this backpack was an adjustable, cushioned pack frame for carrying a loaded duffle bag and other gear. According to Van Coevering, with his wooden backpack "you can carry forty-five or fifty pounds . . . with no more effort than a roll of bedding." Both these changes in equipment—sleeping bags and packs—enhanced tramping's comfort, convenience, and predictability.[31]

Despite these McDonaldized nods toward comfort, tramping during the interwar period continued to be physically challenging because of the heavy loads often carried over long distances. Consequently, the traditional approach for managing tramping's roughness persisted—minimize the load. So when

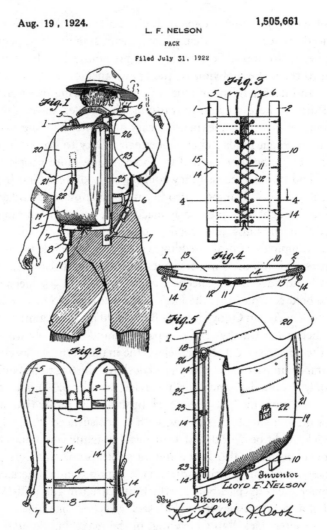

Aug. 19 , 1924.   1,505,661

L. F. NELSON

PACK

Filed July 31, 1922

Figure 7.3. The "Trapper Nelson" packboard of 1924 was a significant advancement in pack design for trampers. From Lloyd F. Nelson, "Pack," patent no. 1,505,661, at "Patent Full-Text Databases," U.S. Patent and Trademark Office, http://patft. uspto.gov/netahtml/PTO/index.html, 1.

Arthur C. Comey published his slim tramping booklet, *Going Light*, in 1924, it was a fast seller. "If we take too much," he began, "especially if our muscles are soft from city life, our burden may cause us so much suffering as to spoil the trip. . . . On the other hand, if we omit essentials discomfort and even real hardship may result. Maximum comfort with minimum weight is our goal." To reach this objective, Comey developed and promoted the "ten-pound pack," which he claimed could be carried with comfort for a week. Providing a carefully detailed list, Comey insisted that it included everything but the food to support a one-to-two-week trip. It covered the minimum needed for maximum enjoyment, though of course not everyone believed him. To those who suggested more items were needed, he replied, "If they are necessary for your comfort, take them," but the tone of his writing suggests that he did not believe any additions were truly indispensable. And to anyone who might suggest fewer pieces, he was "all ears" and willing to "listen closely in the hope of reducing [my] own pack without corresponding disadvantage."[32]

The debate about gear and its weight and necessity would continue up to our day, but it did not lead to a reduction in the number of trampers between the wars. To the contrary, the number and diversity of trampers increased so dramatically after World War I that being one was no longer a novelty, at least as early as 1921. Meanwhile, tramping remained a largely white and middle-class recreation. There is no evidence to suggest it generally appealed to ethnic and racial minorities or was practiced by them. However, rising wages and the diffusion of paid vacations into working-class jobs broadened its appeal among whites. Moreover, tramping no longer appealed almost exclusively to men. Many white women were dedicated trampers by the 1920s, with small groups of them (and no men) tramping long distance through Vermont by 1927. Despite tramping's growing attractiveness, the overall numbers remained small when compared to the popular explosion that would ignite forty years later. Still, Guy and Laura Waterman hit the mark when they declared that "there definitely was a backwoods camping set" during the 1920s and 1930s.[33]

Wilderness for Tramping

Ironically, the roads that increasingly stretched out from urban areas and gave trampers improved opportunities also sliced up wild areas, especially those nearest to cities. The natural landscapes that Robert Dunn had enjoyed near his home in New York and Paul M. Fink near his in Tennessee before World War I rapidly lost their wildness, as roads with automobiles cut through them and auto-oriented recreations grew within them. This sense of loss, especially in regard to public lands, prompted two national responses: a greater interest in and support for packhorse camping and tramping, and an effort to protect "wilderness"—that is, the sacred places where these forms of camping prevailed.[34]

During the interwar years, most of America's wild areas were part of the federal public domain controlled by the National Park and Forest Services.

Between the two agencies, the National Park Service provided the greater
degree of preservation, but its focus was on scenery and geological features
rather than wilderness. The NPS's first two directors, Stephen Mather and
Horace Albright, viewed motor tourism and auto camping as a valid com-
muning with nature while developing a political constituency for park protection. "They lured motorists to the park," wrote historian Paul Sutter, "by
building and improving roads and other tourist facilities." Moreover, they
"packaged" this motoring nature experience as authentic and sold it as a
consumable landscape through speaking tours, negotiations with concessionaires, and by lobbying for roads.[35]

The national parks were spectacularly scenic, and the National Park
Service strove to protect that beauty. After 1922, it even became agency
policy "that overdevelopment of any national park, or any portion of a
national park, is undesirable and should be avoided." In particular, the
NPS wished to emphasize the need for nature protection in order to support
the character-building activities of trampers and other primitive campers.
"Not all of Nature's treasures are to be seen from the seat of an automobile;
one does not receive at twenty miles an hour, the inspiration that results
from a pilgrimage on foot. . . . Someone had said, 'Great views make great
thoughts, great thoughts make great men.' The national parks should be
a real factor in the building of a better, stronger race." Nonetheless, the
parks came to be seen by many as "artificial" and "commercial" as the NPS
developed trails, roads, automobile campgrounds, and other facilities. By
the time scientist John C. Merriam visited Yosemite Valley in 1930, he saw
it as little more than "long stretches of wide road, innumerable buildings,
hotels, automobiles and parking places." No longer was it sacred wilderness,
but "a resort . . . promoted by business for profit." Despite official policy,
for many critics the NPS was too eager to develop its parks and thus undermined national park wildness and its experience.[36]

America's national forests comprised far more land than its national
parks, but they were not viewed as havens from the sort of development that
was seen as damaging the national parks. As a resource and "multiple-use"
agency, the U.S. Forest Service was less oriented toward preservation and
more ambivalent about developments for motorized visitors than was the
National Park Service. Auto camping was poorly supported during the
1920s, and while the motor campers who came to national forests found
a growing network of roads, they were not there for recreationists. Instead
they were being built primarily for lumbering, mining, and the connecting
of isolated communities situated within the nation's forests. "As a result,"
observed historian Sutter, "new roads whittled away at the national forests' substantial roadless acreage more extensively than they did within the

national parks."[37] In addition, the Forest Service's ambivalence toward recreation meant that regional and local foresters were provided few resources to support recreation; many of them adopted such alternatives as permitting summer camps, cottages, and hotels. Unsurprisingly, these private facilities proliferated on those forest lands that were most scenic and accessible by road from urban areas. Under these conditions, some Forest Service voices began to clamor for wilderness protection.

By the 1920s, critics felt that USFS policies threatened to destroy the remaining virgin forests within the system. Fearing that wilderness might soon disappear, Aldo Leopold, Arthur H. Carhart, and other Forest Service officials set about establishing permanently protected areas. Their efforts would ultimately lead to the wilderness preservation system that we know today. As early as 1921, USFS Southwest Region administrator Leopold publicly advocated for the official designation of large "wilderness areas" that would preserve relatively undisturbed nature for nonmotorized camping and associated sports. A packhorse camper himself, Leopold described wilderness as "a continuous stretch of country preserved in its natural state, open to lawful hunting and fishing, big enough to absorb a two weeks' pack trip, and devoid of roads, artificial trails, cottages, or other works of man." The majority of Americans, he admitted, would probably think him wrong. And, as he imagined the situation, they "undoubtedly want all the automobile roads, summer hotels, graded trails, and other modern conveniences that we can give them. But a very substantial minority, I think, want just the opposite." If nothing were done to change Forest Service policy, he warned, the small wild areas that would be left between the roads would be unable to satisfy this minority. Hinting at the ranking that is common among campers, Leopold sneered that these remaining patches "will always be big enough for [car] camping, but they will tend to grow too small for a real wilderness trip" on horseback or foot. Besides, he suggested in subsequent pieces, how could auto campers possibly have anything like the pioneer experience that had produced American culture's "vigorous individualism combined with an ability to organize, a certain intellectual curiosity bent to practical ends, a lack of subservience to stiff social forms, and an intolerance of drones"? "If we think we are going to learn by cruising round the mountains in a Ford, we are largely deceiving ourselves. There is a vast difference between the days of the 'Free Tourist Campground—Wood and Water Furnished' and the Covered Wagon Days." If America was not careful, if it did not cease to build more and more roads into nearby wilderness areas, only the wealthy, who have the time and resources to travel to someplace like Alaska, would ever have the opportunity for a "covered wagon" adventure. The outcome, Leopold clearly implied, would be a loss of "the indigenous part of our Americanism, the qualities that set [our nation] apart as a new rather than an imitative contribution to civilization."[38]

In 1927, former USFS employee Arthur Carhart joined Leopold in his campaign against road building with an article titled "Wilderness, Ltd." According to Carhart, two "bad habits" were destroying the nation's wild landscapes. First, a national history of wilderness clearance had left most Americans accepting of the notion that wildlands needed to be "conquered." Second, and more recently, the country had developed a good-roads habit. Like any habit, when "practiced in moderation," it was "admirable," but that was no longer the case. After more than twenty years of "preaching" by "good-roads apostles . . . there has come into the mass mind of America the fallacious idea that a good road, wherever built, is valuable."[39] These two habits, Carhart argued, were coming together and destroying the remnants of America's original wilderness, which would undermine the value of nature as a recreational retreat from urban life. The mania needed to stop, insisted Carhart. It appears that others were listening.

In 1928 two committee reports on the recreational resources of federal public lands were delivered to the National Conference on Outdoor Recreation (NCOR). Organized by President Calvin Coolidge, NCOR was the most prominent effort by the federal government to address the issue of outdoor recreation since Theodore Roosevelt had called a Governors' Conference on Conservation in 1908. Importantly, the committees shared Leopold's and Carhart's concern. Wilderness, they insisted, had to be "a roadless area" where the simplest, most "primitive" and least modern forms of life could be enjoyed outdoors. Moreover, the committees recommended that wilderness areas be "naturally adapted to camping and allied forms of recreation in connection with canoe, horse, or foot travel." Wilderness, they argued, was not for motor boating, auto camping, or any other recreations that employed motors. These should be enjoyed elsewhere, because places for them could be created almost anywhere.[40]

The following year, 1929, the Forest Service adopted Regulation L-20, the agency's first formal wilderness policy. William B. Greeley, chief forester of the USFS, had felt that the wilderness idea had "merit," so he turned to L. F. Kneipp, the Forest Service's strongest wilderness advocate, to compose Regulation L-20. The regulation identified a new protected-area designation—"primitive area," to support the tramping and similarly nonmotorized recreations that the Forest Service ranked as the best recreational use of these lands. According to officials, primitive areas would "maintain primitive conditions of transportation, subsistence, habitation, and environment to the fullest degree compatible with their highest public use." Using the authority granted by the L-20 Regulation, the USFS established more than seventy primitive areas on more than fourteen million acres during the next ten years. Nevertheless, the regulation did not provide the degree of protection that today's "wilderness" designation delivers, and it would become the focus for further criticism and change during the next decade.[41]

Long-Distance Trails

The Forest Service's new primitive areas, as well as similar spaces in the national parks and elsewhere, were physically challenging to cross. Some trampers, such as Robert Dunn, knew they were truly into nature only when roads and trails disappeared. But as John M. Gould had noted, such trackless, "wild and uninhabited regions" were difficult to negotiate, so for most trampers, trails were desirable, seen as the avenue away from civilization. Indeed, as the twentieth century unfolded and urban-industrial life sprawled across the landscape, trails began to acquire mythic connotations, with links to the Oregon Trail, the Santa Fe Trail, and other pioneer routes. According to historian Glynn Wolar, "the trail not only took the traveler to the wilderness frontier, it *was* the wilderness frontier" for trampers. Regional and long-distance trail building first appeared in parks, forests, and on other lands during the 1910s as hikers, riders, packhorse campers, and trampers demanded access to the wild and beautiful portions of America's public domain.[42]

Recreational trails and local trail systems had appeared even earlier in the western national parks, during the 1900s, 1910s, and 1920s, to provide access to uplifting scenery and as opportunities for quiet and solitude. The USFS, by contrast, generally developed its trails for firefighting and other more utilitarian purposes; only relatively late during these decades did the agency begin to take recreation into account. In the Northeast, however, a new trail-building approach developed. A region-wide awareness had begun to supplant the building of clusters of short trails; local systems were linked together and mapped to form larger systems. The White Mountains of New Hampshire and the Adirondacks of New York each virtually became one large place to hike. An "increasing multitude of feet" were coming to the Adirondacks, crowed Allen Chamberlain in 1920, to enjoy "trunk line trails on attractive routes where the odor of gasolene [*sic*] may not penetrate." The New York State Conservation Commission, he reported, was supporting the region's trail-building effort by issuing new maps showing the extensive possibilities for longer-distance travel. The region's trails were now being used not only by those who came simply for a day trip to Mount Marcy or Whiteface Mountain, "but more and more each year by those men and women who travel foot-free day by day—the ever-growing brotherhood of trampers." As this approach to trails diffused throughout the Northeast, "the full maturing of this new concept produced the 'through trail,'" according to Laura and Guy Waterman. The first of these was Vermont's Long Trail, which was begun in 1910 and took the Green Mountain Club twenty years to complete. Starting at the Massachusetts state line, the trail ran north for 272 miles to the border with Canada. A wave of other long-distance, through trails followed the Long Trail, including the John Muir Trail—the JMT—in California. Theodore S. Solomons and a series of friends and colleagues had had the idea for a trail along the crest of the central Sierra Nevada since the early 1890s. During most of that decade they slowly explored, mapped, and reported parts of the route each summer, with most of the trail identified by the summer of 1897. The trail remained relatively sketchy and unnamed until the summer of 1914, when the Sierra Club decided to seek funding to develop the trail into something more accessible. A committee was formed, and with private donations and state support, construction began. Official designation as the John Muir Trail, along with the location of its path, was first made in 1915, to celebrate the lifework of the famous environmentalist who had died the year before. Work on the trail, however, would be slow, and the project would not be completed for another forty-six years.[43]

Six years after the initiation of the JMT, the longest and most famous of eastern through trails was proposed by Benton MacKaye, a forester, a creative and unconventional planner, and a conservationist. In 1921, he published a revolutionary article titled "An Appalachian Trail: A Project in Regional Planning," which called for a return to premodern lifeways. Suspicious of modern urban life, MacKaye described "civilized" people as "potentially as helpless as canaries in a cage" because they had lost "the ability to cope with nature directly." Modern life had brought benefits, he admitted, but it had also weakened people; active measures, such as the scouting movement, had arisen to counteract the worst aspects of modern life. "We want the strength of progress without its puniness," announced MacKaye. "We want its conveniences without it fopperies. The ability to sleep and cook in the open is a good step forward. But 'scouting' should not stop there." Modern Americans, said MacKaye, also needed the Appalachian Trail—the AT. In MacKaye's vision, the trail would connect a series of "shelter camps," each "a comfortable day's walk apart," and some of these camps would "grow naturally" into permanent settlements. These cooperative "community camps" would house people in "private domiciles" but without private property or profit. The only acceptable activities in these village-like settlements would be "non-industrial" ones, such as recreation and field schooling. Finally, he proposed "food and farm camps," which would be places of production and learning, as well as opportunities for living and employment. The AT was not simply a place to retreat to and have fun. MacKaye amplified tramping's antimodern and pilgrimage aspects for individuals and families into an environment that would remake American society by creating "that counter migration from city to country that has so long been prayed for." If the many urban unemployed and underemployed (rather than the "overworked" typical of the tramping literature) could get out of the city and "walk the skyline" of the Appalachian Trail, they would be able to "develop its varied opportunities . . . for recreation, recuperation and employment." Instead of a single two-week retreat as the antidote for an unsettling existence, MacKaye envisioned a new, pro-rural way of life. Citing the Long Trail as an example, he envisioned the AT as an extension of it and similar efforts in the region. Ideally, he recommended that the new trail stretch from at least from Mount Washington in New Hampshire to Mount Mitchell in North Carolina. Organizationally, the trail would be divided into sections under the control of local groups who would coordinate "under some form of general federated control."[44]

Benton MacKaye, while a lover of the outdoors and a tramper himself, never advocated a tramper's utopia, but he did organize his vision around a trail. After several years of his proselytizing for the AT, the Appalachian Trail Conference (ATC) was organized into a formal body, with five regional divisions. It held its first meeting in Washington, D.C., in 1925, with MacKaye as the first speaker. As he had in his 1921 article, MacKaye continued to promote the idea of a path that would preserve and develop the mountains' crest-line environments as a counterpoint to modern, urban life. MacKaye's dream regularly inspired listeners, but for many of the meeting's other speakers different issues were central. François E. Matthes spoke about the future need for nature-guide and history-guide services, Fred F. Schuetz praised the "tributary trails" that would feed people to and from the Appalachian Trail, and Arthur Comey gave a workshop on how to "go light" when tramping. MacKaye continued to write and speak in favor of the Appalachian Trail, but the tension between his grand vision of a rural alternative to urban life and the more mainstream outdoor recreational concerns of most ATC members was ultimately settled in favor of the latter and made clear in 1930. Myron Avery, the industrious and productive acting chairman of the ATC at the time, penned an article for *Mountain Magazine* that flatly stated the AT's present and future significance. "The Appalachian Trail, as conceived by its proponents and already partly realized, is a footpath for hikers in the Appalachian Mountains, extending from Maine to Georgia, a distance of some 1,300 miles." Its purpose was to provide access to those mountains for "tramping, camping, and outdoor recreation." MacKaye never accepted

Avery's view, arguing that "the mere footpath is no end in itself, but a means of sojourning in the wilderness, whose nurture is your particular care." Walking away from the ATC in 1935, MacKaye would never again be actively involved with the trail and instead would pour his energy into the Wilderness Society, which he helped to found. Nevertheless, his legacy would continue to generate offspring.[45]

A Western Border-to-Border Trail

The growing awareness both within and outside the USFS and the NPS of the fragility of wilderness, as well as the construction of the Long, John Muir, Appalachian, and other through trails during the 1920s, led some westerners to think that a trail equivalent to the one inspired by Benton MacKaye could be created closer to the Pacific Ocean. The first suggestion for a western border-to-border trail came in January 1926 from Catherine Montgomery, a hiker and educator in Bellingham, Washington. She was conversing with Joseph Hazard, a member of Seattle's Mountaineers' club, when she proposed a ridgeline trail "from the Canadian Border to the Mexican Boundary Line," with mile markers and "shelter huts" like "the Long Trail of the Appalachians." No direct evidence ties her suggestion to Oregon's Skyline Trail, a through trail begun in 1920, but being a long-distance tramper herself, Montgomery might have been inspired by it as well as by the Appalachian Trail. Either way, her proposal appealed to Hazard, who persuaded his fellow Mountaineers to embrace the idea, and they, in turn, "promptly contacted all other outdoor organizations. All adopted the project with enthusiasm and organized to promote it."[46] Nevertheless, nothing substantial developed until the spring of 1932, when a Southern California effort began. It would ultimately achieve success.

On January 14, 1932, a committee of five met in Los Angeles to debate a proposal for a new organization whose general aim, they decided, would be to "stimulate interest in wholesome outdoor recreation" and to "preserve our natural resources." They expressed no particular interest in tramping or any other form of camping, nor did they mention anything about trails, either local or long distance. Settling on the name "Mountain League of Los Angeles County," the group was not to be a club composed of individuals, but a federation of interested organizations with representatives from the Sierra Club, the city of Los Angeles's Recreation Department, the U.S. Forest Service, and others. At their meeting's conclusion, the five fanned out to identify and enlist additional supporters from other organizations. In short order, they approached Clinton Clarke of the Pasadena

Boy Scouts, who agreed to chair an "Organizing Committee" along with two of the original five participants. The goal of this committee was to prepare a document detailing the purposes, structure, and likely projects for the proposed league. On March 4, the Mountain League held its first formal meeting to discuss its committee's report. According to Clarke and his committee's other members, the Mountain League's aim would be to survey the county's mountain areas in order to facilitate nature study, conservation, and "mountaineering," obtain support from and give aid to the appropriate public authorities, and become a clearinghouse of information. The organization would be simple, with an executive committee and six standing committees to coordinate work on projects. To begin their efforts, the committee suggested five projects, most of which involved local nature restoration and protection and thus fit in with the objectives of the January meeting. The primary project, however, was something of a departure from the original focus on local mountains—"Extension of the John Muir Trail through the mountains of Southern California from Palmdale to the Mexican line." In spite of this unusual element, the Organizing Committee's report was adopted with some minor structural changes, and the next meeting was set for April 1. At this meeting, an executive committee of fourteen members was formed, including Clinton Clarke, and the following week Clarke emerged as its chair. Although Clarke may not have been present in January, he had moved quickly to become the leader of the Mountain League. In early May, the league again met to organize its several standing committees, and the one focused on trails was tasked with pursuing four issues: uniform trail marking; establishment of overnight camping areas for trampers; coordination and exploration of San Gabriel Mountain trails; and the extension of the John Muir Trail. The first three issues were placed in the charge of others, but Clinton Clarke surfaced as the chair of the subcommittee created to address the trail extension.[47] It seems clear that from the outset Clarke had been focused on the John Muir Trail, and the project would fill his life for the next decade.

Clinton Clarke

Clinton Churchill ("Church") Clarke (1873–1957) was born in Chicago and spent his "boyhood summers camping, fishing, and hunting in northern Michigan and Wisconsin when that country was a true wilderness."

An imposing six feet, three inches tall and a direct descendant of Cotton Mather, Clarke journeyed to New England for his higher education, earning a baccalaureate from Williams College in 1898 and a master of

Figure 7.4. Margaret and Clinton "Church" Clarke's 1927 passport photo. From box 12 (2), Warren Lee Rogers Papers, Huntington Library, San Marino, CA.

arts in "general literary courses" from Harvard University in 1900. With his schooling complete, Clarke chose not to return to his hometown but instead headed off for Southern California, where he settled in Pasadena. Northeast of Los Angeles, this small city held just over nine thousand souls when Clarke arrived but was rapidly growing in size and stature. Heavily promoted by boosters, Pasadena had become a national destination by 1900 and was attracting wealthy winterers, middle-class midwesterners, and a variety of ethnic groups. Clarke and his wife, Margaret, who were married in 1906, found Pasadena and its setting quite attractive and lived there for the rest of their lives (fig. 7.4).[48]

One reason Clarke enjoyed Pasadena was the opportunity it presented for nature recreation in the nearby San Gabriel Mountains. A vigorous man, Clarke continued his youthful affection for "roughing it" after he moved to Southern California. According to him, he "spent summer vacations hiking through the mountains of [Southern] California, and six hiking trips through the Sierra Nevada, pretty well covering and photographing that region." Clarke would be a Sierra Club member for more than thirty years, and at least two of these early adventures were multiweek Sierra Club outings into the Sierra Nevada's backcountry during the summers of 1910 and 1911.[49]

A second reason Pasadena appealed to Clarke was its emerging civic culture. During the first decade of the twentieth century, Pasadenans were self-consciously attempting to create cultural institutions, encourage high-mindedness, and establish the city as a "refined community." Politically a Republican, Clarke supported these progressive efforts, was himself a strong advocate for civic activism, and, importantly, could afford to be deeply involved. Inheritances from his lawyer father and his mother's wealthy family had given him his "own income" for life, which made it possible for him to live quite comfortably with Margaret and to become enthusiastically involved in civic and community affairs.[50] A supporter of local youth, he organized the Pasadena chapter of the Boy Scouts of America in 1916 and served the organization for over thirty-five years in a variety of posts, including president. In addition, Clarke supported service organizations—he was a member of the Pasadena Rotary Club for over twenty-five years—as well as the arts. In 1917, Clarke helped to organize the Pasadena Community Playhouse, where his wife acted, and over the next twenty years held a variety of executive and committee positions. In this context, we can see that when Clarke joined the Mountain League in early 1932, he was simply combining two of his favored pursuits—civic activism and outdoor recreation.

Over the course of the next three months, Clarke and the other members of the trails subcommittee debated the JMT extension but offered no definitive report. At the Mountain League's June 1932 meeting, "Mr. Clarke stated the necessity for immediately determining what is needed throughout the county in the way of trails." But if there was a connection to the JMT extension, it was not made explicit. Instead, Clarke's motivation lay in the ongoing national struggle with the Great Depression. He wanted the local trail information "in order that unemployment agencies may be able to use their help on these trails."[51]

An Extended John Muir Trail

July passed with no update, but then at the league's August 26 meeting, Clarke presented his subcommittee's report, and it offered a radically expanded vision. Using a map that illustrated "the possibilities," Clarke proposed an extended JMT (EJMT) that would now stretch over two thousand miles, from the Mexican border to Canada. As much as one-quarter of the trail would need to be constructed, but much of it already existed and needed only to be linked into a larger system. In effect, Clarke was proposing a sort of grand, western version of the mergers that had linked the local trails of upstate New York into a unified Adirondack region or tied the through trails of New England into the much longer Appalachian Trail. In addition, Clarke reported, he had taken the first steps toward completing the northern extension. He had traveled to San Francisco to confer with L. A. Barrett, the assistant forester for the USFS's Region 5, which included California. Barrett had endorsed Clarke's proposal and told him "that northern California is ready to go with their portion." Clarke had also sent a communication to the National Geographic Society in Washington, D.C., to obtain their backing and had requested the aid of Southern California's Deserts Conservation League. Finally, Clarke recognized that his was an ambitious proposal and that it might alienate other Mountain League members. To calm their concerns and to tie the regional proposal to the local, Clarke illustrated how an EJMT would "form the backbone for [a] network of trails in Los Angeles County."[52]

The minutes for the August 1932 meeting do not record most responses to Clarke's report, but at least one other league member, William V. Mendenhall, forester for the Angeles National Forest in the San Gabriel Mountains of northern Los Angeles County, announced that his office "would place such a trail on their maps and furnish markings" on the physical trail. Other league members may have expressed mixed feelings or offered resistance, but these responses could not have been strong or pointed. Instead, the meeting minutes conclude with a solid affirmation of Clarke's efforts. The top project "for immediate action" by the league would now be the "Extension of the John Muir Trail."[53] Whatever the league's organizers may have imagined in January, by August its primary focus was the JMT extension, which had risen to the top because of the knowledge, efforts, and influence of Clinton Clarke.

Despite Clarke's powerful report to the league, some doubts may have persisted, because the subcommittee quickly produced two additional supportive reports, one that described the EJMT and another that spoke of its construction. The latter consisted of a list of seventeen "points" and clearly identified the trail's intended users as "hikers, horsemen and nature lovers." At the same time, the trail was not intended for someone who wished to visit for a day, but for the extended and physically challenging enjoyment of packhorse campers and trampers. The trail, the report enunciated, "should be located with convenient water places and suitable camping grounds."

The descriptive report, in contrast, was more evocative and recommended that an EJMT consist of six key features:

1. It would be a continuous trail.
2. It would follow the mountain divides (that is, be at or near crests).
3. It would be located primarily on public lands in order to be "under the protection and control of the National Government."
4. "It is absolutely a wilderness trail and touches no improved or cultivated areas except where it crosses main roads or rivers."
5. "It passes through all the outstanding scenic areas of the Pacific Coast."
6. It would be divided into four sections.[54]

Clearly, these characteristics reflected the growing American interest in through trails. Like the AT and other trails, the EJMT would be a single track running along crest lines, and in the spirit of romanticism it would expose users to striking scenery. It would also be administered like the AT—subdivided among four regional authorities. Unlike the AT, the EJMT mostly would be on secured public lands, which was impossible along the Appalachian crests but would make the remaining point more likely: the trail would be wilderness. It is unclear whether the authors meant the trail should run through wilderness areas or that it would be wilderness itself, but this linkage to wilderness demonstrates that the report's authors thought the trail's use would be antimodern, that is, difficult and challenging rather than easy and comfortable. Moreover, the term would have resonated with the period's widespread concern about loss of wilderness, especially to automobiles and roads, and the need for its protection.

Although these reports were produced by a committee, Clinton Clarke's fingerprints are apparent. The league's concern about a through trail emerged with his arrival, he rose to be the league's chief executive, and then he positioned himself on the through trail subcommittee. At the same time, we know that Clarke had extensive personal experience of the Sierra Nevada, a strong interest in outdoor recreation of a challenging nature, and the resources to devote his time to the necessary investigative work. According to Clarke, he had "made a study and survey of the wilderness regions, especially these on the Pacific Coast." And, like Aldo Leopold, Arthur Carhart, and others, he had become "deeply concerned at the encroachment by roads and recreation projects."[55] In particular, it appears that one road, the Angeles Crest Highway, was his nemesis, and its development would prompt much that followed.

When Clinton Clarke arrived in Pasadena in 1900, three key developments were transforming Southern California. First, the population was growing rapidly in Los Angeles County, which had swelled from 101,454 in 1890 to 170,298 in 1900—a nearly 68 percent increase. The city of Pasadena was experiencing a similar expansion, having grown by more than 85 percent during the same period. Nevertheless, the population was still rather meager. But between Clarke's arrival and 1930, the county's population exploded, growing by nearly 1,200 percent, while Pasadena expanded by over 700 percent. In concert with this population increase came the demand for housing, which sprawled across the landscape, swallowing both wild and cultivated land. Second, the automobile was being adopted by the country, and it was especially embraced by Southern Californians. In 1915, for instance, the United States had 43.1 residents per automobile, but the same ratio was only 8.2 in the city of Los Angeles; by 1930, the numbers had dropped to 5.3 and 1.5 respectively. Coincident with the auto's embrace came roadway improvement and extensions. Third, the growth of outdoor recreational walking throughout the San Gabriel Mountains resulted in what historian John W. Robinson termed "the Great Hiking Era." During the first three decades of the twentieth century, dozens of recreational trails came to snake through the mountains, allowing "multitudes of lowland residents, young and old alike, [to enjoy] weekends and holidays rambling over the range." A mild Mediterranean climate meant it was easy to be outdoors, leading these very steep and rugged mountains to be "regarded as a local frontier for exploration and a challenge to the hardy. . . . Action was valued over watching. . . . There was an appreciation of wilderness values. In the mountains a man could put several days between himself and civilization simply by walking." Although Robinson never directly stated it, he described the San Gabriel Mountain wilderness as a sacred, antimodern place where a tramping pilgrim could be transformed. Clinton Clarke was among the multitude who headed out.[56]

The growth of Los Angeles County's population and the people's embrace of the car created an immediate threat to the San Gabriel Mountains. Decade after decade of new homes and subdivisions had swallowed significant portions of the range's foothills in Clarke's hometown of Pasadena, as well as elsewhere. A deep-seated displeasure at this loss likely provided one pillar supporting Clarke's enthusiasm for the Mountain League and its concern for preservation. The other pillar of that support was Clarke's disapproval of the rapid enlargement of Los Angeles County's road system, and it appears to have come to a head following the start of work on the Angeles Crest Highway, the first major motorway into the San Gabriel Mountains. This road, now California State Route 2, runs sixty-six miles from the city of La Cañada Flintridge on the southern slope of the San Gabriel Mountains through Angeles National Forest, with some of the wildest, most rugged landscapes in the region, to Mountain Top Junction along the northern face of the range. The highway, which comes quite close to Pasadena at its western end, had originally been proposed as a "scenic highway" in 1912, but it was also supposed to enhance the firefighting capacity of the U.S. Forest Service, which probably helped win the agency's support. Nevertheless, the highway was envisioned primarily as a recreational venue that would provide access to sublime views north and south. For a variety of reasons, funding was not secured until 1919, and construction did not begin until 1929. Growing indignation at that construction, which was slicing through Clarke's backyard wilderness, likely prompted his participation in the Mountain League in 1932.[57]

In spite of any qualms that individual league members may have held, the organization endorsed the JMT extension in August, and more organizations pledged support at the September meeting, which prompted Clarke into action. In late September, he wrote to Horace Albright, director of the National Park Service, about the league's proposal and brought together his concern about wilderness loss and the through trail. In his letter to Albright, Clarke provided a "preliminary" report on the Mountain League's plan for the EJMT. He began by relating the condition of backcountry trails in Washington State, Oregon, and California and the "camping places" that would become part of the overall trail. "All," he noted, were "in good condition except for a few short stretches." The trail would be open to all, of course, but the users that the league had most in mind were youth organizations like the Boy Scouts and the YMCA. It was hoped that these groups would create organized programs to take young people "exploring" across the mountains. With tramping and related programs in place, the trail ideally would become the "focus" for an outdoor youth movement like those in Germany or the United Kingdom. Such a romantic antimodern movement, Clarke suggested, would balance the negative aspects of modernity. "The TRAIL by providing the opportunity for actual travelling over mountain ranges from one scenic area to another of the Pacific Coast will appeal to the imagination and stimulate a return to a more natural and simpler recreational activity." The modern world, in Clarke's view, had become false by moving toward artificiality and complexity; "roughing it" on the trail would foster a "return" to truth.[58]

Albright thanked Clarke for the Mountain League's report and noncommittally asked the chairman to keep him on the league's mailing list. Sensing possible support, Clarke responded with an expansion of his previous justification for the EJMT. To begin, he offered the same critique as Aldo Leopold and Arthur Carhart before him. "There is an overdevelopment of road building and the automobile type of recreation. Our wildernesses are fast being exploited and uglified." But Clarke's central concern was the EJMT rather than wilderness, so wilderness preservation alone was insufficient. "Something must be done to preserve for future generations not only our scenic areas and the wilderness reserves—so well established in California—but to make it possible for travelers to wander from one to another over nature trails across the United States unaware of the encroachments of civilization." Why did trampers need to "wander" unaware of civilization? Only challenging, physical recreation in nature, rather than just a modernized, passive gazing upon nature, could bring about the "difference" sought by trampers. "The TRAIL by giving opportunity for simple natural recreation will do much to undo the harmful influence of our mechanical, artificial competitive sports programs . . . the JOHN MUIR TRAIL by making possible hiking, exploring expeditions for organizations, will inaugurate this beneficial movement on the Pacific Coast." Clarke felt that this "beneficial movement" was much needed as a corrective to the negative aspects of modern life, but he feared that the Mountain League did not have the authority or influence necessary. Consequently, he offered to let the NPS take over the extension project.[59]

Albright offered Clarke his strong personal support for the extended through trail and also conveyed that support to the superintendents of the national parks that were or would be crossed by the trail, but he did not assume control of it. The trail, he explained, was simply beyond the Park Service's mission. Nonetheless, he remained supportive and ready to cooperate. At the same time, Albright presciently suggested that Clarke be in touch with the Sierra Club about any extensions to the John Muir Trail. As a member of the Sierra Club (like Clarke), Albright feared that the league's application of the trail's name to stretches not currently included might become an issue. Moreover, the name might have little appeal outside California. It was sage advice.[60]

Although Albright declined Clarke's offer to lead the through trail project, Clarke was upbeat in his reply. He thanked Albright for his support and then requested his help with such practical issues as maps, signs, and related trail materials. Finally, he closed his letter with a personal appeal to Albright's sense of fairness and responsibility toward the trampers whom he clearly judged to be the most authentic of campers. "Much has been done for the motor public. Let us do something for the nature lovers. I am confident, Mr. Albright, that given the incentive, opportunity and proper objective there are vast numbers who will gladly hike over the TRAIL, camp beneath the stars, gather around a campfire and experience that most satisfying happiness of the life on the TRAIL."[61]

The extended John Muir Trail would pass through national forests as well as national parks, so Clarke initiated contact with U.S. Forest Service authorities at approximately the same time that he wrote to Albright. His first letter, dated October 3, 1932, went to William V. Mendenhall, a colleague from the Mountain League's executive committee. Mendenhall also happened to be supervisor of Angeles National Forest, which meant he had influence upon the location and development of the unrolling Angeles Crest Highway. The mountains of Southern California, especially the San Gabriel range, were rapidly losing their natural appeal, explained Clarke, and the causes were clear—the increasing presence of "roads, camps, and commercial developments." One way to control these mushrooming modern intrusions might have been to reject them as they were proposed, but Clarke offered a daring and radical alternative. "To preserve a wilderness area in its natural state could not a strip five miles wide on each side of the JOHN MUIR TRAIL be closed to all improvements, etc.?" Clarke was aware that the USFS had enhanced protection for its "wilderness/primitive" areas and that these might or might not be laced with trails.[62] The two features, protection and trails, were not necessarily linked, but for Clarke they could interrelate. Instead of designating an area without roads and other urban developments as wilderness and potentially having its trails run through peripheral areas where roads might possibly pass nearby, he proposed the creation of a wilderness area *centered* on the trail—that is, extending outward from both sides of the trail—which would guarantee a tramper's ability to avoid "the encroachments of civilization." In Clarke's view, the EJMT was itself wilderness, a natural place untarnished by "mechanical" civilization, and if situated correctly, the Forest Service's wilderness areas could act as buffers between the sacred space of the trail and the profane space of conventional life.

The next day, Clarke sent a nearly identical letter to Assistant Forester L. A. Barrett at his San Francisco office. Mountain areas were quickly being "spoiled" for trampers "by an over-building of roads," he warned. We must "provide retreats for the increasing numbers who seek solitude and simple, natural recreation." Trampers, Clarke insisted, needed these sacred spaces to compensate for the crowded, complicated, and inauthentic character of their everyday urban lives. In particular, Clarke encouraged Barrett to position the Northern California portions of the EJMT "to pass through and link up the wilderness areas that you have set aside." At the same time, Clarke appears to have known that most of Northern California's national forests included little or no wilderness, so he again offered his proposal as a way to enhance protection and to improve the tramping experience. "Will it be possible for your Department to include the TRAIL as a part of the wilderness plan and include—say—five miles on each side of the TRAIL as area?"[63]

Unsurprisingly, the Forest Service blanched at Clarke's proposal and would not commit to a wilderness corridor straddling the trail. Supervisor

Mendenhall must have swallowed especially hard when he first read Clarke's letter, because Angeles National Forest is only about twenty miles across. A ten-mile-wide corridor of wilderness would have engulfed nearly half the forest. Moreover, Mendenhall did not share Clarke's concern about roads in national forests. Some portions of Southern California's forests had been heavily developed, Mendenhall admitted in a reply written the day Clarke's letter arrived, but when "you actually scale it on a map," much of these forests remained wilderness. At the same time, he recognized that the EJMT would parallel roads at "numerous places," but the problem was easily solved. For very little expense, "the location can be changed and the trail can be placed out of view of the roads." For Mendenhall, out of sight was out of mind; he was unconcerned about the noise or smells that also came with roadways. Nevertheless, he supported the project, but warned that he had no funds for implementation.[64]

The regional office of the USFS was slow to reply, in contrast to Mendenhall, but it was also more thoughtful. L. A. Barrett, who was "acting forester" while his superior, S. B. Show, presumably attended to other business, sent Clarke Northern California maps with existing and projected trails on them so that the chairman would have a clear sense of their plans. "We have tried to reach as many of the points of scenic interest on the route as we possibly could," reported Barrett. They had even identified an "alternate loop" for trampers who wished to step off the main trail to pass through Lassen National Park. They could not, however, keep the trail in wild areas at all times. "We have found it just impossible to dodge all roads and civilized points." Despite their best efforts, the north–south trail would necessarily have to intersect with several east–west highways. Finally, Barrett closed his letter by turning to Clarke's wilderness-corridor proposal, but he was no more supportive than Mendenhall had been. "I am sorry but it is impracticable to set aside an area on each side of the trail as part of our primitive area system." The L-20 regulation had been inaugurated merely three years before, and it did not provide for "primitive" areas that were organized around a trail. "We just cannot make such a dedication," explained Barrett, "and be consistent with the principles under which such are established."[65] Never one to retreat easily, Clarke would continue to pursue his corridor proposal despite these rejections. At the same time, he turned to other means of support.

The outdoor recreation boom of the 1910s and 1920s had continued into the 1930s, despite the onset of the Great Depression in late 1929. It was, in fact, facilitated by federal programs that aimed to stimulate the national recovery through a variety of enhancements to the nation's recreational infrastructure. In the fall of 1933, one of these newly created programs—the

Civilian Conservation Corps—was beginning to direct its energies toward a variety of new projects across the nation. In an attempt to bring some of those resources to the EJMT, Clarke sent an appeal to Robert Y. Stuart, chief forester of the USFS and a member of the CCC's national advisory council. Should the federal government contribute to the development of the trail, asked Clarke rhetorically? Yes, he responded, because it would have a deeply beneficial impact upon the most impressionable of Americans. "The TRAIL can be the focus, the incentive for the formation and development of the Youth Movement . . . so remarkably successful in Europe." Outdoor recreation organizations were active and popular in Germany, the United Kingdom, and elsewhere in Europe at this time. An extended John Muir Trail would provide many young Americans with opportunities for day trips in the outdoors and, Clarke emphasized, for pioneer-like "cross country exploring trips." Such tramping adventures would especially heighten participants' appreciation for "our mountain wonderlands," but what was more important, they would be pilgrimages away from the everyday. According to Clarke, tramping along the EJMT would counteract the negative aspects of modern young Americans' hectic and "mechanical" lives by "returning" them "to a more natural and simpler recreation program." Since tramping, rather than organized athletics, was what people did when the frontier was explored, the tramper recapitulated this ancestral experience and was thus more likely than someone who played baseball to develop the superior qualities of a premodern American. Moreover, Clarke believed that any portion of the EJMT served this function. This unrecognized perception is clear from his declaration to the USFS's Stuart that the Mountain League was attempting to interest the Boy Scouts, YMCA, American Legion, high schools, and colleges "to program from their central offices outing trips." The league did not, however, imagine that participants would cover the entire trail on one of these trips. Instead, they would enter and exit whichever "sections of the TRAIL" were most accessible and manageable. In other words, tramping along any portion of the EJMT was acceptable, because the entire length was sacred and outside the conventional world.[66]

Clarke was highly defensive of an EJMT that possessed such redemptive power. Since most of the trail ran though natural forests, Clarke again repeated the request that he had recently put to Angeles National Forest supervisor Mendenhall and California's assistant regional forester Barrett, but this time to the top official. "To protect the TRAIL areas from commercial exploitation," he queried Chief Forester Stuart, "can a ruling be made by the Forestry Service and the National Park Service setting aside a strip on either side of the TRAIL as a wilderness area? There has been a serious over-building of roads in our mountain regions and our true wildernesses are fast disappearing before the encroachments of our civilization." Again, Clarke was most likely responding to the construction of the Angeles Crest Highway, but he nevertheless situated his critique within the larger American context. We must do something to protect nature soon, he asserted, or it will be "too late." That something, of course, was the EJMT, which when centered in a wilderness corridor "would preserve at least that much for future nature lovers."[67]

Clarke's characterization of the EJMT as providing a return to "natural" and "simpler" recreation, as being equally enjoyable in any section, and as best centered in a wilderness corridor indicates that he did not perceive it as simply a line within wilderness. Based on his correspondence and other writings, it appears that the EJMT was a sacred path for Clinton Clarke. It was not, in the first instance, merely a route to some sacred place. He did not, for example, argue for the trail because it was the best approach to Half Dome or some other destination. Nor in the second instance was the EJMT simply a route within a sacred place, that is, the surrounding wilderness. Instead, Clarke focused on the EJMT as sacred, while the adjacent wilderness would be a buffer between the trail and civilization.[68] He wished to protect the EJMT because it guided backpackers and others through the ceremonial reenactment of the activities of a nation-forming ancestor—the pioneer. Along this sacred path, backpackers were certain to experience the physical hardships, solitude, and natural beauty that had created the American character. Unlike other forms of camping, however, tramping on the EJMT did not have to be directed toward some sacred destination. A tramper could enter the trail at virtually any point, and as long as he or she moved along the designated pathway, the journey would provide restoration.

Clarke was dismayed by the rejections he received, and the winter of 1933–1934 came and went before he took up his pursuit of a wilderness corridor once more. Robert Stuart had not responded to Clarke's fall letter, so Clarke again wrote to the chief forester in March 1934. In addition, he widened the scope of his pursuit by sending a similar letter to the new director of the National Park Service, Arno Cammerer. Clarke knew that Congress had funded the CCC through the summer of 1934, and he was hopeful that the corps might now help to complete the development of the EJMT. He was also, however, cautious concerning the CCC's involvement, because he recognized that an uncritical application of this New Deal labor could degrade the trail for trampers. The EJMT needed much attention, Clarke would readily admit, but "care should be taken that the primitive wilderness character of the TRAIL be preserved," he cautioned Stuart. According to Clarke, the trail was being "nibbled at" by "commercial interests" that wished to exploit the value of its wildlands. The CCC, if it was not careful, could easily contribute to this slow loss of primitive conditions in national forests by building the sort of modern structures and trails that were often found in national parks. Unknown to Clarke, he was not alone in his cautionary view toward the CCC. The unleashing of the CCC and other New Deal organizations upon the nation's parks and forests was precipitating an organizational response that had been on a slow boil ever since Aldo Leopold and Arthur Carhart had earlier expressed their concerns about the loss of wilderness. In particular, the Wilderness Society would begin to coalesce in the autumn of 1934 when delegates from the American Forestry Association's annual meeting inspected a CCC camp in Tennessee. Distressed by what they found there and by what they had witnessed elsewhere, several of these delegates, including Benton MacKaye and Robert Marshall, joined with other activists, among them Aldo Leopold and Robert Sterling Yard, to officially found the Wilderness Society in January 1935.[69]

Clarke would eventually receive the support of the Wilderness Society and its members, but in the spring of 1934 he remained focused on the immediate protection of the EJMT, so he closed his March 1934 letter to Chief Forester Stuart with a repetition of his previous request. "Will it be possible to set aside five miles of either side of the JOHN MUIR TRAIL as a wilderness area?"[70] As before, Clarke's language seems to suggest that his request for a "wilderness area" was an effort to create a buffer zone to protect his principal interest—the "wilderness trail" that he had been promoting since the summer of 1932.

On this occasion, Clarke did not have to wait long for a reply. Chief Forester Stuart had L. F. Kneipp, the USFS's chief wilderness champion, respond within a week. The Forest Service, Kneipp reminded Clarke, had established the "High Sierra Primitive Area" in the spring of 1931, and since the John Muir Trail mostly ran through it, no buffer zone was necessary. Of course, the original JMT in the central Sierra Nevada constituted only about 10 percent of the EJMT, so Kneipp's letter was a less than satisfactory response to Clarke's proposal. At the same time, it appears that the chief forester's office did not wish to hear anything further from Clarke. If Clarke had any additional questions, Kneipp suggested, he should direct them to S. B. Show, the regional forester in San Francisco.[71]

As requested, Clarke ceased to write to Chief Forester Stuart, but he immediately fired off a letter to L. A. Barrett, Show's assistant, in San Francisco. Clarke was creating a promotional pamphlet about the EJMT in an effort to arouse support for the trail and its protection, especially in the private sector, and he wanted Barrett to provide him with a variety of necessary materials. Moreover, he would soon be in San Francisco and would be pleased to drop in on the assistant forester to show him what he had developed to date. At the same time, Clarke remained deeply concerned about protecting the EJMT. "Already as the TRAIL becomes known commercial interests are beginning to nibble at it and if we are not watchful its primitive and wilderness character will be destroyed." Given this imminent threat, but mindful of previous rebuffs, Clarke softened his proposed solution. "Can not the TRAIL area be set aside as THE JOHN MUIR TRAIL PRIMITIVE AREA?"[72]

The Pacific Crest Trail

Barrett offered no reply for over a month, and when he did, Clarke's proposal was not addressed. Instead Barrett changed the subject to the name of the trail, which had become controversial. Some organizations, especially the Sierra Club but also the USFS in Oregon and Washington, were resisting Clarke's plan to call the entire through trail by the name "John Muir." The Sierra Club thought this appropriation of the name would confuse the supporters of the original trail, which was still under construction, while the northwestern critics disliked the imposition of a California name onto their region. Although he had been cautioned by NPS director Albright, Clarke had heedlessly plowed ahead with his choice for the trail's name, and now he was reaping the consequences. Clarke's determination and bullheadedness were sources of his success, but they also underlay a number of his failures. Consequently, for the remainder of 1934 the trail's name, rather than its creation, consumed Clarke's attention, as it was debated by the USFS, NPS, Sierra Club, and others. At first, Clarke resisted all proposed changes, but the critiques kept coming. Finally in October its current name was first suggested, but not by Clinton Clarke. H. C. Bryant, assistant NPS director for research and education, contacted Clarke in October about a variety of issues, but one was of premier importance—the trail's name. "We have always believed in your fine vision," he crooned, "but some other name must be found" for the EJMT. Living in Washington, D.C., Bryant was familiar with the Appalachian Trail and the use of a distinctive single name for its overall length, while retaining local names, such as "Potomac Trail," for contributing segments. "Would it not be wise," asked Bryant, to try the same approach out west and "hit upon some such name as the 'Cascade Sierra Trail,' the 'Pacific Crest Trail,' or the 'High Pacific Trail'" for the entire length? Recognizing the inevitability of the change and the sensibility of Bryant's suggestion, Clarke finally relented and embraced "Pacific Crest Trail," while retaining the local trail names, including the original John Muir Trail. In less than a month, the Sierra Club, the NPS, and the California region of the USFS also accepted the name that would now become permanent, and the northwest USFS followed about a year later.[73] Although the Pacific Crest Trail's name was now established, Clarke would occasionally raise his wilderness-corridor proposal, but he never did so again with his earlier gusto and optimism. Instead, he brought it up only when he wished to demonstrate to some newly appointed administrator that the idea had been proposed and rejected.

With the trail's name confirmed and his new promotional pamphlet, *The Pacific Crest Trail*, in hand, Clarke turned his attention to creating an "administrating and operating organization" around the PCT. During the fall of 1934 he had pitched a PCT "conference" to the Sierra Club, which had agreed to sponsor it during the late spring of 1935. The idea, Clarke explained to NPS director Cammerer, was to gather "delegates from all the outing clubs and associations, boy scouts, Y.M.C.A., etc. and from the National Forestry and National Park Services" in order to adopt "definite plans and programs concerning the Pacific Crest Trail." The models for this new organization would be "the great Appalachian Trail Conference in the East and the trail organizations of the nations of Europe."[74]

As Clarke and the Sierra Club prepared for the upcoming conference, the first of many subsequent newspaper and magazine articles about the PCT appeared. In March 1935, with spring on the horizon, the *Pasadena Star-News*, the leading newspaper in Clarke's hometown, printed a report that calmly announced the border-to-border trail had been "surveyed," although in reality it had only been mapped. Continuing, the article switched away from the reportorial voice to the more romantically inclined language common to camping promotions in order to encourage the trail's use. Trampers should take to the trail, the paper gushed, because this was no overused and degraded track. Instead, it was a "wilderness trail" that would provide anyone who explored it with a "feast of scenery."[75] This brief article was likely the product of a conversation with Clarke (although he was not mentioned) and began the promotional effort that he would spearhead until World War II. For the next six years, Clarke would expend a great deal of time and money to promote the PCT to the general public in order to raise awareness and to produce a constituency to protect the trail.

Among the Sierra Club members who cooperated with Clarke on the PCT conference's preparation was Ansel Adams, who would become widely renowned as an environmentalist and photographer. At the time, Adams was not only a member of the Sierra Club, but also chair of an environmental group called the Conservation Forum. Hoping to enhance the impact of both organizations, Adams persuaded Clarke to move the PCT conference from its original site, Sierra Club headquarters in San Francisco, to Yosemite Valley, where participants would be close to the John Muir Trail and the conference could be combined with the Conservation Forum's June meeting.

From the sixth to the eighth of June the Conservation Forum's meeting proceeded, but on Friday, June 9, the PCT conference opened, and its first act was to adopt an official name for the organization they were there to found—the "Pacific Crest Trail System Conference" (PCTSC). Modeled after the Appalachian Trail Conference, which organized and directed the development of the AT, the PCTSC would incorporate such existing trails as the Oregon Skyline and the nearby John Muir, create some new trails, such as the Lava Crest, and develop linking trails between all these segments in order to form the PCT. In charge of the PCTSC would be an executive committee consisting of Paul W. Somers (YMCA), C. J. Carlson (Boy Scouts of America), Ansel Adams (Conservation Forum), and Ernest Dawson (Sierra Club), with Clinton Clarke as its chairman, and the organization would be headquartered at Clarke's house in Pasadena. Turning to the trail itself, USFS and NPS officials reported on the trail's route, which was vague to nonexistent for lengthy stretches, and its condition, which varied from poor to good where the route was established.[76] Despite the uncertainties, the route was adopted, but it was also agreed that the unreliable parts of the trail needed to be clarified and that the condition of the entire trail needed to be assessed. A line on a map covering hundreds of square miles was an insufficient guide for someone on the ground. Before additional trampers took to the PCT, it was agreed that someone had to hike the trail to confirm and assess its location and current status. This task was embraced by the YMCA, especially one of its more youthful directors, Warren Lee Rogers.

Warren Lee Rogers

Rogers was born in 1908 at Harbor Springs, Michigan, and moved with his family to Southern California in 1921. He was a victim of childhood polio, and the disease had impaired his ability to walk until anonymous benefactors had provided funding for the surgery that repaired his legs. Rogers was so moved by this generous act that he dedicated himself to a life of service to others. In 1921, Rogers, who was a devout Methodist, began his lifetime involvement with the YMCA, which ultimately awarded him seven "spiritual rags," each symbolizing the attainment of a higher level of blessing on his spiritual journey through life (fig. 7.5).

Despite his confrontation with polio, Rogers loved the out-of-doors and was an avid hiker and wilderness backpacker who answered to the nickname "Step and a Half" and who had first climbed Southern California's 11,503-foot Mount San Gorgonio when he was but fifteen. In the autumn of 1932, a twenty-four-year-old Rogers read an announcement in his hometown newspaper, the *Alhambra Post Advocate*, about a meeting to be held

Figure 7.5. Warren Lee Rogers, circa 1941. Detail from box 62 (16), Warren Lee Rogers Papers, Huntington Library, San Marino, CA.

to discuss a long-distance trail through the region. He attended and met Clinton Clarke, who was presenting the Mountain League's trail proposal. Rogers found that he was in immediate agreement with Clarke on his vision for the trail, and he struck up a friendship that would last their lifetimes and be the basis for a partnership that would nurture and shape the PCT. Thirty-five years younger that Clarke, Rogers would act as the pair's pragmatist and field person, while Clarke would be the visionary. Both would be exceptional advocates for the PCT, but Clarke would primarily focus on correspondence, guidebooks, and other written communications on a year-round basis, while Rogers became the voice the public would hear on the radio or in person when he was not on the trail.[77]

Rogers and Clarke's friendship ultimately led the former, who was a secretary at the Alhambra YMCA by 1935, to agree to organize and guide the initial examination of the PCT. According to the PCTSC's meeting report, the YMCA had adopted "an advanced camping program" that would send "flag-relay exploring expeditions" from local centers over the PCT from Mexico to Canada, beginning June 15, 1935. Each participating center's "knapsacking party" (that is, a small group of backpackers) would take several days to traverse approximately seventy-five miles of trail, compose a "descriptive report" about the distance covered in the official trail logbook, and then "relay" the logbook to the team that would explore the next section of trail. At the time of the PCTSC meeting, it was estimated that the California portion of the PCT could be explored during the summer of 1935 and the states of Oregon and Washington the following summer. It would eventually take twice as long. Filled with romantic-antimodern enthusiasm, the NPS and the USFS offered to cooperate with the YMCA relay teams "as a means of giving the young men in these organizations opportunity for adventure, romance, and the expression of the pioneer spirit that develops leadership and independence." Even these federal agencies linked backpacking and the PCT to the frontier experience, and within a year they were producing official PCT guides in order to support the development of an idealized American character.[78]

Rogers and a YMCA colleague in San Francisco, F. P. Knapp, quickly began to organize relay teams of young men drawn from YMCA centers that were sometimes near and sometimes not so near the PCT. Knapp was the fixed contact point as volunteers were identified and directed to tramp particular stretches of the trail, while Rogers was the official guide along with the tramping relay teams. They had to scramble to begin this task, because the first relay team was scheduled to depart on June 15, a mere six days after the YMCA committed to the project. Despite such a rushed beginning, a starting ceremony was held in San Diego's Balboa Park during the California Pacific International Exposition. Speeches were made, and a "good luck" letter from the exposition's president was given to the first

Figure 7.6. Fourteen California YMCA relay teams tramped the new Pacific Crest Trail System from the Mexico-California border to Yosemite National Park during the summer of 1935. Here, at the Tehachapi railroad station on July 11, the Pasadena and Burbank teams exchanged the logbook kept by all the teams. From box 4, folder "Pacific Crest Trail Conference," William Henry Thrall Papers, Huntington Library, San Marino, CA.

relay team. The team members were then driven thirty-five miles to the international border at Campo, where they began the relays at 10:50 a.m. Between June 15 and August 9, fourteen teams of two to five members, generally ranging in age from fourteen to eighteen, tramped 825 miles north to Tuolumne Meadows in Yosemite National Park.

Clarke was so proud of the teams' accomplishments, he could not resist crowing to NPS director Cammerer. "One team went 35 miles in one day with 45 lb packs. A fine record was made by a team of four that went 14 days without a food depot—the food weight was 35 lbs—through hard Sierra country. One hiker [Warren Rogers] went with all the teams until he wore out his boots, but he covered 485 miles in 32 days with 60 lb pack."[79]

Pacific Crest Trail and Christian Nationalism

As noted, pilgrims usually share some aspects of a pilgrimage, but not all. Individuals also tend to seek particular outcomes from their journeys. Although Clinton Clarke never tramped the PCT himself, he nonetheless expected the trail to bring about a specific transformation. Now, in the midst of the relays, he most clearly announced why he doggedly pursued the creation of the PCT. On July 8, 1935, he sent his "greetings" to the four members of the Pasadena YMCA team, who were then crossing the Mojave Desert from Acton to Tehachapi (fig. 7.6). "The exploration of the Pacific Crest Trail by flag-relay teams," he began,

> is an undertaking of national significance and will have far reaching influence in interesting the young men of our Nation in a more wholesome, robust, adventurous recreational program.
>
> You, young men, are the new pioneers, the new adventurers leading the way to those vast primitive mountain wildernesses in which we can receive inspiration and a renewal of our faith and ideals. Coming into close and friendly companionship with Mother Nature we receive from Her a spiritual and religious revival that will last through the years.
>
> So, your pilgrimage is more than a hiking trip; many follow in your footsteps.
>
> With all Good Wishes for the success of your historical journey.[80]

Clinton Clarke was not as religious as Warren Rogers, but he was clearly a spiritual man and an antimodern nationalist. For him, America's critical population was its young men. When tramping through wilderness, especially on the PCT, they recapitulated a rugged moment in American history to become the "new pioneers" who were on a "pilgrimage" and not just a "hiking trip." Moreover, their efforts were not merely geographic; they were of "national significance" because they would lead America to "a renewal of our faith and ideals." Intimate contact with wild nature, asserted Clarke, would result in the nation's "spiritual and religious revival."

Clarke would repeat his understanding of the importance of PCT tramping on numerous occasions. A letter he wrote in 1940 to James E. West, the chief executive of the Boy Scouts of America, was especially revealing. The religious, spiritual, and humanitarian qualities "that distinguish the Christian man from the dumb brute" have been lost, reasoned Clarke. America's modern, "over-mechanized" society had "stultified" the minds of its youth with "labor-saving devices," "easy entertainments," and more. America's youths were weakened by the character of the modern world, and they needed to be "strengthened through hard work and then freed from most of our materialistic ideas and facts." For this change to occur, he maintained, they must be like the pioneers—get into the wilderness and confront a primitive environment. When the brain has had to think in response to nature and the body to act, the youth will strengthen and "act in a sane and logical manner. Then, and only then, will it be possible to instill those christian virtues and spiritual qualities that can make strong the soul and, thus, sustain and preserve our christian civilization." Tramping for Clarke was more than individual leisure; it was national renewal. These national virtues could only be instilled in trampers, especially when they were on the PCT and organized by groups like the YMCA and the Boy Scouts.[81]

Rogers, in contrast to Clarke, was more religious, but he was also more pragmatic, explicit, and materialist when discussing the PCT or his sense of its purpose and value. He was generally reluctant to speak of any religious connections to tramping and the PCT except to fellow members of the YMCA. When, for instance, he composed *To the Stars through Difficulty*, a six-page pamphlet about tramping and the PCT for the YMCA, Rogers suggested that hiking, camping, and related activities, which were "difficult," moved practitioners closer to God among the heavenly "stars." In one section, he specified the connections by asserting that every youth organization in Washington State, Oregon, and California ought to follow the YMCA's example of wilderness camping on the trail, especially on the PCT. Why? "Because by holding their camping interest and loyalty to a Christian program we can set their character for social and religious well being; because it is an educational project where the boy learns by doing and maintaining a healthy interest in the romance and adventure of the day; [and] because each one learns to take his turn and do his share towards the maintenance of a party—a lasting lesson in Christian conduct and social adjustment." Rogers clearly felt that tramping was an important tool for fostering "Christian" virtues, but unlike Clarke he did not overtly link them to the national character.[82]

The majority of Rogers's personal communications about the PCT contained few religious comments. Instead, he mostly made note of management issues, statistics, and conditions. In a November 1937 letter to Clarke, for example, Rogers related that he had recently spoken to approximately seven hundred grammar school children about the PCT. To increase the mood and sense of outdoor adventure, he had taken along a topographical map and had lit lamps on it. "It was," he reported, "well received." In addition to promoting the PCT through school presentations, Rogers spoke publicly to business organizations, service groups, college students, and others, but he was proudest of the programs he developed and presented on radio. Sometimes these programs were simple fifteen-minute question-and-answer exchanges that focused on the status of the PCT. Others, such as "Pacific Crest Campfires," were longer, more orchestrated programs that consisted of a variety of elements, including music, stories, and PCTS news. During these events, Rogers tried to metaphorically link appealing values to the PCT, especially through references to the frontier and its way of life. Although his programs were modeled on more professional ones that followed a strict ordering of elements—sponsors' announcements, entertainment, listener letters, and news, for instance—Rogers dramatized his by situating these components within a nineteenth-century "West" of the imagination. He used camp songs, terms like "pardner" and "mailbag," and references to the listeners as "sitting around the campfire." Such allusions heightened his listeners' sense of historic depth and the cultural significance of the PCT. By merging the trail with visions of America's pioneers and the impact they had on the nation's formation, he effectively fused the two together. Tramping the trail became more than time out of doors; it was converted into a journey through a mythic past. Tramping could transform the tramper. It could be pilgrimage.[83]

During the subsequent summers of 1936 through 1938, twenty-six additional YMCA relay teams tramped north from Tuolumne Meadows to Blaine, Washington, where a completion ceremony was held at the International Peace Arch at 3 p.m. on August 11, 1938. Rogers participated in the event and noted the dignitaries present: "There was official representation for the Premier of British Columbia, the Mayor of New Westminster, B.C., the Governor of Washington, the Mayor of Bellingham, Washington, and the Mayor of Seattle, Washington. Governor Clarence D. Martin signed the 'End of the Trail' statement on the final page of the log book at the Capitol Building, Olympia, Washington, and the Seal of the State of Washington was stamped on the page at high noon, August 12, 1938." The presence of these officials demonstrated that the YMCA relays had drawn much public attention. And along the way, the teams had explored and evaluated routes to determine where the PCT should best lie. This information would lead to the first detailed field guide and map of the entire trail system (fig. 7.7).

In all, thirty YMCA centers sponsored forty teams of 140 trampers who covered approximately twenty-three hundred miles during 193 days on the trail. As their official guide, Rogers accompanied twenty-five of these teams over seventeen hundred miles during the four seasons. Coverage of the relay teams by their local newspapers stimulated national exposure for the PCT, with supportive articles appearing in such publications as *American Forests*, the *Christian Science Monitor*, *Sunset*, and *Travel*.[84]

The route identified by the YMCA relay teams has more or less remained the PCT's path to the present. In Oregon and Washington little change has occurred, although some stretches of the trail were relocated from time to time for a variety of reasons. The entire length also deteriorated from lack of maintenance during World War II. However, it was in California,

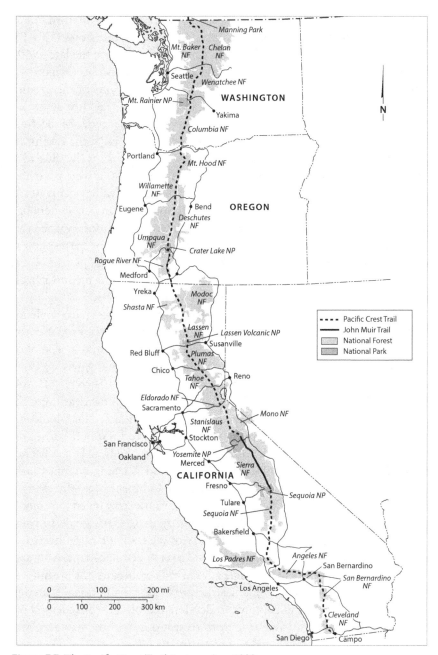

Figure 7.7. The Pacific Crest Trail System, circa 1938.

especially south of the Sierra Nevada, where long stretches remained murky for decades. The situation was so uncertain that the authors of 1977's *The Pacific Crest Trail, Volume 1: California* observed that until the late 1960s, "Anyone who wanted to walk or ride the PCT from Mexico to Oregon—or vice versa—was pretty much on his own for large portions of the existing 1600-mile distance." The situation began to improve in 1965 just as America's largest backpacking boom took off. The USFS held a series of meetings about a route for the PCT with representatives from the NPS, the California Division of Parks and Beaches, and various local governments. By the end of the year a route had been drawn onto maps, and these later were presented to the PCT Advisory Council created by the National Trail Systems Act of 1968. The council settled on a route in 1972, but unfortunately not enough fieldwork had been done. Indeed, the 1977 guidebook's authors warned that the PCT maps released to the public in June 1972 "did not correspond to what was on the ground in many places." Nevertheless, maps from other sources and commercially produced guides were sufficient for most backpackers until the trail was officially completed in June 1993.[85]

Neither Clinton Clarke nor Warren Rogers lived to witness the completion of the PCT. Rogers had become the PCTSC's executive secretary in November 1935, and Clarke assumed its presidency in 1936. Clarke's reputation peaked around this time, and he was appointed to a Special Advisory Committee for Hiking for the National Park Service by Interior Secretary Harold Ickes. Clarke would retain the PCTSC's presidency until his death, but the organization would wither over the next five years as he acted high-handedly and argued with many allied groups. By the time World War II began, the PCTSC was largely moribund. After the war ended, the U.S. Forest Service completed a great deal of trail work in Oregon and Washington, but Clarke was never able to induce USFS authorities in California to fully develop the PCT in their region. Despite these setbacks, Clarke continued to promote the trail, publishing *The Pacific Crest Trailway* in 1945. A guide to backpacking the entire trail, it included a history of the trail, a natural history of the region, a "daily log" of hiking goals, and a set of detailed maps. Although it was published but once, *The Pacific Crest Trailway* became the preeminent guide to the PCT until the 1960s. Clarke produced no additional materials about the PCT, but he did continue to develop and promote his ideas about the social and personal value of nature recreation. No one, however, was listening anymore, and Clarke died quietly in 1957.[86]

After the last YMCA relay was run in 1938, Rogers devoted much energy to promoting the PCT through radio programs and talks. By his own estimate, he had made more than a thousand presentations by 1980. In addition to organizing and leading relays, Rogers was a YMCA secretary for twenty-one years, often running camping programs, until he retired from the organization in 1952. Subsequently, he worked for a variety of nonprofit organizations in Southern California, including one that helped to create the Los Angeles Times Summer Camp Fund.[87] Rogers never resigned from the PCTSC, and his enthusiasm for the trail never wavered. When Clinton Clarke passed away, Rogers cheerfully took up the cause of its completion.

Rogers obtained Clarke's PCT files after the latter's death, and for two decades he was one of the few sources that hikers could turn to for reliable information. When the National Trails System Act was passed in 1968, it designated the USFS as the PCT's manager and established a PCT Advisory Council. In 1970, the U.S. secretary of agriculture appointed Rogers to the council, and he served on it for more than sixteen years. In addition to this public service, Rogers founded the Pacific Crest Club in 1972. When backpacking had boomed in the late 1960s and early 1970s, so many hikers were contacting Rogers about the PCT that he began this international organization to coordinate and facilitate the transfer of information. Members received a magazine, *Pacific Crest Quarterly*, which included stories about recent long-distance backpackers, tips about hiking the PCT, and updates on the most recent route changes. As interest in backpacking and the PCT continued to mount, the club merged in 1977 with the PCTSC's successor organization, the Pacific Crest Trail Conference, to form today's Pacific Crest Trail Association. Rogers also supported the use of the PCT through his Pocket Map and Food Pack businesses. The former was an early producer of PCT maps, while the latter delivered food supplies to backpackers. These caches made it easier for a backpacker to pursue a long journey. Warren Rogers passed away about one year before the PCT's golden spike ceremony in 1993, but both his and Clarke's efforts to create and nurture the trail were not forgotten. Today a monument commemorates their accomplishment.[88]

Like other campers, Clinton C. Clarke and Warren L. Rogers shared some of their ideas about the value of backpacking with others, but they also pursued personal goals both when on the Pacific Crest Trail and when promoting it. Rogers saw hiking the trail as an activity that recapitulated the frontier experience and could foster Christian virtues. His vision was relatively optimistic and accepting. By contrast, Clarke was more of a nationalist who overtly linked backpacking to the character and durability of America. An antimodernist, he looked upon the country and saw a decline that needed treatment in order to restore America's "Christian civilization." His prescription was the Pacific Crest Trail. For both these men and for many more backpackers both before and after them, a wilderness experience could return hikers to everyday life in an improved state. They could return from these pilgrimages "with a difference."

THE DECLINE AND PROMISE OF AMERICAN CAMPING

Camping in all its various modes continues to be one of America's most popular leisure activities. In its 2014 report on participation in outdoor recreation, the Outdoor Foundation identified camping as the fourth-most-popular activity by participation rate, with only running/jogging, biking, and fishing as more popular. According to its analysis, a total of 14 percent of Americans ages six and older, or 40.1 million, engaged in car, backpacking, and RV camping, the three principal modes explored in this book. Moreover, a close look at the report also reveals that these three camping modes are among the most popular outdoor activities for a wide range of ethnic and racial groups, even though participation rates vary widely. Among African Americans, camping is ranked fifth in popularity, yet the participation rate of 4 percent is noticeably lower than for the population as a whole. Asian Americans also rated camping as fourth in popularity, but in their case the participation rate was 11 percent, much closer to the national average. Both whites and Latinos also gave camping a popularity rank of four, but the participation rates were again different, with the former being above the national rate at 16 percent, while the latter came nearer the nation at 13 percent.[1] This snapshot, however, masks a recent trend.

Camping's Decline

Despite camping's strong and pervasive popularity today, the zenith of its national appeal occurred in the past. It is impossible to precisely quantify

Figure E.1. The "Four Vagabonds," Harvey Firestone, Thomas Edison, and John Burroughs (*second, third, and fourth from left*) and Henry Ford (*third from right*) with some of their staff and customized camping vehicles at Green Island, New York, in August 1919. Courtesy of the Henry Ford, Dearborn, MI.

such trends, but camping's cultural significance appears to have peaked with the explosion of auto campers who hit the motor-camping trail during the decade following World War I. Articles about equipment, techniques, and destinations, as well as colorful accounts of camping adventures, peppered mainstream newspapers and magazines like *McClure's, Saturday Evening Post, and Ladies' Home Journal* even as they saturated such specialized periodicals as *Outing, Field & Stream*, and the *American Angler*. In addition, advertisements of all sizes for supplies and equipment could easily be found in these periodicals, while an expanding array of catalogs offered goods for campers.

Camping became such a cultural phenomenon during these years that industrialists Henry Ford and Harvey Firestone, inventor Thomas Edison, and author John Burroughs organized annual auto-camping adventures for themselves and their families (fig. E.1). The exploits of these "Four Vagabonds" were closely followed in the popular press, with even U.S. president Warren G. Harding joining them on one occasion. This heightened and

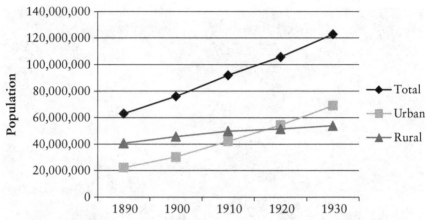

Figure E.2. Urban and rural populations of the United States. Between 1890 and 1930, rural populations grew only slightly, but urban populations expanded greatly. By 1930, America's cities contained over fifteen million more residents than its rural areas. Source: *Statistical History of the United States from Colonial Times to the Present* (Stamford, CT: Fairfield Publishers, 1965), 9.

widespread popularity should be understood as a reflection of the continuing and rapid urbanization that was sweeping through America, transforming it from a largely rural country in 1910 to a distinctly urban one by 1930 (fig. E.2).[2]

In contrast to camping's cultural pinnacle, its numerical peak came near the end of the twentieth century, although the timing depends on which numbers are examined. For over a century, the most consistent and direct collector of camping statistics has been the National Park Service, which measures the annual number of visitors to the parks, monuments, and other lands that it manages. According to the NPS, camping peaked in 1981, when just over 11.2 million visitors stayed overnight in tents or recreational vehicles in its campgrounds or backpacked through NPS wilderness areas. That number was never achieved again. Instead, the number of campers declined slowly and has stabilized at around seven million annually during the twenty-first century. Raw numbers, however, can mislead. If instead the peak is determined to be the year when the largest percentage of visitors also camped, then 1979 ranks as first. In that year, 5 percent of the almost 10.3 million visitors camped on NPS lands. In 1981, by contrast, the 11.2 million campers were only 4.7 percent of NPS visitors, and that number now has shrunk to approximately 2.6 percent (fig. E.3).[3]

However, since most camping occurs outside the national parks, it makes sense to turn also to one of the alternative methods that have been developed to assess camping's long-term scale and scope. The most reliable

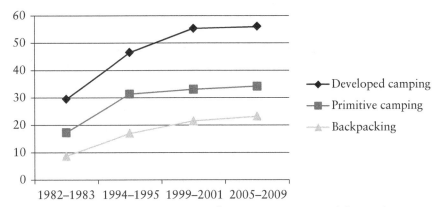

Figure E.3. U.S. camping participants (in millions). Source: H. K. Cordell, "Outdoor Recreation Trends and Futures: A Technical Document Supporting the Forest Service 2010 RPA Assessment" (Asheville, NC: U.S. Forest Service, Southern Research Station, 2012), 33, 35.

and durable of these tools is the National Survey on Recreation and the Environment (NSRE) and its predecessor, the National Survey on Recreation (NSR). Beginning in 1960, a total of nine NSRs and NSREs have been conducted. The NSRE divides camping into three major categories: "developed" (in designated areas with tables, comfort stations, and other amenities); "primitive" (in both non-specified and designated areas, but without amenities); and "backpacking." According to the NSRE, the number of American campers grew dramatically over the last five decades, especially at first. During the summer surveys of the early 1960s, approximately 9 percent of respondents said they participated in any of the three forms of camping, but by the time of the 1982–1983 survey, summer participation had more than doubled to 19 percent. In following years, the pattern of growth continued, albeit at a slowing pace. The total number of camping participations (developed + primitive + backpacking) climbed from 55.5 million in the 1982–1983 survey to 94.9 million in 1994–1995, 109.9 million in 1999–2001, and 113.4 million in 2005–2009. By this measure, camping's prevalence peaked during the most recent survey.

If, however, we measure participation as a percent of the total population age sixteen and older (the baseline population used to develop the number of overall participants), then a different pattern appears. Developed camping's participation rate rose from 17.0 percent of the population in the 1982–1983 survey to 25.8 percent in 1999–2001, but then it declined to 23.8 percent during 2005–2009. Similarly, primitive camping climbed from 9.9 percent in 1982–1983 to 15.6 percent in 1994–1995, remained nearly the same at 15.5 percent in 1999–2001, and then decreased slightly to 14.5 percent in

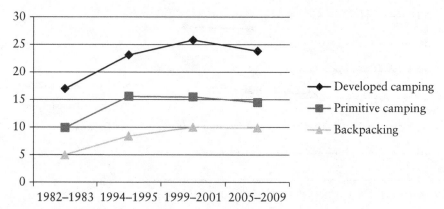

Figure E.4. U.S. camping partipants as a percentage of the 16+ population. Source: H. K. Cordell, "Outdoor Recreation Trends and Futures: A Technical Document Supporting the Forest Service 2010 RPA Assessment" (Asheville, NC: U.S. Forest Service, Southern Research Station, 2012), 37–38.

2005–2009. Backpacking, in contrast, increased from 5.0 percent in 1982–1983 to 10.0 percent in 1999–2001 but then largely held steady at 9.9 percent in 2005–2009 (fig. E.4). By this measure, camping's popularity peaked a bit later than suggested by the National Park Service statistics—near the end of the twentieth century, when the greatest percentage of Americans participated. The total number of American campers may have continued to increase during the twenty-first century, but it did not do so as rapidly as did the baseline population. When the two surveys are considered together, it seems clear that camping's overall popularity peaked in the past and will likely decrease during coming decades.[4]

Recently, several publications bemoaned the decrease in camping and other nature-based recreations in America. One of the best known of these was Richard Louv's *Last Child in the Woods: Saving Our Children from Nature-Deficit Disorder*. In an extended polemic, Louv argued the need for nature-based recreations, stating that "direct exposure to nature is essential for healthy childhood development and for the physical and emotional health of children and adults." Relatedly, Oliver R. W. Pergams and Patricia A. Zaradic analyzed a variety of sources, including camping frequency, to reach a similar conclusion. According to their analyses, the popularity of camping (excluding backpacking) had increased for decades but began to decrease in 1987. Backpacking, by contrast, had become slightly more popular during the same period. The authors were not certain of the cause or causes for the drop in camping specifically, but they suggested that the root cause for a decrease in nature-based recreation may be "videophilia," which they defined as "the new human tendency to focus on sedentary activities involving electronic media." Critics rejected Pergams and Zaradic's conclusions, arguing instead that any shift was the result of "sampling error." "While some forms of outdoor recreation are decreasing," insisted Maarten H. Jacobs and Michael J. Manfredo, "other forms are increasing." They and other authors pointed out, for example, that even as surveys documented that hunting was on the wane, wildlife viewing was increasing. *Heading Out* has nothing to add to these sampling critiques, but it does suggest that the changing character of American cities, along with the process of McDonaldization, rather than videophilia alone, contributed to the decrease in the number of campers.[5]

On the one hand, *Heading Out* argues that the American embrace of camping was driven by cultural concerns; it did not, as Richard Louv argued, have its roots in nature. Campers were pilgrims in search of transformation, so they had to move "out" of their customary world. Everyday life for campers was lived in modernizing cities, which despite the many benefits, they found unsatisfying and distressing. Their romantic antimodern response was not to flee cities permanently but to temporarily travel outside their urban lives and to engage in historically, socially, and even family-saturated activities. By "roughing it," campers affirmed their senses of identity and belonging even as they found relief and restoration. Over time, however, camping tended to become less challenging, because, like much in the modern world, it was subject to McDonaldization. Manifestations included the proliferation of such specialized gear as ultralight tents, insulated coolers, and aluminum trailers, as well as the standardization of automobile campgrounds along lines first proposed by E. P. Meinecke. McDonaldization transformed camping for the same reason it transformed many other aspects of modern life—it offered greater efficiency, calculability, predictability, and control, and not only to campers, but to equipment manufacturers and environmental managers as well. McDonaldization promised, for example, enhanced comfort for the family who camped using a recreational vehicle, elevated sales and profits for the manufacturer who could standardize production and create new product niches, and increased environmental protection for managers who could designate exactly where and for how long campers could stay. Overall, McDonaldization led to an easing of the challenges that all campers face. In the pithy words of Elon Jessup, it transformed camping, no matter how practiced, into "roughing it smoothly."[6] But was "smooth" the ideal way to "rough it"? Might a reduction in roughness somehow be responsible for a reduced number of campers? One conclusion *Heading Out* suggests is that however much camping's participation numbers rose because McDonaldization made it more convenient, comfortable, and appealing to more people, that same McDonaldization may also be responsible for the slow decline of recent decades as some forms of camping became too comfortable and convenient, and therefore too much like everyday life. For an increasing number of individuals, camping no longer offered a way to "head out."

At the same time, it is critical to note that McDonaldization unevenly affected the different camping modes, even if it was immanent in American society. Motorized camping, whether with a recreational vehicle or in a car with a tent, was sharply affected, becoming the most comfortable and convenient mode. A late-nineteenth century horse-wagon camper would hardly recognize his successors. Backpacking was also noticeably affected, but essential elements of it remained unaltered—backpackers continued to walk and to carry their own equipment and supplies. The "roughness" of backpacking was "smoothed," but not very much. Similarly, the fact that motorized camping became the "smoothest" of modes helps to explain why the NSRE's surveys agreed with the analysis of Pergams and Zaradic when they indicated that the number of "developed" and "primitive" campers decreased in recent years. It appears possible that many of these former campers found their chosen forms of camping to be increasingly like life at home and therefore not worth pursuing. Campers cannot "return with a difference" if they cannot get "out" of their customary world. If such has been the case, the growth and steadiness of backpacking as measured by Pergams and Zaradic and by the NSRE would appear to confirm it. Today's backpackers undoubtedly use lighter tents and enjoy a wider range of foods than their predecessors, but they must still walk and carry their load. Their camping experience, unlike that of motorized campers, remains in fundamental ways as rough as that of their predecessors, and therefore the contrast with everyday life is sharp, effective, and appealing.

Camping's Promise

On the other hand, fewer Americans may be camping because America's cities changed. Campers long denounced modern life as polluted, constraining, confusing, alienating, and more, but the symbol of that ire usually had a name—city. The title of this book reflects campers' enduring desire to head out of their accustomed urban worlds. But as this book demonstrates, the "nature" that satisfied campers varied greatly. For some campers, only a complete absence of anything motorized would do, but for others, the beach alongside a highway was fine. This variance suggests that there is a difference of views among campers about how un-urban their nature needs to be.

Heading Out suggests that the decrease in campers may also be caused by an improvement in the nature of American cities.

When camping began, America was rapidly urbanizing and industrializing. The environmental differences between cities, towns, farms, and wildlands were increasing, and these different places were increasingly discrete and isolated from one another. Cities, in particular, included little that was green and growing. In recent years, however, the distinctions between these places began to fade as the qualities of one were incorporated into the other. "Urban agriculture" is no longer an oxymoron; the U.S. Army Corps of Engineers recently began a billion-dollar restoration of the Los Angeles River; and the Museum of the City of New York showcased the increased sustainability that will come from planting more street trees, building cleaner power plants, creating new parks, and more. As efforts like these appeared, the livability of American cities increased and the differences between them and wildlands decreased. In these years of decreasing campers, Americans began to blend their cities and nature back together. As urban, suburban, rural, and wild places became less distinct and the cities became more natural, campers, especially those satisfied with a relatively modernized experience, decreasingly felt a need to make a pilgrimage to nature "out there." Instead, they increasingly found it around themselves in everyday life. With this change in mind, I conclude by noting that to the degree that camping is decreasingly common because Americans less frequently feel distressed by everyday life and any urge to "head out," to that degree it is a sign that we are finally discovering how to create a city where we are comfortable, which is indeed good news.[7]

NOTES

Introduction

1. Gerard Delanty, "Modernity," in *Blackwell Encyclopedia of Sociology*, ed. George Ritzer (Malden, MA: Blackwell, 2007), 3068. Marshall Berman, in *All That Is Solid Melts into Air: The Experience of Modernity* (New York: Simon & Schuster, 1982), 17, divided the modern period into three parts. In its first era, which lasted about three centuries, people were only mildly conscious of the nature of the change that gradually altered their world, and traditional social relations continued to dominate. During its second era, which ran from around the end of the eighteenth century until the beginning of the twentieth, the pace of modernization increased. "A great modern public," declares Berman, "came abruptly and dramatically to life," and its members became aware that they lived in a revolutionary and contradictory era, yet they also recalled life in a more traditional, premodern world. In its third era, from the early twentieth century to today, modernity spread worldwide. Robert David Sack, *Place, Modernity, and the Consumer's World: A Relational Framework for Geographical Analysis* (Baltimore: Johns Hopkins University Press, 1992), 5, argues, "strong claims can be made that attitudes, values and beliefs . . . are as important to modernity as the economic component." Anthony Giddens, *Conversations with Anthony Giddens: Making Sense of Modernity* (Stanford, CA: Stanford University Press, 1998), 94, considers modernity to be "vastly more dynamic than any previous type of social order," and, echoing Sack, he points out that "unlike any preceding culture, [it] lives in the future, rather than the past."

2. See Roy Rosenzweig, *Eight Hours for What We Will* (New York: Cambridge University Press, 1983), and Witold Rybczynski, *Waiting for the Weekend* (New York: Viking, 1991). T. J. Jackson Lears, *No Place of Grace: Antimodernism and the Transformation of American Culture, 1880–1920* (New York: Pantheon Books, 1981), includes chapters on a variety of antimodern responses, including the rise of the martial ideal, medievalism, and others. Clifford Putney, *Muscular Christianity: Manhood and Sports in Protestant America, 1880–1920* (Cambridge, MA: Harvard University Press, 2003).

3. For an extensive discussion of the origins, breadth, and impact of romanticism see Jacques Barzun, *Classic, Romantic, and Modern*, 2nd ed. (Boston: Little, Brown, 1961).

4. Thomas Jefferson, *Notes on the State of Virginia* (Boston: Wells and Lilly, 1829), 171–73. See also Morton White and Lucia White, *The Intellectual versus the City: From*

Thomas Jefferson to Frank Lloyd Wright (Cambridge, MA: Harvard University Press, 1962); Thomas Bender, *Toward an Urban Vision: Ideas and Institutions in Nineteenth-Century America* (Lexington: University Press of Kentucky, 1975); and Andrew Lees, *Cities Perceived: Urban Society in European and American Thought, 1820–1940* (New York: Columbia University Press, 1985). Peter J. Schmitt, *Back to Nature: The Arcadian Myth in Urban America* (Baltimore: Johns Hopkins University Press, 1990). Lears, *No Place*, delves deeply into the ambivalence that was common among all sorts of antimodernists.

5. Joseph E. Taylor, *Pilgrims of the Vertical: Yosemite Rock Climbers and Nature at Risk* (Cambridge, MA: Harvard University Press, 2010); John Ruskin, *Modern Painters*, vol. 2 (London: George Allen, 1906), 16.

6. John Ruskin, *The Stones of Venice*, vol. 2, *The Sea Stories* (Boston: Dana Estes & Co., 1900), 162.

7. David Schuyler, *Apostle of Taste: Andrew Jackson Downing, 1815–1852* (Baltimore: Johns Hopkins University Press, 1996), 136. See also Roger B. Stein, *John Ruskin and Aesthetic Thought in America, 1840–1900* (Cambridge, MA: Harvard University Press, 1967). Laura Wood Roper, *FLO: A Biography of Frederick Law Olmsted* (Baltimore: Johns Hopkins University Press, 1973), 40, 72; Barbara Novak, *Nature and Culture: American Landscape Painting, 1825–1875*, rev. ed. (New York: Oxford University Press, 1995). Most Americans were moved by Ruskin's writings, but Stillman knew and deeply respected Ruskin personally. See "W. J. Stillman and John Ruskin," *The Decorator and Furnisher* 11, no. 5 (1888): 160; Stephen L. Dyson, *The Last Amateur: The Life of William J. Stillman* (Albany: SUNY Press, 2014); and James Schlett, *A Not Too Greatly Changed Eden: The Story of the Philosophers' Camp in the Adirondacks* (Ithaca, NY: Cornell University Press, 2015). Laura Waterman and Guy Waterman, *Forest and Crag: A History of Hiking, Trail Blazing, and Adventure in the Northeast Mountains* (Boston: Appalachian Mountain Club, 1989), 69–74.

8. Susan Fenimore Cooper, *Rural Hours* (New York: G. P. Putnam, 1850); Vera Norwood, *Made from This Earth: American Women and Nature* (Chapel Hill: University of North Carolina Press, 1993), 27. See also Douglas C. Sackman, "Putting Gender on the Table: Food and the Family Life of Nature," in *Seeing Nature through Gender*, ed. Virginia Scharff (Lawrence: University Press of Kansas, 2003), 178.

9. Philip G. Terrie, *Contested Terrain: A New History of Nature and People in the Adirondacks* (Syracuse, NY: Syracuse University Press, 1997); Charles Fenno Hoffman, *Wild Scenes in the Forest and Prairie* (New York: Richard Bentley, 1843), iv; J. T. Headley, *The Adirondack; or, Life in the Woods* (New York: Baker and Scribner, 1849). Warder H. Cadbury, introduction in William H. H. Murray, *Adventures in the Wilderness*, ed. William K. Verner (Syracuse, NY: Adirondack Museum / Syracuse University Press, 1989), 62, provides a list of the additional, post-Hoffman books published around this time. Headley, *Adirondack*, ii. According to Terrie, *Contested Terrain*, 45, Headley was "in search of mental and physical health after suffering what was apparently a nervous breakdown." Innumerable modern Americans would take up camping over the next 150-plus years for much the same reason. Headley, *Adirondack*, 168; Headley, *Adirondack*; and T. Addison Richards, "A Forest Story. II—The Adirondack Woods and Waters," *Harper's New Monthly Magazine*, June–November 1859, 454–66. See also Philip G. Terrie, "Romantic Travelers in the Adirondack Wilderness," *American Studies* 24, no. 2 (1983): 59–75.

10. Schlett, *Not Too*, is an extended history of the Philosophers' Camp. The Saturday Club was an informal monthly gathering of writers, scientists, historians, and others. See Edward Waldo Emerson, *The Early Years of the Saturday Club, 1855–1870* (Boston: Houghton Mifflin, 1918). Jack Robinson, "Matters in Boston: Discoveries in Art—A Group of Statuary by Ball Hughes—The Cup and Ball—The Adirondack Club—Miscellaneous," *New York Times*, March 18, 1859. According to Schlett, *Not Too*, 3, the *New York Evening Post* sent a reporter to the location while the camp was in progress to cover the story. See Don Carlos, "A Trip to the Saranac Lakes," *New York Evening Post*, August 30, 1858; "Agassiz, Emerson, Lowell, Holmes, and Stillman in the Woods," *Saint Paul Daily Minnesotian*, September 7,

1858; F. S. Stallknecht and Charles E. Whitehead, "An August Sporting Tour," *Frank Leslie's New Family Magazine*, November 13–20, 1858, 336–49; and Robinson, "Matters in Boston."

11. For an insightful, early look into camping's social role see Henry M. Busch, "Camping," in *Encyclopedia of the Social Sciences*, ed. E. R. A. Seligman (New York: Macmillan, 1930), 168–70.

12. I use the term "pilgrimage" as a metaphor, not as the description of a religious practice. As metaphor, pilgrimage has been used to explain a variety of leisure travel, including theme park visits, summer vacations, and tourism. See Alexander Moore, "Walt Disney World: Bounded Ritual Space and the Playful Pilgrimage Center," *Anthropological Quarterly* 53 (1980): 207–18; Susan Sessions Rugh, *Are We There Yet? The Golden Age of American Family Vacations* (Lawrence: University Press of Kansas, 2008); Nelson H. H. Graburn, "Tourism: The Sacred Journey," in *Hosts and Guests: The Anthropology of Tourism*, 2nd ed., ed. V. L. Smith (Philadelphia: University of Pennsylvania Press, 1989), 21–36; and John F. Sears, *Sacred Places: American Tourist Attractions in the Nineteenth Century* (New York: Oxford University Press, 1989). Rugh and Sears both argued that the nature tourists who camped at such places as Yosemite and Yellowstone were engaged in pilgrimage. Thomas R. Dunlap, *Faith in Nature: Environmentalism as Religious Quest* (Seattle: University of Washington Press, 2004), similarly argued that visits to wilderness are often pilgrimages. On the larger roles, forms, and meanings of pilgrimage in American life see Gwen Kennedy Neville, *Kinship and Pilgrimage: Rituals of Reunion in American Protestant Culture* (New York: Oxford University Press, 1987). She concludes that the initial colonization of the United States during the seventeenth century by Protestants who had rejected Roman Catholic pilgrimage contributed greatly to an American culture resistant to religious pilgrimage. For more on pilgrimage in general see Victor W. Turner and Edith Turner, *Image and Pilgrimage in Christian Culture* (New York: Columbia University Press, 1978), and John Eade and Michael J. Sallnow, eds. *Contesting the Sacred: The Anthropology of Christian Pilgrimage* (New York: Routledge, 1991). Barbara Myerhoff, "Pilgrimage to Meron: Inner and Outer Peregrinations," in *Creativity/Anthropology*, eds. Smadar Lavie, Kirin Narayan, and Renato Rosaldo (Ithaca, NY: Cornell University Press, 1993), 218. No clear characteristics define the holiness or sanctity of a place, but R. H. Jackson and R. Henrie, "Perception of Sacred Space," *Journal of Cultural Geography* 3 (1983): 94, offer a useful definition of one: "That portion of the earth's surface which is recognized by individuals or groups as worthy of devotion, loyalty or esteem. Space is sharply discriminated from the non-sacred or profane world around it. Sacred space does not exist naturally, but is assigned sanctity as man defines, limits and characterizes it through his culture, experience and goals." See also Chris Park, *Sacred Worlds: An Introduction to Geography and Religion* (New York: Routledge, 1994), and Victor W. Turner, "The Center Out There: Pilgrim's Goal," *History of Religions* 12 (1973): 191–230. On historic sites see Wilbur Zelinsky, "Nationalistic Pilgrimages in the United States," in *Pilgrimage in the United States*, eds. G. Rinschede and S. M. Bhardwaj (Berlin: Dietrich Reimer, 1990), 253–67; and, for naturalistic ones, see Patrick McGreevy, "Niagara as Jerusalem," *Landscape* 28, no. 2 (1985): 26–32; and Taylor, *Pilgrims*. On Graceland see Derek Alderman, "Writing on the Graceland Wall: On the Importance of Authorship in Pilgrimage Landscapes," *Tourism Recreation Research* 27, no. 2 (2002): 27–33; Linda Kay Davidson and David M. Gitlitz, eds., *Pilgrimage: From the Ganges to Graceland, An Encyclopedia* (Santa Barbara, CA: ABC-CLIO, 2002), 204–6; and Karal Ann Marling, *Graceland: Going Home with Elvis* (Cambridge, MA: Harvard University Press, 1996). On Walt Disney World see Moore, "Walt Disney World." According to Neville, *Kinship*, this urban-to-rural pilgrimage pattern gave America its southern cemetery or church homecomings, camp meetings at rural grounds, and more. Sears, *Sacred Places*, 5–6, concluded that the Protestant rejection of pilgrimage led to a closely related phenomenon, tourism, which was how he categorized camping. Neville's perspective smoothly aligns with that of Linda H. Graber, *Wilderness as Sacred Space* (Washington, DC: Association of American Geographers, 1976), ix, who argued that

the reverence for wild areas was "a focus for religious feeling" but that the "religious essence of the wilderness ethic" tended to be overshadowed by attempts to protect it through secular justifications. William Cronon, "The Trouble with Wilderness; or, Getting Back to the Wrong Nature," in *Uncommon Ground: Toward Reinventing Nature*, ed. W. Cronon (New York: W. W. Norton, 1995), 69–90, similarly argued that Americans view wilderness, not cities, as their legitimate home.

13. For a comprehensive overview of pilgrimage and these beliefs see Linda Kay Davidson and David M. Gitlitz, introduction in Davidson and Gitlitz, *Pilgrimage*, xvii–xxiii.

14. See Robert H. Stoddard, "Defining and Classifying Pilgrimages," in *Sacred Places, Sacred Spaces: The Geography of Pilgrimage*, eds. Robert H. Stoddard and Alan Morinis (Baton Rouge, LA: LSU Press, 1997), 41–60, on the contrast between pilgrimages to a specific destination versus circumambulations.

15. Eade and Sallnow, *Contesting the Sacred*; Turner, "Center," 227. On who qualifies as an authentic pilgrim on the path to Santiago de Compostela see Nancy Louise Frey, *Pilgrim Stories: On and Off the Road to Santiago* (Berkeley: University of California Press, 1998), 50ff.

16. Timothy Egan, "Roughing It, 90's-Style: A Sea of Fibreglass," *New York Times*, July 2, 1995.

17. Lears, *No Place*, 96; Steven M. Gelber, *Hobbies: Leisure and the Culture of Work in America* (New York: Columbia University Press, 1999), 196. See also Kathleen Franz, *Tinkering: Consumers Reinvent the Early Automobile* (Philadelphia: University of Pennsylvania Press, 2005).

18. George Ritzer, *The McDonaldization of Society 5* (Los Angeles: Pine Forge, 2008), 1, 13–14. Ritzer does not argue that the McDonald's chain caused this process, but rather that it is the paradigm for this modern phenomenon. His work is based on the writings of the nineteenth- and early twentieth-century social theorist Max Weber.

19. Horace Kephart, *Camping and Woodcraft: A Handbook for Vacation Campers and for Travelers in the Wilderness, Two Volumes in One*, introduction by George Ellison and Janet McCue (Gatlinburg, TN: Great Smoky Mountains Association, 2011).

20. Elon Jessup, *Roughing It Smoothly; How to Avoid Vacation Pitfalls* (New York: G. P. Putnam's Sons, 1923).

21. Paul S. Sutter, *Driven Wild: How the Fight against Automobiles Launched the Modern Wilderness Movement* (Seattle: University of Washington Press, 2002), offers a compelling explanation for how the increasing presence of automobiles in America's protected areas led to the creation of wilderness—a place where one could camp without motorized vehicles. Grant W. Sharpe, Charles H. Odegaard, and Wenonah Finch Sharpe, *Park Management* (New York: John Wiley & Sons, 1983), 222.

22. Camping remains largely unexplored as an American cultural phenomenon, but authors have begun to look into its history, permutations, and elements in recent years. See Cindy Aron, *Working at Play: A History of Vacations in the United States* (New York: Oxford University Press, 1999); Warren James Belasco, *Americans on the Road: From Autocamp to Motel, 1910–1945* (Baltimore: Johns Hopkins University Press, 1979); Matthew De Abaitua, *The Art of Camping: The History and Practice of Sleeping under the Stars* (New York: Penguin, 2011); Charlie Hailey, *Campsite: Architectures of Duration and Place* (Baton Rouge, LA: LSU Press, 2008); Charlie Hailey, *Camps: A Guide to 21st-Century Space* (Cambridge, MA: MIT Press, 2009); Phoebe Kropp, "Wilderness Wives and Dishwashing Husbands: Comfort and the Domestic Arts of Camping in America, 1880–1910," *Journal of Social History* 43, no. 1 (2009): 5–30; Phoebe S. Kropp Young, "Sleeping Outside: The Political Natures of Urban Camping," in *Cities and Nature in the American West*, ed. Char Miller (Reno: University of Nevada Press, 2010), 171–91; Rugh, *Are We There Yet?*; Schmitt, *Back to Nature*; Sears, *Sacred Places*; Susan Snyder, *Past Tents: The Way We Camped* (Berkeley, CA: Heyday Books, 2006); David Wescott, *Camping in the Old Style* (Salt Lake City: Gibbs Smith, 2000); and, Dan White, *Under the Stars: How America Fell in Love with Camping* (New York: Henry Holt, 2016).

1. Adventures in the Wilderness

1. "Our Summer Resorts," *New York Daily Tribune*, July 5, 1870.
2. Ibid.
3. I liberally borrow biographical material from Warder H. Cadbury, introduction in William H.H. Murray, *Adventures in the Wilderness*, ed. William K. Verner (Syracuse, NY: Adirondack Museum / Syracuse University Press, 1989); Alfred L. Donaldson, *The Adirondacks* (New York: Century, 1921); H. J. Griswold, "W. H. H. Murray, by a Classmate," *New Haven Register*, June 26, 1904; Ruby Murray Orcutt, "Personal Impression of the Life and Works of William H. H. (Adirondack) Murray," October 16, 1931, William H. H. Murray Collection (MS 69–13), Adirondack Museum, Blue Mountain Lake, NY (hereafter WHHM Collection); and Harry V. Radford, *Adirondack Murray: A Biographical Appreciation* (New York: Broadway Publishing, 1906).
4. Radford, *Adirondack Murray*, 49. The best-known members of the Knickerbocker Group were Washington Irving, James Fenimore Cooper, and William Cullen Bryant. Cadbury, introduction, 14, cites from an "unidentified clipping" in the WHHM Collection.
5. Ruby Murray Orcutt, W. H. H. Murray's daughter, quips in "Personal Impression," 2, about the marriage: "He had complained of the slowness of his brother-in-law's courtship. Apparently he was on the dot with his own." Ibid., 2–3. Daniel Justin Herman, *Hunting and the American Imagination* (Washington, DC: Smithsonian Institution Press, 2001).
6. Radford, *Adirondack Murray*, 69, gives the dates from Murray's annual vacations as 1864 to 1877. However, Cadbury, introduction, 32, notes that the first confirmed date for any of Murray's Adirondack trips is September 3, 1866. For a short time, Osprey Island became known as Murray's Island. See Cadbury, introduction, 35. Donaldson, *Adirondacks*, 199, relates that Murray camped on the island only during the summers of 1867, 1868, and 1869. Ruby M. Orcutt to Mr. Meeks, Madison, CT, January 31, 1949, WHHM Collection, 1.
7. W. H. H. "Adirondack" Murray, "Reminiscences of My Literary and Outdoor Life," Part 1, *Independent* 57 (1904): 198–99.
8. Ibid., 197. Jonathan Edwards was a highly regarded American preacher, philosopher, and theologian during the eighteenth century. See George M. Marsden, *Jonathan Edwards: A Life* (New Haven, CT: Yale University Press, 2003).
9. Murray, "Reminiscences," Part 1, 200.
10. Ibid. See William H. H. Murray and Fields, Osgood & Co., "Agreement," February 10, 1869, WHHM Collection, 1.
11. William H. H. Murray, *Adventures in the Wilderness; or, Camp-Life in the Adirondacks* (Boston: Fields, Osgood, 1869); "Current Literature," *Overland Monthly* 3 (July 1869): 101; "Two Books on the Adirondacks," *Nation*, July 15, 1869, 240; *New York Times*, April 12, 1869; "the same house have issued," unattributed newspaper clipping on page 9 in a scrapbook in "Scrapbooks, Clippings, Notebooks, Ledgers, and Diaries," WHHM Collection.
12. The printing number is taken from a July 7, 1869, letter from Joseph (formerly Josephus) Cook to his parents, but the size of the printings is unknown. See Frederick G. Bascom, ed., *Letters of a Ticonderoga Farmer: Selections from the Correspondence of William H. Cook and His Wife and Their Son, 1851–1885* (Ithaca, NY: Cornell University Press, 1946), 88. The five hundred per week is from W. H. H. "Adirondack" Murray, "Reminiscences of My Literary and Outdoor Life," Part 2, *Independent* 57 (1904): 278.
13. Cadbury, introduction, 49, points out that no detailed count of visitors exists but accepts this range as reasonably accurate. Ibid., 40.
14. The mountain was discussed in Laura Waterman and Guy Waterman, *Forest and Crag: A History of Hiking, Trail Blazing, and Adventure in the Northeast Mountains* (Boston: Appalachian Mountain Club, 1989), 73. Cadbury, introduction, 40, identifies Wachusett as "very probably" the Philadelphia painter George B. Wood. Wachusett, "With the Multitudes in the Wilderness. I. Introductory," *Boston Daily Advertiser*, July 17, 1869.

15. Radford, *Adirondack Murray*, 60–61. This "best route" is laid out in Murray, *Adventures*, 41–44, but subsequent "tourist editions" typically directed campers to Plattsburgh on Lake Champlain, where they caught the train to the Ausable station and then the stages to Martin's hotel. See, for example, George F. Field, "Plattsburg Route to the Adirondacks," in William H. H. Murray, *Tourist's Edition: Murray's Adventures in the Adirondacks, with Maps and Illustrations* (Boston: Fields, Osgood, 1869), 1–8. Wachusett, "With the Multitudes. I."

16. Quoted in Donaldson, *Adirondacks*, 194.

17. *The Statistical History of the United States from Colonial Times to the Present* (Stamford, CT: Fairfield Publishers, 1965), 13–14; Robert E. Gallman, "Gross National Product in the United States, 1834–1909," in *Output, Employment, and Productivity in the United States after 1800*, ed. D. S. Brady (Washington, DC: National Bureau of Economic Research, 1966), 7–10; John B. Bachelder, *Popular Resorts, and How to Reach Them*, 3rd ed. (Boston: John B. Bachelder, 1875), 15. David Strauss, "Toward a Consumer Culture: 'Adirondack Murray' and the Wilderness Vacation," *American Quarterly* 39 (1987): 270, termed the urban embrace of the region as "inevitable."

18. Murray, *Adventures*, 22. J. T. Headley, *The Adirondack; or, Life in the Woods* (New York: Baker and Scribner, 1849), i, had claimed "an attack on the brain" to justify his trip into the wilds during the 1840s. Herman, *Hunting*, 195, states that "the middle-class public adored [Murray] as if it had feverishly awaited a prophet to undo the Puritan strictures on field sports." See also Strauss, "Toward a Consumer Culture," and Philip G. Terrie, *Contested Terrain: A New History of Nature and People in the Adirondacks* (Syracuse, NY: Syracuse University Press, 1997), 61–82. Philip G. Terrie, "Romantic Travelers in the Adirondack Wilderness," *American Studies* 24, no. 2 (1983): 60. Cindy Aron, *Working at Play: A History of Vacations in the United States* (New York: Oxford University Press, 1999), and Maitland C. De Sormo, *The "Murray Rush" in Retrospect or, With the Multitude in the Adirondacks* (Burlington, VT: George Little Press, 1989), both pointed toward Murray's writing skill to explain the rush. Cadbury, introduction, recognized Murray's style as significant but did not give it the greatest weight.

19. Headley, *Adirondack*, 288; Cadbury, introduction, 63. Donaldson, *Adirondacks*, 196, also identifies this element as crucial. The earliest American guidebooks had appeared during the 1820s, and they were having a noticeable impact on wilderness recreation in the Northeast during the 1860s and 1870s. See Richard Gassan, "The First American Tourist Guidebooks," *Book History* 8 (2005): 51–74, and Waterman and Waterman, *Forest and Crag*, 195–96.

20. John F. Sears, *Sacred Places: American Tourist Attractions in the Nineteenth Century* (New York: Oxford University Press, 1989), 3, recounted that landscape gardening, landscape painting, and widely read essays on the beautiful, sublime, and picturesque had stimulated Americans' interest in natural scenery beginning in the 1820s and 1830s. Mircea Eliade, *The Sacred and the Profane: The Nature of Religion* (New York: Harcourt, Brace, 1957), referred to such sacred places as "hierophanic," i.e., a place that becomes sacred when it is identified with some divine manifestation or with an overpoweringly significant event. One of these landscape painters, William Stillman, co-organized the 1858 Philosophers' Camp. See the previous chapter.

21. Murray, *Adventures*, 193, 188. See Victor W. Turner, "The Center Out There: Pilgrim's Goal," *History of Religions* 12 (1973): 191–230. Patrick McGreevy, "Niagara as Jerusalem," *Landscape* 28, no. 2 (1985): 26–32, made this same point about the characterization of a contemporary destination, Niagara Falls.

22. Headley, *Adirondack*, ii–iii, I; T. B. Thorpe, "A Visit to 'John Brown's Tract,'" *Harper's New Monthly Magazine* 19 (1859): 160.

23. One reviewer, Munroe, "Books in Boston," *New York Times*, April 12, 1869, wrote that Murray suggested that readers "rough it," but the term is not used in *Adventures in the Wilderness*. Murray, *Adventures*, 8. Hans Huth, *Nature and the American: Three Centuries of Changing Attitudes* (Lincoln: University of Nebraska Press, 1972), and Peter Schmitt, *Back to Nature: The Arcadian Myth in Urban America* (Baltimore: Johns Hopkins University Press, 1990), stressed that urban Americans were drawn to the Adirondacks by the "Arcadian impulse" common in American society, but they did not connect it to pilgrimage. Murray, *Adventures*, 11, 10, 11–12.

24. Victor W. Turner and Edith Turner, *Image and Pilgrimage in Christian Culture* (New York: Columbia University Press, 1978), 250–55, referred to this social leveling as *communitas*. It is a common characteristic of pilgrimage. See Cadbury, introduction, 64–65, for more on why Murray went camping.

25. Murray, *Adventures*, 19, 51, 58–59.

26. Ibid., 12–14. McGreevy, "Niagara," found that tourist-pilgrims to Niagara Falls also expected extraordinary events. Murray, *Adventures*, 14.

27. See Peggy A. Russo and Paul Finkelman, eds., *Terrible Swift Sword: The Legacy of John Brown* (Athens: Ohio University Press, 2005); Murray, *Adventures*, 43. Nancy Louise Frey, *Pilgrim Stories: On and Off the Road to Santiago* (Berkeley: University of California Press, 1998), 41–42, 175–76, 221–22, discussed this nostalgia for the past along pilgrim pathways. See Benedict Anderson, *Imagined Communities: Reflections on the Origin and Spread of Nationalism* (London: Verso/NLB, 1983), concerning such imagined communities. According to Wilbur Zelinsky, "Nationalistic Pilgrimages in the United States," in *Pilgrimage in the United States*, ed. G. Rinschede and S. M. Bhardwaj (Berlin: Dietrich Reimer, 1990), 253–67, secular pilgrimages to nationally significant, historic sites, memorials, and museums began around the middle of the nineteenth century in the United States.

28. The reporter clearly had read *Adventures*, because his articles focused on featured items in the text: transportation, insects, guides, adventures while hunting and fishing, scenery, accommodations, costs, crowding, and the character of visitors. Wachusett, "With the Multitudes. I."

29. Wachusett, "With the Multitudes in the Wilderness. II. The Dearth of Guides and the Pest of Mosquitoes," *Boston Daily Advertiser*, July 19, 1869.

30. Ibid.

31. "Murray's Fools Again—a Plea for the Wilderness," *New York Daily Tribune*, August 17, 1869.

32. Frey, *Pilgrim Stories*, found that contemporary pilgrims who hike and bike to Santiago de Compostela use the same epithet against pilgrims who ride in motor vehicles—"tourists." John Eade and Michael J. Sallnow, eds., *Contesting the Sacred: The Anthropology of Christian Pilgrimage* (New York: Routledge, 1991), 5, examined "how the practice of pilgrimage and the sacred powers of a shrine are constructed as varied and possibly conflicting representations by the different sectors of the cultic constituency, and indeed by those outside it as well." See also Frey, *Pilgrim Stories*, and Chris Park, *Sacred Worlds: An Introduction to Geography and Religion* (New York: Routledge, 1994).

33. Kate Field, "Among the Adirondacks; Murray's Fools—a Plain Talk about the Wilderness," *New York Daily Tribune*, August 12, 1869. Field was a frequent correspondent for this newspaper. "Summer Resorts," *New York Daily Tribune*, August 14, 1869.

34. T. B. Thorpe, "The Abuses of the Backwoods," *Appletons' Journal of Popular Literature, Science, and Art* 2 (1869): 564.

35. Field, "Among the Adirondacks." See Gary Scharnhorst, *Kate Field: The Many Lives of a Nineteenth-Century American Journalist* (Syracuse, NY: Syracuse University Press, 2008), and Lilian Whiting, *Kate Field: A Record* (Boston: Little, Brown, 1899). Field wrote art criticism concerning music, painting, and drama as well as her own short comedies. Her social circle included Anthony Trollope, whom she had met while traveling in England, Ralph Waldo Emerson, Henry Wadsworth Longfellow, Louisa May Alcott, Benjamin Pierce, Charles Sumner, and James T. Fields of Fields, Osgood & Co., the publisher of Murray's book. According to Whiting, 212, Field wrote in her diary: "On July 5th I started for the Adirondacks with mother, and the Rev. Mr. Murray was of our party. . . . Returned August 1." According to Joseph Cook, Murray's own vacation lasted two months. See Bascom, *Letters*, 89. Field, "Among the Adirondacks."

36. Wachusett, "With the Multitude in the Wilderness. IV. Feeble and Feminine Tourists," *Boston Daily Advertiser*, July 22, 1869. "Lectures Last Evening: Miss Kate Field on 'The Adirondacks,'" *New York Times*, November 10, 1869. Field's presentation was the very first in the "Star Course of Lectures" created by Philadelphian entrepreneur T. B. Pugh. This

series became very well known in the Northeast and continued into the 1880s. It ultimately involved many leading performers, including Mark Twain. Kate Field, "In and Out of the Woods," in *The Atlantic Almanac of 1870* (Boston: Fields, Osgood, 1869), 52. According to Whiting, *Kate Field*, 222–23, Field gave this Adirondack lecture on numerous occasions between 1869 and 1871.

37. Thorpe, "Abuses," 564–65. On the shifting roles of women and men in late nineteenth-century American life see Ann Douglas, *The Feminization of American Culture* (New York: Knopf, 1977). The biting interactions between Thorpe on the one hand and Field, Murray, and Wachusett on the other neatly mimic the gender interactions surrounding men's and women's views toward mountains and mountain climbing. See Susan R. Schrepfer, *Nature's Altars: Mountains, Gender, and American Environmentalism* (Lawrence: University Press of Kansas, 2005).

38. Field, "Among the Adirondacks"; "Murray's Fools Again"; "Summer Resorts." Death statistics are from Dan Ruggiero, "A Glimpse at the Colorful History of TB: Its Toll and Its Effect on the U.S. and the World," in *TB Notes 2000* (Atlanta: Centers for Disease Control, 2000), 2.

39. Field, "Among the Adirondacks."

40. W. H. H. Murray, "The Adirondacks; Mr. Murray's Reply to His Calumniators," *Boston Journal*, October 30, 1869. Trudeau had visited the Adirondacks for pleasure before the Murray Rush and then again in May 1873 in an effort to recover from or at least retard his rapidly advancing tuberculosis. The disease retreated, prompting Trudeau to remain in the region and to later open the first of hundreds of American sanatoriums for the control and sometimes cure of tuberculosis. Sanatoriums dwindled away after the discovery of antibiotics in the 1940s. See David L. Ellison, *Healing Tuberculosis in the Woods: Medicine and Science at the End of the Nineteenth Century* (Westport, CT: Greenwood, 1994); Stephen H. Gehlbach, *American Plagues: Lessons from Our Battles with Disease* (New York: McGraw-Hill, Medical Publications Division, 2005); and Edward Livingston Trudeau, *An Autobiography* (Garden City, NY: Doubleday, 1916).

41. Murray, "Adirondacks."

42. Charles Hallock, "Raquette Club," *Harper's New Monthly Magazine* 41 (1870): 321. Cadbury, introduction, 54, identified the article's author as Hallock, who was a widely read writer of books about fishing, hunting, and other field sports.

43. Winslow C. Watson, *A Descriptive and Historical Guide to the Valley of Lake Champlain and the Adirondacks* (Burlington, VT: R. S. Styles' Steam Printing, 1871), 101, 112; S.R. Stoddard, *The Adirondacks Illustrated* (Albany, NY: Weed, Parsons, 1874), 120.

44. H. Perry Smith and E. R. Wallace, *The Modern Babes in the Wood or Summerings in the Wilderness; To Which Is Added a Reliable and Descriptive Guide to the Adirondacks* (Hartford, CT: Columbian Book Co., 1872). E. R. Wallace, *Descriptive Guide to the Adirondacks and Handbook of Travel to Saratoga Springs, Schroon Lake, Lakes Luzerne, George and Champlain, the Ausable Chasm, the Thousand Islands, Massena Spring and Trenton Falls* (New York: American News Co., 1875).

45. William H. H. Murray, "*My Record as a Lecturer*," WHHM Collection, 2–3; Murray, "Reminiscences," Part 2, 278.

46. This biographical material is again drawn from Cadbury, introduction; Donaldson, *Adirondacks*; Griswold, "W. H. H. Murray"; Orcutt, "Personal Impression"; and Radford, *Adirondack Murray*. Quoted in Cadbury, introduction, 27.

2. The Art of Camping

1. H. Perry Smith and E. R. Wallace, *The Modern Babes in the Wood or Summerings in the Wilderness; To Which Is Added a Reliable and Descriptive Guide to the Adirondacks* (Hartford, CT: Columbian Book Co., 1872), 432–40; E. R. Wallace, *Descriptive Guide to the*

Adirondacks and Handbook of Travel to Saratoga Springs, Schroon Lake, Lakes Luzerne, George and Champlain, the Ausable Chasm, the Thousand Islands, Massena Spring and Trenton Falls (New York: American News Co., 1875), 238–60. Smith's section was a literary description of his travels in the Adirondack region. Wallace chose to publish his more applied section alone after Murray's *Adventures in the Wilderness* demonstrated the public's desire for a practical camping guidebook. See chapter 1.

2. See John B. Bachelder, *Key to Bachelder's Isometrical Drawing of the Gettysburg Battle-Field* (New York: C. A. Alvord, Printer, 1864); *Gettysburg: Description of the Painting of the Repulse of Longstreet's Assault Painted by James Walker* (New York: John B. Bachelder, 1870); *Descriptive Key to the Painting of the Repulse of Longstreet's Assault at the Battle of Gettysburg* (New York: John B. Bachelder, 1870); John B. Bachelder, *Bachelder's Illustrated Tourist's Guide of the United States* (Boston: John B. Bachelder, 1873); *Popular Resorts, and How to Reach Them*, 2nd ed. (Boston: John B. Bachelder, 1874), 9. One of the two volumes of *Bachelder's Illustrated Tourist's Guide of the United States* was subtitled "Popular Resorts and How to Reach Them." The author obviously built upon that foundation for this "second" edition.

3. Bachelder, *Popular Resorts*, 2nd ed., 10, 11.

4. John B. Bachelder, *Popular Resorts, and How to Reach Them*, 3rd ed. (Boston: John B. Bachelder, 1875), 13.

5. See Warren Belasco, *Americans on the Road, from Autocamp to Motel, 1910–1945* (Cambridge, MA: MIT Press, 1979), which discusses the resentment people felt toward the constraints placed on them by employers, railroads, resorts, etc.

6. Bachelder, *Popular Resorts*, 3rd ed., 13, 15, 17. Canoe and boat camping are not mentioned by Bachelder but were well known in his day and should be seen as regional variations on horse-and-wagon camping because they provided the same comforts and opportunities when water was present.

7. Hallock founded and directed *Forest and Stream* from 1873 to 1880. See Charles Hallock, *An Angler's Reminiscences: A Record of Sport, Travel and Adventure, with Autobiography of the Author* (Cincinnati: Sportsmen's Review, 1913). Fred Beverly, "Three Months in Florida for a Hundred Dollars," in *Camp Life in Florida: A Handbook for Sportsmen and Settlers*, comp. Charles Hallock (New York: Forest and Stream, 1876), 73.

8. Bachelder, *Popular Resorts*, 3rd ed., 18. Bachelder's caution was reasonable. In 1877, a Yellowstone National Park camper, George Cowan, was shot and abandoned by Nez Perce Indians who were fleeing U.S. Army cavalry. See Hiram Martin Chittenden, *The Yellowstone National Park* (Cincinnati: R. Clarke, 1895); Mrs. George F. Cowan, "Reminiscences of Pioneer Life: A Trip to the National Park in 1877—an Account of the Nez Perce Raid from a Woman's Standpoint—Incidents and Accidents," in *Old Yellowstone Days*, ed. Paul Schullery (Boulder, CO: Associated University Press, 1979), 1–25; John Sears, *Sacred Places: American Tourist Attractions in the Nineteenth Century* (New York: Oxford University Press, 1989); Mark David Spence, *Dispossessing the Wilderness: Indian Removal and the Making of the National Parks* (New York: Oxford University Press, 1999); and Jerome A. Greene, *Nez Perce Summer, 1877: The US Army and the Nee-Me-Poo Crisis* (Helena: Montana Historical Society, 2001).

9. "The Tent under the Beech," *Scribner's Monthly* 8, no. 4 (1874): 499. Other contemporary camping publications were, for example, S. R. Stoddard, *The Adirondacks Illustrated* (Albany. NY: Weed, Parsons, 1874), and "Adirondack Adventures," *Appleton's Journal* 14 (December 11, 1875): 754–57.

10. John M. Gould, *Hints for Camping and Walking: How to Camp Out* (New York: Scribner, Armstrong, 1877), 33, 93–95; "How to Camp Out," *Nation*, April 19, 1877, 240.

11. For example see S. Anna Gordon, *Camping in Colorado: With Suggestions to Gold Seekers, Tourists and Invalids* (New York: Author's Publishing Co., 1879), who describes her and her family's adventures as they camped in the Rocky Mountains near Denver. Dillon Wallace, "Camping Suggestions for the Novice," *Outing*, July 1909, 505.

12. Thomas G. Appleton, "A Month in the Adirondacks," in *Windfalls* (Boston: Roberts Bros., 1878), 34. See, for example, Lucy J. T___, "From a Lady Who Loves 'Camping,'"

American Angler, July 14, 1883, 22–23, and George Elmer Browne, "Canoeing Down the Androscoggin," *Outing*, July 1898, 358–68. Helen S. Clark, "Camping in the Woods," *Outing*, August 1891, 417.

13. Nessmuk, *Woodcraft* (New York: Forest and Stream, 1884), vii; "From Camp," *Overland Monthly*, July 1883, 112. Similar urban indictments can be found in James Weir Jr., "A Little Excursion into Savagery," *Outing*, July 1895, 305–9, and T. C. Yard, "Practical Camping-Out Near Home," *Outing*, June 1899, 269–73.

14. Hubert P. Dyer, "A Tramp in the High Sierras," *Outing*, July 1895, 301; Emily H. Palmer, "Family Camping," *Outing*, September 1895, 479. In the language of Victor Turner, camping was *liminal*, an ambiguous, inter-structural period between everyday life's structure. See *The Ritual Process: Structure and Anti-Structure* (New York: Aldine, 1969). Appleton, "Month in the Adirondacks," 34–35.

15. Elisabeth Woodbridge, "On a Connecticut Stillwater," *Outlook*, June 3, 1905, 324; Gwen Kennedy Neville, *Kinship and Pilgrimage: Rituals of Reunion in American Protestant Culture* (New York: Oxford University Press, 1987), 20–21. See also Edward Relph, *Place and Placelessness* (London: Pion, 1976), on the connections between placelessness and modernity.

16. Dan Beard, "The Art of Camping," *World's Work* 6 (1903): 3539. See A. Judd Northrup, *Camps and Tramps in the Adirondacks and Grayling Fishing in Northern Michigan* (Syracuse, NY: Davis, Bardeen, 1880), 13–14, who records that when he was young and living in the country he had hunted and fished, but now "I had almost forgotten all the experiences . . . in that regard . . . while I was entirely ignorant of the special delights of forest camp life."

17. See Patrick McGreevy, "Niagara as Jerusalem," *Landscape* 28, no. 2 (1985): 26–32, and Yi-Fu Tuan, *Space and Place: The Perspective of Experience* (Minneapolis: University of Minnesota Press, 1977), 6.

18. "A Glimpse of the Adirondacks," *Catholic World* 24 (November 1876): 263–64. See Northrup, *Camps and Tramps*; Clark, "Camping"; and "The Spectator," *Outlook*, January 25, 1908, 165–66, which also took note of scenery, campfires, and hiking on their camping trips. These are not the only practices and elements commonly mentioned; others include reading, nature study, animals, plants, painting, hunting, fishing, and more. At the same time, we must remember that camping is voluntary, so its rituals have not been monolithic but plural, fragmentary, and idiosyncratic. See Victor Turner and Edith L. B. Turner, *Image and Pilgrimage in Christian Culture* (New York: Columbia University Press, 1978), 243–55.

19. See, for example, A. Radclyffe Dugmore, "The Camp Fire and How to Make It," *Country Life in America*, June 1909, 179–80; Dan Beard, "How to Make a Winter Camp," *Outing*, March 1904, 742–44; and A. D. Gillette and S. McAndrew, "Camp Cookery," *Outing*, May 1896, 120–24.

20. See David Chidester and Edward T. Linenthal, introduction in *American Sacred Space*, ed. D. Chidester and E. T. Linenthal (Bloomington: Indiana University Press, 1995), 9. Kephart was a prolific writer. His extensive bibliography is listed on Western Carolina University's web exhibit, "Horace Kephart: Revealing an Enigma," http://www.wcu.edu/library/DigitalCollections/Kephart/. I borrow biographical material from Horace Kephart, "Horace Kephart," *North Carolina Library Bulletin* 5 (1922): 49–52, which is a reminiscence about the author's life; George Ellison, introduction in *Our Southern Highlanders: A Narrative of Adventure in the Southern Appalachians and a Study of Life among the Mountaineers*, by Horace Kephart (Knoxville: University of Tennessee Press, 1984), ix–xlvi; Michael Frome, *Strangers in High Places: The Story of the Great Smoky Mountains*, expanded ed. (Knoxville: University of Tennessee Press, 1980); Martin W. Maxwell, "Horace Kephart: An Introduction to His Life and Work" (master's thesis, Wake Forest University, 1982); and Jim Casada, introduction in *Camping and Woodcraft: A Handbook for Vacation Campers and for Travelers in the Wilderness*, by Horace Kephart, facsimile ed. (Knoxville: University of Tennessee Press, 1988), vii–xxxiii. Casada, introduction, xxvi, estimated that 1906's *The Book of*

Camping and Woodcraft and its various revised versions had appeared in "approximately three score printings."

21. Horace Kephart, *The Book of Camping and Woodcraft: A Guidebook for Those Who Travel in the Wilderness* (New York: Outing Publishing Co., 1906), 37, 43–44. In *Camp Cookery* (New York: Outing Publishing Co., 1910), 7, Kephart comments that "on general principles I object to naming firms or brands; but when a good thing is not generally procurable in average stores, there would be no use in mentioning it without telling the reader where to get it."

22. Kephart, *Book of Camping*, 70, 81.

23. Ibid., xiv.

24. Nancy Louise Frey, *Pilgrim Stories: On and Off the Road to Santiago* (Berkeley: University of California Press, 1998), also reports that not everyone who chose to travel the *camino* to Santiago de Compostela found the pilgrimage transformative. Kephart, *Book of Camping*, 8.

25. Horace Kephart, "A Month in the Woods for $30," *Collier's Outdoor America*, November 13, 1909, 30–31.

26. Kephart, *Camp Cookery*, 49.

27. Horace Kephart, "Camping," in *Camping and Woodcraft* (New York: Macmillan, 1917), 19–20. This book has two complete sections—"Camping" and "Woodcraft." Each is separately paginated. Overall, it is a revised version of his earlier *The Book of Camping and Woodcraft*.

28. The frontier and its nationalist implications have played a major role in the formation of America's problematic "wilderness ethic." See William Cronon, "The Trouble with Wilderness; or, Getting Back to the Wrong Nature," *Environmental History* 1, no. 1 (1996): 7–28, and replies by Samuel P. Hays, Michael P. Cohen, and Thomas R. Dunlap.

29. The association was meeting in Chicago where the Columbian Exposition was also under way. See Frederick Jackson Turner, *The Significance of the Frontier in American History*, ed. Harold P. Simonson (New York: Frederick Ungar, 1963). Lee Clark Mitchell, *Witnesses to a Vanishing America: The Nineteenth-Century Response* (Princeton, NJ: Princeton University Press, 1981), 90. Mitchell also examines a variety of other influential Americans who shared Turner's concern about the country's future, including George Bird Grinnell, Theodore Roosevelt, Frederick Remington, and Owen Wister.

30. See David M. Wrobel, *Promised Lands: Promotion, Memory, and the Creation of the American West* (Lawrence: University Press of Kansas, 2002), on the cultural impact of these intellectual and popular interests. He concludes that this passion for the frontier remained strong from approximately 1880 to 1930. It also, however, lived on in film westerns. See Peter C. Rollins and John C. O'Connor, eds., *Hollywood's West: The American Frontier in Film, Television, and History* (Lexington: University of Kentucky Press, 2005).

31. Other camping authors in this period also made covert and overt connections to pioneers and the frontier. See, for example, Warwick S. Carpenter, "Lure of the Adirondack Gold," *Outing*, February 1911, 522–32, and Ernest Thompson Seton, *Rolf in the Woods: The Adventures of a Boy Scout with Indian Quonab and Little Dog Shookum* (Garden City, NY: Doubleday, Doran, 1911). Horace Kephart, "Bits of Woodcraft," *Outing*, November 1901, 152.

32. Kephart, *Book of Camping*, xi–xii.

33. Ibid., 193, 219–20. Rockahominy is generally now known as hominy.

34. Ibid., 2.

35. Ibid., 1–2.

36. Ibid., 6. According to James Morton Turner, "Nothing troubled the woodsman more than being labeled a tenderfoot." The experienced, thoughtful camper took neither too much nor too little equipment. See Turner, "From Woodcraft to 'Leave no Trace': Wilderness, Consumerism and Environmentalism in Twentieth Century America," *Environmental History* 7, no. 3 (2002): 465.

37. The articles appeared in the *Religious Telescope* of Dayton, Ohio, from January 4, 1893, to February 8, 1893. Frederick Jackson Turner was born one year before Kephart, and his father, who was a newspaper editor in Wisconsin, also wrote columns about the region's pioneer history. See Allan G. Bogue, *Frederick Jackson Turner: Strange Roads Going Down* (Norman: University of Oklahoma Press, 1998).

38. Kephart, "Horace," 49–50.

39. Ibid. Alpheus Hyatt (1838–1902) was a prominent neo-Lamarckian, first editor of the scientific journal *American Naturalist*, and first president of Woods Hole laboratory. See Samuel Henshaw, "Alpheus Hyatt," *Science* 15 (February 21, 1902): 300–302.

40. Letter from Kephart to Fiske, January 15, 1887, and quoted in Ellison, introduction, xvii; Kephart, "Horace," 50–51. The *Nation* article (February 2, 1888, p. 96) is an untitled, unsigned piece that discusses a copyright problem.

41. Letter from Kephart to Fiske, December 9, 1888, and quoted in Maxwell, "Horace Kephart," 12. Kephart's response to parenthood was not unique, but part of what Ann Douglas, in *The Feminization of American Culture* (New York: Knopf, 1977), 327, argued was a "militant crusade for masculinity" and a deep concern for the "feminization" of American culture at this time.

42. The library today is part of the University of Missouri–St. Louis campus.

43. Clarence E. Miller, "Horace Kephart, a Personal Glimpse," *Missouri Historical Society Bulletin* 16 (July 1959): 305–6. Kephart hired Miller as an assistant librarian "after perhaps the briefest interview on record." Subsequently, Miller became head librarian for the same institution. Kephart, "Horace," 51.

44. Letter from Kephart to Fiske, March 12, 1894, and quoted in Casada, introduction, xvi.

45. Miller, "Horace Kephart," 307. Letter from Mrs. L. K. (Margaret) Wonref to Mr. McLean, December 18, 1931, and quoted in Maxwell, "Horace Kephart," 24. Although the Kepharts never divorced, their separation was effectively permanent. Miller, "Horace Kephart," 308.

46. Kephart, *Our Southern Highlanders*, 29–30. Kephart, "Horace," 51.

47. Kephart, "Horace," 51. The Appalachians were not "primitive," "backwards," or a "frontier," in spite of Kephart's impression of them. Western North Carolina was a poor, rural American setting much like many others. For an insightful history of the region's misperception see Henry D. Shapiro, *Appalachia on Our Mind: The Southern Mountains and Mountaineers in the American Consciousness, 1870–1920* (Chapel Hill: University of North Carolina Press, 1978). According to the introduction by George Ellison and Janet McCue in *Camping and Woodcraft: A Handbook for Vacation Campers and for Travelers in the Wilderness*, by Horace Kephart (Gatlinburg, TN: Great Smoky Mountains Association, 2011), liv–lv, Kephart had been at work on a manuscript about woodcraft "for several years" prior to moving to Dayton. To support himself after he arrived in western North Carolina Kephart began to write the camping articles that would become the book. The review is in "Out of Door Life in New Books: Farming, Camping, Gardening and Rambling Talks—Essays on the Birds and the Flowers" *New York Times*, June 22, 1907.

48. Horace Kephart, "Woodcraft," in *Camping and Woodcraft* (New York: Macmillan, 1917), 14–15.

49. Ellison, introduction, ix; Ellison and McCue, introduction, lv–lvi.

50. See Daniel S. Pierce, *The Great Smokies: From Natural Habitat to National Park* (Knoxville: University of Tennessee Press, 2000).

51. The numbers here are suggestive rather than definitive and do not include fiction or revised editions. Books are derived from the Library of Congress and Harvard University catalogs, while the magazine articles come from *Poole's Index to Periodical Literature, Nineteenth Century Readers' Guide to Periodical Literature,* and *Readers' Guide to Periodical Literature.* On the rise of magazines see Frank Luther Mott, *A History of American Magazines,* 5 vols. (Cambridge, MA: Harvard University Press, 1938–1968); and on the impact of the economic depression see Douglas Steeples and David O. Whitten, *Democracy*

in Desperation: The Depression of 1893 (Westport, CT: Greenwood, 1998). The Yellowstone National Park figures are from U.S. Department of the Interior, *Report of the Secretary of the Interior for the Fiscal Year* (Washington, DC: Government Printing Office), 64 for 1895; 119–20 for 1900; and 185 for 1906. The summary national park visitor numbers are recorded in *The Statistical History of the United States from Colonial Times to the Present* (Stamford, CT: Fairfield Publishers, 1965), 222. These statistics are necessarily suggestive rather than definitive because the national parks did not gather visitor numbers in any consistent format at the time.

52. Miss M. F. Whitman, "Camp Life for Ladies" (August 2, 1879), in *Clipping Book Number Two* (Boston: Appalachian Mountain Club), 8c; Martha Coman, "The Art of Camping: A Woman's View," *Outlook*, June 7, 1902, 376, 373; Mrs. N. E. Corthell, "A Family Trek to the Yellowstone," *Independent*, June 29, 1905, 1466. See C., S.E.D., "Over the Hills," *Boston Daily Evening Traveller*, August 11, 1883, who reported on an Appalachian Mountain Club camping trip where approximately half the thirty-nine participants were women. For more on early women campers see Cindy Aron, *Working at Play: A History of Vacations in the United States* (New York: Oxford University Press, 1999).

53. Bachelder, *Popular Resorts*, 3rd ed., 15.

54. Wallace, *Descriptive Guide*, 248–49. See also Phoebe Kropp, "Wilderness Wives and Dishwashing Husbands: Comfort and the Domestic Arts of Camping in America, 1880–1915," *Journal of Social History* 43 (2009): 5–30, which insightfully examines camping and its comforts during this era to reveal how middle-class urban residents understood and accommodated modernity.

55. Robert David Sack, "The Consumer's World: Place as Context," *Annals of the Association of American Geographers* 78 (1988): 642–64; McGreevy, "Niagara"; and Tuan, *Space and Place*.

56. Kate Douglas Wiggin, *A Summer in a Cañon: A California Story* (Boston: Houghton, Mifflin, 1893), v. See Alfred L. Donaldson, *The Adirondacks* (New York: Century, 1921), and Paul Schneider, *The Adirondacks: A History of America's First Wilderness* (New York: Henry Holt, 1997), for more on Sabattis.

57. Clara D. Gamble, "Camping on the East Shore, Lake Michigan," *Country Life in America*, July 1909, 310. A contemporary of Clara Gamble, George H. Walsh, estimated that some equipment, such as tents, could last "indefinitely, when properly kept in storage," but that most other items would last only four to six years. See Walsh, "Outfitting the Camper and Hunter," *Independent*, August 20, 1908, 426. According to *Statistical History*, 139, the per capita GNP at the time was $349.

58. Earl Pomeroy, *In Search of the Golden West: The Tourist in Western America* (New York: Knopf, 1957), 125, noted that the Southern Pacific and Denver and Rio Grande Railroads would drop campers "in the midst of the mountains" by the 1890s. For a well-documented, carefully developed, and effectively illustrated history of early Adirondack boating see Hallie E. Bond, *Boats and Boating in the Adirondacks*, intro. Philip G. Terrie (Blue Mountain Lake, NY: Adirondack Museum / Syracuse University Press, 1995). See also Jerry Stelmok and Rollin Thurlow, *The Wood and Canvas Canoe: A Complete Guide to Its History, Construction, Restoration, and Maintenance* (Gardiner, ME: Harpswell, 1987). For a collection of recent canoe camping accounts by women see Judith Niemi and Barbara Wieser, eds., *Rivers Running Free: Canoeing Stories by Adventurous Women* (Seattle: Seal, 1987).

59. Nessmuk, *Woodcraft*, 129.

60. Bogue, *Frederick Jackson Turner*, 12–13. Turner's passion for outdoor recreation and the impact it had on his views about the American frontier are explored in Ray A. Billington, "Young Fred Turner," in *Frederick Jackson Turner: Wisconsin's Historian of the Frontier*, ed. Martin Ridge (Madison: State Historical Society of Wisconsin, 1993), 13–25. Frederick Jackson Turner to Max Farrand, September 27, 1908, in Wilbur R. Jacobs, *The Historical World of Frederick Jackson Turner, with Selections from His Correspondence* (New Haven, CT: Yale University Press, 1968), 15.

61. Turner to Farrand, 40–41. The mining company was a subsidiary of US Steel Corporation. Neither Frederick Jackson Turner nor Caroline Mae Turner provided the cook's name in their vacation accounts. Landry's name is noted in their daughter's photographic album from the same vacation. See Dorothy K. Turner, "Hunters Island and Nipegon 1908," Huntington Library, San Marino, CA, inside cover. The weight is mentioned in Turner to Farrand, 42. Caroline Mae (Sherwood) Turner, "Journal of a Camping Trip, When the Turners Camped with Mr. & Mrs. C. R. Van Hise in Ontario, Canada," Huntington Library, San Marino, CA, 1908, second p. 6, obverse. (This journal is handwritten on loose sheets with the pagination only on one side of each sheet and beginning twice, but separated by a section with dates alone.)

62. Caroline Turner, "Journal," 4 reverse. Van Hise was referring to William Hogarth (1697–1764), a satirical English painter and engraver as well as an art theorist. Turner to Farrand, 41.

63. Caroline Turner, "Journal," 10 reverse.

64. Turner to Farrand, 41. Bogue, *Frederick Jackson Turner*, 202, reports that Turner became an expert on American Indian policy, but he "did not have a sympathetic understanding of tribal cultures." Bogue also quotes a 1906 letter to Charles Van Hise where Turner referred to the Paiute as "the most degrated [sic] & disgusting and lo down aggregation of grasshopper eating savages that disgrace the West." Turner to Farrand, 42–43.

65. Aron, *Working at Play*, 184ff.

66. "An Act to Set Apart a Certain Tract of Land Lying Near the Headwaters of the Yellowstone River as a Public Park, Approved May 1, 1872 (17 Stat.32)," in *America's National Park System: The Critical Documents*, ed. Lary M. Dilsaver (Lanham, MD: Rowman & Littlefield, 1994), 28. When Congress "set apart" Yellowstone and subsequent national park lands from the ordinary world's profane development, it made them sacred. Apartness is a fundamental characteristic of any sacred space, along with otherworldliness, orderliness, and wholeness. See Yi-Fu Tuan, "Sacred Space: Exploration of an Idea," in *Dimensions of Human Geography*, ed. K. W. Butzer (Chicago: University of Chicago, Department of Geography, 1978), 84–99; and Sears, *Sacred Places*. On early local campers see Langdon Smith and William Wyckoff, "Creating Yellowstone: Montanans in the Early Park Years," *Historical Geography* 29 (2001): 93–115; Harry J. Norton, *Wonder-land Illustrated, or, Horseback Rides through the Yellowstone National Park* (Virginia City, MT: H. J. Norton, 1873); Earl of Dunraven, *The Great Divide: Travels in the Upper Yellowstone in the Summer of 1874* (London: Chatto & Windus, 1876). John B. Bachelder, *Popular Resorts, and How to Reach Them*, 4th ed. (Boston: John B. Bachelder, 1876), 18. Today Garden of the Gods is a Colorado Springs, CO, municipal park.

67. Mircea Eliade, *The Sacred and the Profane: The Nature of Religion* (New York: Harcourt, Brace, 1957), 42. Wilbur Zelinsky, "Nationalistic Pilgrimages in the United States," in *Pilgrimage in the United States*, ed. G. Rinschede and S. M. Bhardwaj (Berlin: Dietrich Reimer, 1990), 259, divides National Park Service–managed sites into three categories: nationalistic, Civil War, and other. The last includes all the natural scenic and recreational parks. Zelinsky's division is mistaken because its first category focuses on *historic*-nationalistic sites and misses the *cultural*-nationalistic values wrapped up in the last. Each national park was also "home," a "center" on the American landscape, and in the top rank of camping destinations. Although the idea of "multiple centers" may seem contradictory, it is not, since national parks represent, in the words of geographer Yi-Fu Tuan, *Space and Place*, 150, "a concept in mythic thought rather than a deeply felt value bound to unique events and locality." Like many forms of pilgrimage, camping developed its destinations at a variety of geographic scales. Any natural site away from a town could transform a camper, but the wilder, more scenic national parks were deemed to be higher in the American camping hierarchy and thus more desirable. The mythic character of the national parks is also revealed by their spatial distribution. If the sites had been selected according to some economic rationale, they would not have all been in the west, but would have been distributed for greater accessibility and improved efficiency.

See Chris Park, *Sacred Worlds: An Introduction to Geography and Religion* (New York: Routledge, 1994).

68. Much of this biographical material is drawn from William M. Slaughter's excellent introduction in Mary Bradshaw Richards, *Camping Out in the Yellowstone, 1882*, ed. William M. Slaughter (Salt Lake City: University of Utah Press, 1994), ix–xxxi. See Aron, *Working at Play*, on self-improvement and vacations.

69. See Chittenden, *Yellowstone*; Cowan, "Reminiscences"; Sears, *Sacred Places*; Spence, *Dispossessing*; and Greene, *Nez Perce Summer*.

70. Richards, *Camping Out*, 12; *Statistical History*, 139.

71. Richards, *Camping Out*, 10–11. The letters were assembled in 1910 and published as a book, which subsequently was edited and reprinted as Richards, *Camping Out*, in 1994.

72. Richards, *Camping Out*, 11.

73. Ibid., 21–23. On the national park as frontier see, for instance, her reference to a "prospector" on p. 27, Jack Baronett on p. 43, and the "trail of the Indian and the pioneer" on p. 90.

74. Ibid., 12.

75. Ibid., 15, 16, 17–18.

76. See Judith Meyer, *The Spirit of Yellowstone: The Cultural Evolution of a National Park* (Lanham, MD: Rowman & Littlefield, 1996), on the historic perception of Yellowstone as a unique place. Richards, *Camping Out*, 20.

77. Aubrey L. Haines, *The Yellowstone Story: A History of Our First National Park*, vol. 1 (Yellowstone National Park, WY: Yellowstone Library and Museum Association, 1977), 354, attributes the nickname to a February 28, 1872, story in the *Helena Herald* titled "Our National Park," which applied the term "Wonderland" to the park. Haines also asserts that the name was inspired by Lewis Carroll's *Alice in Wonderland*, published in 1865. See also Chris Magoc, *Yellowstone: The Creation and Selling of an American Landscape, 1870–1903* (Albuquerque: University of New Mexico Press, 1999). I thank Peter Blodgett for bringing this history to my attention. Richards, *Camping Out*, 37–38.

78. Richards, *Camping Out*, 86, 88. Richards quote came from Philippians 4:7.

79. Richards, *Camping Out*, 102. The Richardses' party was particularly lucky because the Grand Geyser's period was variable. Mary knew this, mentioning two Bostonians who, after waiting for three days, failed to see it erupt. Ibid., 106.

80. Marguerite S. Shaffer, *See America First: Tourism and National Identity, 1880–1940* (Washington, DC: Smithsonian Institution Press, 2001), argued that many forms of American tourism, including national park visits, were secular pilgrimages and that they served to create and reinforce American national identity. Campers, however, often distinguished themselves from "tourists," whom they deemed inauthentic.

3. Let's Hit the Motor Camping Trail

1. Canoe pricing taken from two catalogs: Sears, Roebuck and Co., *Spring 1923* (Chicago, 1923), 780, and Abercrombie & Fitch Co., *Camp and Trail* (New York, 1927), 43. A common wall tent for four people, by contrast, cost approximately twenty-five to forty-five dollars from the same outfitters. The 1925 per capita annual income for the United States was $647: see *Statistical History of the United States from Colonial Times to the Present* (Stamford, CT: Fairfield Publishers, 1965), 7, 139. For Rinehart's and the Santa Fe Railroad's impacts see Earl Pomeroy, *In Search of the Golden West: The Tourist in Western America* (New York: Knopf, 1957), 153–54. Dillon Wallace, *The Camper's Handbook* (New York: Fleming H. Revell, 1936), 85.

2. Hrolf Wisby, "A Practical Automobile Touring Outfit," *Scientific American*, March 1, 1902, 134–35.

3. Daniel M. G. Raff and Manuel Trajtenberg, "Quality-Adjusted Prices for the American Automobile Industry: 1906–1940," in *The Economics of New Goods*, ed. Timothy F. Bresnahan and Robert J. Gordon (Chicago: University of Chicago Press, 1997), 77; James J. Flink, *The Automobile Age* (Cambridge, MA: MIT Press, 1990), 33. The 1906 per capita annual income for the United States was $236, but it rose to $301 in 1908 and to $331 in 1916; see *Statistical History*, 7, 139. At the other extreme, the 1910 Packard 30 limousine cost $5,450; see Flink, *Automobile Age*, 35, 37.

4. Cindy S. Aron, *Working at Play: A History of Vacations in the United States* (New York: Oxford University Press, 1999), 209. Robert S. Lynd and Helen Merrell Lynd, *Middletown: A Study in American Culture* (New York: Harcourt, Brace, 1929), 254–55, reported that people were mortgaging their homes to buy cars, but that "75 to 90 per cent of the cars purchased locally are bought on time payment, and a working man earning $35.00 a week frequently plans to use one week's pay each month as a payment for his car." George Thomas Kurian, *Datapedia of the United States: American History in Numbers* (Lanham, MD: Bernan, 2004), 19–20, 307–8. National Automobile Chamber of Commerce, *Facts and Figures of the Automobile Industry* (New York, 1925), 18; and National Automobile Chamber of Commerce, *Facts and Figures of the Automobile Industry, 1931 Edition* (New York, 1931), 46. Lynd and Lynd, *Middletown*, 251.

5. "The Cost of a Transcontinental Auto Journey," *Sunset*, September 1924, 48–49. It would have remained a costly vacation for many if not most Americans, however. According to *Statistical History*, 7, 139, the U.S. per capita annual income in 1924 was only $642, or approximately $1.76 per day. The "cheaper than staying home" argument would continue for many decades. See Susan Sessions Rugh, *Are We There Yet? The Golden Age of American Family Vacations* (Lawrence: University Press of Kansas, 2008), 122–23, and Peter Boag, "Outward Bound: Family, Gender, Environmentalism, and the Postwar Camping Craze, 1945–1970," *Idaho Yesterdays* 50, no. 1 (2009): 3–15.

6. Elon Jessup, *The Motor Camping Book* (New York: G. P. Putnam's Sons, 1921), 3. See Warren James Belasco, *Americans on the Road: From Autocamp to Motel, 1910–1945* (Cambridge, MA: MIT Press, 1979), about the frustration and sense of helplessness that many late nineteenth- and early twentieth-century Americans felt toward railroads. At the same time, if one changed campgrounds daily, the routine of erecting, occupying, and breaking camp could be restricting, too. As John Jakle, *The Tourist: Travel in Twentieth-Century North America* (Lincoln: University of Nebraska Press, 1985), 156, noted, "Camping could offer freedom in theory, but not always in actuality." Belasco also delves into the "gypsy" image claimed by many early automotive enthusiasts. In addition to *The Motor Camping Book*, Jessup wrote *Roughing It Smoothly: How to Avoid Vacation Pitfalls* (New York: G. P. Putnam's Sons, 1923) and *Camp Grub: An Out-of-Doors Cooking Manual* (New York: E. P. Dutton, 1924). He also wrote books on golf, winter sports, and canoeing. He again became a freelance writer after he departed *Outing* magazine, frequently contributing pieces to the *New York Times* until 1952. Jessup, *Motor Camping*, 5. Jessup's work as a correspondent had taken him to a variety of domestic and foreign destinations, including Serbia, Sweden, and Holland.

7. Jessup, *Roughing It*, 203. Kathleen Franz, *Tinkering: Consumers Reinvent the Early Automobile* (Philadelphia: University of Pennsylvania Press, 2005), 58–66, provides a persuasive and insightful critique of this "companionate" view of auto camping, which presents masculine domesticity and family interactions as increased. Franz argues that it also limited women's access to mechanical knowledge and reinforced traditional gender relations. See also Belasco, *Americans*, and Flink, *Automobile Age*.

8. Gary Cross, *Time and Money: The Making of Consumer Culture* (New York: Routledge, 1993), 78–81, 95. See also Aron, *Working at Play*, 183–205.

9. Emerson Hough, *Maw's Vacation: The Story of a Human Being in the Yellowstone* (Saint Paul, MN: J. E. Haynes, 1921), 5–6.

10. Elon Jessup, "The Flight of the Tin Can Tourists," *Outlook*, May 25, 1921, 166. The Vagabonds would auto camp together again in 1923 and 1924. See Norman Brauer,

There to Breathe the Beauty: The Camping Trips of Henry Ford, Thomas Edison, Harvey Firestone, John Burroughs (Dalton, PA: Norman Brauer, 1995). Belasco, *Americans*, 74; Earl C. May, "The Argonauts of the Automobile," *Saturday Evening Post*, August 9, 1924, 25; Frank E. Brimmer, *Motor Campcraft* (New York: Macmillan, 1923), 1; Frank E. Brimmer, "Autocamping—the Fastest-Growing Sport," *Outlook*, July 16, 1924, 439; Frank E. Brimmer, *Coleman Motor Campers Manual* (Wichita, KS: Coleman Lamp Co., 1926), 4.

11. Automobiles were initially banned from the national parks, but they entered Mount Rainier National Park in 1908, General Grant NP in 1910, Crater Lake NP in 1911, Glacier NP in 1912, Yosemite and Sequoia NPs in 1913, Mesa Verde NP in 1914, and Yellowstone NP in 1915. For more on the sometimes contentious lifting of the ban see Richard Bartlett, "Those Infernal Machines in Yellowstone Park," *Montana, the Magazine of Western History* 20, no. 3 (1970): 16–29; Richard Lilliard, "The Siege and Conquest of a National Park," *American West*, January 1968, 29–32, 67–72; and David Louter, *Windshield Wilderness: Cars, Roads, and Nature in Washington's National Parks* (Seattle: University of Washington Press, 2006). Marion Clawson and Carlton S. Van Doren, eds., *Statistics on Outdoor Recreation*, Part 1, *The Record through 1956*, and Part 2, *The Record since 1956* (Washington, DC: Resources for the Future, 1984), 22–23. Theodore Catton, *National Park, City Playground: Mount Rainier in the Twentieth Century* (Seattle: University of Washington Press, 2006), 91, reported that hotel occupancy plummeted at Mount Rainier National Park between 1931 and 1933 and then remained depressed for years, while campground use in the park increased. An analysis by the U.S. Department of the Interior, *Report of the Director of the National Park Service to the Secretary of the Interior* (Washington, DC: Government Printing Office) for the years 1920 to 1925 reveals that the combined visitation to Crater Lake, General Grant, Glacier, Mesa Verde, Mount Rainier, Rocky Mountain, Sequoia, Wind Cave, Yellowstone, and Yosemite National Parks grew from 205,857 in 1916 to 1,040,949 in 1925, a 405 percent increase, but that the number of automobiles entering during the same period rose from 29,358 to 257,426, a 777 percent increase. Lloyd M. Brett, letter to Secretary of the Interior, September 30, 1915, RG 79, Records of the National Park Service, appendix 1, Central Files, 1907–1939 (hereafter NPS-1), National Parks: Yellowstone, Reports, Annual, box 240, U.S. National Archives, College Park, MD (hereafter NA), 3. Three privately operated "camping companies" operated permanent tourist settlements of fixed, tent-based accommodations at Yellowstone National Park in 1915—Wylie Permanent Camping Co., Shaw & Powell Camping Co., and Hefferlin Camps. For a history of these concessionaires see Richard A. Bartlett, *Yellowstone: A Wilderness Besieged* (Tucson: University of Arizona Press, 1985); and on the management of all early national park concessions see Peter J. Blodgett, "Striking a Balance: Managing Concessions in the National Parks, 1916–1933," *Forest & Conservation History* 34, no. 2 (1990): 60–68. Horace M. Albright, letter to Director, National Park Service, September 27, 1923, NPS-1, National Parks: Yellowstone, Reports, Annual, box 241, NA, 8–9. National Park Service, *A Study of the Park and Recreation Problem of the United States* (Washington, DC: Government Printing Office, 1941), 14, 18.

12. The number of magazine articles is derived from an analysis of *Readers' Guide to Periodical Literature* for the period. Articles that focused on countries outside the United States or on backpacking, canoe camping, packhorse camping, and camping with an automobile trailer are excluded. The book publication figures are derived from the Library of Congress and Harvard University catalogs, and while they are similarly edited for locale and technique, manufacturer catalogs, archival collections, and publications produced by local, state, and national government agencies are also excluded.

13. Hrolf Wisby, "Camping Out with an Automobile," *Outing*, March 1905, 739. Robert Sloss, "Camping in an Automobile," *Outing*, May 1910, 236–37, made a similar comparison between the horse and automobile: "Annihilator of distances that it is, the automobile makes possible many things to the outdoor man that would be beyond his reach, if he had only shank's mare to depend upon." Many Americans have felt that technology and nature can be reconciled. Leo Marx, *The Machine in the Garden: Technology and the Pastoral Ideal in*

America (New York: Oxford University Press, 1964), referred to their blending as the "middle landscape." See also Jennifer Price, *Flight Maps: Adventures with Nature in Modern America* (New York: Basic Books, 1999), who explored what she called the mixing of "nature and artifice." Louter, *Windshield Wilderness*, investigated the vision and impact of those Americans who, like Wisby and Sloss, found automobiles and wilderness compatible, even beneficial. Paul S. Sutter, *Driven Wild: How the Fight against Automobiles Launched the Modern Wilderness Movement* (Seattle: University of Washington Press, 2002), took the opposite tack to insightfully reveal the connections between the wilderness movement's leading advocates and their rejection of cars in the wild.

14. "Home Comforts in Outdoor Life," *Craftsman*, June 1913, 340. This urban-escape refrain would continue to be heard among car campers for decades to come. See Boag, "Outward Bound," who identifies it as a commonly identified motivator during the post–World War II era. J. C. Long, "The Week-End Wild Man," *Outlook*, July 12, 1922, 466; Wilborn J. Deason, *Nature's Silent Call* (Waukegan, IL: Bunting, 1925), 6–7; Long, "Week-End Wild Man," 466; "Neighbors for a Night," *Literary Digest*, August 30, 1924, 45.

15. Ryland P. Madison, "An Automobile Camping Trip," *Country Life in America*, June 11, 1911, 52.

16. Sloss, "Camping," 236.

17. Wallace, *Camper's Handbook*, 10–11.

18. J. W. Sutphen, "Desert Camps," *Outing*, May 1916, 152; "Home Comforts," 340–41; "Sleeping in the Car," *Outing*, May 1919, 106.

19. Sutphen, "Desert Camps," 152; Sloss, "Camping," 236.

20. "Neighbors for a Night," 44.

21. Ibid. According to this article, 45, "The sagebrusher is so called to distinguish him from a dude." Dudes arrived at Yellowstone National Park on the train, while the sagebrusher, "cutting loose from effeteness," brought all the family, including the dog, "and lets his adventurous, pioneering spirit riot here in the mountain air." See also Horace M. Albright and Frank J. Taylor, *"Oh Ranger!" A Book about the National Parks* (Palo Alto, CA: Stanford University Press, 1928). "Neighbors for a Night," 46. Robert Sterling Yard, "The People and the National Parks," *Survey* 48, no. 13 (1922): 583, agreed that campers "redemocratized" in a national park as they sat "around the evening camp fire with a California grape grower, a locomotive engineer from Massachusetts and banker from Michigan. Here the social differences so insisted on at home just don't exist." As a consequence of this mingling, Yard insisted, one found a "total absence of sectionalism. . . . In the national parks all are just Americans." Chris Park, in *Sacred Worlds: An Introduction to Geography and Religion* (New York: Routledge, 1994), noted that political integration and social mixing are common features of pilgrimage.

22. Charles G. Percival, "Coast to Coast Tour," in *Percival's Motor Tourist Camp Manual* (New York: American Tourist Camp Association, 1927), 4; Long, "Week-End Wild Man," 466.

23. "The Call of the Open Road," *Country Life*, June 2, 1923, 112; Wallace, *Camper's Handbook*, 11. Deason, *Nature's Silent Call*, 3, asserts that the human desire to get into the wild is instinctual and offers a Lamarckian explanation for why "the white man, with his superior intellect, often loses or at least disregards these forces of instinct."

24. "Call of the Open Road," 112. A tourist-camper dichotomy was persistent, if vague and flexible. The authors of prescriptive literature before auto camping became common, such as Horace Kephart, sometimes condemned the use of guides and other conveniences, dismissing anyone who used them as "tourists" rather than campers. See chapter 2.

25. "Home Comforts," 340. William Cronon, "The Trouble with Wilderness; or, Getting Back to the Wrong Nature," in *Uncommon Ground: Toward Reinventing Nature*, ed. W. Cronon (New York: W. W. Norton, 1995), 78, pointed out that "one went to the wilderness not as a producer but as a consumer." Consequently, it is unsurprising that camping should change as a result of consumerist pressure.

26. "Call of the Open Road," 112; Brimmer, *Motor Campcraft*, 15.

27. Thaddeus S. Dayton, "Camping Out with an 'Auto,' " *Harper's Weekly*, September 2, 1911, 12; Wisby, "Camping Out," 739, 745. Franz, *Tinkering*, 25–40, talks about the rapid growth of the automobile accessory industry and its merchants during the 1910s and 1920s, including auto-camping items. An example of a running-board carrier design can be found in Jessup, *Motor Camping*, chapter 3.

28. "Get Ready Now for Vacation Days," *Field and Stream*, June 1917, 179; "Hawkeye Basket Refrigerator," *Field and Stream*, July 1920, 320.

29. "Motor Rambling," *Field and Stream*, July 1920, 289. The outfit's items and prices were not listed in the advertisement. Instead the reader was directed to request a catalog. See Abercrombie & Fitch Co., *Camp and Trail*, 44. By comparison, the F. J. Burch Co., Pueblo, CO, sold a nine-piece "auto camp outfit for two persons," including tent, bed, chairs, stove, table, basin, and two bags, for forty-eight dollars. See *Outers' Recreation*, June 1923, 49. Brimmer, *Coleman*, 7, estimated that "the average outfit of thousands of campers cost $198 entire; replacement for outfits that had been in use averaged $58 a year."

30. "Carry Your Camp on the Running Board," *Field and Stream*, June 1917, 185; "Campers! Be Sure to Take Along Carnation Milk," *Outing*, September 1918, 385; "Listerine for the Camp First Aid Kit," *Literary Digest*, July 3, 1920, 92.

31. National Bureau of Economic Research, "Census U.S. Decennial County Population Data, 1900–1990," http://www.nber.org/data/census-decennial-population.html.

32. Gas lighting's history is detailed in a Smithsonian Institution exhibit catalog by William E. Worthington Jr., *Beyond the City Lights: American Domestic Gas Lighting Systems* (Washington, DC: Smithsonian Institution, 1985).

33. Early electric lightbulbs used carbon filaments, which glowed at approximately fifteen to thirty candlepower and were not bright by twenty-first-century standards. Tungsten filament lightbulbs, which can produce much greater light, were introduced in 1911.

34. According to Herb Ebendorf, "The Coleman Story," unpublished manuscript, Coleman Company Inc. records (Wichita, KS, n.d.), 2, Coleman had eyesight so poor that he could not read at night by oil, gas, or electric lights, but when he first encountered a gasoline-pressure lamp on a February 1899 evening in a shop in Blocton, Alabama, he found "he could read the gold labels on the apothecary jars and, on closer inspection, read the lettering on the cartons holding the patent medicine bottles." After some inquiries and contemplation, he concluded that these lamps held more promise for him than did typewriters. Herb Ebendorf, *Gas from Gasoline* (Wichita, KS: Coleman Co., 1985), 11.

35. Ebendorf, "Coleman Story," 22. Ebendorf was the Coleman Company historian.

36. Ibid., 20. The production figures are from "Coleman Shipping Records, 1905–1933," Charleen Becker, compiler, unpublished manuscript, Coleman Company Inc. records (Wichita, KS, 1997).

37. Ebendorf, "Coleman Story," 23; Bliss Isely, "The Coleman Company's Forty Years," unpublished manuscript, Coleman Company Inc. records (Wichita, KS, ca. 1940), 34; "For Campers," *Field and Stream*, June 1917, 185. All figures are from "Coleman Shipping Records," which reports that the company sold eight lantern versions during 1917 for a combined total of 23,685 units shipped. In 1918, it shipped 27,884 Quick-Lite lanterns alone, plus 9,761 units of six other lantern versions.

38. Herb Ebendorf, "Notes on the Gasoline Camp Stove," unpublished manuscript, Coleman Company Inc. records (Wichita, KS, 1983), 1; "Coleman Shipping Records."

39. "Coleman Stove Expert on Tour of Tourist Camps," *Wichita Beacon*, July 16, 1925, 2; Brimmer, *Coleman*, 14; Ebendorf, "Coleman Story," 40, 37, 38.

40. "When do we eat?," advertising brochure, Coleman Company Inc. records (Wichita, KS, n.d.), promoted Coleman camp stoves numbers 2 and 9. A mid-1920s date is inferred because the company switched production from the number 1 camp stove to numbers 2 and 9 in mid-1924 and continued to produce them through the remainder of the decade. See "Coleman Shipping Records." Brimmer, *Coleman*, 36.

41. Brimmer, *Coleman*, 6, 9. Coleman Lamp Company, "Coleman Camp Stove—It's a Miniature Kitchen Range," advertising brochure (Wichita, KS, n.d.). Coleman Lamp and Stove Company, "Coleman Camp Stove—'The Smooth Way to Rough It,'" advertising brochure (Wichita, KS, n.d.). The date is inferred because the company's name has changed on the brochure from the Coleman Lamp Company to the Coleman Lamp and Stove Company, which Ebendorf, "Coleman Story," 28, records as occurring in April 1926.

42. Mary Crehore Bedell, *Modern Gypsies: The Story of a Twelve Thousand Mile Motor Camping Trip Encircling the United States* (New York: Brentano's, 1924), 12–13. Mary was born in 1870 and Fred in 1868.

43. Frederic F. Van de Water, *The Family Flivvers to Frisco* (New York: D. Appleton, 1927), 25, 26, 27. Frederic, born in 1890, was thirty-six at the time of the vacation, but his wife's age is uncertain.

44. Bedell, *Modern Gypsies*, 34–35, 56, 76.

45. Ibid., 144; Jan Gordon and Cora J. Gordon, *On Wandering Wheels: Through Roadside Camps from Maine to Georgia in an Old Sedan Car* (New York: Dodd, Mead, 1928), 50; Van de Water, *Family Flivvers*, 49, 50.

46. Charles Erskine Scott Wood, "June 27–August 1, 1928 trip from Los Gatos to Bend, Oregon and back," handwritten notes in bound journal, folder 4, box 29, Papers of C. E. S. Wood, Huntington Library, San Marino, CA, June 27. The diary's title is incorrect because Wood's notes indicated that the camping trip began on June 20, 1928. The journal is not paginated but is subdivided by date.

47. Maud M. Keck, "Amateur Campers," *Sunset*, May 1922, 92. See also Wood, "June 27," June 30, on his trials with mice.

48. Van de Water, *Family Flivvers*, 132, 133.

49. Keck, "Amateur Campers," 91; Bedell, *Modern Gypsies*, 129–130; italics in original.

50. Van de Water, *Family Flivvers*, 30, 32; Wood, "June 27," June 27; Van de Water, *Family Flivvers*, 55. Gordon and Gordon, *On Wandering Wheels*, 87. At the same time, on p. 83, they note that among the auto-camping couples who did not really like to camp, but were doing so because it was simply inexpensive, the men were least satisfied. Franz, *Tinkering*, 58–73, thoughtfully explored the issue of "motor wives" and how the period's expanding array of equipment may have only made the gender inequality of camping chores more entrenched. Erica Morin, "'No Vacation for Mother': Traditional Gender Roles in Outdoor Travel Literature, 1940–1965," *Women's Studies* 41 (2012): 436–56, reached a related conclusion about camping's gender responsibilities during later decades, especially after World War II. According to the back cover of Charmaine Severson, *The I Hate to Camp Book* (New Canaan, CT: Tobey, 1973), "This book is for those wives and mothers who, every summer, find it impossible to avoid the 'great outdoors.'" In contrast, Boag, "Outward Bound," argues that post–World War II car camping provided a satisfying arena for the practice of idealized gender roles by both women and men.

51. Virginia Scharff, introduction in *Twenty Thousand Roads: Women, Movement, and the West* (Berkeley: University of California Press, 2003), 3; Keck, "Amateur Campers," 90–91. Kathryn Hulme, *How's the Road?* (San Francisco: Kathryn Hulme, 1928), recounts a similar, if longer, trip by her and "Tuny," a woman friend, from New York to San Francisco in June 1923. Marguerite S. Shaffer, "Seeing America First: The Search for Identity in the Tourist Landscape," in *Seeing and Being Seen: Tourism in the American West*, ed. David M. Wrobel and Patrick T. Long (Lawrence: University Press of Kansas, 2001), 182, called Hulme and her friend's travels "a declaration of independence" and an assertion of "their rights as women to enjoy the public sphere defined by the road and the automobile." Bedell, *Modern Gypsies*, 73–74; Van de Water, *Family Flivvers*, 188, 187. For similar accounts of women auto campers see Winifred Hawkridge Dixon, *Westward Hoboes* (New York: C. Scribner's Sons, 1921), and Joanne Wilke, *Eight Women, Two Model Ts, and the American West* (Lincoln: University of Nebraska Press, 2007). On competing discourses see Park, *Sacred Worlds*, and

John Eade and Michael J. Sallnow, eds., *Contesting the Sacred: The Anthropology of Christian Pilgrimage* (New York: Routledge, 1991).

52. Keck, "Amateur Campers," 91.

53. Wood, "June 27," June 23; Bedell, *Modern Gypsies*, 11; Van de Water, *Family Flivvers*, 12.

54. Keck, "Amateur Campers," 91; Van de Water, *Family Flivvers*, 59; "Call of the Open Road," 112.

55. Van de Water, *Family Flivvers*, 49. Herbert Evison, "The Problem of the Gypsy Automobilist," *American Forestry* 31 (May 1925): 273–74, also rejects this type of camper and argues that the U.S. Forest Service should require a fee for the use of its developed campgrounds. Belasco, *Americans*, 105–28, explores "pay camps" as a response to "undesirables" staying at free municipal auto campgrounds.

56. Bedell, *Modern Gypsies*, 11. For another example of discovery while on a pilgrimage see Simon Coleman and John Elsner, *Pilgrimage Past and Present: Sacred Travel and Sacred Space in the World Religions* (London: British Museum Press, 1995), 66–67, who discuss Malcolm X's unexpected self-discoveries on the hajj to Mecca. Van de Water, *Family Flivvers*, 85–86. Infantile paralysis was a common name for the infectious disease poliomyelitis. See Patrick McGreevy, "Niagara as Jerusalem," *Landscape* 28, no. 2 (1985): 26–32, who discusses how visitors to Niagara Falls have similarly expected unusual occurrences.

57. Gordon and Gordon, *On Wandering Wheels*, 85.

58. Bedell, *Modern Gypsies*, 129, 144–45.

59. Van de Water, *Family Flivvers*, 14, 15, 16.

60. Ibid., 6. Van de Water is also discussing the conversion of distant, relatively abstract spaces into meaningful places through personal experience, which is common on pilgrimages. See Nancy Louise Frey, *Pilgrim Stories: On and Off the Road to Santiago* (Berkeley: University of California Press, 1998). Van de Water, *Family Flivvers*, 144; Leo A. Borah, "Patriotic Pilgrimage to Eastern National Parks," *National Geographic*, June 1934, 663. Frey, *Pilgrim Stories*, notes that current pilgrims to Santiago de Compostela similarly are pleased to be following the same route as their predecessors.

61. The Van de Waters were, in effect, becoming more authentic as their long travel became more apparent. Frey, *Pilgrim Stories*, found that the authenticity of a pilgrim to Santiago de Compostela also rose among other pilgrims the longer she or he had been on the road. Van de Water, *Family Flivvers*, 43.

62. Van de Water, *Family Flivvers*, 194, 203, 200.

63. Ibid., 199. Gwen Kennedy Neville, *Kinship and Pilgrimage: Rituals of Reunion in American Protestant Culture* (New York: Oxford University Press, 1987), 20, argues that Americans, whose culture is embedded in Protestant Christianity, tend to regard rural areas as home. "The actual repeated journey made by the Protestant pilgrim is not one of going *out* as in the classical pilgrimage but one going *back* periodically as a way of escaping the individuation and depersonalization experienced as a member of a scattered, mobile, and often anonymous urban industrial society." The motor-camping Van de Waters apparently felt this way when at Yellowstone National Park. The Van de Waters' conclusion that Yellowstone was "home" fits into the common American perception that the nation's true home is in wilderness. See Cronon, "Trouble," who offers a thoughtful and influential argument about the historic American relationship between wild and urban areas.

64. Van de Water, *Family Flivvers*, 200. Frey, *Pilgrim Stories*, notes that some contemporary pilgrims feel more "European" after completing their travels to Santiago de Compostela. Bedell, *Modern Gypsies*, 172; Wood, "June 27," June 24.

65. Van de Water, *Family Flivvers*, 240.

66. Ibid., 8, italics in original; Bedell, *Modern Gypsies*, 261, 262. Frey, *Pilgrim Stories*, notes that a return from pilgrimage does not guarantee a permanent transformation, so many pilgrims seek to repeat their travels.

4. The Garage in the Forest

1. Sacred places are not all equal. Rather, they occur at a variety of scales, and some rank higher than others. William Cronon, "The Trouble with Wilderness; or, Getting Back to the Wrong Nature," in *Uncommon Ground: Toward Reinventing Nature*, ed. William Cronon (New York: W. W. Norton, 1995), 75–76, noted how wild places had been perceived at different scales by John Muir, Henry David Thoreau, and William Wordsworth. Thomas R. Dunlap, *Faith in Nature: Environmentalism as Religious Quest* (Seattle: University of Washington Press, 2004), 71, similarly argued that Sigurd Olson ranked wilderness above other types of protected nature. See also Chris Park, *Sacred Worlds: An Introduction to Geography and Religion* (New York: Routledge, 1994).

2. Warren James Belasco, *Americans on the Road: From Autocamp to Motel, 1910–1945* (Cambridge, MA: MIT Press, 1979), 71.

3. J. W. Gregg, "The Automobile Camping Ground—a New Element in Park Design," *Architect and Engineer* 57 (1919): 64–65. Plans from other sites were soon available to guide small towns that were considering how to improve their own auto campgrounds. See, for example, Rolland Schanel Wallis, *Tourist Camps* (Ames: Iowa State College of Agriculture and Mechanic Arts, 1923), and Calvert S. Winsborough, "Automobile Tourist Camping Grounds," *Roads and Streets*, May 1923: 987–92.

4. Gregg, "Automobile Camping Ground," 64; Wallis, *Tourist Camps*, 40; Mary Crehore Bedell, *Modern Gypsies: The Story of a Twelve Thousand Mile Motor Camping Trip Encircling the United States* (New York: Brentano's, 1924), 171–72; Earl Pomeroy, *In Search of the Golden West: The Tourist in Western America* (New York: Knopf, 1957), 148; and Belasco, *Americans*, 72. Rebecca N. Porter, "The New Hospitality," *Scribner's Magazine*, June 1921, 735. The size and layout of Overland Park are noted in Belasco, *Americans*, 71–72. Elon Jessup, "The Flight of the Tin Can Tourist," *Outing*, May 25, 1921, 168, asserts that Overland Park had been "an old race track" before it became a campground. According to Belasco, *Americans*, 71–72, Seattle and Omaha had similarly extensive municipal auto camps. Frank E. Brimmer, "Autocamping—the Fastest-Growing Sport," *Outlook*, July 16, 1924, 439. Private organizations dedicated to the promotion of named highways like the Ocean-to-Ocean Highway or the Lincoln Highway were common at this time. The National Park-to-Park Highway Association formed in 1916 to create and promote a highway that would pass through eleven states and link the twelve western national parks together for motor campers. See Lee Whitely and Jane Whitely, *The Playground Trail: The National Park-to-Park Highway; To and through the National Parks of the West in 1920* (Boulder, CO: Johnson Printing, 2003).

5. Fees and other controls are discussed in Belasco, *Americans*, 121–27. Herbert Evison, "The Problem of the Gypsy Automobilist," *American Forests and Forest Life* 31 (May 1925): 273. The limits of private campgrounds are highlighted in John A. Jakle, *The Tourist: Travel in Twentieth-Century North America* (Lincoln: University of Nebraska Press, 1985), 160. This trend toward privatization and catering to short-stay travelers would lead to the motor court and motel. See Belasco, *Americans*. Marion Clawson and Carlton S. Van Doren, eds., *Statistics on Outdoor Recreation*, Part 1, *The Record through 1956*, and Part 2, *The Record Since 1956* (Washington, DC: Resources for the Future, 1984), 63.

6. Earl E. Bachman, *Recreation Facilities: A Personal History of Their Development in the National Forests of California* (San Francisco: Government Printing Office, 1967), 2; U.S. Forest Service, *Handbook for Campers in the National Forests in California* (Washington, DC: Government Printing Office, 1915), 3.

7. William C. Tweed, "Recreation Site Planning and Improvements in National Forests, 1891–1942," Forest Service, FS-354 (Washington, DC: Government Printing Office, 1980), 4. Before 1918, Frank Waugh wrote several publications that touched on camping. See, for instance, Frank A. Waugh, *The Natural Style in Landscape Gardening* (Boston: R. G. Badger,

1917). The Agricultural College is now the University of Massachusetts. USFS chief forester Henry Graves and assistant forester Edward A. Sherman hired Waugh to tour the national forests and offer his recommendations. According to Tom Wolf, *Arthur Carhart: Wilderness Prophet* (Boulder: University Press of Colorado, 2008), 37, Waugh and Sherman were "personal friends." Frank Waugh, *Recreation Uses on the National Forests* (Washington, DC: US Department of Agriculture, Forest Service, 1918), 8.

8. Carhart's background is discussed in Robert W. Cermak, "In the Beginning: The First National Forest Recreation Plan," *Parks and Recreation* 9, no. 11 (1974): 20–31, and Wolf, *Arthur Carhart*; Arthur H. Carhart, "Recreation in the Forests," *American Forestry* 26 (1920): 269.

9. Hamel's response to the request for campground facilities is noted in Cermak, "In the Beginning," 22; See also Wolf, *Arthur Carhart*, 25, 86–89, and Jack McCrory, letter to the author, June 15, 2004. Cermak, "In the Beginning," 30. See also Arthur H. Carhart, "Historical Development of Outdoor Recreation," in *Outdoor Recreation Literature: A Survey; Report to the Outdoor Recreation Resources Review Commission by the Librarian of Congress* (Washington, DC: Government Printing Office, 1962), 112, for his interpretation of the development of these campgrounds. According to Tweed, "Recreation Site Planning," 8–9, this public-private collaboration became a model for national forest development during the 1920s. Bachman, *Recreation Facilities*, 2–3, relates that during this same decade, the California State Automobile Association, the Automobile Association of Southern California, and the Rotary Club worked cooperatively with the Forest Service to develop public camping facilities in California's national forests.

10. Quoted in Bachman, *Recreation Facilities*, 3. The 1925 appropriation amount is in Tweed, "Recreation Site Planning," 12. Ibid., 12–13. Carhart, "Historical Development," 115, provided the fire budget figure. The 1920 and 1930 values are from Kenneth O. Maughan, "Recreational Development in the National Forests: A Study of the Present Recreational Use and a Suggested Plan for Future Development together with a Recreational Management Plan for the Wasatch National Forest, Utah," *Bulletin of the New York State College of Forestry at Syracuse University* 7, no. 1a (May 1934): 39. The 1940 figure is from Clawson and Van Doren, eds., *Statistics*, 36. The U.S. Forest Service initially responded slowly to the arrival of recreationists in general and to motor campers specifically. See Donald F. Cate, "Recreation and the U.S. Forest Service: A Study of Organizational Response to Changing Demands" (PhD diss., Stanford University, 1963); Tweed, "Recreation Site Planning"; and Bachman, *Recreation Facilities*.

11. The national parks were administered by the U.S. Army before 1916. See H. Duane Hampton, *How the U.S. Cavalry Saved Our National Parks* (Bloomington: Indiana University Press, 1971). Lary M. Dilsaver, "Stemming the Flow: The Evolution of Controls on Visitor Numbers and Impact in National Parks," in *The American Environment: Interpretations of Past Geographies*, ed. Lary M. Dilsaver and Craig E. Colten (Lanham, MD: Rowman & Littlefield, 1992), 238. Whitely and Whitely, *Playground Trail*; Richard West Sellars, *Preserving Nature in the National Parks: A History* (New Haven, CT: Yale University Press, 1997), 59–60.

12. Stephen T. Mather, "Progress in the National Parks," *Sierra Club Bulletin* 11, no. 1 (1920): 5; Franklin K. Lane, letter to Stephen T. Mather, May 13, 1918, in *America's National Park System: The Critical Documents*, ed. Lary M. Dilsaver (Lanham, MD: Rowman & Littlefield, 1994), 50; Belasco, *Americans*, 93 on the 1919 statistic and Peter J. Schmitt, *Back to Nature: The Arcadian Myth in Urban America* (Baltimore: Johns Hopkins University Press, 1990), 162 on the 1922 statistic; Lary M. Dilsaver and William C. Tweed, *Challenge of the Big Trees* (Three Rivers, CA: Sequoia Natural History Association, 1990), 139. Stanford E. Demars, *The Tourist in Yosemite, 1855–1985* (Salt Lake City: University of Utah Press, 1991), 101. By comparison, only twenty-eight hundred stayed in Yosemite Valley's hotels and hotel camps.

13. Bedell, *Modern Gypsies*, 148; Frederic F. Van de Water, *The Family Flivvers to Frisco* (New York: D. Appleton, 1927), 203.

14. At the same time, campers had to be a hardy and well-prepared lot because drinking water and sanitary facilities were generally scarce. Demars, *Tourist*, 55, 62; see also Linda Wedel Greene, *Yosemite: The Park and Its Resources*, 3 vols. (Washington, DC: U.S. Department of the Interior, National Park Service, 1981), 458. Ethan Carr, *Wilderness by Design: Landscape Architecture and the National Park Service* (Lincoln: University of Nebraska Press, 1998), 88; Linda Flint McClelland, *Building the National Parks: Historic Landscape Design and Construction* (Baltimore: Johns Hopkins University Press, 1998), 144. See also Carr, *Wilderness by Design*, 88–89. See Dilsaver and Tweed, *Challenge*, 138–39 on Sequoia National Park, and Theodore R. Catton, *National Park, City Playground: Mount Rainier in the Twentieth Century* (Seattle: University of Washington Press, 2006) on Mount Rainier National Park.

15. See Dilsaver, "Stemming the Flow," 236, 251–52.

16. Mary Bradshaw Richards, *Camping Out in the Yellowstone, 1882*, ed. William W. Slaughter (Salt Lake City: University of Utah Press, 1994), 38. U.S. Department of the Interior, *Report of the Secretary of the Interior for the Fiscal Year Ended June 30, 1892* (Washington, DC: Government Printing Office, 1892), 134. A few years later, in the summer of 1905, the superintendent of Mount Rainier National Park moved beyond simple scrutiny and suasion: he had a camper arrested for cutting green timber. See Catton, *National Park*, 45. Henry F. Lincoln, letter to C. C. Smith, August 29, 1908, RG 79, Records of the National Park Service, Central Files, 1907–1939 (hereafter NPS-1), "Sanitation," box 196, U.S. National Archives, College Park, MD (hereafter NA), 2. Smith was a captain in the Fourteenth U.S. Cavalry and acting superintendent of Sequoia and General Grant National Parks. R. B. Dole, letter to Secretary of the Interior, December 30, 1913, RG 79, Records of the National Park Service, appendix 2, Central Classified Files, 1907–1949 (hereafter NPS-2), "Yosemite-Sanitation-General," box 536, NA, 3. The multi-decadal struggle to manage sewage and garbage in Yosemite is detailed in Craig E. Colten and Lary M. Dilsaver, "The Devil in the Cathedral: Sewage and Garbage in Yosemite National Park," in *Cities and Nature in the American West*, ed. Char Miller (Reno: University of Nevada Press, 2010), 154–70.

17. Demars, *Tourist*, 139.

18. See L. F. Kneipp, "Camping Sites in Public Parks and Forests," *Annals of the American Academy of Political and Social Science* 116 (1924): 62–66, on the damage at and around campgrounds. See also "Motor Camping Presents Many Problems: Poor Conditions in Some Sites a Drawback to Out-Door Life—Fail to Attract Even the Hardened Traveler," *Automobile Topics* 75, no. 1 (August 16, 1924): 37–39, 44, on the poor conditions at many public municipal campgrounds; and McClelland, *Building*, 277, on the abandonment of park campgrounds. Robert Marshall, *The People's Forests* (New York: Harrison Smith and Robert Haas, 1933), 185.

19. Vegetation management policies are discussed in Dilsaver and Tweed, *Challenge*, 144. Punchard is quoted in *Annual Report of the Department of the Interior for the Fiscal Year Ended June 30, 1920* (Washington, DC: Government Printing Office, 1920), 336. White quoted in Dilsaver and Tweed, *Challenge*, 136; Fry's efforts are detailed ibid. An increase in public use can follow an effort to mitigate the environmental damage caused by earlier use. See Lary M. Dilsaver and William Wyckoff, "Agency Culture, Cumulative Causation and Development in Glacier National Park, Montana," *Journal of Historical Geography* 25 (1999): 75–92.

20. Dilsaver, "Stemming the Flow," 243; Dilsaver and Tweed, *Challenge*, 136; John R. White, "Superintendent's Monthly Report for May 1924," NPS-1, Sequoia-Monthly Reports 1920–1925, "From Oct. 1, 1923 to July 13, 1925," box 193, NA, 5.

21. John R. White, "Superintendent's Monthly Report for October 1925," Superintendent's Monthly Reports, SEQU 1919–1928, "Manuscript T," box 1, Library, Sequoia National Park, Three Rivers, CA (hereafter LSNP), 3. William A. Taylor, letter to John R. White, November 17, 1925, box 275, LSNP.

22. E. P. Meinecke, "Memorandum on the Effects of Tourist Traffic on Plant Life, Particularly Big Trees, Sequoia National Park, California, May 13–16, 1926," Archives, Library, U.S. Forest Service, Region 5 (Vallejo, CA), 1.

23. I liberally borrow biographical material from Frederick S. Baker, "We Present: Emilio Pepe Michael Meinecke," *Journal of Forestry* 46 (1948): 302; W. W. Wagener, Carl Hartley, and J. S. Boyce, "Emilio Pepe Michael Meinecke," *Phytopathology* 47 (1957): 633; and "Dr. E. P. Meinecke, 88, Famed Botanist, Dies," *San Francisco Examiner,* February 10, 1957.

24. Baker, "We Present," 302.

25. Ibid., 303; Wagener, Hartley, and Boyce, "Emilio," 634; and "Emilio Pepe Michael Meinecke (1869–1957)," *Journal of Forestry* 55 (1957): 316.

26. See *Proceedings of the National Parks Conference Held at Berkeley, California, March 11, 12, and 13, 1915* (Washington: Government Printing Office, 1915), 5, which mistakenly lists "C. P. Meinecke" as an attendee. See Carl Hartley, letter to E. P. Meinecke, August 3, 1925, RG 54, Records of the Bureau of Plant Industry, Soils, and Agricultural Engineering, entry 80, box 47, NA. John R. White, "Superintendent's Monthly Report for May 1926," Superintendent's Monthly Reports, SEQU 1919–1928, "Manuscript T," box 1, LSNP, 2.

27. Meinecke, "Memorandum," 12; E. P. Meinecke, "Tree Giants in the Sequoia Groves Are Menaced by Tourists," in *Yearbook of Agriculture—1927* (Washington, DC: Government Printing Office, 1928), 633; Meinecke, "Memorandum," 3, 9, 10, 4, 11.

28. Meinecke, "Memorandum," 2. Meinecke made no overt references to pilgrimage or to the redwoods as specifically sacred, but he was deeply concerned not to introduce urban-style management to the site. Meinecke, "Memorandum," 11–19; see also Dilsaver and Tweed, *Challenge,* 144–45, 148. The vegetation in Giant Forest was so damaged that the park's Ash Mountain nursery was expanded a few years later to supply new trees and shrubs. See Dilsaver and Tweed, *Challenge,* 148. The final phase of revegetation began in 1974, but the park continued to have campgrounds in the Giant Forest area until the late 1990s when these facilities were finally removed and the sites restored; the project was completed in 2005. See National Park Service, Sequoia and Kings Canyon National Parks, "Giant Forest Restoration Overview," https://www.nps.gov/seki/learn/historyculture/gfmain.htm.

29. E. P. Meinecke, letter to Haven Metcalf, June 9, 1927, RG 54, Records of the Bureau of Plant Industry, Soils, and Agricultural Engineering, entry 80, box 59, NA; and E. P. Meinecke, *A Report upon the Effect of Excessive Tourist Travel on the California Redwood Parks* (Sacramento: California State Printing Office, 1928), 1. Meinecke finished the first version of this report by June 1927, but the final version, which also included new material on Big Basin State Park, was not published until March 1928. See E. P. Meinecke, letter to Haven Metcalf, March 24, 1928, RG 54, Records of the Bureau of Plant Industry, Soils, and Agricultural Engineering, entry 80, box 59, NA. Meinecke, *Report,* 7, 13. According to Meinecke, Rider's request for his analysis was part of California's effort to expand its number of state parks; see E. P. Meinecke, letter to Haven Metcalf, January 13, 1928, RG 54, Records of the Bureau of Plant Industry, Soils, and Agricultural Engineering, entry 80, box 59, NA.

30. Meinecke, *Report,* 12.

31. Ibid., 13, 14, 15.

32. E. P. Meinecke, letter to Stephen T. Mather, September 30, 1927, box 275, LSNP, 1, 4.

33. National park system visitors, for example, increased from 1,059,000 in 1920 to 3,248,000 in 1929. See Clawson and Van Doren, *Statistics,* 22. E. P. Meinecke, letter to Haven Metcalf, April 5, 1929, RG 54, Records of the Bureau of Plant Industry, Soils, and Agricultural Engineering, entry 80, box 74, NA. Meinecke retained the NPS consultancy until he retired. In recognition of his skill and the respect he had earned, his superiors allowed him to direct the pathology office from San Francisco. All Meinecke's peers elsewhere in the bureau were required to work from Washington, D.C. See California District, Forest Service, USDA, "Government Personnel Changes in California," memorandum to California District, Forest Service, July 13, 1929, RG 54, Records of the Bureau of Plant Industry, Soils, and Agricultural Engineering, entry 80, box 63, NA; and Wagener, Hartley, and Boyce, "Emilio," 633. E. P. Meinecke, "Committee on Forest Pathology" (San Francisco, December 12, 1930), RG 54, Records of the Bureau of Plant Industry, Soils, and Agricultural Engineering, entry 80, box 67, NA.

34. Horace M. Albright, memorandum to Superintendents of All the National Parks and Muir Woods National Monument, April 1, 1931, box 275, LSNP. Horace M. Albright, "A Forestry Policy for the National Parks," in Dilsaver, *America's National Park System*, 96, 97, but originally approved on May 6, 1931. Albright's use of the BPI as a consulting agency fits neatly with President Herbert Hoover's view that federal experts should provide assistance to individuals, companies, and governments, but that these should not be controlled by the central government's bureaucrats. See also Kendrick A. Clements, *Hoover, Conservation, and Consumerism: Engineering the Good Life* (Lawrence: University Press of Kansas, 2000).

35. E. P. Meinecke, letter to Haven Metcalf, July 3, 1931, RG 54, Records of the Bureau of Plant Industry, Soils, and Agricultural Engineering, entry 80, box 74, NA. See also Bachman, *Recreation Facilities*, 4–5. E. P. Meinecke, letter to Haven Metcalf, July 24, 1931, RG 54, Records of the Bureau of Plant Industry, Soils, and Agricultural Engineering, entry 80, box 74, NA; E. P. Meinecke, letter to Haven Metcalf, San Francisco, April 8, 1932, RG 54, Records of the Bureau of Plant Industry, Soils, and Agricultural Engineering, entry 80, box 81, NA; E. P. Meinecke, "A Camp Ground Policy" (n.p.p., April 2, 1932), Camping, L3415, Office of Library, Archives and Graphics Research, National Park Service—Harpers Ferry (WV) Center. A printed version, E. P. Meinecke, *A Camp Ground Policy* (n.p.p., 1932), Emilio P. Meinecke Papers, box 8, California Academy of Sciences Library (San Francisco), shortly followed the mimeograph. All page references are to the printed version of the report.

36. Meinecke, *Camp Ground Policy*, 2, 10.

37. Ibid., 12.

38. Ibid., 11.

39. Ibid.

40. Ibid., 11, 9. The source for this romantic-era practice in America was the designer Andrew Jackson Downing (1815–1852), who emphasized the need for harmony between the artificial and the natural in a designed landscape. He inspired Frederick Law Olmsted, Calvert Vaux, and many succeeding park designers. Downing drew his ideas from eighteenth- and early nineteenth-century English landscape designers. See Carr, *Wilderness by Design*; McClelland, *Building*; Robert C. Pavlik, "In Harmony with the Landscape: Yosemite's Built Environment, 1913–1940," *California History* 69, no. 2 (1990): 182–95; and Craig E. Colten and Lary M. Dilsaver, "The Hidden Landscape of Yosemite National Park," *Journal of Cultural Geography* 22, no. 2 (2005): 27–50. Meinecke, *Camp Ground Policy*, 9, 11.

41. Meinecke, *Camp Ground Policy*, 12, 13.

42. Ibid., 14.

43. Meinecke reported in early May 1932 that his office was about to send out fifty mimeographed copies of "A Camp Ground Policy" to USFS supervisors in California; see E. P. Meinecke, letter to Haven Metcalf, May 4, 1932, RG 54, Records of the Bureau of Plant Industry, Soils, and Agricultural Engineering, entry 80, box 81, NA. The USFS ordered three thousand printed copies of the report in August 1932, and they were being distributed by early October; see E. P. Meinecke, letter to Haven Metcalf, August 25, 1932, RG 54, Records of the Bureau of Plant Industry, Soils, and Agricultural Engineering, entry 80, box 81, NA, and E. P. Meinecke, letter to Haven Metcalf, October 3, 1932, RG 54, Records of the Bureau of Plant Industry, Soils, and Agricultural Engineering, entry 80, box 81, NA. The training courses are discussed in Tweed, "Recreation Site Planning," 15.

44. Meinecke, letter to Metcalf, April 8, 1932.

45. L. P. Bradstreet, letter to John D. Coffman, October 2, 1933, RG 79, Records of the National Park Service, Central Classified File, 1907–1949, 0–601.03 Part 1, General, Lands, Camp Sites, box 378, NA, 1; E. P. Meinecke, letter to Haven Metcalf, July 8, 1932, RG 54, Records of the Bureau of Plant Industry, Soils, and Agricultural Engineering, entry 80, box 81, NA, 4; McClelland, *Building*, 281.

46. E. P. Meinecke, letter to John R. White, May 10, 1932, box 42, LSNP. Handwritten note by White on his copy of report. See John R. White, letter to E. P. Meinecke, May 20, 1932, box 42, LSNP. John R. White, letter to General Foreman, May 20, 1932, NPS-2, Sequoia and Kings Canyon National Parks, 601–03 Camp Sites, 1925–1932, box 424, NA.

47. Lemuel L. Garrison, *The Making of a Ranger: Forty Years with the National Parks*, Russell Dickenson, introduction (Salt Lake City: Howe Bros., 1983), 62; Irvin D. Kerr, letter to Chief Ranger [L. F. Cook], June 29, 1932, NPS-2, Sequoia and Kings Canyon National Parks, 601–03 Camp Sites, 1925–1932, box 424, NA. Cook argued for roads and sites at the Firwood Campground in L. F. Cook, letter to Superintendent, Sequoia National Park, September 23, 1931, box 42, LSNP. His sketch can be found at L.F. Cook, "Firwood Camp—Suggested Camp Layout," hand-drawn plan, September 9, 1932, box 42, LSNP.

48. Garrison, *Making of a Ranger*, 62. Garrison was a seasonal ranger at this time, but he would rise to become superintendent of a series of national parks, including Yosemite and Yellowstone, as well as becoming chair of the Mission 66 Steering Committee. See Ethan Carr, *Mission 66: Modernism and the National Park Dilemma* (Amherst: University of Massachusetts Press, 2007). Garrison, *Making of a Ranger*, 63.

49. Garrison, *Making of a Ranger*, 62–63.

50. "Camp Ground Improvement Manual" (San Francisco: U.S. Forest Service, California Region, 1933), 3; E. P. Meinecke, letter to Haven Metcalf, June 17, 1933, RG 54, Records of the Bureau of Plant Industry, Soils, and Agricultural Engineering, entry 80, box 88, NA. Superintendent quoted in Cathy A. Gilbert and Gretchen A. Luxenburg, *The Rustic Landscape of Rim Village, 1927–1941, Crater Lake National Park, Oregon* (Seattle: National Park Service, Cultural Resources Division, Pacific Northwest Region, 1990), at http://www.nps.gov/crla/rim/rimvill.htm.

51. Bachman, *Recreation Facilities*, 5, 38.

52. Greene, *Yosemite*, 729, 839–60; Demars, *Tourist*, 139.

53. E. P. Meinecke, "Camp Planning and Camp Reconstruction" (n.p.p.: U.S. Forest Service, California Region, [1934]), 6, 10, 11, 9, 11, 20. Were Meinecke's campground proposals unprecedented? The simple answer is no. Both Arthur Carhart and Frank Waugh had suggested some spatial control of campers during the 1910s and 1920s. Each, however, had achieved only limited success in persuading the Forest Service to implement his vision. See Tweed, "Recreation Site Planning," 6–9. During these same years, municipal campgrounds also had experimented with bounded campgrounds incorporating designated and developed campsites, such as the previously discussed plan by J. W. Gregg for Marysville, California. In addition, zoning to control impacts had become a standard urban planning tool by the 1920s. See M. Christine Boyer, *Dreaming the Rational City: The Myth of American City Planning* (Cambridge, MA: MIT Press, 1983), and Patricia Burgess, *Planning for the Private Interest: Land Use Controls and Residential Patterns in Columbus, Ohio, 1900–1970* (Columbus: Ohio State University Press, 1994). The NPS had embraced zoning by the 1920s at such parks as Grand Canyon, Mount Rainier, and Yosemite; see Carr, *Wilderness by Design*. Likewise, Meinecke's proposal strongly suggests the sort of suburban developments that were proliferating during the 1910s, 1920s, and 1930s; see Kenneth T. Jackson, *Crabgrass Frontier: The Suburbanization of the United States* (New York: Oxford University Press, 1985), and Dolores Hayden, *Building Suburbia: Green Fields and Urban Growth, 1820–2000* (New York: Vintage Books, 2003). Nevertheless, no surviving documents clearly indicate that Meinecke was consciously aware of any precedents to his campground plans. Given how widely and frequently he traveled and the variety of park and forest staff that he met, however, Meinecke must have either come across or been introduced to some similar designs. Unfortunately, their impact on him cannot be ascertained.

54. T. G. Taylor and W. L. Hansen, "Public Campground Planning," miscellaneous publication 13 (Logan: Utah Agricultural Experiment Station and School of Forestry, Utah State Agricultural College, October 1934), 2. "Public Camp Manual" (San Francisco: U.S. Forest Service, California Region, 1935), 4, has a direct reference to Meinecke's "Camp Planning and Camp Reconstruction." Carr, *Wilderness by Design*, 281. McClelland, *Building*, 336ff. Herbert Maier and his handbook are discussed in Carr, *Wilderness by Design*, and McClelland, *Building*. Albert H. Good, ed., *Park Structure and Facilities* (Washington, DC: National Park Service, 1935), 32; McClelland, *Building*, 281. Philip F. King of the NPS sent copies of Meinecke's "A Campground Policy" and "Camp Planning and Camp Reconstruction"

to W. T. Foster, a counterpart at Canada's Parks Branch in 1956, calling them "first rate," for example. See King, letter to Foster, September 14, 1956, RG 79, Records of the National Park, appendix 3, Administrative Files, 1949–1971, box 2175, L66 Foreign Parks and Historic Sites, Canada, 1954–1967, NA.

55. See Dilsaver and Tweed, *Challenge*, 170ff., and Demars, *Tourist*, 101, 102.

56. Belasco, *Americans*, 106. See Platt National Park, "Rules and Regulations," mimeographed handout, July 7, 1926, NPS-2, 208 Rules and Regulations, General, 1937–1947, box 230, NA. Apparently Mount Rainier National Park had instituted a two-week limit in 1924, but it came in the form of a superintendent's order, which can be temporary and easily reversed. Platt NP inaugurated its time limit in the form of a regulation, which is intended to be permanent. See National Park Service, "Conference of Superintendents and Field Officers, Washington, D.C., November 19 to 23, 1934, Volume 1, Pages 1 to 199, Sessions of November 19th and 20th," unpublished report, NPS-2, 0–1.1 General, Superintendents' Conference, Program and Letters, 1934, box 2, NA, 17. L. F. Cook, "Dr. Meinecke Suggestions," handwritten note, October 5, 1932, box 42, LSNP; L. F. Cook, memorandum to Superintendent, Sequoia National Park, "Camp Situation at Giant Forest," September 15, 1933, box 42, LSNP; Ford E. Spigelmyre, memorandum to Superintendent, Sequoia National Park, "Public Camp Administration," October 18, 1934, box 42, LSNP; Daniel J. Tobin to C. G. Thomson, September 26, 1934, box 42, LSNP; National Park Service, "Conference, 1934," 116–22; U.S. Department of the Interior, National Park Service, "Rules and Regulations," June 6, 1935, NPS-2, 208 Rules and Regulations, General, 1937–1947, box 230, NA, 3; U.S. Department of the Interior, National Park Service, "Rules and Regulations," June 18, 1936, NPS-2, 208 Rules and Regulations, General, 1937–1947, box 230, NA, 3; Lemuel A. Garrison, "Camper Activities in Yosemite Valley," *Yosemite Nature Notes* 18, no. 6 (1939): 73.

57. Thomas C. Vint and E. P. Meinecke, "Stoves and Fireplaces in Public Camp Grounds," March 29, 1935, NPS-2, box 378, 0–601–03, Stoves and Fireplaces, box 378, NA; E. P. Meinecke, "Recreation Planning: A Discussion," *Journal of Forestry* 35, no. 12 (December 1937): 1120–28.

58. E. P. Meinecke, letter to John D. Coffman, December 6, 1937, NPS-2, box 378, 0–601.03 Part 1, General, Lands, Camp Sites, box 378, NA, 7; E. P. Meinecke, "The Need for Non-urban Outdoor Recreation and the Types of Recreation Involved" and "Camp Grounds and Picnic Grounds," in "Recreation Report," unpublished manuscript, 1938, E. P. Meinecke Papers, box 19, California Academy of Sciences (San Francisco), 10. It does not appear that this report was ever published, because no search has found a copy, and Meinecke did not list it among his publications.

59. E. P. Meinecke, letter to Newton B. Drury, October 2, 1944, E. P. Meinecke Papers, box 6, California Academy of Sciences (San Francisco); E. P. Meinecke, "Relocation of Public and Operator Developments in Sequoia National Park," typed manuscript, E. P. Meinecke Papers, box 6, California Academy of Sciences (San Francisco), 13.

5. Liberalizing the Campground

1. Quoted in Warren James Belasco, *Americans on the Road: From Autocamp to Motel, 1910–1945* (Baltimore: Johns Hopkins University Press, 1979), 62. Frank E. Brimmer, *Coleman Motor Campers Manual* (Wichita, KS: Coleman Lamp Co., 1926), inside back cover. R. L. Duffus, "America Works Hard at Play," *New York Times Sunday Magazine*, September 1, 1929, 21.

2. The patterns, limits, and challenges faced by African Americans as they pursued nature-based and other recreations at this time was reported in William H. Jones, *Recreation and Amusement among Negroes in Washington, D.C.* (1927; Westport, CT: Negro Universities Press, 1970); Forrester B. Washington, "Recreational Facilities for the Negro," *Annals of the American Academy of Political and Social Science* 140 (1928): 272–82; Charles S.

Johnson, *The Negro in American Civilization* (New York: Henry Holt, 1930), 299–310, 457–58; and Gunnar Myrdal, *An American Dilemma: The Negro Problem and Modern Democracy* (1944; New York: Harper & Row, 1962), 346–47. For more on the history of African American recreation in a variety of public and private settings see Craig Allan Kaplowitz, "A Breath of Fresh Air: Segregation, Parks, and Progressivism in Nashville, Tennessee, 1900–1920," *Tennessee Historical Quarterly* 57 (1998): 132–49; Aaron V. Wunsch, "From Private Privilege to Public Place: A Brief History of Parks and Park Planning in Charlottesville," *Magazine of Albemarle County History* 56 (1998): 77–117; Mark S. Foster, "In the Face of 'Jim Crow': Prosperous Blacks and Vacations, Travel and Outdoor Leisure, 1890–1945," *Journal of Negro History* 84 (1999): 130–49; Jearold Winston Holland, *Black Recreation: A Historical Perspective* (Chicago: Burnham, 2002); Brian Alnutt, " 'The Negro Excursions': Recreational Outings among Philadelphia African Americans, 1876–1926," *Pennsylvania Magazine of History and Biography* 129 (January 2005): 73–104; James E. Wells, Geoffrey L. Buckley, and Christopher G. Boone, "Separate but Equal? Desegregating Baltimore's Golf Courses," *Geographical Review* 98 (2008): 151–70; Scott E. Giltner, *Hunting and Fishing in the New South: Black Labor and White Leisure after the Civil War* (Baltimore: Johns Hopkins University Press, 2008); and Brian Katen, "Parks Apart: African American Recreational Landscapes in Virginia," in *Proceedings: CELA 2008–2009 Teaching + Learning Landscape* (Edmond, OK, 2009), 131–38. See also Cindy S. Aron, *Working at Play: A History of Vacations in the United States* (New York: Oxford University Press, 1999), 206–36. A more scholarly version of this chapter can be found at Terence Young, " 'A Contradiction in Democratic Government': W. J. Trent, Jr. and the Struggle to Desegregate National Park Campgrounds," *Environmental History* 14 (October 2009): 651–82. For an insightful evaluation of the more recent situation see Carolyn Finney, *Black Faces, White Spaces: Reimagining the Relationship of African Americans to the Great Outdoors* (Chapel Hill: University of North Carolina Press, 2014). Washington, "Recreational Facilities," 272; Johnson, *Negro*, 457. William G. Crawford Jr., "The Long Hard Fight for Equal Rights: A History of Broward Country's Colored Beach and the Fort Lauderdale Beach 'Wade-Ins' of the Summer of 1961," *Tequesta: The Journal of the Historical Association of Southern Florida* 67 (2007): 19–51.

    3. Great Smoky Mountains National Park, Shenandoah National Park, and Mammoth Cave National Park in Kentucky were all authorized in May 1926 but became available for public use at different times. Great Smoky Mountains was established for "full development" in June 1934, Shenandoah was "fully established" in December 1935, and Mammoth Cave was "established" in July 1941. See *The National Parks: Index, 2009–2011* (Washington, DC: U.S. Department of the Interior, 2011), 47, 80, and 88. Congress also authorized the National Park Service to create a multitude of "recreational demonstration areas" (RDAs) with the various states during the 1930s, and it transferred the National Military Parks from the War Department to the National Park Service in 1933. In the South, RDAs were often racially segregated. See William O'Brien, "The Strange Career of a Florida State Park: Uncovering a Jim Crow Past," *Historical Geography* 35 (2007): 160–84. Civilian Conservation Corps camps were also racially segregated when the work was performed in southern states. See Owen Cole, *The African-American Experience in the Civilian Conservation Corps* (Tallahassee: University Press of Florida, 1999); Neil Maher, *Nature's New Deal: The Civilian Conservation Corps and the Roots of the American Environmental Movement* (New York: Oxford University Press, 2008); and Timothy B. Smith, "Black Soldiers and the CCC at Shiloh National Military Park," *CRM: The Journal of Heritage Stewardship* 3 (2006): 73–84.

    4. On displacement of indigenous populations see Robert H. Keller and Michael E. Turek, *American Indians and National Parks* (Tucson: University of Arizona Press, 1998); Mark David Spence, *Dispossessing the Wilderness: Indian Removal and the Making of the National Parks* (New York: Oxford University Press, 1999); and Philip Burnham, *Indian Country, God's Country* (Covelo, CA: Island Press, 2000). The superintendents' statement is quoted in Marguerite S. Shaffer, *See America First: Tourism and National Identity, 1880–1940* (Washington, DC: Smithsonian Institution Press, 2001), 126.

5. See Durwood Dunn, *Cades Cove: The Life and Death of a Southern Appalachian Community, 1818–1937* (Knoxville: University of Tennessee Press, 1988); Margaret Lynn Brown, *The Wild East: A Biography of the Great Smoky Mountains* (Gainesville: University Press of Florida, 2000); Daniel S. Pierce, *The Great Smokies: From Natural Habitat to National Park* (Knoxville: University of Tennessee Press, 2000); Darwin Lambert, *The Earth-Man Story, Starring Shenandoah Skyline* (New York: Exposition Press, 1972); and Justin Reich, "Re-creating the Wilderness: Shaping Narratives and Landscapes in Shenandoah National Park," *Environmental History* 6 (2001): 95–117. See E. K. Burlew, letter to Carter Glass, March 6, 1939, RG 48, Department of the Interior, Office of the Secretary, Central Classified Files, 1937–1953, National Park Service, General, Racial Discrimination, box 3791 (hereafter DOI—Racial), U.S. National Archives, College Park, MD (hereafter NA), 2; and Harry Byrd to E. K. Burlew, March 9, 1939, DOI—Racial, NA. See Jerrold M. Packard, *American Nightmare: The History of Jim Crow* (New York: St. Martin's, 2002).

6. L. E. Wilson, letter to Harold L. Ickes, September 10, 1936, RG 79, Records of the National Park Service, appendix 2, Central Classified Files, 1907–1949 (hereafter NPS-2), 601–03 Shenandoah, Lands (General), Camp Sites, box 1650, NA. A. E. Demaray, letter to L. E. Wilson, September 18, 1936, NPS-2, 601–03 Shenandoah, Lands (General), Camp Sites, box 1650, NA.

7. Walter White, letter to Harold L. Ickes, January 21, 1937, NPS-2, 601–03 Shenandoah, Lands (General), Camp Sites, box 1650, NA. For more on the history of the NAACP during this period see Mark V. Tushnet, *The NAACP's Legal Strategy against Segregated Education, 1925–1950* (Chapel Hill: University of North Carolina Press, 1987); Kenneth Robert Janken, *White: The Biography of Walter White, Mr. NAACP* (New York: New Press, 2003); Manfred Berg, *"The Ticket to Freedom": The NAACP and the Struggle for Black Political Integration* (Gainesville: University Press of Florida, 2005); and Gilbert Jonas, *Freedom's Sword: The NAACP and the Struggle against Racism in America, 1909–1969* (New York: Routledge, 2005). White and Ickes had been corresponding about federal involvement in racial issues since shortly after the latter was appointed interior secretary in 1933, and they were both on the Virgin Islands Advisory Council that was formed in February 1934. See T. H. Watkins, *Righteous Pilgrim: The Life and Times of Harold L. Ickes, 1874–1952* (New York: Henry Holt, 1990), 503; Nancy J. Weiss, *Farewell to the Party of Lincoln: Black Politics in the Age of FDR* (Princeton, NJ: Princeton University Press, 1983), 51; and Janken, *White*, 176ff. White greatly respected Ickes, who he said was "throughout his life an unequivocal battler for justice to the Negro," in Walter White, *A Man Called White: The Autobiography of Walter White* (New York: Viking, 1948), 181–82. The NAACP embraced other segregation issues at around this time. Late in the following year, 1938, the black press and a variety of black organizations began to call for racial integration throughout the military. The NAACP took up this issue officially and vigorously in the spring of 1940. See Weiss, *Farewell*, 274ff; and Harvard Sitkoff, *A New Deal for Blacks: The Emergence of Civil Rights as a National Issue* (New York: Oxford University Press, 1978), 302ff.

8. Harold L. Ickes, letter to Walter White, February 4, 1937, NPS-2, 601–03 Shenandoah, Lands (General), Camp Sites, box 1650, NA. Three months later, the Memphis chapter of the NAACP requested the NPS to provide "proper provision for Negroes" at the Shelby Forest Recreation Demonstration Project. Along with many supporting churches, clubs, and fraternities, the Memphis chapter stated that there were no "rural parks for out-door recreation available to Negroes" in the area. It contended that this situation condemned "Negro Youth, during leisure hours, to the streets of Memphis and makes them the easy prey of places of vice and disease." Grace T. Hamilton, letter to Conrad L. Wirth, May 13, 1937, RG 79, Records of the National Park Service, appendix 30, Recreational Demonstration Area Program Files, 1934–1947, Recreation Facilities for Negroes, box 17, NA. After this single exchange, further contact with the NPS came only through the NAACP's central office.

9. J. R. Eakin, letter to William P. Gamble, September 18, 1933, NPS-2, 601–02, box 1101, NA. See also A. D. Lambert, "Shenandoah National Park, an Administrative

History" (typed, unpublished manuscript; Luray, VA, Shenandoah National Park, 1979), 254, who records that Arno Cammerer, assistant director of the National Park Service, noted the need for African American accommodations at Shenandoah National Park in late 1932, but no controversy was involved at the time.

10. T. Arnold Hill, letter to Harold L. Ickes, June 25, 1935, NPS-2, National Park Service Recreational Areas, box 379, NA.

11. Hill and Ickes became friends while the former was executive secretary of the Chicago Urban League from 1916 to 1925. He changed from acting to executive secretary of the National Urban League during 1925. See "T. Arnold Hill," *Journal of Negro History* 32 (1947): 528–29; and Guichard Parris, "Hill, T(homas) Arnold," in *Dictionary of American Negro Biography*, ed. Rayford Logan and Michael R. Winston (New York: W. W. Norton, 1982), 311–13. Watkins, *Righteous Pilgrim*, 199–201, details Ickes's involvement with the NAACP during these years. Weiss, *Farewell*, 51, also mentions Ickes's time as the NAACP chapter's president, and she quotes Ickes as saying that "'the prevention of discrimination against the Negro race' was a subject that was 'very close' to his heart." T. A. Walters, letter to T. Arnold Hill, July 3, 1935, NPS-2, National Park Service Recreational Areas, box 379, NA. Theodore Augustus Walters was assistant secretary of the interior from 1933 until he died of pneumonia in 1937. See "Milestones," *Time*, December 6, 1937, http://www.time.com/time/magazine/article/0,9171,758568,00.html.

12. Weaver graduated in 1934 from Harvard University with a PhD in economics. According to Watkins, *Righteous Pilgrim*, 645–47, Weaver was hired in November 1933 to be an assistant to Clark Foreman, Ickes's first adviser for Negro affairs. Weaver took over Foreman's post in early 1936. See also Sitkoff, *New Deal*; and Janken, *White*. Robert C. Weaver, letter to Arno B. Cammerer, July 1, 1936, NPS-2, General, Lands, Camp Sites, box 378, NA. Arno B. Cammerer, letter to Robert C. Weaver, July 6, 1936, NPS-2, General, Lands, Camp Sites, box 378, NA. Beginning in 1934, the federal government provided funds to purchase "submarginal agricultural lands" for conversion into dozens of state parks. The National Park Service administered this "recreational demonstration area" program throughout the decade. See Linda Flint McClelland, *Building the National Parks: Historic Landscape Design and Construction* (Baltimore: Johns Hopkins University Press, 1998), 414–20. Robert C. Weaver, letter to Harold L. Ickes, August 17, 1936, NPS-2, General, Lands, Camp Sites, box 378, NA. Cammerer to Weaver, July 6, 1936; Arno B. Cammerer, letter to A. E. Demaray and Conrad L. Wirth, September 30, 1936, NPS-2, General, Lands, Camp Sites, box 378, NA; and Arno B. Cammerer, letter to Charles S. Johnson, May 27, 1937, NPS-2, National Park Service Recreational Areas, box 379, NA. Great Smoky Mountains National Park superintendent J. R. Eakin conveyed to Cammerer that if the proposed African American campground was constructed in his park, the number of African American campers "would undoubtedly increase." J. R. Eakin, letter to Director [Arno B. Cammerer], April 25, 1938, NPS-2, 601–03, box 1101, NA.

13. Johnson was Robert E. Park's first African American student and a graduate of the University of Chicago. He ultimately rose to become Fisk University's president and a nationally renowned expert on race relations. He was a well-known, prolific author and knew Eleanor Roosevelt personally when he sent his letter to Cammerer. See Patrick J. Gilpin and Marybeth Gasman, *Charles S. Johnson: Leadership beyond the Veil in the Age of Jim Crow* (Albany: SUNY Press, 2003). Charles S. Johnson, letter to Arno B. Cammerer, April 23, 1937, NPS-2, National Park Service Recreational Areas, box 379, NA; Cammerer to Johnson, May 27, 1937. Charles S. Johnson, letter to Arno B. Cammerer, June 8, 1937, NPS-2, National Park Service Recreational Areas, box 379, NA. Johnson to Cammerer, June 8, 1937. Arno B. Cammerer, letter to A. E. Demaray, July 24, 1937, NPS-2, Shenandoah, Lands (General), Camp Sites, box 1650, NA.

14. Biographical details about William J. Trent Jr. come from Greta Tilley, "'Unheralded Hero': He's Devoted Life to Improving World for Black America," *Greensboro (NC) News and Record* (March 10, 1985); Eric Pace, "William Trent, 83, Director of Negro College

Fund," *New York Times*, November 29, 1993; and personal communications with Judy Scales-Trent, W. J. Trent's daughter. See "W. J. Trent, Jr. Gets New Job under Federal Works Agency," *Norfolk Journal and Guide*, July 28, 1939, on Trent's 1936 work for the Weaver survey. Judy Scales-Trent, e-mail with author, June 20, 2006, related the story of Weaver's recommendation of Trent.

15. Bethune would become one of the best-known advocates for equal civil rights. See Rackham Holt, *Mary McLeod Bethune: A Biography* (Garden City, NY: Doubleday, 1964); Weiss, *Farewell*; and Andrea Davis Pinkney, *Let It Shine: Stories of Black Women Freedom Fighters* (San Diego: Harcourt, 2000). See Willard M. Kiplinger, *Washington Is Like That* (New York: Harper & Bros., 1942), 147–62; Albert W. Hamilton, "The Black Cabinet," *Common Sense* 12 (1943): 97–99; and Weiss, *Farewell*, 136–55.

16. W. J. Trent Jr., letter to Mary McLeod Bethune, December 21, 1938, William J. Trent Jr. Papers (hereafter TrPa), Interior Department, Articles Statements Speeches, box 1, Moorland-Spingarn Research Center, Howard University, Washington, DC (hereafter MSRC). The quote is from Judy Scales Trent, e-mail with author, June 20, 2006. Trent's hunting is mentioned in William J. Trent, letter to William J. Trent Jr., December 4, 1944, TrPa, Personal Correspondence, box 1, MSRC.

17. Both Salomon and Evison were well established in their fields. See, for instance, Julian Harris Salomon, "Camping Trends and Public Areas," in *American Planning and Civic Annual, 1938*, ed. H. James (Washington, DC: American Planning and Civic Association, 1938), 146–51; and Herbert Evison, ed., *A State Park Anthology* (Washington, DC: National Conference on State Parks, 1930). W. J. Trent Jr., "New Deal Recreation Program for Negroes" (unpublished speech, Washington, DC, n.d. [1939]), TrPa, Interior Department, Articles Statements Speeches, box 1, MSRC, 1. W. J. Trent Jr., letter to T. Edward Davis, December 21, 1938, TrPa, Interior Department, Articles Statements Speeches, box 1, MSRC; and W. J. Trent Jr., "The Government and Organized Camping among Negroes," *National Educational Outlook among Negroes*, February 1939, 23.

18. W. J. Trent Jr., letter to Mary McLeod Bethune, December 23, 1938, TrPa, Interior Department, Articles Statements Speeches, box 1, MSRC, 5.

19. W. J. Trent Jr., letter to the Secretary [Harold L. Ickes], January 3, 1939, NPS-2, folder named "Parks General, Conference * Wash DC Santa Fe, 1939," box 10, NA, 1.

20. Donald S. Libbey, Secretary, "[Minutes—] Superintendents' Conference, Washington, D.C., January 7, 1939," NPS-2, folder named "Parks General, Conference * Wash DC Santa Fe, 1939," box 10, NA, 1. W. J. Trent Jr., *Negro and National Parks: A Discussion before the Superintendents of the National Parks*, NPS-2, folder named "Parks General, Conference * Wash DC Santa Fe, 1939," box 10, NA, 1.

21. Ibid., 3, 5, 6.

22. Ibid., 8, 2, 8.

23. Eakin to Director, April 25, 1938, placed the total number of visitors at 727,243 at Great Smoky Mountains National Park. Libbey, Secretary, "[Minutes—]," 1. "Accommodations for Negroes," in *Recommendations of the National Park Superintendents' Conference, January 1939*, NPS-2, folder named "Parks General, Conference * Wash DC Santa Fe, 1939," box 10, NA, 12.

24. Michael Fletcher, "Inherently Unequal," *Crisis* 111, no. 3 (May–June 2004): 24–31. See also White, *Man Called White*, 142. When Ickes assumed the secretary's office he needed a departmental solicitor, so he consulted with Felix Frankfurter of Harvard University and Supreme Court justice Louis Brandeis. Both recommended the thirty-three-year-old Margold. See Jeanne Nienaber Clarke, *Roosevelt's Warrior: Harold L. Ickes and the New Deal* (Baltimore: Johns Hopkins University Press, 1996), 39–40. Phineas Indritz, letter to Solicitor [Nathan R.] Margold, January 12, 1939, DOI—Racial, NA, 3, 9. Indritz would go on to become a renowned New Deal liberal and civil rights activist. See *New York Times* obituary of October 26, 1997.

25. Nathan R. Margold, letter to Secretary [Harold L.] Ickes, January 17, 1939, DOI—Racial, NA, 1–2.

26. Roosevelt quoted in Watkins, *Righteous Pilgrim*, 638. Associate Director [A. E. Dema-ray], memorandum to Director [Arno B. Cammerer], February 11, 1939, NPS-2, Shenandoah, Lands (General), Camp Sites, box 1650, NA, 1. Harold L. Ickes, *The Secret Diary of Harold L. Ickes*, vol. 2, *The Inside Struggle, 1936–1939* (New York: Simon & Schuster, 1954), 105–6. See also Rixey Smith and Norman Beasley, *Carter Glass: A Biography* (New York: Longmans, Green, 1939), who noted how Glass defended Virginia's poll taxes against President's Roosevelt's efforts to eliminate such taxes and Glass's acidic, public disagreement with Ickes over the use of federally funded public works projects. Both episodes occurred in 1938.

27. Ebert Keiser Burlew (but known universally as "E.K.") had been with the Interior Department since 1923. Ickes, who considered Burlew quick, reliable, and efficient, appointed him one of his two personal assistants. See Watkins, *Righteous Pilgrim*, 329.

28. Carter Glass, letter to E. K. Burlew, March 7, 1939, DOI—Racial, NA. Harry F. Byrd, letter to E. K. Burlew, March 9, 1939, DOI—Racial, NA.

29. W. J. Trent Jr., "The Government and Organized Camping among Negroes, Part II," TrPa, Interior Department, Correspondence, 1939, box 1, MSRC, 1, 5.

30. W. J. Trent Jr. to Harold L. Ickes, March 20, 1939, TrPa, Federal Works Agency, Correspondence, box 1, MSRC.

31. A. E. Demaray, letter to Director [Arno B. Cammerer], March 25, 1939, NPS-2, Shenandoah, Lands (General), Camp Sites, box 1650, NA. Also present at the meeting were E. K. Burlew, Assistant Interior Secretary Oscar L. Chapman, and Acting Associate Director John R. White. According to Harold L. Ickes, "Diary," unpublished manuscript, Harold L. Ickes Papers, Library of Congress (Washington, DC), 3067, the secretary had torn into Director Cammerer on December 3, 1938.

32. The quotes are from A. E. Demaray, letter to the Secretary [of the Interior, Harold Ickes], April 7, 1939, DOI—Racial, NA. The development at Lewis Mountain is detailed in the attachments to A. E. Demaray, memorandum to E. K. Burlew, March 14, 1939, NPS-2, Recreational Areas, 1935–48, box 1651, NA.

33. Henderson was well known at the time for his civil rights work in the Washington area and has since been called "the father of black basketball." See James H. M. Henderson and Betty F. Henderson, *Molder of Men: Portrait of a "Grand Old Man," Edwin Bancroft Henderson* (New York: Vantage, 1985). Edwin B. Henderson, letter to Secretary Harold L. Ickes, April 5, 1939, NPS-2, Shenandoah, Lands (General), Camp Sites, box 1650, NA.

34. Walter White, letter to Harold L. Ickes, April 10, 1939, NPS-2, Shenandoah, Lands (General), Camp Sites, box 1650, NA.

35. The time and day of the heart attack are noted in a letter from Horace M. Albright, the NPS director before Cammerer, to John D. Rockefeller Jr. See Joseph W. Ernst, ed., *Worthwhile Places: Correspondence of John D. Rockefeller, Jr. and Horace M. Albright* (New York: Fordham University Press for Rockefeller Archive Center, 1991), 186. Ickes, "Diary," 3265–66. Harry Slattery, letter to Mr. Secretary [Harold L. Ickes], April 19, 1939, DOI—Racial, NA. Slattery shortly would become the head of the Rural Electrification Administration. See D. Clayton Brown, *Electricity for Rural America: The Fight for the REA* (Westport, CT: Greenwood, 1980).

36. W. J. Trent Jr., letter to Mr. [E. K.] Burlew, May 9, 1939, DOI—Racial, NA. Ickes simply wrote the word "approved" adjacent to the portion of this memorandum that included the recommendation.

37. Harold L. Ickes, letter to Secretary Walter White, May 11, 1939, DOI—Racial, NA. Walter White, letter to Secretary Harold L. Ickes, May 15, 1939, DOI—Racial, NA.

38. E. K. Burlew, letter to Acting Director A. E. Demaray, May 19, 1939, DOI—Racial, NA.

39. White served as superintendent of Sequoia National Park from 1920 to 1938 and again from 1941 to 1947. He worked in the National Park Service headquarters in the interim. See Lary M. Dilsaver and William C. Tweed, *Challenge of the Big Trees* (Three Rivers, CA: Sequoia Natural History Association, 1990). John R. White, memorandum to Miss [Isabelle F.] Story, May 23, 1939, DOI—Racial, NA. A. E. Demaray, memorandum to First Assistant Secretary [E. K. Burlew], May 25, 1939, DOI—Racial, NA.

40. A. E. Demaray, letter to Edwin B. Henderson, May 25, 1939, NPS-2, Shenandoah, Lands (General), Camp Sites, box 1650, NA.

41. W. J. Trent Jr., letter to First Assistant Secretary [E. K. Burlew], June 19, 1939, DOI—Racial, NA. A. E. Demaray, letter to First Assistant Secretary [E. K. Burlew], June 22, 1939, DOI—Racial, NA.

42. W. J. Trent Jr., letter to Henry S. Percival, October 25, 1939, TrPa, Interior Department, Correspondence, 1939, box 1, MSRC. Ickes was apparently pleased with Trent's work and decided that Trent should change posts. Judy Scales-Trent, e-mail with author, June 20, 2006. Soon Trent's title changed to racial relations officer and the agency was renamed the Federal Works Agency. Henry S. Percival, letter to William J. Trent Jr., November 20, 1939, TrPa, box 1, Interior Department, Correspondence 1939, MSRC.

43. Walter White, letter to Mr. [William J.] Trent, February 19, 1940, NPS-2, Shenandoah, Lands (General), Camp Sites, box 1650, NA. W. J. Trent Jr., memorandum to Secretary [Harold L.] Ickes, February 24, 1940, NPS-2, Shenandoah, Lands (General), Camp Sites, box 1650, NA. Trent's ongoing concern about federally sanctioned racial segregation was not limited to the national parks. According to Truman K. Gibson, *Knocking Down Barriers: My Fight for Black America* (Evanston, IL: Northwestern University Press, 2005), 81, in the fall of 1940, Trent persuaded Gibson, a family friend, to come to Washington to meet William Hastie, a member of the "black cabinet" and civilian aide to the secretary of war, who wanted Gibson for his assistant. Gibson visited for one week, and during an evening's poker game, "Trent and [Robert] Weaver poured out all the arguments about duty, responsibility, and challenge" to persuade Gibson to take the post. In particular, Gibson found "the challenge of tackling segregation in the army registered strongly with me," which suggests that Trent advocated its end in the national parks and beyond. Gibson accepted Hastie's offer and became personally involved in many of the meetings, discussions, and debates that culminated in President Truman's Executive Order 9981 in July 1948, which declared a policy of equal treatment in the military and began the end of racial segregation in the armed forces. Harold L. Ickes, letter to W. J. Trent Jr., March 6, 1940, NPS-2, Shenandoah, Lands (General), Camp Sites, box 1650, NA.

44. W. J. Trent Jr., letter to E. K. Burlew, July 31, 1940, DOI—Racial, NA. E. K. Burlew, letter to Mr. [A. E.] Demaray, August 6, 1940, DOI—Racial, NA.

45. Lassiter had suffered a heart attack in December 1939 and did not return to duty until late spring 1940. Nonetheless, he had more than six months before his episode and several after to inform Chief Ranger Stephens about the policy. See Reed Engle, "Segregation/Desegregation: Laboratory for Change," National Park Service, https://www.nps.gov/shen/learn/historyculture/segregation.htm. J. R. Lassiter, memorandum to the Director, National Park Service, August 14, 1940, NPS-2, Shenandoah, Lands (General), Camp Sites, box 1650, NA.

46. A. E. Demaray, memorandum to Superintendent [J. R. Lassiter], August 23, 1940, NPS-2, Shenandoah, Lands (General), Camp Sites, box 1650, NA.

47. J. R. Lassiter, letter to the Director, National Park Service, September 3, 1940, DOI—Racial, NA; and A. E. Demaray, letter to Mr. [E. K.] Burlew, September 7, 1940, DOI—Racial, NA.

48. E. K. Burlew, letter to Mr. [A. E.] Demaray, September 10, 1940, DOI—Racial, NA; and E. K. Burlew, letter to Mr. W. J. Trent Jr., September 10, 1940, DOI—Racial, NA.

49. J. R. Lassiter, memorandum to Director, National Park Service, September 16, 1940, NPS-2, Shenandoah, Lands (General), Camp Sites, box 1650, NA; E.K. Burlew, letter to W. J. Trent Jr., September 23, 1940, DOI—Racial, NA.

50. J. R. Lassiter, memorandum to Director, National Park Service, August 1, 1940, NPS-2, Shenandoah, Lands (General), Camp Sites, box 1650, NA. Lassiter lost his superintendent's post in October 1941. As a consequence of the race-related conflicts detailed here and others, he was transferred to Santa Fe, New Mexico, to be a regional engineer with a cut in grade and a 10 percent reduction in salary. See Lambert, "Shenandoah," 279–82.

51. Walter Magnes Teller, letter to Newton B. Drury, October 4, 1940, NPS-2, Shenandoah, Lands (General), Camp Sites, box 1650, NA, about segregation as a violation of

democracy, but see also, for example, Walter Gellhorn, letter to Harold L. Ickes, May 26, 1939, NPS-2, Shenandoah, Lands (General), Camp Sites, box 1650, NA; Sadie Evans Gough, letter to Harold L. Ickes, June 19, 1939, NPS-2, Shenandoah, Lands (General), Camp Sites, box 1650 NA; Millicent E. Selsam, letter to Harold L. Ickes, July 7, 1939, NPS-2, Shenandoah, Lands (General), Camp Sites, box 1650, NA; Richard Grobstein, letter to Harold L. Ickes, July 5, 1940, NPS-2, Shenandoah, Lands (General), Camp Sites, box 1650, NA; George F. Miller, letter to President [Franklin D. Roosevelt], July 6, 1940, NPS-2, Shenandoah, Lands (General), Camp Sites, box 1650, NA; Arthur Ernst, letter to Harold L. Ickes, September 23, 1940, NPS-2, Shenandoah, Lands (General), Camp Sites, box 1650, NA; Robert O. Ballou, letter to S. K. Padover, January 17, 1941, NPS-2, Shenandoah, Lands (General), Camp Sites, box 1650, NA; Norma E. Boyd, letter to W. J. Trent Jr., April 2, 1941, TrPa, Federal Works Agency—Correspondence, box 1, MSRC; and Lambert, "Shenandoah," 281. According to J. R. Lassiter and Theodore T. Smith, letter to Director [Arno B. Cammerer], February 28, 1940, NPS-2, Shenandoah, Lands (General), Camp Sites, box 1650, NA, "the Rangers at the checking stations [of Shenandoah National Park] have been bitterly assailed for allowing the joint use of picnic grounds," but a year later, Oliver G. Taylor, "A Report on Developments for Public Use in Shenandoah National Park with Particular Reference to Racial Use" (January 23, 1941), NPS-2, Shenandoah, Lands (General), Camp Sites, box 1650, NA, 2, reported that visitors had "made no written complaint" at the park. The author found no complaint letters anywhere else among the archival record. As a consequence of his poor health and the strongly negative opinion that Ickes held of him, Cammerer resigned as NPS director in June 1940. Drury became the new director on August 20, 1940. The study was Taylor, "Report." The quote is from Newton B. Drury, letter to Superintendent [J. R.] Lassiter, February 25, 1941, NPS-2, Shenandoah, Lands (General), Camp Sites, box 1650, NA. On Trent's support see W. J. Trent Jr., letter to E. K. Burlew, April 4, 1941, NPS-2, Shenandoah, Lands (General), Camp Sites, box 1650, NA; E. K. Burlew, letter to W. J. Trent Jr., April 14, 1941, DOI—Racial, NA; and W. J. Trent Jr., letter to E. K. Burlew, May 3, 1941, DOI—Racial, NA.

52. Archibald MacLeish, letter to Harold L. Ickes, April 7, 1942, TrPa, Federal Works Agency—Correspondence, box 1, MSRC.

53. W. J. Trent Jr., letter to E. K. Burlew, May 19, 1942, NPS-2, General, Camp Sites (Colored), box 378, NA.

54. Harold L. Ickes, letter to Archibald MacLeish, May 21, 1942, NPS-2, General, Camp Sites (Colored), box 378, NA. E. K. Burlew, letter to Director [Newton B. Drury], May 21, 1942, NPS-2, Shenandoah, Lands (General), Camp Sites, box 1650, NA; E. K. Burlew, letter to Director [Newton B.] Drury, May 22, 1942, NPS-2, General, Camp Sites (Colored), box 378, NA. See, for example, Newton B. Drury, letter to Superintendent [J. R. Lassiter], May 26, 1942, NPS-2, Shenandoah, Lands (General), Camp Sites, box 1650, NA.

55. Newton B. Drury, memorandum to First Assistant Secretary [E. K.] Burlew, June 12, 1942, NPS-2, General, Camp Sites (Colored), box 378, NA. The Blue Ridge Parkway's superintendent had reported in August 1941 that Bluff Park's African American picnic area had been converted to a joint-use area, and only the white picnic area continued to be segregated. In light of this report, Drury's statement that three new areas were under development may be inaccurate. Also, no picnic or campground areas were segregated along the North Carolina portion of the Blue Ridge Parkway by June 1943, even as all the leisure areas in Virginia were closed for the duration of the war. See Stanley W. Abbot, letter to Newton Drury, August 14, 1941, NPS-2, Blue Ridge, Supt's Report, box 2718, NA, which noted the conversion of the African American picnic area and the retention of the whites-only area at Bluff Park. Stanley W. Abbot, "Recreational Parks," in Annual Report of the Blue Ridge Parkway, Roanoke, VA, June 30, 1943, NPS-2, Blue Ridge, Supt's Report, box 2718, NA, n.p., reported that no segregated areas existed in any recreational area along the North Carolina stretch of the parkway by June 1943. It also noted that all the Virginia areas were closed because of a state ban on pleasure driving during World War II. According to Stanley W. Abbot, "Pine Spur," in Annual Report of the Blue Ridge Parkway, Roanoke, VA, June 30, 1941, NPS-2, Blue Ridge, Supt's Report, box 2718, NA, n.p., the Pine Spur area prior to June 1941 was

an African American–only picnic and ball-playing area, not a campground. "This attractive area, twenty-five miles south of Roanoke was developed for negro use through the encouragement of the Negro Advisor to the Secretary." Newton B. Drury, memorandum to Regional Director, Region One, June 15, 1942, NPS-2, General, Camp Sites (Colored), box 378, NA.

56. Walton Onslow, memorandum to First Assistant Secretary [E. K. Burlew], June 19, 1942, RG 48, Department of the Interior, Office of the Secretary, Central Classified Files, 1937–1953, War Information, box 2860, NA. Ickes's approval is handwritten across the bottom of the letter.

57. Tilley, "Unheralded."

6. A Clearer Picture of This Country

1. "Nixon Praises Foundation Projects," *Caravanner* 17 (November–December 1971): 2.
2. Ibid., 2.
3. Roger B. White, *Home on the Road: The Motor Home in America* (Washington, DC: Smithsonian Institution Press, 2000), 3.
4. I borrow the term "tinkering" from the revealing work of Kathleen Franz, *Tinkering: Consumers Reinvent the Early Automobile* (Philadelphia: University of Pennsylvania Press, 2005), 8.
5. White, *Home*, 13; "This Auto Is a Flat on Tires: Motor-Driven Gypsy Van with Kitchen, Running Water, Beds, Tables, and Even a Roof Garden," *New York Times*, August 22, 1915; White, *Home*, 24ff.
6. White, *Home*, 17ff; Earl Pomeroy, *In Search of the Golden West: The Tourist in Western America* (New York: Knopf, 1957), 148.
7. Melville F. Ferguson, *Motor Camping on Western Trails* (New York: Century, 1925), 120.
8. Ibid., 120–21. Ferguson does not identify whether the motor-home camper repaired the bridge. According to Carlton M. Edwards, *Homes for Travel and Living: The History and Development of the Recreation Vehicle and Mobile Home Industries* (East Lansing, MI: Carl Edwards & Associates, 1977), 122, motor homes became significant only "when they achieved 2% or more of the [recreational vehicle] market," which occurred in 1965.
9. David A. Thornburg, *Galloping Bungalows: The Rise and Demise of the American House Trailer* (Hamden, CT: Archon Books, 1991), 7–8. This book provides an overview of the history of travel trailers and their more sedentary cousins, mobile homes. Edwards, *Homes*, 7, sets the date of the first American camping trailer at 1915. See also Allan D. Wallis, *Wheel Estate: The Rise and Decline of Mobile Homes* (New York: Oxford University Press, 1991), 37.
10. Franz, *Tinkering*, 30, reported that catalogs were a principal source of travel trailer parts between 1910 and 1930. Sears, Roebuck & Co., *Fall 1918* (Chicago: Sears, Roebuck & Co., 1918), 1512. Warren James Belasco, *Americans on the Road: From Autocamp to Motel, 1910–1945* (Cambridge, MA: MIT Press, 1979), 52; Ferguson, *Motor*, 299.
11. "Camping De Luxe," *Outing*, September 1916, 686. Among the firms this article identified as producing camp trailers were the Cosy Camp and Auto Trailer Co., the Auto-Kamp Equipment Co., the Warner Manufacturing Co., and the Shattuck Trailer Co. "Double-filled, army khaki duck" is an extra strong but light canvas cloth. It continues to be employed in the manufacture of high-end, custom tents. See Davis Tent and Awning Co., http://davistent.com/html/index.html.
12. On Curtiss see Thornburg, *Galloping Bungalows*, 10–11, and Russ Banham, *Wanderlust: Airstream at 75* (Old Saybrook, CT: Greenwich Publishing Group, 2005), 38. On the Chenango Trailer Co. see Wallis, *Wheel Estate*, 36, and "The Chenango Camp Trailer," *Hood Release*, Summer 2008, 5–6.

13. Elon Jessup, *The Motor Camping Book* (New York: G. P. Putnam's Sons, 1921), 137, 146. The August 17, 1922, issue is quoted in Donald F. Wood, *RVs and Campers: 1900 through 2000; An Illustrated History* (Hudson, WI: Iconografix, 2002), 27.

14. J. C. Long and John D. Long, *Motor Camping* (New York: Dodd and Mead, 1923), 2–3.

15. See also Franz, *Tinkering*, 15–25, who argues that "motor tourists" used tinkering and accessories to soften travel's roughness and to maintain the standards of comfort they pursued at home. White, *Home*, 14, similarly argues that some auto campers were "simply reluctant to leave the comforts of home behind." I modify these positions by arguing that, on the one hand, trailer and tent camping stands apart from other types of auto-based tourism because it is premised on the experience of roughness, while on the other hand, McDonaldization is widespread within modernity. It modifies camping, but is not exclusive to it or closely related activities. See George Ritzer, *The McDonaldization of Society 5* (Los Angeles: Pine Forge, 2008). Los Angeles Trailer Company, "Your Camping Trip," *Sunset*, July 1916, 76. Chenango Equipment Manufacturing Co. brochure, *Summer Outings*, 1924, on "Pop-Up Camper History," http://www.popupcamperhistory.com/chenango1924brochure.html#, 13; "Camping in Autos Has Become Popular," *New York Times*, June 18, 1916; Long and Long, *Motor Camping*, 49.

16. According to his obituary, *New York Times*, June 18, 1968, Ferguson had been a reporter for the *Philadelphia Record* since May 1895 and became its editor in 1926, shortly after this book was published. Ferguson, *Motor*, vii.

17. Ferguson, *Motor*, 3–4.

18. Ibid., 6, 9.

19. Ibid., 9–10.

20. Ibid., 28, 270.

21. Ibid., 118.

22. Ibid., 141–42, 143.

23. "200,000 Trailers," *Fortune*, March 1937, 107; Thornburg, *Galloping Bungalows*, 6, 14–15, 7; "200,000 Trailers," 108.

24. Wallis, *Wheel Estate*, 51; "The Covered Wagon Company," PDF document, Mount Clemens Public Library, http://www.libcoop.net/mountclemens/local%20history/covered%20wagon.pdf; Wallis, *Wheel Estate*, 51; "200,000 Trailers," 108.

25. Thornburg, *Galloping Bungalows*, 37; Franz, *Tinkering*, 12. For more on Hoovervilles see Joan Crouse, *The Homeless Transient in the Great Depression: New York State, 1929–1941* (Albany: SUNY Press, 1986). Belasco, *Americans*, 167.

26. See "No Depression for Trailers," *Business Week*, October 5, 1938, 18–20, and Burnham Finney, "New Coach Trailer Industry," *New York Times*, December 8, 1936. Thornburg, *Galloping Bungalows*, 39, discusses the ratio between home-built and factory-built trailers. The decline in tent trailer sales was so precipitous that the Chenango Trailer Company, for example, shifted production to hard-body trailers before going out of business in 1936. Nevertheless, the popularity of low-cost collapsible trailers rose again in the mid-1950s when hard-body travel trailers generally became more "deluxe," "self-contained," and thus costly. The tops and sides of these newer collapsibles were, however, more likely to consist of anything from light textiles to solid panels rather than canvas. See Edwards, *Homes*, 27, 33. "200,000 Trailers," 107, 214, 110, 214. See also Thornburg, *Galloping Bungalows*, 12; "200,000 Trailers," 110. The Covered Wagon Company moved to the Detroit suburb of Mount Clemens in 1934, according to "The Covered Wagon Company." *Fortune*'s estimate of the size of the industry is suggestive rather than definitive. According to Thornburg, *Galloping Bungalows*, 39, the *National Used Car Market Report* listed approximately eight hundred manufacturers in the fall of 1936. Moreover, the Great Lakes region was not the only area where trailer manufacturers were located. Early in 1936, *Sunset* magazine found eighty-five manufacturers in Los Angeles alone. Thornburg, *Galloping Bungalows*, 40, estimated that as many as two thousand companies

may have existed between 1930 and 1940. T. H. Watkins, "Home on the Road," *American West* 13, no. 5 (1976): 39.

27. *Readers' Guide Retrospective* online database records 3 articles whose subject was "automobile trailers" between 1920 and 1930, but 111 between 1930 and 1940. Wallis, *Wheel Estate,* 43; "200,000 Trailers," 229.

28. Wallis, *Wheel Estate,* 50, provides an insightful examination of this developing distinction between the three markets. Kozy Coach Co., "'Home Sweet Home' Wherever You Roam," advertisement, in Bryan Burkhart, Phil Noyes, and Allison Arieff, *Trailer Travel: A Visual History of Mobile America* (Salt Lake City: Gibbs Smith, 2002), 41; "Hitting the Trail—1935 Style," *Popular Mechanics,* July 1935, 41; Covered Wagon Co., "Announcing Three New 1937 Covered Wagon Trailer Coaches with Exclusive Shermanite Steel Bodies and Steel Chassis," advertisement, in Burkhart, Noyes, and Arieff, *Trailer Travel,* 43.

29. These ads were reproduced in Burkhart, Noyes, and Arieff, *Trailer Travel,* 41.

30. Freeman Marsh, *Trailers* (New York: Coward-McCann, 1937), 6, 9, 10. The *New York Times,* February 26, 1937, described Marsh's book as "an attempt to answer all questions about trailers." Gene Lindberg, "New Covered Wagon," in Charles Edgar Nash, *Trailer Ahoy!* (Lancaster, PA: Intelligencer Printing Co., 1937), 88. Susan Sessions Rugh, *Are We There Yet? The Golden Age of American Family Vacations* (Lawrence: University Press of Kansas, 2008), 127–29, artfully relates how travel trailer ads in the post–World War II era suggested that campers could go anywhere in trailers, that trailers were homelike and comfortable yet offered campers the opportunity to escape and to express their "pioneering spirit."

31. Bryan Burkhart and David Hunt, *Airstream: The History of the Land Yacht* (San Francisco: Chronicle Books, 2000), 40. See also Wallis, *Wheel Estate,* 54, who termed Byam an "industry pioneer"; Banham, *Wanderlust,* 58, who called Byam "visionary"; and Michael Aaron Rockland, *Homes on Wheels* (New Brunswick, NJ: Rutgers University Press, 1980), 59, who referred to Byam as the recreation-vehicle industry's "prophet." Much of this biographical material is drawn from Banham, *Wanderlust.*

32. Byam quoted in Banham, *Wanderlust,* 37; ibid. Byam initially opened a factory in 1931 in Culver City, California, but moved to Los Angeles before production began. Ibid.

33. Thornburg, *Galloping Bungalows,* 46; Banham, *Wanderlust,* 41, 46; Burkhart and Hunt, *Airstream,* 65; Banham, *Wanderlust,* 46; Burkhart and Hunt, *Airstream,* 66–67. See also Wallis, *Wheel Estate,* 54–55.

34. Airstream Trailer Co., *Airstream Trailers: America's Finest,* brochure (Los Angeles: Airstream Trailer Co., [1937]), 4, 5, 8. Airstream Trailer Co., *The "Clipper" Airstream Trailer,* brochure (Los Angeles: Airstream Trailer Co., [1938]). Airstream Trailer Co., *Airstream Trailers,* 9, 6.

35. Airstream Trailer Company, *Airstream Trailers,* 16; Banham, *Wanderlust,* 51; Thornburg, *Galloping Bungalows,* 49ff; Roger B. White, "At Home on the Highway," *American Heritage* 37, no. 1 (1985): 104; E. P. Meinecke, "The Trailer Menace—a Voice from the Past," *Journal of Forestry* 70, no. 5 (1972): 280 (originally published in 1935); Aldo Leopold, "Conservation Esthetic," *Bird-Lore* 40, no. 2 (1938): 101, and reprinted in the July 1938 issue of the National Park Service's *Park Service Bulletin.* See also "What about Trailer Squatters?," *Business Week,* December 19, 1936, 20; and J. Edgar Hoover, "Camps of Crime," *American Magazine,* February 1940, 14–15. At the same time, some National Park Service personnel found no problems with trailer camping. See John White, letter to Director, National Park Service, July 30, 1938, RG 79, Records of the National Park Service, appendix 2, Central Classified Files, 1907–1949, Sequoia National Park, box 1603, National Archives, College Park, MD (hereafter NA).

36. Burkhart and Hunt, *Airstream,* 32. See Rugh, *Are We There Yet?,* 122ff, who explores this period at length. White, "At Home," 104; Edwards, *Homes,* 35.

37. Byam initially pursued a partnership with the Curtiss-Wright Company, but it was unsuccessful. See Banham, *Wanderlust,* 52–54. The origins of the caravan are mentioned in

Wally Byam, *Trailer Travel Here and Abroad: The New Way to Adventurous Living* (New York: David McKay, 1960), 27. "Trailer Caravan Will Visit Central America," *Los Angeles Times,* June 24, 1951. The *Los Angeles Times* articles were written on July 22, 1951, October 28, 1951, and November 4, 1951, by Jean Jacques in a column titled "Trailering." The closing of applications and the expected turnout are mentioned in the last article. Banham, *Wanderlust,* 52–57, 62. Byam may have come up with the idea of caravans on his own, but precedents exist. For example, the "Tin Can Tourists" had traveled together in groups or separately to meet at predetermined sites as early as the 1920s, and R. T. Baumberger, owner of the Columbia Trailer Company in Los Angeles, organized his first caravan tour in 1933. See Wallis, *Wheel Estate,* 43–45, and Thornburg, *Galloping Bungalows,* 42.

38. Wally Byam, *Fifth Avenue on Wheels* (Los Angeles: Cambridge, 1953), 5. The Wally Byam Creed is reproduced in Burkhart and Hunt, *Airstream,* 83.

39. Byam, *Fifth Avenue,* 5, 6; Wally Byam, "Nothing Can Beat Romance of Traveling by Trailer," *Caravanner* 1 (June 1954): 1.

40. See Byam, *Trailer Travel.* Norma Miller, "Through Europe by Trailer Caravan," *National Geographic Magazine,* June 1957, 769–816, quote on 808; Carolyn Bennett Patterson, *Of Lands, Legends, and Laughter: The Search for Adventure with National Geographic* (Golden, CO: Fulcrum, 1998), 63.

41. Banham, *Wanderlust,* 89; Patterson, *Of Lands,* 64. This biographical material is drawn primarily from Carolyn Bennett Patterson's autobiography, *Of Lands.*

42. The Wally Byam Foundation: Humanitarian Works by His Followers Will Honor Wally Byam's Memory," *Caravanner* 8, no. 9 (1962): 3. Funding for the foundation came from the Airstream Company. See Banham, *Wanderlust,* 100.

43. "Airstreams Aid U.S. Foreign Service: 12 USIA Families Going Overseas Study America Via Trailer Tours," *Caravanner* 9, no. 7 (1963): 1; and Edward R. Murrow, letter to Carolyn Patterson, February 18, 1963, reproduced in the *Caravanner* 9, no. 7 (1963): 3. Patterson quoted in "Airstreams Aid," 3; Murrow to Patterson, February 18, 1963; Patterson, *Of Lands,* 66.

44. See Banham, *Wanderlust,* 84; "Airstreams Aid," 1.

45. According to "Wally's Foundation: Returning Foreign Service Officer Revisits America in an Airstream," *Caravanner* 11, no. 3 (1965): 2, the two-year program was formally launched in August 1964. Three fully equipped and furnished Airstream trailers and their Ford tow cars were turned over to the State Department. The Wally Byam Foundation paid for the gasoline and oil, while the participants paid for their food, any toll charges, and all personal expenses during their three- to four-week camping vacations. The program's expansion to include the State Department is noted in "Foundation Trailers Aid World Understanding," *Caravanner* 10, no. 11 (1964): 3. "Airstreams Aid," 1; William F. Keyes, "Foreign Service Officer Finds Trailer Leave Successful, Fun," *Caravanner* 11, no. 7 (1965): 2; John Alden Mason Jr., "USIA Officer Stationed in Brazil Recalls Foundation-Sponsored Tour," *Caravanner* 11, no. 9 (1965): 3.

46. Frederick T. Kelley, letter to Helen Byam Schwamborn, March 29, 1965, folder—New York Wire 3-23-00, Airstream Company records (Jackson Center, OH). NB, this folder and others from the Airstream Company records were marked with names that did not refer to what was in them when the author examined them during the summer of 2006. They appeared to be reused folders named during a previous use. Wally Byam Foundation, *Caravan America: A Program of the Wally Byam Foundation,* brochure, folder—New York Wire 3-23-00, Airstream Co. records (Jackson Center, OH), [11].

47. L. D. Aikman, memorandum to F. G. Vosburgh, April 14, 1965, Library #510-1-4383 I See America First: Diary of a President's Dau[ghter] 1 of 1, National Geographic Society Library, Washington, DC (hereafter Library #510). See Mrs. Duncan Aikman, letter to Mrs. Bess Abell, Social Secretary for the White House, May 6, 1965, Library #510; and Office of the Press Secretary, letter to Mrs. Johnson, White House, June 3, 1965, in Library #510. Lynda Bird Johnson, "I See America First: Diary of the President's Daughter," *National Geographic,* December 1965, 875, 877.

48. Wally Byam Foundation, *Caravan America*, [3, 7, 26].
49. "'Caravan America' Crosses Nation," *Caravanner* 13, no. 4 (July–August 1967): 2. According to Wally Byam Foundation, "General Procedures and Instructions for Caravan America," May 17, 1967, unpublished handout, folder—New York Wire 1997–2000, Airstream Company records (Jackson Center, OH), 4, the only U.S. cities visited by the British and French participants were Washington, D.C., Salt Lake City, Los Angeles, and San Francisco. "'Caravan America' Crosses Nation," 2.
50. "'Caravan America' Delights French," *Caravanner* 13, no. 5 (September–October 1967): 2.
51. Wally Byam Foundation, *Caravan America*, [29]. "Diplomats Tour U.S. in Caravan of Airstreams," *Caravanner* 13, no. 5 (September–October 1967): 1, 5; and Kathleen Teltsch, "Envoys See 'Other' U.S. in 5-Week Caravan Tour," *New York Times*, October 12, 1967. The two sources disagree on the number of participants. According to the latter, only thirteen families took part.
52. Teltsch, "Envoys"; "Argentines Learn U.S. from Auto," *Los Angeles Times*, December 7, 1967.
53. Rediscover America lasted until at least 1974. See "U.S. Foreign Service Officer on Leave Served by Byam Foundation's Program," *Caravanner* 21, no. 1 (January–February 1975): 2. The German visit is detailed in Ray Loren, "Foundation Guests Criss-Cross U.S.," *Caravanner* 18, no. 5 (September–October 1972): 2, 5; and the inclusion of foreign journalists is described in Catherine Elmore, "15 Journalists Visiting U.S. in Foundation's Airstreams," *Caravanner* 20, no. 2 (May–June 1974): 2. Virgil Ericson, "Caravan America Tour 7: Petaluma, CA. to Dayton, OH., July 29–Aug. 20, 1976," unpublished, typed manuscript, folder—New York Wire March, Airstream Company records (Jackson Center, OH), 2–3.
54. Patterson, *Of Lands*, 74, 75.
55. Carolyn Bennett Patterson, letter to Charles H. Manchester, June 15, 1978, Carolyn Bennett Patterson Papers, Caravan America Correspondence and Miscellaneous—1976–1978, box 3, Special Collections Department, Mitchell Memorial Library, Mississippi State University (Mississippi State, MS).

7. A Renewal of Our Faith and Ideals

1. U.S. Department of the Interior, Bureau of Outdoor Recreation, *Trails for America: Report on the Nationwide Trails Study* (Washington, DC: Government Printing Office, 1966), 3; Lary Dilsaver, compiler, "An Act to Establish a National Trails System, and for Other Purposes," in *America's National Park System: The Critical Documents* (Lanham, MD: Rowman & Littlefield, 1994), 325, 330–31, 335; U.S. Forest Service, "History of Pacific Crest Trail," http://www.fs.fed.us/pct/pacific_crest_trail_history.html; Jonathan Gaw, "Long and Winding Road: New Segment Completes Pacific Crest Trail after 25 Years," *Los Angeles Times*, June 2, 1993.
2. Colin Fletcher, *The Complete Walker: The Joys and Techniques of Hiking and Backpacking* (New York: Knopf, 1969), 320; Charles Cook, *The Essential Guide to Wilderness Camping and Backpacking in the United States* (New York: Michael Kesend, 1994), ix–x.
3. Christopher McCandless, *Back to the Wild: The Photographs and Writings of Christopher McCandless*, ed. Mary Ellen Barnes (St. George, UT: Twin Star, 2011), 191.
4. David Green, *A Pacific Crest Odyssey: Walking the Trail from Mexico to Canada* (Berkeley, CA: Wilderness Press, 1979), 27; Cindy Ross, *Journey on the Crest: Walking 2600 Miles from Mexico to Canada* (Seattle: Mountaineers, 1987), viii, 14; Cheryl Strayed, *Wild: From Lost to Found on the Pacific Crest Trail* (New York: Knopf, 2012), 4, 5. Strayed's explanation for a backpacking trip recalls Joel T. Headley's explanation for his 1849 camping trip (see introduction) as well as those of many subsequent campers and camping enthusiasts.

5. On returning with a difference see Barbara Myerhoff, "Pilgrimage to Meron: Inner and Outer Peregrinations," in *Creativity/Anthropology*, ed. Smadar Lavie, Kirin Narayan, and Renato Rosaldo (Ithaca, NY: Cornell University Press, 1993), 218; Fletcher, *Complete Walker*, 7–8; Green, *Pacific Crest Odyssey*, 116; Ross, *Journey*, 309, 310; Strayed, *Wild*, 311.

6. Robert Dunn, "The Wilderness near Home," *Outing*, July 1904, 472, includes the earliest identified use of the term "back-pack," but he did not apply the object's name to the camping technique, and the name did not catch on with other trampers. According to the database *Readers Guide Retrospective*, the next reference to a "back pack" is Jack Van Coevering, "Cushioned Back Pack," *Popular Science*, July 1934, 77, and the first time the mode of camping is given its current name is by Clinton C. Clarke, "Backpacking on the Pacific Crest Trail," in Boy Scouts of America, *Adventuring for Senior Scouts* (New York, 1938), 415–29. However, Clarke's term did not become common until the early 1960s.

7. Laura and Guy Waterman, *Forest and Crag: A History of Hiking, Trail Blazing, and Adventure in the Northeast Mountains* (Boston: Appalachian Mountain Club, 1989), 29–32. One colleague who joined Partridge on an 1821 trip was a twenty-year-old George Perkins Marsh, who would go on to become an ambassador to the Ottoman Empire and elsewhere, and author of one of the first books with a modern environmentalist theme, 1864's *Man and Nature*. See David Lowenthal, *George Perkins Marsh: Prophet of Conservation* (Seattle: University of Washington Press, 2000).

8. Waterman and Waterman, *Forest and Crag*, 119–20.

9. Ibid., 79–91; Philip G. Terrie, "Urban Man Confronts the Wilderness: The Nineteenth-Century Sportsman in the Adirondacks," *Journal of Sport History* 5, no. 3 (1978): 8; Philip G. Terrie, "Romantic Travelers in the Adirondack Wilderness," *American Studies* 24, no. 2 (1983): 61.

10. John B. Bachelder, *Popular Resorts, and How to Reach Them* (Boston: John B. Bachelder, 1874), 9 (italics in original). Although it is not noted in this book, it is a second edition. See chapter 1.

11. Weston continued to give public lectures for most of his life. Phil Howell, "Racewalking History in the United States" (2010), http://www.runtheplanet.com/resources/historical/rwushistory.asp; and Nick Harris, Helen Harris, and Paul Marshall, *A Man in a Hurry: The Extraordinary Life and Times of Edward Payson Weston, the World's Greatest Walker* (London: DeCoubertin, 2012). The *New York Times* published articles about "Weston, the Pedestrian," on October 29 and 30, November 1, 4, 5, 6, 8, 9, 10, 12, 13, 14, 15, 16, 17, 18, 19, 20, 21, 22, 24, 26 (2), 27, 29, and December 1, 1867. "The Pedestrian Mania," *New York Times*, December 1, 1867, 4. Howell, "Racewalking"; Waterman and Waterman, *Forest and Crag*, 151ff. According to Waterman and Waterman, 156, some of these clubs had colorful names like "Pemigewasset Perambulators." For a contemporary account of the exploits of Edward Payson Weston see "Pedestrianism," *New York Times*, May 13, 1874, 4.

12. John B. Bachelder, *Popular Resorts, and How to Reach Them*, 3rd ed. (Boston: John B. Bachelder, 1875), 13.

13. Ibid., 15.

14. Ibid., 14, 19, 13, 20.

15. Bachelder's term "pedestrianism" did not endure. Within a few years the term "tramping" became the dominant one. See, for example, William H. Hobbs, "Outfit for a Tramping and Camping Trip," *Outing*, June 1895, 207–12. For other authors who ranked tramping as best see Horace Kephart, *The Book of Camping and Woodcraft* (New York: Outing Publishing Co., 1906); George D. Baird, "Mountain Camping in California," *Country Life in America*, June 1906, 193–94; and Claude P. Fordyce, "A Tramp up Rifle Creek Canyon, with Suggestions for an Outfit," *Country Life in America*, June 1909, 193–95.

16. John M. Gould, *Hints for Camping and Walking; How to Camp Out* (New York: Scribner, Armstrong, 1877), 5, 6, 114. Biographical materials on Gould are drawn from John M. Gould, "The Biography of John Mead Gould," http://johnmeadgould.com/. Gould, *Hints*, 15, about the speed and costs.

17. Gould, *Hints*, 107, 15 (italics in original), 16, 19, 20.

18. Ibid., 22; Waterman and Waterman, *Forest and Crag*, 257.

19. Gould, *Hints*, 15, 14 (italics in original). Gould was a member of a hiking club, the Portland White Mountain Club, and such organizations were active promoters and developers of trails and trail systems during the 1870s, 1880s, and beyond. See Waterman and Waterman, *Forest and Crag*, 206ff.

20. Gould, *Hints*, 30, 26.

21. Tramping articles included Hobbs, "Outfit"; Dunn, "Wilderness"; and Baird, "Mountain Camping." George Washington Sears, *Woodcraft* (New York: Forest and Stream, 1884), 1, 3. Sears's reputation has been so widespread and deeply positive that publications recently have appeared about him. See George Washington Sears, *Canoeing the Adirondacks with Nessmuk: The Adirondack Letters of George Washington Sears*, ed. Dan Brenan (Blue Mountain Lake, NY: Adirondack Museum / Syracuse University, 1993); and Christine Jerome, *An Adirondack Passage: The Cruise of the Canoe Sairy Gamp* (New York: HarperCollins, 1994).

22. Ratio from a sample of advertisements in popular magazines published between 1912 and 1918.

23. Waterman and Waterman, *Forest and Crag*, 256ff. The advertisements aimed at trampers likely had little impact because of the overwhelming focus on weight. A "Perfection Pneumatic Mattress" might offer more comfortable sleep, but its five to eight pounds would discourage most trampers. See Pneumatic Manufacturing Co., "Good Sleeping on Any Ground," *Outing*, April–September 1915, 20; Stewart Edward White, "Camp Equipment," *Outing*, December 1906, 405. Note that this was a multi-installment article appearing in several issues.

24. White, "Camp Equipment," 405. Few authors praised winter camping, but one of them, Horace Kephart, "Outfit for Walking Trips," *Outing*, December 1915, 259, allowed for thirty pounds in winter instead of summer's twenty-five pounds. Paul M. Fink, *Backpacking Was the Only Way* (Johnson City: Research Advisory Council, East Tennessee State University, 1975), 1–11; Dan Beard, "How to Pack and Unpack in the Woods," *Outing* 46, August 1905, 370.

25. Hobbs, "Outfit," 209, 210, 212.

26. Stewart Edward White, "Camp Equipment," *Outing* 49, no. 5 (1907): 678; Kephart, "Outfit," 263; Fink, *Backpacking*, 3.

27. U.S. Department of the Interior, *Report of the Secretary of the Interior for the Fiscal Year Ended June 30, 1892* (Washington, DC: Government Printing Office, 1892), 134; U.S. Department of the Interior, *Report of the Secretary of the Interior for the Fiscal Year Ended June 30, 1896* (Washington, DC: Government Printing Office, 1896), 100.

28. On purported "American" qualities see Roderick Nash, *Wilderness and the American Mind*, 5th ed. (New Haven, CT: Yale University Press, 2014). Fink, *Backpacking*, ix; Dunn, "Wilderness," 473; Fink, *Backpacking*, vii; Harriet Monroe, "Camping above the Yosemite: A Summer Outing with the Sierra Club," *Putnam's Magazine*, May 1909, 219, 221.

29. Dunn, "Wilderness," 469; Hobbs, "Outfit," 207; Monroe, "Camping," 223.

30. Trampers, like other campers, indeed like all pilgrims, are motivated for many reasons. The categories identified here are more suggestive than exhaustive. See Chris C. Park, *Sacred Worlds: An Introduction to Geography and Religion* (New York: Routledge, 1994), for a discussion of pilgrims' many motivations. For examples of continuing motivations to tramp see Laura Thornborough, "Tramping in the Great Smokies," *American Forests and Forest Life* 33 (August 1927): 463–66, 512, on the "allure" of wild scenery; Claude P. Fordyce, "Touring Our National Parks Afoot," *Country Life*, June 1921, 41–43; Arthur C. Comey, *Going Light* (New Haven, CT: New England Trail Conference, 1924); and Stephen Graham, *The Gentle Art of Tramping* (New York: D. Appleton, 1926), for references to the negative aspects of modern urban life. See Poirier Tent and Awning Company, "Hit the Trail," *Field and Stream*, July 1920, 340, for references to links between tramping and a pioneer past. And see Arthur

H. Carhart, "Wilderness, Ltd.," *Independent*, May 1927, 509–10, for references to both of the last two. *The Statistical History of the United States from Colonial Times to the Present* (Stamford, CT: Fairfield Publishers, 1965), 222–23. See also Robert Marshall, "The Forest for Recreation and a Program for Forest Recreation," in *A National Plan for American Forestry* (Washington, DC: Government Printing Office, 1933), 464–65. These park and forest statistics are themselves of questionable quality, but they do indicate a trend toward increased recreational use during these years.

31. Waterman and Waterman, *Forest and Crag*, 458; Leibold & Co., "O Joy! Sleeping Bag with Lightning Fastener," *Pacific Sportsman*, July 1927, 19; Waterman and Waterman, *Forest and Crag*, 459; Van Coevering, "Cushioned," 77.

32. Comey, *Going Light*, 1; Waterman and Waterman, *Forest and Crag*, 460; Comey, *Going Light*, 1.

33. Waterman and Waterman, *Forest and Crag*, 349. Gary Cross, *Time and Money: The Making of Consumer Culture* (New York: Routledge, 1993), and Cindy Aron, *Working at Play: A History of Vacations in the United States* (New York: Oxford University Press, 1999), examined the impacts of the increase in vacations on leisure-time activities. See also Peter J. Schmitt, *Back to Nature: The Arcadian Myth in Urban America* (Baltimore: Johns Hopkins University Press, 1990), and chapter 3. Waterman and Waterman, *Forest and Crag*, 457.

34. On the sacred character of wilderness see Linda H. Graber, *Wilderness as Sacred Space* (Washington, DC: Association of American Geographers, 1976), and Thomas R. Dunlap, *Faith in Nature: Environmentalism as Religious Quest* (Seattle: University of Washington Press, 2004). On the role of roads, autos, and auto-oriented recreations in the creation of a wilderness movement see Glynn Gary Wolar, "The Conceptualization and Development of Pedestrian Recreational Wilderness Trails in the American West, 1890–1940: A Landscape History" (PhD diss., University of Idaho, 1998); Paul Sutter, *Driven Wild: How the Fight against Automobiles Launched the Modern Wilderness Movement* (Seattle: University of Washington Press, 2002); and Paul Sutter, "Putting Wilderness in Context: The Interwar Origins of the Modern Wilderness Idea," in *American Wilderness: A New History*, ed. Michael Lewis (New York: Oxford University Press, 2007), 167–85.

35. Sutter, "Putting," 170–71. See also David Louter, *Windshield Wilderness: Cars, Roads, and Nature in Washington's National Parks* (Seattle: University of Washington Press, 2006), 5–6. See Marguerite Shaffer, "Performing Bears and Packaged Wilderness: Reframing the History of National Parks," in *Cities and Nature in the American West*, ed. Char Miller (Reno: University of Nevada Press, 2010), 137–53.

36. Roger W. Toll, "Superintendents' Resolution on Overdevelopment," in Dilsaver, *America's National Park System*, 57, 59. John C. Merriam quoted in Schmitt, *Back to Nature*, 171.

37. Sutter, "Putting," 171.

38. A range of authors have intensively explored the roles of USFS personnel and others in the creation of America's wilderness preservation system. See, for example, Schmitt, *Back to Nature*; Nash, *Wilderness*; Sutter, *Driven Wild*; and Sutter, "Putting." Aldo Leopold, "The Wilderness and Its Place in Forest Recreational Policy," *Journal of Forestry* 19, no. 7 (1921): 719, 720; Aldo Leopold, "Wilderness as a Form of Land Use," *Journal of Land and Public Utility Economics* 1, no. 4 (1925): 401; Aldo Leopold, "Conserving the Covered Wagon," in *The River of the Mother of God and Other Essays by Aldo Leopold*, ed. Susan L. Flader and J. Baird Callicott (Madison: University of Wisconsin Press, 1991), 128–29; Leopold, "Wilderness as a Form," 401.

39. Arthur H. Carhart, "Wilderness, Ltd.," *Independent*, May 1927, 509.

40. Chauncey J. Hamlin and National Conference on Outdoor Recreation, *A Report Epitomizing the Results of Major Fact-Finding Surveys and Projects Which Have Been Undertaken under the Auspices of the National Conference on Outdoor Recreation* (Washington, DC: Government Printing Office, 1928); Joint Committee on Recreational Survey of Federal Lands of the American Forestry Association and the National Parks Association, *Recreation*

Resources of Federal Lands: Report of the Joint Committee on Recreational Survey of Federal Lands of the American Forestry Association and the National Parks Association to the National Conference on Outdoor Recreation (Washington, DC: National Conference on Outdoor Recreation, 1928), 89.

41. James M. Glover, *A Wilderness Original: The Life of Bob Marshall* (Seattle: Mountaineers, 1986), 94, 116. According to Sutter, "Putting," 176, "primitive" became the new name for "wilderness" because some agency personnel thought the former term better suggested the intended means of access, while the latter hinted at pristine conditions. Some of the areas under consideration for designation had previously been logged, e.g., in Maine, so "primitive" seemed the more appropriate term. See also L. F. Kneipp, "What Shall We Call Protected Recreation Areas in National Forests?," in *American Civic Annual*, ed. Harlean James (Washington, DC: American Civic Association, 1929), 34–36. M. Rupert Cutler quoted on Forest History Society, "1929: Forest Service L-20 Regulation for Primitive Areas," http://www.foresthistory.org/ASPNET/policy/Wilderness/1929_L-Reg.aspx. Forest History Society, "1929."

42. Wolar, "Conceptualization," 11. Waterman and Waterman, *Forest and Crag*, 347; and Wolar, "Conceptualization," 10.

43. Wolar, "Conceptualization," 22–23; Allen Chamberlain, "Making the Tramper's Dream Come True," *Conservationist* 3, no. 8 (August 1920): 115, 118; Waterman and Waterman, *Forest and Crag*, 347; Theodore S. Solomons, "The Beginnings of the John Muir Trail," *Sierra Club Bulletin* 25, no. 1 (1940): 29–40; Walter L. Huber, "The John Muir Trail," *Sierra Club Bulletin* 15, no. 1 (1930): 37–46.

44. Benton MacKaye, "An Appalachian Trail: A Project in Regional Planning," *Journal of the American Institute of Architects* 9, no. 10 (1921): 325, 328, 327, 328.

45. Brian B. King, "Trail Years: A History of the Appalachian Trail Conference," *Appalachian Trailway News*, Special 75th Anniversary Issue (July 2000), 4. Avery quoted ibid., 9. Avery was elected chairman of the ATC in 1931 and would hold the post for twenty-one years. MacKaye quoted ibid., 11.

46. Catherine Montgomery quoted in Joseph T. Hazard, *Pacific Crest Trails from Alaska to Cape Horn* (Seattle: Superior, 1946), 57. See also Barney Mann, "Where the Pacific Crest Trail Begins: Is It Campo? Manning Park? No, It's Montgomery," *PCT Communicator*, March 2011, 8–11. Hazard, *Pacific Crest Trails*, 57. According to Hazard, the local Forest Service personnel were cooperative but focused on a trail or trails between the Canadian and California borders, which are the northern and southern edges of USFS Region 6. In 1928, Fred W. Cleator, supervisor of recreation, USFS Region 6, "named, announced, and developed the Cascade Crest Trail" (58). According to the U.S. Forest Service brochure *Oregon Skyline Trail—Pacific Crest System, Guide No. 35* (Portland, 1936), the Skyline Trail, which was also within this same USFS region, was begun in 1920 and itself was assembled from "many pieces of rough trails."

47. "Meeting of Committee to Define Purposes—January 14," January 14, 1932, reverse, Mountain League Minutes & Organization, box 4, Papers of William Henry Thrall, ca. 1873–1962, Huntington Library, San Marino, CA (hereafter PWHT). The goal of the organizing committee is noted in "Motions Carried at Meeting of Mountain League, March 4, 1932," Mountain League Minutes & Organization, box 4, PWHT. The standing committees were trails, map, publication, conservation, finance, and publicity. See "Report of the Organization Committee for the Proposed Mountain League of Los Angeles County," March 1932, Series 1: vol. 1, Pacific Crest Trail System History Correspondence, 1932–1936, Papers of Warren Lee Rogers, 1912–1992, Huntington Library, San Marino, CA (hereafter PWLR), 1. The minutes of the April 1 and April 8, 1932, meetings are recorded in "Mountain League Minutes," May 6, 1932, Mountain League Minutes & Organization, box 4, PWHT, 1.

48. Clinton C. Clarke, letter to Roland C. Geist, October 22, 1943, Series 1: vol. 15, Pacific Crest Trail System: Correspondence, Reports . . . (1940–1946), PWLR, 1. Robert Winter, "Pasadena, 1900–1910: The Birth of 'Its Culture,'" *Southern California Quarterly*

91, no. 3 (2009): 295–317. Additional biographical material comes from Clinton Clarke's obituary, "Cotton Mather Descendent Dies Here," *Pasadena Star-News*, February 2, 1957; and Wolar, "Conceptualization," 330–31. Margaret R. Clarke was born in San Francisco in 1883 and was a well-known Southern California actress. She starred in dozens of stage productions at the Pasadena Playhouse between 1910 and 1938. See "Mrs. Margaret Clarke, 70, of Playhouse Fame Dies," *Los Angeles Times*, July 17, 1953.

49. The quotes are from Clarke, letter to Geist, October 22, 1943. Barney Mann, "Discovering Dad: A Dusty Trail Leads to Clinton Clarke's Handmade Journal," *PCT Communicator*, December 2010, 16. For analyses of the Sierra Club's outings see Michael P. Cohen, *The History of the Sierra Club, 1892–1970* (San Francisco: Sierra Club Books, 1988), and Anne F. Hyde, "Temples and Playgrounds: The Sierra Club in the Wilderness, 1901–1922," *California History* 66, no. 3 (1987): 208–20.

50. Winter, "Pasadena," 295. The description of Clarke is from the U.S. Census of 1910. In the 1920 Census, at age forty-two, he was described as "retired." These descriptions are quoted in Bradford Caslon, "Richard V. LeGrand—149 N. El Molino Ave., Pasadena," http://oldhomesoflosangeles.blogspot.com/2012/10/richard-v-legrand-149-n-el-molino-ave.html. Clarke's California certificate of death listed his occupation as "financier" and his business as "investments." He simply drew a line through the "occupation" section of both his 1927 and 1930 passports, which are in Series 1: Clarke Personal, 1927–1953, box 12, PWLR.

51. "June 3 Executive Committee Meeting," June 3, 1932, Mountain League Minutes & Organization, box 4, PWHT, 1.

52. "Report. Mountain League Meeting 8/26/32," Mountain League Minutes & Organization, box 4, PWHT, 1.

53. Ibid.

54. The release date or date for these two reports is uncertain, but they are located between documents dated March 1932 at the earliest and September 1932 at the latest. "The John Muir Trail—Methods of Construction and Operation," Series 1: vol. 1, Pacific Crest Trail System History Correspondence, 1932–1936, box 1, PWLR, 1. "The John Muir Trail—Description," Series 1: vol. 1, Pacific Crest Trail System History Correspondence, 1932–1936, box 1, PWLR, 1.

55. Clarke, letter to Geist, October 22, 1943.

56. The county figures are from Science in the City, "Population Growth by Single Year Los Angeles County, 1850–1998," http://www.laep.org/target/science/population/table.html, while the Pasadena figures are from Los Angeles Almanac, "General Population by City, Los Angeles County, 1850–1900," http://www.laalmanac.com/population/po25.htm, and from Los Angeles Almanac, "General Population by City, Los Angeles County, 1910–1950," http://www.laalmanac.com/population/po26.htm. See Greg Hise, *Magnetic Los Angeles: Planning the Twentieth-Century City* (Baltimore: Johns Hopkins University Press, 1997). Scott Bottles, *Los Angeles and the Automobile: The Making of the Modern City* (Berkeley: University of California Press, 1987), 93; John W. Robinson, *The San Gabriels: Southern California Mountain Country* (San Marino, CA: Golden West Books, 1977), 127.

57. Tom Chester and Jane Strong, "Angeles Crest Highway (SR2)," http://tchester.org/sgm/places/sr2.html. It is unclear when Clinton Clarke first conceived the idea of a grand western through trail. He may have heard about Catherine Montgomery's suggestion, it may have emerged during a conversation with another outdoor enthusiast, or he may have come up with it alone. Glynn Gary Wolar, in "Conceptualization," 333, argues that Clarke came up with the idea long before 1932. Wolar reports that one of Clarke's acquaintances, Will Thrall, claimed in a November 1934 speech that Clarke had begun to imagine a "western counter to the Appalachian Trail as early as 1924." As Wolar notes, if Thrall is correct, then Clarke's idea of a border-to-border trail *precedes* that of Catherine Montgomery. A review of Thrall's speech, however, revealed that "10" years had been handwritten over "two" years on the original typed manuscript. I propose that ten here means "many" rather than an exact quantitative value. I suspect that Thrall had learned from Clarke that the latter had been

pondering the value, location, and production of a through trail for some time when the Mountain League became the vehicle to carry his proposal. Clarke *may* have first conceived of the trail in 1924, but 1929, 1930, or 1931 seems far more likely. See William Thrall, "Radio Speech," November 16, 1934, USGS So. Calif. Blueprint, box 4, PWHT, 2.

58. "Minutes—Mountain League Meeting 9/16/32," Mountain League Minutes & Organization, box 4, PWHT, 1, record that representatives from the Junior Chamber of Commerce, the Pacific Electric Railroad, the "Motor Transit," and, most ironically, the Automobile Club of Southern California initially pledged support for the EJMT. Clinton C. Clarke, letter to Horace M. Albright, September 23, 1932, Series 1: vol. 1, Pacific Crest Trail System History Correspondence, 1932–1936, box 1, PWLR, 1, 2.

59. Clinton C. Clarke, letter to Horace M. Albright, October 14, 1932, Series 1: vol. 1, Pacific Crest Trail System History Correspondence, 1932–1936, box 1, PWLR, 2, 1.

60. Clarke sent similar appeals and justifications to the superintendents of Crater Lake, Lassen, and Sequoia National Parks. See Clinton C. Clarke, letter to E. C. Solinsky, November 2, 1932; Clinton C. Clarke, letter to L. W. Collins, n.d.; and Clinton C. Clarke, letter to J. R. White, November 1, 1932. All are located in Series 1: vol. 1, Pacific Crest Trail System History Correspondence, 1932–1936, box 1, PWLR. Horace M. Albright, letter to Clinton C. Clarke, November 1, 1932, Series 1: vol. 1, Pacific Crest Trail System History Correspondence, 1932–1936, box 1, PWLR, 1. Despite Albright's membership, no evidence suggests that he had contacted anyone at the Sierra Club about the EJMT. Wolar, "Conceptualization," 336–37.

61. Clinton C. Clarke, letter to Horace M. Albright, November 12, 1932, Series 1: vol. 1, Pacific Crest Trail System History Correspondence, 1932–1936, box 1, PWLR, 2.

62. Clinton C. Clarke, letter to William V. Mendenhall, October 3, 1932, Series 1: vol. 1, Pacific Crest Trail System History Correspondence, 1932–1936, box 1, PWLR, 1. Clarke's "camps" referred to both the individual cabins built in large numbers in some forest canyons and the summer camps developed by nonprofit organizations and local governments. See Robinson, *San Gabriels*. Clarke here is using an older term. The Forest Service had adopted Regulation L-20 in 1929, which renamed their "wilderness" category as "primitive" instead. They would again use "wilderness" after the adoption of the U-1, U-2, and U-3 regulations in 1939. See Samuel P. Hays, *The American People & The National Forests: The First Century of the U.S. Forest Service* (Pittsburgh: University of Pittsburgh Press, 2009), 87.

63. Clinton C. Clarke, letter to L. A. Barrett, October 4, 1932, Series 1: vol. 1, Pacific Crest Trail System History Correspondence, 1932–1936, box 1, PWLR, 1.

64. Approximately 12 percent of this national forest is currently designated wilderness. See "Angeles National Forest. Special Places," http://www.fs.usda.gov/attmain/angeles/special places. William V. Mendenhall, letter to Clinton C. Clarke, October 4, 1932, Series 1: vol. 1, Pacific Crest Trail System History Correspondence, 1932–1936, box 1, PWLR, 1.

65. S. B. Show, letter to Clinton C. Clarke, February 28, 1933, Series 1: vol. 1, Pacific Crest Trail System History Correspondence, 1932–1936, box 1, PWLR, 1, 2.

66. See Sutter, "Putting," and Neil M. Maher, *Nature's New Deal: The Civilian Conservation Corps and the Roots of the American Environmental Movement* (New York: Oxford University Press, 2008). Clinton C. Clarke, letter to R. Y. Stuart, October 23, 1933, Series 1: vol. 1, Pacific Crest Trail System History Correspondence, 1932–1936, box 1, PWLR, 1. See John A. Williams, *Turning to Nature in Germany: Hiking, Nudism, and Conservation, 1900–1940* (Stanford, CA: Stanford University Press, 2007). Clarke, letter to Stuart, October 23, 1933, 1.

67. Clarke, letter to Stuart, October 23, 1933, 2.

68. It has long been understood that a pilgrim's journey may be as significant as any destination and that some forms of behavior associated with sacred space tend to challenge basic principles of geographic behavior. See, for instance, Linda Kay Davidson and David M. Gitlitz, introduction in *Pilgrimage: From the Ganges to Graceland; an Encyclopedia* (Santa Barbara, CA: ABC-Clio, 2002), xvii–xxiv, about the importance of both journeys

and destinations in pilgrimage. Paul Wheatley, *The Pivot of the Four Quarters: A Preliminary Enquiry into the Origins and Character of the Ancient Chinese City* (Chicago: Aldine, 1971), explored the impact of Chinese beliefs on the design of early cities. Dallen J. Timothy and Daniel H. Olsen, eds., *Tourism, Religion and Spiritual Journeys* (New York: Routledge, 2006), examined how religion and spirituality have shaped modern tourism and travel. One geographer, Robert H. Stoddard, "Pilgrimages along Sacred Paths," *National Geographical Journal of India* 33, no. 4 (1987): 448–56, argued that the same challenge occurs with behavior on what he termed "sacred paths." All movement to sacred places requires people to traverse earth space, but Stoddard contends that it is crucial to distinguish whether the movement occurs along what he calls a "route" or a "path." The former is the case when the movement is neither prescribed nor significant itself. Most routes to Mecca, for instance, are socially, economically, and politically important, but they generally lack any spiritual significance for someone on a hajj. Few pilgrims ever militate for the protection of routes. A path, by contrast, refers to a line of movement that a pilgrim follows because the track is itself spiritually meaningful; many paths have been protected by pilgrims and spiritual authorities. See, for example, "Via Dolorosa," in Davidson and Gitlitz, *Pilgrimage*, 1:277–78. Regardless of this distinction, whether movement is along a route or a path cannot be fixed by an observer. As Stoddard, "Pilgrimages," 451, cautioned, that distinction "may depend on the perceptions of pilgrims." This buffering seems to possess two aspects. On the one hand it safeguarded the trail from exploitation by developers, and on the other hand it guaranteed that the experience of moving along the trail would be natural and acceptable for Clarke's "nature lovers."

69. Clinton C. Clarke, letter to R. Y. Stuart, March 15, 1934, Series 1: vol. 1, Pacific Crest Trail System History Correspondence, 1932–1936, box 1, PWLR; Clinton C. Clarke, letter to Arno B. Cammerer, March 19, 1934, Series 1: vol. 1, Pacific Crest Trail System History Correspondence, 1932–1936, box 1, PWLR. The two letters' contents are nearly identical. Wolar, "Conceptualization," 342–43. Clarke, letter to Stuart, March 15, 1934, 1. "Overdeveloped" trails prompted three Wilderness Society members to launch protests against the NPS at about this time. See "Women Members Protest against Elaborate National Park Trails," *Living Wilderness* 3, no. 3 (1937): 8–12. Sutter, "Putting," 173.

70. Clarke, letter to Stuart, March 15, 1934, 1.

71. L. F. Kneipp, letter to Clinton C. Clarke, March 21, 1934, Series 1: vol. 1, Pacific Crest Trail System History Correspondence, 1932–1936, box 1, PWLR, 1.

72. Stuart was shortly succeeded by Ferdinand A. Silcox. Clarke would soon contact the new chief forester. Wolar, "Conceptualization," 352. Clinton C. Clarke, letter to L. A. Barrett, March 28, 1934, Series 1: vol. 1, Pacific Crest Trail System History Correspondence, 1932–1936, box 1, PWLR, 1.

73. S. B. Show, letter to Clinton C. Clarke, May 14, 1934, Series 1: vol. 1, Pacific Crest Trail System History Correspondence, 1932–1936, box 1, PWLR. Although the letter was from the regional forester, Barrett signed it for him. H. C. Bryant, letter to Clinton C. Clarke, October 19, 1934, Series 1: vol. 1, Pacific Crest Trail System History Correspondence, 1932–1936, box 1, PWLR, 1; Clinton C. Clarke, letter to C. J. Buck, October 26, 1934, Series 1: vol. 1, Pacific Crest Trail System History Correspondence, 1932–1936, box 1, PWLR, 1. S. B. Show, letter to Clinton C. Clarke, November 3, 1934; H. C. Bryant, letter to Clinton C. Clarke, November 7, 1934; and William E. Colby, letter to Clinton C. Clarke, November 21, 1934. The Northwest region of the USFS initially rejected the name Pacific Crest Trail but later relented. C. J. Buck, letter to Clinton C. Clarke, November 5, 1934; and C. J. Buck, letter to Clinton C. Clarke, November 15, 1935. All five previous letters are in Series 1: vol. 1, Pacific Crest Trail System History Correspondence, 1932–1936, box 1, PWLR.

74. Clinton C. Clarke, *The Pacific Crest Trail* (Pasadena, CA: Clinton C. Clarke, 1935); Clinton C. Clarke, letter to Arno B. Cammerer, January 28, 1935, Series 1: vol. 1, Pacific Crest Trail System History Correspondence, 1932–1936, box 1, PWLR, 1; Clinton C. Clarke, letter to W. V. Mendenhall, March 24, 1935, Series 1: vol. 1, Pacific Crest Trail System History Correspondence, 1932–1936, box 1, PWLR, 1.

75. "Trail Survey to Canada Finished," *Pasadena Star-News*, March 1935. This imprecisely dated clipping is located in Series 1: vol. 5, PCT System Publicity, Advertising, Bulletins (correspondence; 1934–1940), box 3, PWLR.

76. Clinton C. Clarke, "Report: The Pacific Crest Trail System Conference of the Conservation Forum," June 1935, Pacific Crest Trail Conference, box 4, PWHT, 2, 1.

77. Warren Rogers's attraction to wilderness stands in contrast to Methodism's rare investment of wilderness with spiritual and moral meaning. For more on wilderness and religion see Mark Stoll, "Religion 'Irradiates' the Wilderness," in *American Wilderness: A New History*, ed. Michael Lewis (New York: Oxford University Press, 2007), 35–53. Wolar, "Conceptualization," 339–41; Warren L. Rogers, "Background Data Pacific Crest Trail Activities," Series 7: "My Story," Autobiographical, folder 4, box 62, PWLR, 1.

78. Clarke, "Report," 1–2. According to Warren L. Rogers, *The PCT Relays* (Santa Ana, CA: Warren L. Rogers, 1968), 5, Charles G. Norman, another YMCA member attending the Conservation Forum meeting in Yosemite, first proposed that this organization explore the complete trail. Clarke, "Report," 2. On the same page of this report was noted that the Boy Scouts of America also volunteered to "provide for a detailed survey of the entire Trail . . . with descriptive and photographic reports." However, the organization later withdrew its offer.

79. F. P. Knapp, letter to Warren Rogers, June 20, 1935, Series 2: Y-Relays, folder 1, box 14, PWLR, 1; Rogers, *PCT*, 4; Warren L. Rogers, "Tell the Story of the Y.M.C.A. Pacific Crest Trail Relay Hike," mimeographed pamphlet, Series 2: Y-Relays, folder 6, box 15, PWLR, 7; Clinton C. Clarke, letter to Arno B. Cammerer, September 16, 1935, Series 1: vol. 1, Pacific Crest Trail System History Correspondence, 1932–1936, box 1, PWLR, 2.

80. Clinton C. Clarke, letter to Knapsackers of the Pasadena Young Men's Christian Association, July 8, 1935, Series 1, vol. 2, Pacific Crest Trail System History, Organization, Development, Clubs, Personal Correspondence, 1932–1935, box 2, PWLR, 1.

81. Clinton C. Clarke, letter to James E. West, April 17, 1940, Series 1: vol. 1, Pacific Crest Trail System History Correspondence, 1938–1941, box 1, PWLR, 1–2.

82. Warren L. Rogers, "To the Stars through Difficulty" (1937), mimeographed pamphlet, Series 1: vol. 4, PCT System Bulletins, Data Reports (correspondence; 1933–1937), box 3, PWLR, 6. The title comes from a Latin phrase: "Ad astra per ardua."

83. Warren Rogers, letter to Clinton C. Clarke, November 1, 1937, Series 2: Y-Relays, folder 6, box 15, PWLR, 1. Rogers was active in his public promotion of the PCT during the late 1930s. For example, between September 1936 and August 1937, without a budget, he set up window displays in Marysville, California, and Portland, Oregon, as well as exhibits in Pasadena, Asilomar (during a conference), Balboa (another conference), and Whittier, California. He participated in radio programs on KFVD (Los Angeles), KQW (San Jose), and KOIN (Portland). He gave illustrated talks to schools, clubs, and chambers of commerce (more than three dozen in sum); composed newspaper stories (approximately three hundred column inches), answered more than three hundred mail queries; held innumerable personal discussions with people planning to hike the PCT; and distributed more than eleven hundred pieces of mimeographed and printed materials about the PCT. See Warren L. Rogers, letter to Board of Directors, PCTS Conference, September 4, 1937, Series 1: vol. 4, PCT System Bulletins, Data Reports (correspondence; 1933–1937), box 3, PWLR, 1–2. Warren L. Rogers, "Radio Program," n.d., and Warren L. Rogers, "Radio Program Outline," n.d. Both are located in Series 2: Y-Relays, folder 6, box 15, PWLR, and appear to have been written in 1935 or 1936.

84. Rogers, *PCT*, 8–9. "Map of the Pacific Crest Trail System. The 24 Famous Mountains. Log of Daily Itinerary" (Pasadena, CA, n.d.) was likely published in 1938 or 1939 after the YMCA relays were completed. Rogers, *PCT*, 3, 8, 12; and Rogers, "Tell the Story," 7. Robert O. Foote, "The Wilderness Way," *American Forests* 42, no. 9 (1936): 395–99; "Pacific Coast Hikers Can Walk 2300 Miles," *Christian Science Monitor*, July 10, 1936; "A Trail Down the Backbone of the West," *Sunset*, July 1936, 29–30; and Leverett G. Richards, "The Skyline Trail from Mexico to Canada," *Travel*, July 1937, 36–38, 46.

85. Clinton C. Clarke, letter to John E. Sieker, September 17, 1942, Series 1: vol. 15, Pacific Crest Trail System: Correspondence, Reports . . . (1940–1946), box 8, PWLR, 1; Jeffrey P. Schaffer, Ben Schifrin, Thomas Winnett, and J. C. Jenkins, *The Pacific Crest Trail, Volume 1: California*, 2nd ed. (Berkeley, CA: Wilderness, 1977), 2, 3.

86. Clinton C. Clarke, "Bulletin," November 1935, Series 7: "My Story" Autobiographical, folder 4, box 62, PWLR, lists Rogers's appointment as executive secretary. Letters mailed to and from Clarke list him as president beginning in 1936. Clarke, letter to Geist, 1. Clinton C. Clarke, *The Pacific Crest Trailway* (Pasadena, CA: Clinton C. Clarke, 1945). See, for example, Clinton C. Clarke, "A National Physical Training Program" (April 1949), unpublished typescript, Collection, Pacific Crest Trailway, vol. 2, Huntington Library, San Marino, CA. "Cotton Mather Descendent Dies Here."

87. Warren L. Rogers, "Background Data Pacific Crest Trail Activities" (n.d.), Series 7: "My Story" Autobiographical, box 62, PWLR, 1; Warren L. Rogers, letter to Daniel G. Aldrich Jr., October 15, 1965, Series 7: "My Story" Autobiographical, box 62, PWLR, 1.

88. Mark Antony Rossi, "The Final Frontiersman: Warren L. Rogers," July 1991, Series 7: "My Story" Autobiographical, box 62, PWLR, 4; Pacific Crest Trail Association, "Media Fact Sheet," http://www.pcta.org/about-us/media/media-fact-sheet/. The pocket map and food pack businesses are noted in Denise Dobbs, "The Papers of Warren Lee Rogers, 1912–1992: Finding Aid," typescript file, 2007, Huntington Library, San Marino, CA, 3.

Epilogue

1. According to the Outdoor Foundation, *2014 Outdoor Participation Report* (Washington, DC: Outdoor Foundation, 2014), 13, none of the top three activities were substantially more popular than camping. The number-one activity—running/jogging—attracted 20 percent of Americans, or 57.5 million participants. Outdoor Foundation, *2014 Outdoor*, 33. The camping and other outdoor recreation participation rates among the racial/ethnic groups in the Outdoor Foundation's report are nearly the same as those reported elsewhere in recent years. See Myron Floyd, "Race, Ethnicity, and Use of the National Park System," *Social Science Research Review* 1, no. 2 (1999): 1–24, and Patricia A. Taylor, Burke D. Grandjean, and James H. Gramann, *National Park Service Comprehensive Survey of the American Public, 2008–2009: Racial and Ethnic Diversity of National Park System Visitors and Non-visitors*, Natural Resource Report NPS/NRSS/SSD/NRR—2011432 (Fort Collins, CO: National Park Service, 2011). The dramatically lower participation rates of African Americans are comprehensively and thoughtfully examined in Carolyn Finney, *Black Faces, White Spaces: Reimagining the Relationship of African Americans to the Great Outdoors* (Chapel Hill: University of North Carolina Press, 2014).

2. Norman Brauer, *There to Breathe the Beauty: The Camping Trips of Henry Ford, Thomas Edison, Harvey Firestone, John Burroughs* (Dalton, PA: Norman Brauer, 1995), and Steven Watts, *The People's Tycoon: Henry Ford and the American Century* (New York: Knopf, 2005), 258–65. According to *Statistical History of the United States from Colonial Times to the Present* (Stamford, CT: Fairfield Publishers, 1965), 9, some 45.6 percent of the population lived in urban areas in 1910, 51.2 percent in 1920, and 56.1 percent in 1930.

3. U.S. National Park Service, "Annual Summary Report (1904—Last Calendar Year)," https://irma.nps.gov/Stats/SSRSReports/National Reports/Annual Visitation Summary Report (1979—Last Calendar Year). We must be cautious when relying on National Park Service numbers because they can shift for reasons unrelated to camping's popularity and so fail to indicate trends correctly. For example, the total number of national park units increased from 271 in 1979 to 370 in 2014, but many of the new national historic sites (as well as others) do not provide camping facilities. As a consequence, total national park visitors likely increased, while the camping numbers remained at or near the same level and thus reduced the percentage of national park visitors who were campers. In addition, changes in policy at some heavily

visited national parks have reduced the number of campers in popular but environmentally deteriorating areas without providing alternatives for lost sites. See, for example, U.S. National Park Service, "Summary Guide for the Merced Wild and Scenic River Draft Comprehensive Management Plan and Environmental Impact Statement" (January 2013), http://www.nps.gov/yose/parkmgmt/upload/mrp-deis-sum-guide-optimize-web.pdf. Furthermore, the scale of national park infrastructure held steady for decades while the size of many recreational vehicles expanded, making their use increasingly difficult to impossible in many national park campgrounds. Many of these campers have gone elsewhere. See John Hoeffel, "Where RVs Dare Not Go," *American Demographics* 18, no. 2 (1996): 15. Despite this need for caution when reading NPS statistics, they are closely tracked by the car and RV camping statistics amassed over the last decade by the Outdoor Foundation. See Outdoor Foundation, *Outdoor Recreation Participation Report 2012* (Boulder, CO: Outdoor Foundation, 2012), 53; and Outdoor Foundation, *2014 Outdoor*, 40.

4. H. Ken Cordell, "Outdoor Recreation Trends and Futures: A Technical Document Supporting the Forest Service 2010 RPA Assessment," Gen.Tech.Rep. SRS-150 (Asheville, NC: U.S. Forest Service, Southern Research Station, 2012), 6–7. To be included in either the "developed" or "primitive" categories, a camper must live or be able to bring his motor vehicle within one-quarter mile of the campsite. If he has to walk any farther, that is backpacking. U.S. National Park Service, *1982–1983 Nationwide Recreation Survey* (Washington, DC: U.S. Department of the Interior, National Park Service, 1986), 19. The total camping participation numbers do not represent the total number of individual campers, since an individual could participate in any or all three camping modes during a single year. Cordell, "Outdoor," 33, 35, 37–38.

5. For publications concerned about the decrease in camping and related outdoor activities see Richard Louv, *Last Child in the Woods: Saving Our Children from Nature-Deficit Disorder* (Chapel Hill: Algonquin Books of Chapel Hill, 2005); Oliver R. W. Pergams and Patricia A. Zaradic, "Is Love of Nature in the US Becoming Love of Electronic Media? 16-Year Downtrend in National Park Visits Explained by Watching Movies, Playing Video Games, Internet Use and Oil Prices," *Journal of Environmental Management* 80 (2006): 387–93; Oliver R. W. Pergams and Patricia A. Zaradic, "Evidence for a Fundamental and Pervasive Shift Away from Nature-Based Recreation," *Proceedings of the National Academy of Sciences* 105 (2008): 2295–300; and Peter Kareiva, "Ominous Trends in Nature Recreation," *Proceedings of the National Academy of Sciences* 105 (2008): 2757–58. Richard Louv, "Last Child in the Woods," http://richardlouv.com/books/last-child/; Pergams and Zaradic, "Evidence," 2299; Pergams and Zaradic, "Is Love," 392; Maarten H. Jacobs and Michael J. Manfredo, "Decline in Nature-Based Recreation Is Not Evident," *Proceedings of the National Academy of Sciences* 105 (2008): E40. See also H. Ken Cordell, "The Latest on Trends in Nature-Based Outdoor Recreation," *Forest History Today*, Spring 2008, 4–10; and H. Ken Cordell, Carter J. Betz, and Gary T. Green, "Nature-Based Outdoor Recreation Trends and Wilderness," *International Journal of Wilderness* 14, no. 2 (2008): 7–13.

6. Elon Jessup, *Roughing It Smoothly: How to Avoid Vacation Pitfalls* (New York: G. P. Putnam's Sons, 1923).

7. Hillary Rosner, "Los Angeles River: From Concrete Ditch to Urban Oasis," *National Geographic*, July 18, 2014, http://news.nationalgeographic.com/news/2014/07/140719-los-angeles-river-restoration-kayaking-greenway/; Museum of the City of New York, "Growing and Greening New York," https://mcny.org/exhibition/growing-and-greening-new-york. The idea that cities need not be sites of degeneration but can be places for the mutual regeneration of nature and society is increasingly explored by scholars and students. See, for instance, the John T. Lyle Center for Regenerative Studies at the California State Polytechnic University, Pomona, http://www.cpp.edu/~crs/.

INDEX